Introducing Translation Studies

Introducing Translation Studies remains the definitive guide to the theories and concepts that make up the field of translation studies. Providing an accessible and up-to-date overview, it has long been the essential textbook on courses worldwide.

This fourth edition has been fully revised and continues to provide a balanced and detailed guide to the theoretical landscape. Each theory is applied to a wide range of languages, including Bengali, Chinese, English, French, German, Italian, Punjabi, Portuguese and Spanish. A broad spectrum of texts is analysed, including the Bible, Buddhist sutras, *Beowulf*, the fiction of García Márquez and Proust, European Union and UNESCO documents, a range of contemporary films, a travel brochure, a children's cookery book and the translations of *Harry Potter*.

Each chapter comprises an introduction outlining the translation theory or theories, illustrative texts with translations, case studies, a chapter summary and discussion points and exercises.

New features in this fourth edition include:

■ new material to keep up with developments in research and practice, including the sociology of translation, multilingual cities, translation in the digital age and specialized, audiovisual and machine translation
■ revised discussion points and updated figures and tables
■ new, in-chapter activities with links to online materials and articles to encourage independent research
■ an extensive updated companion website with video introductions and journal articles to accompany each chapter, online exercises, an interactive timeline, weblinks, and PowerPoint slides for teacher support

This is a practical, user-friendly textbook ideal for students and researchers on courses in Translation and Translation Studies.

Jeremy Munday is Professor of Translation Studies at the University of Leeds, UK, and is a qualified and experienced translator. He is author of *Style and Ideology in Translation* (Routledge 2008) and *Evaluation in Translation* (Routledge 2012), editor of *The Routledge Companion to Translation Studies* (2009) and co-author, with Basil Hatim, of *Translation: An Advanced Resource Book* (Routledge 2004).

Praise for this edition

'Jeremy Munday's *Introducing Translation Studies* has long been admired for its combination of theoretical rigour and down-to-earth explanation, and this new edition will further confirm its place as the go-to introduction for students and teachers alike. Its further incorporation of ideas from the Chinese context is particularly welcome.'
Robert Neather, *Hong Kong Baptist University, China*

'An even better fourth edition of a widely popular and commonly used book in Translation Studies (TS). Munday's volume is a sound and accessible introduction to TS, combining scholarly rigor with reader-friendly style and an excellent didactic orientation, which will continue to make this book highly attractive to students, teachers and newcomers.'
Sonia Colina, *University of Arizona, USA*

Praise for the third edition

'This book provides a comprehensive and precise coverage of the major theories of translation ... The discussion and research points at the end of each topic will be welcomed by students, teachers and researchers alike ... written in exceptionally clear and user-friendly style ... Readers who may have no previous knowledge of translation studies will also find the book interesting and illuminating.'
Susan Xu Yun, *SIM University, Singapore*

'Whether you are a researcher, teacher, practitioner or learner of translation, you should read this book to get a comprehensive view of translation theories of the world, at present and in the past. This book is extremely useful as the starting point for understanding translation theories. It is deep enough for you to get adequate details and broad enough to let you know which directions to follow in your further research.'
Chris Shei, *Swansea University, UK*

'Jeremy Munday covers it all in this up-to-date book. It covers most, if not all, aspects of translation, whether they are theoretical or practical. This book is also an essential resource of knowledge for professional, academic, and practicing translators. Many approaches to translation are clearly and thoroughly explained.'
Said M. Shiyab, *UAE University, UAE*

'It would be difficult to find a better introduction to the complex field of translation studies ... A real must for everybody interested in this discipline.'
María Sánchez, *University of Salford, UK*

'This updated edition of *Introducing Translation Studies* provides a clear, thorough, and balanced introduction to major past and current trends in translation studies. It will be of great assistance to translation instructors and students seeking an updated overview of the field.'
Françoise Massardier-Kenney, *Kent State University, USA*

Introducing Translation Studies

Theories and applications

Fourth Edition

JEREMY MUNDAY

Routledge
Taylor & Francis Group

LONDON AND NEW YORK

Fourth edition published 2016
by Routledge
2 Park Square, Milton Park, Abingdon, Oxon OX14 4RN

and by Routledge
711 Third Avenue, New York, NY 10017

Routledge is an imprint of the Taylor & Francis Group, an informa business

First edition published by Routledge 2001
Second edition published by Routledge 2008
Third edition published by Routledge 2012

British Library Cataloguing in Publication Data
A catalogue record for this book is available from the British Library

Library of Congress Cataloging in Publication Data
Names: Munday, Jeremy, author.
Title: Introducing translation studies : theories and applications / by
Jeremy Munday.
Description: Fifth Edition. | Milton Park ; New York : Routledge, 2016. |
Includes bibliographical references and index.
Identifiers: LCCN 2015039263 | ISBN 9781138912540 (pbk.) | ISBN 9781138912557
(pbk.) | ISBN 9781315691862 (ebk.)
Subjects: LCSH: Translating and interpreting.
Classification: LCC P306 .M865 2016 | DDC 418/.02—dc23
LC record available at http://lccn.loc.gov/2015039263

ISBN: 978-1-138-91254-0 (hbk)
ISBN: 978-1-138-91255-7 (pbk)
ISBN: 978-1-315-69186-2 (ebk)

Typeset in Berthold Akzidenz Grotesk
by RefineCatch Limited, Bungay, Suffolk
Printed in Great Britain by Ashford Colour Press Ltd,
Gosport, Hants

Para Cristina,
que me ha hecho feliz

Contents

A visual tour of *Introducing Translation Studies*   x
List of figures and tables   xiii
Acknowledgements   xv
List of abbreviations   xvii

Introduction   1

Chapter 1 Main issues of translation studies   7
    1.1   The concept of translation   8
    1.2   What is translation studies?   10
    1.3   An early history of the discipline   13
    1.4   The Holmes/Toury 'map'   16
    1.5   Developments since Holmes   21
    1.6   The van Doorslaer 'map'   22
    1.7   Discipline, interdiscipline or multidiscipline?   24

Chapter 2 Translation theory before the twentieth century   29
    2.0   Introduction   30
    2.1   'Word-for-word' or 'sense-for-sense'?   30
    2.2   Early Chinese and Arabic discourse on translation   33
    2.3   Humanism and the Protestant Reformation   38
    2.4   Fidelity, spirit and truth   40
    2.5   Early attempts at systematic translation theory:
            Dryden, Dolet, Tytler and Yán Fù   42
    2.6   Schleiermacher and the valorization of the foreign   47
    2.7   Towards contemporary translation theory   49

Chapter 3 Equivalence and equivalent effect   58
    3.0   Introduction   59
    3.1   Roman Jakobson: the nature of linguistic meaning and equivalence   59
    3.2   Nida and 'the science of translating'   62
    3.3   Newmark: semantic and communicative translation   71
    3.4   Koller: equivalence relations   74
    3.5   Later developments in equivalence   77

Chapter 4 Studying translation product and process   86
      4.0   Introduction   87
      4.1   Vinay and Darbelnet's model   88
      4.2   Catford and translation 'shifts'   95
      4.3   Option, markedness and stylistic shifts in translation 98
      4.4   The cognitive process of translation   100
      4.5   Ways of investigating cognitive processing   103

Chapter 5 Functional theories of translation   113
      5.0   Introduction   114
      5.1   Text type   114
      5.2   Translatorial action   124
      5.3   Skopos theory   126
      5.4   Translation-oriented text analysis   131

Chapter 6 Discourse and Register analysis approaches   141
      6.0   Introduction   142
      6.1   The Hallidayan model of language and discourse   142
      6.2   House's model of translation quality assessment   145
      6.3   Baker's text and pragmatic level analysis: a coursebook
             for translators   149
      6.4   Hatim and Mason: the levels of context and discourse 156
      6.5   Criticisms of discourse and Register analysis approaches
             to translation   159

Chapter 7 Systems theories   169
      7.0   Introduction   170
      7.1   Polysystem theory   170
      7.2   Toury and descriptive translation studies   174
      7.3   Chesterman's translation norms   186
      7.4   Other models of descriptive translation studies: Lambert and van
             Gorp and the Manipulation School   189

Chapter 8 Cultural and ideological turns   197
      8.0   Introduction   198
      8.1   Translation as rewriting   199
      8.2   Translation and gender   205
      8.3   Postcolonial translation theory   208
      8.4   The ideologies of the theorists   213
      8.5   Translation, ideology and power in other contexts   214

Chapter 9 The role of the translator: visibility, ethics and sociology 222
      9.0   Introduction   223
      9.1   The cultural and political agenda of translation   223
      9.2   The position and positionality of the translator   233

9.3   The sociology and historiography of translation   236
9.4   The power network of the translation industry   239
9.5   The reception and reviewing of translations   241

Chapter 10 Philosophical approaches to translation   249
10.0   Introduction   250
10.1   Steiner's hermeneutic motion   250
10.2   Ezra Pound and the energy of language   258
10.3   The task of the translator: Walter Benjamin   260
10.4   Deconstruction   262

Chapter 11 New directions from the new media   274
11.0   Introduction   275
11.1   Audiovisual translation   275
11.2   Localization, globalization and collaborative translation   287
11.3   Corpus-based translation studies   291

Chapter 12 Research and commentary projects   302
12.0   Introduction   303
12.1   Consilience in translation studies   303
12.2   Translation commentaries   306
12.3   Research projects in translation studies   314

Notes   319
Bibliography   328
Index   361

A visual tour of *Introducing Translation Studies*

Pedagogical features

Introducing Translation Studies offers a variety of ways to help lecturers introduce this vibrant discipline, and to help students understand the key concepts and issues.

Key conc
■ **Definitic** **translating and interpreting.**
of translating is long established, I
The pr on studies is new.

KEY CONCEPTS   Each chapter opens with a series of straightforward definitions of the key concepts that the chapter will cover.

Key texts
Gabriela Saldanha (eds) (2009) *The*
Baker, Mo *Studies, Part II: History and Traditions,* 2n
of Tra outledge.

KEY TEXTS   Essential articles and books in the topic area.

Case stud
e study considers two series of transl
The followi rmal and dynamic equivalence. The three
from translations from the Hebrew of the openi
book of the Old Testament of the Christian Bible.[10]

CASE STUDIES   Case studies in each chapter to give focus and insight into the theories discussed.

Exploratio on: The term 'translation'
re used for 'translation' in the languag
h word(s) agins. What do these terms suggest abo
za their slation?

EXPLORATION   Within each chapter there are links to extra journal material on the ITS companion website to encourage further exploration of ideas.

Discussion d research points
t the analysis in the case study. Are the
Look a with the analysis? What does this tell us a
kind of model? The analysis focuses on the seven pi

DISCUSSION AND RESEARCH POINTS   At the end of each chapter are a number of questions that can be set as assignments, or discussed in class. They can also serve as a platform for related research project ideas.

FURTHER READING Additional sources for
students to explore particular issues raised in the
chapter.

Companion website

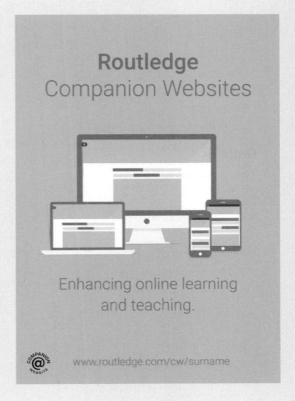

www.routledge.com/cw/munday

Introducing Translation Studies also
includes a comprehensive companion
website of online resources for both
students and lecturers. These include:

Student resources

- Video presentation by the author on
  each chapter, discussing the key
  issues for students to consider
- Interactive timeline to explain how
  translation theories have evolved since
  the first theorists
- Multiple-choice questions to test
  understanding of definitions and
  concepts
- Additional discussion questions and
  further reading

Lecturer resources

- PowerPoint presentations for each chapter, which can be downloaded and annotated,
  providing lecturers with a ready-made foundation for lecture preparation
- Free access to journal articles with accompanying teaching notes

Figures and tables

Figures

1.1	Holmes's 'map' of translation studies	17
1.2	The applied branch of translation studies	20
1.3	Translation strategies	23
1.4	Translation procedures	24
3.1	Nida's three-stage system of translation	63
5.1	Reiss's text types and text varieties	116
5.2	Text type and relevant criteria for translation	122
6.1	The Hallidayan model of language	143
6.2	Revised scheme for analysing and comparing original and translated texts	146
7.1	Conditions when translation is in primary position in polysystem	173
7.2	Toury's initial norm and the continuum of adecuate and acceptable translation	178
7.3	Initial, preliminary and operational norms	179
8.1	Control factors inside and outside the literary system	201
9.1	Domestication and foreignization: ethical and discursive levels	228
10.1	Steiner's hermeneutic motion	252
11.1	Concordance sample of *loom large*	297
11.2	Concordance sample of *se cierne(n)*	298

Tables

3.1	Example of componential analysis	66
3.2	Comparison of Newmark's semantic and communicative translation	72
3.3	Characteristics of research foci for different equivalence types	76
4.1	Segmentation of text into units of translation	106
5.1	Functional characteristics of text types and links to translation methods	115
6.1	Register variables and their typical realizations	145
6.2	Forms of cohesion	152
7.1	Comparison of Toury's and Chesterman's norms	188
11.1	Multimodal transcription model	282
12.1	Example translation specification sheet	307
12.2	Comparison of terminology for orientation of strategies	311
12.3	Types of research questions	315
12.4	Types of hypotheses	315

Acknowledgements

I would like to thank the following copyright holders for giving permission to reproduce the following: Figure 1.1, reproduced from G. Toury, *Descriptive Translation Studies – And Beyond*, revised edition copyright 2012, Amsterdam and Philadelphia, PA: John Benjamins. Figures 1.3 and 1.4 reproduced from L. van Doorslaer 'Risking conceptual maps', in Yves Gambier and Luc van Doorslaer (eds) *The Metalanguage of Translation*, special issue of *Target* 19.2: 217–33, reissued in Benjamins Current Topics 20 in 2009. Figure 5.2, reproduced from M. Snell-Hornby, *Translation Studies: An Integrated Approach*, copyright 1998, Amsterdam and Philadelphia, PA: John Benjamins. All the above reproduced with kind permission by John Benjamins Publishing Company, www.benjamins.com. Figure 3.1, reproduced from E. Nida and C. R. Taber, *The Theory and Practice of Translation*, copyright 1969, Leiden: E. J. Brill. Figure 6.2, reproduced from J. House, *Translation Quality Assessment: Past and Present*, copyright 2015, Routledge. Table 5.1, translated and adapted from K. Reiss, *Möglichkeiten und Grenzen der Übersetzungskritik*; the original is copyright of K. Reiss. While every effort has been made to trace copyright holders and obtain permission, this may not have been possible in all cases. Any omissions brought to the publisher's attention will be remedied at the earliest opportunity.

The case study in Chapter 8 is a revised and abridged version of an article of mine: 'The Caribbean conquers the world? An analysis of the reception of García Márquez in translation', published in *Bulletin of Hispanic Studies*, 75.1(1998): 137–44.

Introducing Translation Studies has evolved over time, but I acknowledge my sincere debt to Lawrence Venuti (Temple University, USA) for his encouragement with the initial project and for his detailed comments and suggestions on drafts of the first edition.

My thanks also go to Rana Nayar (Reader, Department of English at Panjab University, Chandigarh, India) for his assistance with the case study in Chapter 9. I also thank colleagues at the Universities of Leeds, Surrey and Bradford for their support during the writing of the various editions of this book, and to my students at all those institutions and universities where I have been lucky enough to be invited to speak, who have responded to versions of this material. My thanks also to all who have contacted me with comments on the earlier editions with suggestions for revision, to those journal reviewers who have made constructive suggestions and most particularly to the reviewers of the proposal and drafts for this fourth edition.

There are many other translation studies colleagues who have offered suggestions and help in many ways. I thank them all.

I would also like to express my extreme gratitude to Louisa Semlyen, Laura Sandford and everyone at Routledge, who have been so very supportive and patient throughout the writing and editing process. Also to Anna Callander for her careful attention to detail. And thanks to Jacob Blakesley and Falih Al-Emara for help with the index. Any remaining errors or deficiencies are of course mine alone.

Finally, but most of all, my thanks to Cristina, whose love and help mean so much to me, and to Nuria and Marina, who continue to add so much more to my life.

Jeremy Munday
London, August 2015

Abbreviations

@AC	Before Common Era
AC	Common Era
DTS	descriptive translation studies
SL	source language
ST	source text
TL	target language
TT	target text

Introduction

Translation studies is the now established academic discipline related to the study of the theory, practice and phenomena of translation. This book brings together and clearly summarizes the major strands of translation studies, in order to help readers acquire an understanding of the discipline and the necessary background and tools to begin to carry out their own research. It also presents and discusses theoretical frameworks into which professional translators and trainee translators can place their own practical experience.

The first three editions of *Introducing Translation Studies* (2001, 2008 and 2012) presented a practical introduction to an already diverse field. This fourth edition, while maintaining the structure and much of the material, is **fully revised** and **updated**. New content has been included throughout, 'exploration boxes' have been inserted within the text to link to full-text articles available on the *Introducing Translation Studies* companion website (http://www.routledge.com/cw/munday) and other material has been located online. The website also contains new video summaries of each chapter and revised PowerPoint presentations that may be customized by the tutor.

However, the general structure of the book remains the same. It sets out to give a critical but balanced survey of many of the most important trends and contributions to translation studies in a single volume, written in an accessible style. The different contemporary models are applied to illustrative texts in brief case studies so that the reader can see them in operation. The new research contained in these case studies, together with the 'discussion and research points' sections, is designed to encourage further exploration and understanding of translation issues.

The book is designed to serve as a **coursebook** for undergraduates and postgraduates in translation, translation studies and translation theory, and as a **solid theoretical introduction** for students, researchers, instructors and professional translators. The aim is to enable the readers to develop their understanding of the issues and associated technical language (**metalanguage**), and to begin to apply the models themselves. The reader is also encouraged to carry out a closer examination of specific issues and to pursue further reading in those areas that are of greatest interest. In this way, the book may provide a stimulating introduction to a range of theoretical approaches to translation that are relevant both for those engaged in the academic study of translation and for the professional linguist.

Each of the chapters surveys a major area of the discipline. Each is designed to be self-standing, so that readers with a specific focus can quickly find the descriptions that are of most interest to them. However, conceptual links between chapters are cross-referenced and the book has been structured so that it can function as a coursebook. The twelve chapters might be covered in one or two weeks, depending on the length of the course, to fit into a semesterized system. The discussion and research points additionally provide substantial initial material for students to begin to develop their own research.

The progression of ideas is also from the introductory (presenting main issues of translation studies in Chapter 1) to the more complex, as the students become more accustomed to the terminology and concepts. In general, the progression is chronological, from pre-twentieth-century theory in Chapter 2 to linguistic-oriented theories (Chapters 3 to 6) and to more recent developments from cultural studies such as postcolonialism (Chapter 8), and from sociology (Chapter 9) and new technologies (Chapter 11). But it is also conceptual, since some of the earlier theories and concepts, such as equivalence and universals of translation, are constantly being revisited (e.g. in Chapter 10).

Clarity has been a major consideration, so each chapter follows a similar **format** of:

- an introductory table clearly presenting key terms and ideas;
- the main text, describing in detail the models and issues under discussion;
- 'exploration boxes' with links to relevant full-text articles online and with self-study or classroom activities;
- an illustrative case study, which applies and evaluates the main model of the chapter;
- suggestions for further reading;
- a brief evaluative summary of the chapter;
- a series of discussion and research points to stimulate further thought and research;
- links to the **ITS website** (www.routledge.com/cw/munday) where each chapter is accompanied by a video summary, multiple-choice recall test,

customizable PowerPoint slides, extra research articles, further reading hints and research project questions. Extra case studies in other languages appear.

In common with other anthologies and introductory books, this volume is necessarily selective. The theorists and models covered have been chosen because of their strong influence on translation studies and because they are particularly representative of the approaches in each chapter. Much other worthy material has had to be excluded due to space constraints and the focus of the book, which is to give a clear introduction to a number of theoretical approaches. Over recent years, the field has continued to expand dramatically with a considerable increase in the number of publications and the borrowing of concepts from new fields such as cognitive studies, sociology, literary theory and corpus linguistics. It is not practicable, and indeed would be impossible, to attempt to be fully comprehensive. I am also aware that the organization of the book inevitably gives preference to those theorists who have advanced major new ideas and gives less than sufficient due to the many scholars who work in the field producing detailed case studies or less high-profile work.

For these reasons, detailed suggestions are given for **Further reading**. These are designed to encourage students to go to the primary texts, to follow up ideas that have been raised in each chapter and to investigate the research that is being carried out in their own countries and languages. In this way, the book should ideally be used in conjunction with the readers mentioned in section 1.2 and be supported by an institution's library resources. An attempt has also been made to refer to many works that are readily available, either in recent editions or reprinted in one of the anthologies. The emphasis is on encouraging reflection, investigation and awareness of the new discipline, and on applying the theory to both practice and research.

A major issue has been the choice of languages for the texts used in the illustrative case studies. There are examples or texts from Chinese, English, French, German, Italian, Portuguese and Spanish. Some additional examples are given from Arabic, Bengali, Dutch, Punjabi and Russian. Yet the case studies are written in such a way as to focus on the theoretical issues and should not exclude those unfamiliar with the specific language pairs. A range of text types is offered. The earlier editions included the Bible, *Beowulf*, the fiction of García Márquez and Proust, European Union and UNESCO documents, a travel brochure, a children's cookery book, the translations of *Harry Potter* and subtitled films from Bengali, French and German. This fourth edition expands to discuss website localization, other types of technical translation, videogame transcreation and crowdsourced translations, amongst others.

A guide to chapters

The book is organized as follows.

Chapter 1 discusses what we mean by 'translation' and what the scope is of the discipline of translation studies. It discusses the three types of translation defined by Jakobson: intralingual, interlingual and intersemiotic. It then presents the well-known Holmes/Toury conceptual map of the discipline, and critiques it with new conceptualizations and knowledge structures used in the construction of the online publications database, the Benjamins *Translation Studies Bibliography*.

Chapter 2 describes some of the major issues that are discussed in writings about translation up to the twentieth century. This huge range of over 2,000 years, beginning with Cicero in the first century @AC, focuses on the 'literal vs. free' translation debate, an imprecise and circular debate from which theorists have emerged only in the last sixty years. The chapter describes some of the classic writings on translation over the years, making a selection of the most well-known and readily available sources. It aims to initiate discussion on some of the key issues.

Chapter 3 deals with the concepts of meaning, equivalence and 'equivalent effect'. Translation theory in the 1960s under Eugene Nida shifted the emphasis to the receiver of the message. This chapter encompasses Nida's model of translation transfer, influenced by Chomsky's generative grammar, and his concepts of formal equivalence and dynamic equivalence. Newmark's similarly influential categories of semantic translation and communicative translation are also discussed, as is Koller's analysis of equivalence.

Chapter 4 overviews attempts that have been made to describe the product and process of translation. These include classifications of the linguistic changes or 'shifts' which occur in translation. The main model described here is Vinay and Darbelnet's classic taxonomy, but reference is also made to other traditions, such as Loh's English-Chinese model, and to Catford's linguistic model. The latter part of the chapter introduces some of the work that has been conducted from a cognitive perspective, which seeks to explain message processing and how translation as communication is achieved. This section covers the interpretive model of the Paris School, Gutt's work on relevance theory and recent advances in empirical studies.

Chapter 5 covers Reiss and Vermeer's text-type and skopos theory of the 1970s and 1980s and Nord's text-linguistic approach. In this chapter, translation is analysed according to text type and function in the TL culture, and prevailing concepts of text analysis – such as word order, information structure and thematic progression – are employed. Hybrid and multimodal text genres are also discussed.

Linked closely to the previous chapter, Chapter 6 moves on to consider House's recently modified Register analysis model and the development of discourse-oriented approaches in the 1990s by Baker, and Hatim and Mason, who make use of Hallidayan linguistics to examine translation as communication within a sociocultural context.

Chapter 7 investigates systems theories and the field of target-oriented 'descriptive' translation studies, following Even-Zohar, Toury and the work of the Manipulation School.

Chapter 8 examines the cultural and ideological approaches in translation studies. These start with Lefevere's work of the 1980s and early 1990s – which itself arose out of a comparative literature and Manipulation School background – and move on to more recent developments in gender studies and translation (in Canada), to postcolonial translation theories (in India) and other ideological implications of translation. The chapter then focuses on a case study of translation from Asia.

Chapter 9 looks at the role of the translator and the ethics of translation practice. It begins by following Berman and Venuti in examining the foreign element in translation and the 'invisibility' of the translator. The idea explored is that the practice of translation, especially in the English-speaking world, is considered to be a derivative and second-rate activity, and that the prevailing method of translation is 'naturalizing'. The role of 'agents' such as literary translators and publishers is also described and linked to recent work on the sociology and historiography of translation, incorporating theories from Bourdieu, Latour and Luhmann.

Chapter 10 investigates a range of philosophical issues around language and translation, ranging from Steiner's 'hermeneutic motion', Pound's use of archaisms, Walter Benjamin's 'pure' language, and Derrida and the deconstruction movement. These question some of the basic tenets of translation theory.

Chapter 11 looks at the challenges presented by the unprecedented growth in new technologies. It discusses audiovisual translation, the most prominent of the new research areas, but also localization processes in translation practice and corpus-based translation studies. These technological advances have forced a dramatic revision of some long-held beliefs and the reassessment of central issues such as equivalence and translation universals.

Chapter 12 brings together some of the distinct strands of the discipline in Chesterman's call for 'consilience'. It then discusses how research advances may be achieved, with the reaching out to other disciplines, and proposes specific advice for those working on reflexive translation commentaries and MA or PhD research projects.

CHAPTER 1

Main issues of translation studies

Key concepts

- **Definitions of translating and interpreting.**
- **The practice of translating is long established, but the discipline of translation studies is relatively new.**
- **In academic circles, translation was previously relegated to just a language-learning activity.**
- **A split has persisted between translation practice and theory.**
- **The study of (usually literary) translation began through comparative literature, translation 'workshops' and contrastive analysis.**
- **James S. Holmes's 'The name and nature of translation studies' is considered to be the 'founding statement' of a new discipline.**
- **Translation studies has expanded hugely, and is now often considered an interdiscipline.**

Key texts

Holmes, James S. (1988b/2004) 'The name and nature of translation studies', in Lawrence Venuti (ed.) (2004), *The Translation Studies Reader*, 2nd edition, London and New York: Routledge, pp. 180–92.

Jakobson, Roman (1959/2012) 'On linguistic aspects of translation', in Lawrence Venuti (ed.) (2012), *The Translation Studies Reader*, 3rd edition, London and New York: Routledge, pp. 126–31.

Snell-Hornby, Mary (2006) *The Turns of Translation Studies*, Amsterdam and Philadelphia: John Benjamins, Chapter 1.

van Doorslaer, Luc (2007) 'Risking conceptual maps', in Yves Gambier and Luc van Doorslaer (eds) *The Metalanguage of Translation*, special issue of *Target* 19.2: 217–33.

1.1 The concept of translation

Watch the introductory video on the companion website.

The main aim of this book is to introduce the reader to major concepts and models of translation studies. Because the research being undertaken in this field is now so extensive, the material selected is necessarily only representative and illustrative of the major trends. For reasons of space and consistency of approach, the focus is on written translation rather than oral translation (the latter is commonly known as **interpreting** or **interpretation**), although the overlaps make a clear distinction impossible (cf. Gile 2004). More subtly, interpreting is defined, by Otto Kade, as 'a form of Translation (in the wider sense) in which (a) the source language text is presented only once and thus cannot be reviewed or replayed, and (b) the target language text is produced under time pressure, with little chance for correction and revision' (Pöchhacker 2009: 133, following Kade 1968).[1]

The English term **translation**, first attested in around 1340,[2] derives either from Old French *translation* or more directly from the Latin *translatio* ('trans-porting'), itself coming from the participle of the verb *transferre* ('to carry over'). In the field of languages, **translation** today has several meanings:

(1)   the general subject field or phenomenon ('I studied translation at university')
(2)   the product – that is, the text that has been translated ('they published the Arabic translation of the report')
(3)   the process of producing the translation, otherwise known as translating ('translation service').

The **process of translation** between two different written languages involves the changing of an original written text (the **source text** or **ST**) in the original verbal language (the **source language** or **SL**) into a written text (the **target text** or **TT**) in a different verbal language (the **target language** or **TL**):

Source text (ST)   ⟶   Target text (TT)
in source language (SL)   in target language (TL)

Thus, when translating a product manual from Chinese into English, the ST is Chinese and the TT is English. However, internationalization and communication practices have meant that this traditional conceptualization of translation needs to be broadened to include those contexts in which there is no clearly defined source text. This may be because there are multilingual versions of the same text, each of which is deemed to be equally valid (e.g. the Acquis body of European Union law), or because of an 'unstable' source text that is subject to constant updating or adaptation, each iteration of which requires a modification of existing target texts rather than a completely new translation (e.g. a multilingual website). The traditional ST-TT configuration is the most prototypical of 'interlingual translation', one of the three categories of translation described by the Russo-American structuralist Roman Jakobson (1896–1982) in his seminal paper 'On linguistic aspects of translation'. Jakobson's categories are as follows:

(1) **intralingual** translation, or 'rewording' – 'an interpretation of verbal signs by means of other signs of the same language'

(2) **interlingual** translation, or 'translation proper' – 'an interpretation of verbal signs by means of some other language'

(3) **intersemiotic** translation, or 'transmutation' – 'an interpretation of verbal signs by means of signs of non-verbal sign systems'.

(Jakobson 1959/2012: 127)

These definitions draw on **semiotics**, the general science of communication through signs and sign systems, of which language is but one (Cobley 2001, Malmkjær 2011). The use of the term **semiotics** is significant here because translation is not always limited to verbal languages. **Intersemiotic translation**, for example, occurs when a written text is translated into a different mode, such as music, film or painting. Examples would be Jeff Wayne's famous 1978 musical version of H. G. Wells's science-fiction novel *The War of the Worlds* (1898), which was then adapted for the stage in 2006, or Gurinder Chadha's 2004 Bollywood *Bride and Prejudice* adaptation of Jane Austen's *Pride and Prejudice*. **Intralingual translation** would occur when we produce a summary or otherwise rewrite a text in the same language, say a children's version of an encyclopedia. It also occurs when we rephrase an expression in the same language. In the following example, *revenue nearly tripled* is a kind of intralingual translation of the first part of the sentence, a fact that is highlighted by the trigger expression *in other words*.

In the decade before 1989 revenue averaged around [NZ]$1 billion a year while in the decade after it averaged nearly [NZ]$3 billion a year – in other words, revenue nearly tripled.[3]

It is **interlingual translation**, between two different verbal sign systems, that has been the traditional focus of translation studies. However, as we shall see as the book progresses, notably in Chapters 8 to 10, the very notion of 'translation proper' and of the stability of source and target has been challenged. The question of what we mean by 'translation', and how it differs from 'adaptation', 'version', 'transcreation' (the creative adaptation of video games and advertising in particular, see section 11.1.8), 'localization' (the linguistic and cultural adaptation of a text for a new locale, see section 11.2) and so on, is a very real one. Sandra Halverson (1999) claims that translation can be better considered as a **prototype** classification, that is, that there are basic core features that we associate with a prototypical translation, and other translational forms which lie on the periphery.

Much of translation theory has until recently also been written from a western perspective and initially derived from the study of Classical Greek and Latin and from Biblical practice (see Chapter 2). By contrast, Maria Tymoczko (2005, 2006, 2007: 68–77) discusses the very different words and metaphors for 'translation' in other cultures, indicative of a **conceptual orientation** where the goal of close lexical fidelity to an original may not therefore be shared, certainly in the practice of translation of sacred and literary texts. For instance, in India there is the Bengali *rupantar* (= 'change of form') and the Hindi *anuvad* (= 'speaking after', 'following'), in the Arab world *tarjama* (= 'biography') and in China *fan yi* (= 'turning over'). Each of these construes the process of translation differently and anticipates that the target text will show a substantial change of form compared to the source.[4] Tymoczko (2007: 107–39) also frames the 'cross-cultural' concept of translation as an interface of representation, transmission and transculturation.

1.1 Exploration: The term 'translation'

Which word(s) are used for 'translation' in the languages you work with? Explore their origins. What do these terms suggest about the conceptualization of translation?

1.2 What is translation studies?

Throughout history, written and spoken translations have played a crucial role in interhuman communication, not least in providing access to important texts for

scholarship and religious purposes. As world trade has grown, so has the importance of translation. By 2015, the global market for outsourced translation, interpreting and related technologies was estimated to exceed US$38 billion, while
international organizations such as the European Union translate between
24 languages and spend some €456 million per year on translation and interpreting
services.[5] Yet the study of translation as an academic subject only really began in the
second half of the twentieth century. In the English-speaking world, this discipline is
now generally known as **'translation studies'**, thanks to the Dutch-based US
scholar James S. Holmes (1924–1986). In his key defining paper delivered in 1972,
but not widely available until 1988, Holmes describes the then nascent discipline as
being concerned with 'the complex of problems clustered round the phenomenon of
translating and translations' (Holmes 1988b/2004: 181). By 1995, the time of the
second, revised, edition of her *Translation Studies: An Integrated Approach*, Mary
Snell-Hornby was able to talk in the preface of 'the breathtaking development of
translation studies as an independent discipline' and the 'prolific international discussion' on the subject (Snell-Hornby 1995, preface). Little more than a decade later,
the editors of the second edition of the *Routledge Encyclopedia of Translation*
comment on 'new concerns in the discipline, its growing multidisciplinarity, and its
commitment to break away from its exclusively Eurocentric origins, while holding on
to the achievements of the past decades' (Baker and Saldanha 2009: xxii).

There are four very visible ways in which translation studies has become
more prominent. Unsurprisingly, these reflect a basic tension between the practical side of professional translating and the often more abstract research activity
of the field. First, just as the demand for translation has soared, so has there been
a vast expansion in **specialized translating and interpreting programmes**
at both undergraduate and postgraduate level. These programmes, which attract
thousands of students, are mainly oriented towards training future professional
commercial translators and interpreters and serve as highly valued entry-level
qualifications for the professions. The types of translation covered at each institution vary. These may include MAs in applied translation studies, scientific and
technical translation, conference and bilateral interpreting, audiovisual translation, specialized Sign Language and audio description. A smaller number of
programmes focus on the practice of literary translation. In Europe, literary translation is also supported by the RECIT network of centres where literary translation is studied, practised and promoted.[6] The first of these was set up in Straelen,
West Germany, in 1978.

Second, the past decades have also seen a proliferation of **conferences,
books and journals** on translation in many languages. Longer-standing

international translation studies journals such as *Babel* (the Netherlands) and *Meta* (Canada), first published in 1955, were joined by TTR (*Traduction, terminologie, rédaction*, Canada) in 1988, *Target* (the Netherlands) in 1989, *Perspectives* (Denmark) in 1993 and *The Translator* (UK) in 1995.

Online accessibility is increasing the profile of certain publications including open access journals such as *The Journal of Specialised Translation* and *New Voices* (see www.routledge.com/cw/munday). In addition, there is a whole host of other journals devoted to single languages, modern languages, applied linguistics, comparative literature and others where articles on translation are often published.

1.2 Exploration: Translation studies journals

The companion website for *Introducing Translation Studies* includes a list of major translation studies journals.

The front and backlists of publishers such as Bloomsbury, John Benjamins, Multilingual Matters, Peter Lang, Palgrave, Rodopi and Routledge (including St Jerome publishing) have significant series in translation studies. There are also various professional publications dedicated to the practice and study of translation. In the UK these include *The Linguist* of the Chartered Institute of Linguists, *The ITI Bulletin* of the Institute of Translating and Interpreting and *In Other Words*, the literary-oriented publication of the Translators Association.

Third, as the number of publications has increased so has the demand for **general and analytical instruments** such as anthologies, databases, encyclopedias, handbooks and introductory texts. Their number is ever-growing. Among these are *Translation Studies* (Bassnett 1980/1991/2002/2013), *Contemporary Translation Theories* (Gentzler 1993/2001), *The Routledge Encyclopedia of Translation Studies* (Baker and Malmkjær 1998; Baker and Saldanha 2009), *Dictionary of Translation Studies* (Shuttleworth and Cowie 1997), *Introducing Translation Studies* (Munday 2001/2008/2012), *The Routledge Companion to Translation Studies* (Munday 2009), *Critical Concepts: Translation Studies* (Baker 2009), *Critical Readings in Translation Studies* (Baker 2010), *Exploring Translation Theories* (Pym 2010/2014), the *Handbook of Translation Studies* (Gambier and van Doorslaer 2010 onwards), *The Oxford Handbook of Translation Studies* (Malmkjær and Windle 2011), *Theories of Translation* (Williams 2013), *The Routledge Handbook of Translation Studies* (Millán and Bartrina 2013) and

A Companion to Translation Studies (Bermann and Porter 2014). The best-known searchable online bibliographies are *Translation Studies Bibliography* (John Benjamins/Routledge) and the free-access *BITRA* (University of Alicante).[7]

Fourth, **international organizations** have also prospered. The Fédération Internationale des Traducteurs (International Federation of Translators, FIT) was established in 1953 by the Société française des traducteurs and its president Pierre-François Caillé (1907–79). It brought together national associations of translators. In more recent years, translation studies scholars have banded together nationally and internationally in bodies such as the Canadian Association for Translation Studies/Association canadienne de traductologie (CATS, founded in Ottawa in 1987), the European Society for Translation Studies (EST, Vienna, 1992), the European Association for Studies in Screen Translation (ESIST, Cardiff, 1995), the American Translation and Interpreting Studies Association (ATISA, Kent, OH, 2002), the International Association for Translation and Intercultural Studies (IATIS, Seoul, 2004) and the Asia-Pacific Forum on Translation and Intercultural Studies (Hangzhou-Tsinghua, 2011). International conferences on a wide variety of themes are held in an increasing number of countries. From being a relatively quiet backwater in the early 1980s, translation studies has now become one of the most active and dynamic new areas of multidisciplinary research.

1.3 An early history of the discipline

Writings on the subject of translating go far back in recorded history. The **practice of translation** was crucial for the early dissemination of key cultural and religious texts and concepts. In the west, the different ways of translating were discussed by, among others, Cicero and Horace (first century @AC) and St Jerome (fourth century AC). As we shall see in Chapter 2, their writings were to exert an important influence up until the twentieth century. In St Jerome's case, his approach to translating the Greek Septuagint Bible into Latin would affect later translations of the Scriptures. Indeed, in western Europe the translation of the Bible was to be the battleground of conflicting ideologies for well over a thousand years and especially during the Reformation in the sixteenth century. In China, it was the translation of the Buddhist sutras that inaugurated a long discussion on translation practice from the first century AC.

While the practice of translation is long established, the study of the field developed into an academic discipline only in the latter part of the twentieth century. Before that, translation had often been relegated to an element of language learning. In fact, from the late eighteenth century to the 1960s and beyond, language learning in secondary schools in many countries had come to be dominated by what was known as **grammar-translation** (Cook 2010: 9–15). Applied to Classical Latin and Greek and then to modern foreign languages, this centred on the rote study of the grammatical rules and structures of the foreign language. These rules were both practised and tested by the translation of a series of usually unconnected and artificially constructed sentences exemplifying the structure(s) being studied. This is an approach that persists even today in certain contexts. Typical of this is the following rather bizarre and decontextualized collection of sentences to translate into Spanish, for the practice of Spanish tense use. They appear in K. Mason's *Advanced Spanish Course*, still to be found on some secondary school courses in the UK until the 1990s:

(1) The castle stood out against the cloudless sky.
(2) The peasants enjoyed their weekly visits to the market.
(3) She usually dusted the bedrooms after breakfast.
(4) Mrs Evans taught French at the local grammar school.

(Mason 1969/1974: 92)

The gearing of translation to language teaching and learning may partly explain why academia considered it to be of secondary status. Translation exercises were regarded as a means of learning a new language or of reading a foreign language text until one had the linguistic ability to read the original. Study of a work in translation was generally frowned upon once the student had acquired the necessary skills to read the original. Grammar-translation therefore fell into increasing disrepute, particularly in many English-language countries, with the rise of alternative forms of language teaching such as the **direct method** and the **communicative approach** from the 1960s and 1970s (Cook 2010: 6–9, 22–26). The communicative approach stressed students' natural capacity to learn language and attempts to replicate 'authentic' language-learning conditions in the classroom. It often privileged spoken over written forms, at least initially, and generally avoided use of the students' mother tongue. This led to the abandoning of translation in language learning. As far as teaching was concerned, translation then tended to become restricted to higher-level and university language courses and professional translator training. It is only relatively recently that there has been a move to restore translation to language teaching (see Cook 2010: 125–53, for examples).

In 1960s USA, starting in Iowa and Princeton, literary translation was promoted by the **translation workshop** concept. This was based on the reading and practical criticism workshops of Cambridge critic I. A. Richards (1893–1979) from the 1920s and on later creative writing workshops. The translation workshops were intended as a platform for the introduction of new translations into the target culture and for the discussion of the finer principles of the translation process and of understanding a text.[8] Running parallel to this approach was that of **comparative literature**, where literature is studied and compared transnationally and transculturally, necessitating the reading of some works in translation.

Another area in which translation became the subject of research was **contrastive linguistics**. This is the study of two languages in contrast in an attempt to identify general and specific differences between them. It developed into a systematic area of research in the USA from the 1930s onwards and came to the fore in the 1960s and 1970s. Translations and translated examples provided much of the data in these studies (e.g. Di Pietro 1971, James 1980 and later Connor 1996). The contrastive approach heavily influenced important linguistic research into translation, such as Vinay and Darbelnet (1958) and Catford (1965), even if it did not incorporate sociocultural and pragmatic factors nor sufficiently the role of translation as a communicative act. The continued application of linguistics-based models has demonstrated their obvious and inherent link with translation. Among the specific models used are those related to generative grammar, functional linguistics and pragmatics (see Chapters 3 to 6).

The more systematic, linguistic-oriented, approach to the study of translation began to emerge in the 1950s and 1960s. There are a number of now classic examples:

- Andrei Fedorov's *Osnovy obshchey teorii perevoda* [Foundations of a General Theory of Translation] (1953/1968), described by Mossop (2013) and shown by Pym (2016) to have heavily influenced Vinay and Darbelnet and Loh (below);
- Jean-Paul Vinay and Jean Darbelnet produced their *Stylistique comparée du français et de l'anglais* (1958), a contrastive study of French and English which introduced key terminology for describing translation. It was not translated into English until 1995;
- Alfred Malblanc (1944/1963) did the same for translation between French and German and Loh Dian-yang for Chinese and English (Zhang and Pan Li 2009; Pym 2016);
- Georges Mounin's *Les problèmes théoriques de la traduction* (1963) examined linguistic issues of translation;

■ Eugene Nida (1964a) incorporated elements of Chomsky's then fashionable generative grammar as a theoretical underpinning of his books, which were initially designed to be practical manuals for Bible translators.

This more systematic approach began to mark out the territory of the 'scientific' investigation of translation. The word *science* was used by Nida in the title of his 1964 book (*Toward a Science of Translating*, 1964a). The German equivalent, *Übersetzungswissenschaft*, was taken up by Wolfram Wilss in his teaching and research at the Universität des Saarlandes at Saarbrücken, by Werner Koller in Heidelberg and by the Leipzig School, where scholars such as Otto Kade and Albrecht Neubert became active (see Snell-Hornby 2006). At that time, even the name of the emerging discipline remained to be determined, with other candidates staking their claim, such as *translatology* and its counterparts *Translatologie* in German, *traductologie* in French and *traductología* in Spanish (e.g. Vázquez-Ayora 1977 and the substantial contribution of Hurtado Albir 2001).

1.4 The Holmes/Toury 'map'

A seminal paper in the development of the field as a distinct discipline was James S. Holmes's 'The name and nature of translation studies' (Holmes 1988b/2004). In his *Contemporary Translation Theories*, Gentzler (2001: 93) describes Holmes's paper as 'generally accepted as the founding statement for the field.' Snell-Hornby (2006: 3) agrees. Interestingly, in view of our discussion above of how the field evolved from other disciplines, the published version was an expanded form of a paper Holmes originally gave in 1972 in the translation section of the Third International Congress of Applied Linguistics in Copenhagen (Holmes 1972). Holmes drew attention to the limitations imposed at the time because translation research, lacking a home of its own, was dispersed across older disciplines (languages, linguistics, etc.). He also stressed the need to forge 'other communication channels, cutting across the traditional disciplines to reach all scholars working in the field, from whatever background' (1988b/2004: 181).

Crucially, Holmes put forward an overall framework, describing what translation studies covers. This framework was subsequently presented by the leading Israeli translation scholar Gideon Toury as in Figure 1.1.

In Holmes's explanations of this framework (Holmes 1988b/2004: 184–90), the objectives of the 'pure' areas of research are: (1) the description of the

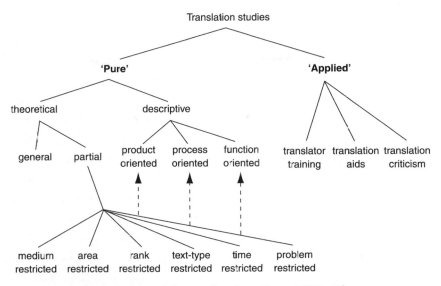

Figure 1.1   Holmes's 'map' of translation studies (from Toury 1995: 10)

phenomena of translation; and (2) the establishment of general principles to explain and predict such phenomena (**translation theory**). The **'theoretical'** branch is divided into general and partial theories. By 'general', Holmes is referring to those writings that seek to describe or account for every type of translation and to make generalizations that will be relevant for translation as a whole (one example would be Toury's 'laws' of translation; see Chapter 7). 'Partial' theoretical studies are restricted according to the parameters discussed below (medium, text-type, etc.).

The descriptive branch of 'pure' research in Holmes's map is known as **descriptive translation studies** (DTS, see Chapter 7). It may examine: (1) the product; (2) the function; and (3) the process.

(1)   **Product-oriented DTS** examines existing translations. This may involve the description or analysis of a single ST–TT pair or a comparative analysis of several TTs of the same ST (into one or more TLs). These smaller-scale studies can build up into a larger body of translation analysis looking at a specific period, language or text/discourse type. Examples would be translation in the twenty-first century, in the English<>Chinese language pair, or of scientific reports. Larger-scale studies can be either diachronic (following development over time) or synchronic (at a single point or period in time). Holmes (ibid.: 185) foresees that 'one of the eventual goals of

product-oriented DTS might possibly be a general history of translations – however ambitious such a goal might sound at this time'.

(2)   By **function-oriented DTS**, Holmes (ibid.) means the description of the 'function [of translations] in the recipient sociocultural situation: it is a study of contexts rather than texts'. Issues that may be researched include which texts were translated when and where, and the influences that were exerted. For example, the study of the translation and reception of Shakespeare into European languages, or the subtitling of contemporary cartoon films into Arabic. Holmes terms this area 'socio-translation studies'. Nowadays it would probably be called the sociology and historiography of translation. It was less researched at the time of Holmes's paper but is more popular in current work on translation studies (see Chapters 8 and 9).

(3)   **Process-oriented DTS** in Holmes's framework is concerned with the psychology of translation, i.e. it is concerned with trying to find out what happens in the mind of a translator. Work from a cognitive perspective includes think-aloud protocols (where recordings are made of translators' verbalization of the translation process as they translate). More recent research using new technologies such as eye-tracking shows how this area is now being more systematically analysed (see section 4.4).

The results of DTS research can be fed into the theoretical branch to evolve either a general theory of translation or, more likely, partial theories of translation 'restricted' according to the subdivisions in Figure 1.1.

■   **Medium-restricted theories** subdivide according to translation by machine and humans, with further subdivisions according to whether the machine/computer is working alone (automatic machine translation) or as an aid to the human translator (computer-assisted translation), to whether the human translation is written or spoken and to whether spoken translation (interpreting) is consecutive or simultaneous.

■   **Area-restricted theories** are restricted to specific languages or groups of languages and/or cultures. Holmes notes that language-restricted theories (e.g. for the Japanese<>English pair) are closely related to work in contrastive linguistics and stylistics.

■   **Rank-restricted theories** are linguistic theories that have been restricted to a level of (normally) the word or sentence. At the time Holmes was writing, there was already a trend towards text linguistics, i.e. analysis at the level of the text, which has since become far more popular (see Chapters 5 and 6 of this book).

■ **Text-type restricted theories** look at discourse types and genres; e.g. literary, business and technical translation. Text-type approaches came to prominence with the work of Reiss and Vermeer, among others, in the 1970s (see Chapter 5).

■ The term **time-restricted** is self-explanatory, referring to theories and trans-lations limited according to specific time frames and periods. The history of translation falls into this category.

■ **Problem-restricted theories** may refer to certain problems such as equivalence (a key issue that came to the fore in the 1960s and 1970s) or to a wider question of whether so-called 'universals' of translation exist.

Despite this categorization, Holmes himself is at pains to point out that several different restrictions may apply at any one time. Thus, the study of the prefaces to the new English translations of novels by Marcel Proust, analysed in Chapter 2, would be area restricted (translation from Parisian French into English), text-type restricted (prefaces to a novel) and time restricted (1981 to 2003).

The **'applied'** branch of Holmes's framework concerns applications to the practice of translation:

■ **translator training:** teaching methods, testing techniques, curriculum design;

■ **translation aids:** such as dictionaries and grammars;

■ **translation criticism:** the evaluation of translations, including the marking of student translations and the reviews of published translations.

Another area Holmes mentions is **translation policy**, where he sees the transla-tion scholar advising on the place of translation in society. This should include what place, if any, it should occupy in the language teaching and learning curriculum.

There are drawbacks to the structure. The divisions in the 'map' as a whole are in many ways artificial, and Holmes himself points out that the theoretical, descrip-tive and applied areas do influence one another. The main merit of the divisions is, as Toury states (1991: 180; 2012: 93), that they allow a clarification and a division of labour between the various areas of translation studies which, in the past, have often been confused. The divisions are still flexible enough to incorporate develop-ments such as the technological advances of recent years (see Chapter 11).

Even a cursory glance at Figure 1.1 shows the applied side to be under-developed. However, it is not difficult to expand it, as in Figure 1.2:

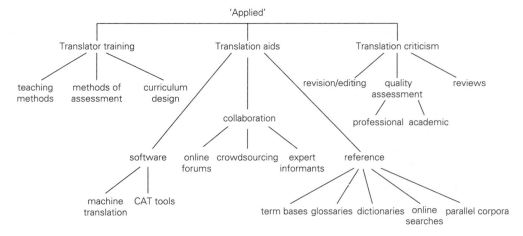

Figure 1.2   The applied branch of translation studies

While the general categories have been retained, we have filled in the detail, particularly for translation aids with the explosion in the use of computer-assisted translation tools (CAT tools) and in automatic online translation.

Although it may have dated, the crucial role played by Holmes's paper is in the delineation of the potential of translation studies. The map is still often employed as a point of departure, even if subsequent theoretical discussions have attempted to rewrite parts of it (e.g. Pym 1998, Hatim and Munday 2004, Snell-Hornby 2006, van Doorslaer 2007, see below). Also, present-day research has transformed the 1972 perspective. The fact that Holmes devoted two-thirds of his attention to the 'pure' aspects of theory and description surely indicates his research interests rather than a lack of possibilities for the applied side. 'Translation policy' is nowadays far more likely to be related to the ideology, including language policy and hegemony, that determines translation than was the case in Holmes's description. The different restrictions, which Toury identifies as relating to the descriptive as well as the purely theoretical branch in the discontinuous vertical lines in Figure 1.1, might well include a discourse-type as well as a text-type restriction. Inclusion of interpreting as a sub-category of human translation would also be disputed by many scholars. In view of the very different requirements and activities associated with interpreting, and despite inevitable points of overlap, it would probably be best to consider interpreting as a parallel field or 'sub-discipline', under the title of '**interpreting studies**' (see Pöchhacker 2004, 2009). **Audiovisual translation** (see Díaz Cintas and Remael 2007) and **sign language interpreting** might claim similar status. Additionally, as Pym points out (1998: 4), Holmes's map omits any mention of the individuality of the style, decision-making and working practices of human translators involved in the translation process. Yet it was precisely the split between theory and practice that Holmes, himself both a literary translator and a researcher, sought to overcome.

1.3 Exploration: Location in the Holmes/Toury map

Look at a recent issue of widely available online journals such as *Meta* and *JosTrans* (and, where possible, *Target, The Translator* and other journals). Try and locate each article within the Holmes/Toury 'map' (Figures 1.1 and 1.2). How easy is it to do so? Where would you locate your own work or studies in this schema?

1.5 Developments since Holmes

The surge in translation studies since Holmes has seen different areas of the map come to the fore. **Contrastive linguistics** generally fell by the wayside, but has resurfaced thanks to the advances in **machine translation** and **corpus-based studies** (see Chapter 11). The linguistics-oriented 'science' of translation has continued strongly in Germany, but the concept of **equivalence** associated with it has been questioned and reconceived (see Chapter 3). Germany has seen the rise of theories centred around **text types** and text **purpose** (the skopos theory of Reiss and Vermeer, see Chapter 5). The Hallidayan influence of **discourse analysis** and systemic functional grammar, which views language as a communicative act in a sociocultural context, came to prominence in the early 1990s, especially in Australia and the UK. It was applied to translation in a series of works by scholars such as Bell (1991), Baker (1992/2011), Hatim and Mason (1990, 1997), Calzada Pérez (2007), Munday (2008, 2012) (see Chapter 6). The late 1970s and the 1980s also saw the rise of a **descriptive approach** that had its origins in comparative literature and Russian Formalism (see Chapter 7). A pioneering centre was Tel Aviv, where Itamar Even-Zohar and Gideon Toury pursued the idea of the literary **polysystem** in which, among other things, different literatures and genres, including translated and non-translated works, compete for dominance. The polysystemists worked with a Belgium-based group including José Lambert and the late André Lefevere (who subsequently moved to the University of Austin, Texas), and with the UK-based scholars Susan Bassnett and Theo Hermans. A key volume was the collection of essays edited by Hermans, *The Manipulation of Literature: Studies in Literary Translation* (Hermans 1985a), which gave rise to the name of the

'Manipulation School'. Bassnett and Lefevere's volume *Translation, History and Culture* (1990) then introduced the term 'cultural turn'. This dynamic, culturally oriented approach held sway for much of the following decade (Chapter 8).

The 1990s saw the incorporation of new approaches and concepts: Canadian-based translation and gender research led by Sherry Simon, the Brazilian Cannibalist School promoted by Else Vieira, and postcolonial translation theory with the prominent figures of the Bengali scholars Tejaswini Niranjana and Gayatri Spivak (Chapter 8). In the USA, the cultural studies-oriented analysis of Lawrence Venuti called for greater visibility and recognition of the translator (Chapter 9). Developments continued at an ever-increasing pace in the new millennium, with special interest devoted to, for example, translation, globalization and resistance (Cronin 2003, Baker 2006, Boéri and Maier 2010, Marais 2014), the sociology and historiography of translation (e.g. Inghilleri 2005a, Wolf and Fukari 2007, Rundle 2014, Vorderobermeier 2014) and process-oriented research (e.g. O'Brien 2011). Research activity, as well as the practice of translation, has also been revolutionized by new technologies. These new areas include machine and automatic translation, audiovisual and multimodal translation, localization and corpus-based translation studies (see Chapter 11). Furthermore, the international reach of the discipline has expanded enormously with research and training in Asia (e.g. Chan 2004, Cheung 2006, 2009, Sato-Rossberg and Wakabayashi 2012) and the Arab world (Selim 2009) in particular.

1.6 The van Doorslaer 'map'

In order to deal with such a breadth of work, a new conceptual tool was developed for the Benjamins *Translation Studies Bibliography*, as explained by van Doorslaer (2007). In the new maps, a distinction is drawn between 'translation' and 'translation studies', reflecting the different centres of interest of research.[9] 'Translation' looks at the act of translating and, in the new map (van Doorslaer 2007: 223), is subdivided into:

- lingual mode (interlingual, intralingual);
- media (printed, audiovisual, electronic);
- mode (covert/overt translation, direct/indirect translation, mother tongue/ other tongue translation, pseudo-translation, retranslation, self-translation, sight translation, etc.);
- field (political, journalistic, technical, literary, religious, scientific, commercial).

Translation studies (ibid.: 228–31) is subdivided into:

- approaches (e.g. cultural approach, linguistic approach);
- theories (e.g. general translation theory, polysystem theory);
- research methods (e.g. descriptive, empirical);
- applied translation studies (criticism, didactics, institutional environment).

Alongside these is a 'basic transfer map' (ibid.: 226) of terminology to describe the linguistic manoeuvres that, despite the cultural turn, remain central to the concrete translating process. This consists of strategies, procedures/techniques, 'errors', rules/norms/conventions/laws/universals and translation tools. Figures 1.3 and 1.4 display the taxonomy of 'strategies' and 'procedures'.

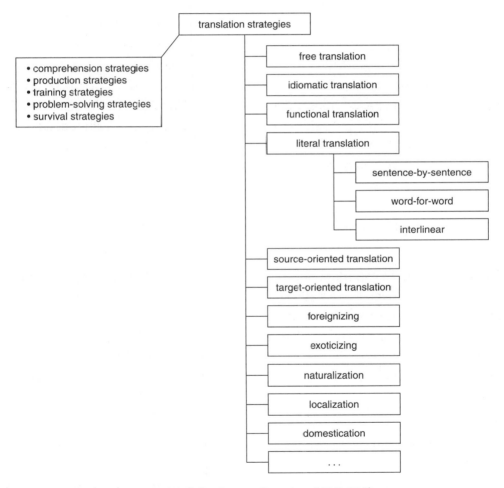

Figure 1.3 Translation strategies (following van Doorslaer 2007: 226)

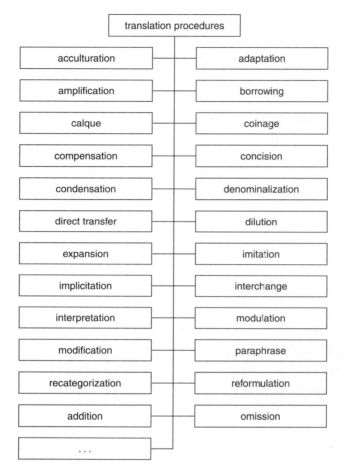

Figure 1.4   Translation procedures (following van Doorslaer 2007: 227)

The distinction is an important one, even if it is sometimes blurred in the literature: a **strategy** is the overall orientation of a translated text (e.g. literal translation, see Chapter 2) while a **procedure** is a specific technique used at a given point in a text (e.g. borrowing, calque, see Chapter 4).

Linguistic transfer of course still occurs within a sociocultural and historical context and institutional environment that place their own constraints on the process.

1.7 Discipline, interdiscipline or multidiscipline?

A notable characteristic of recent research has been its **interdisciplinarity**. In the first edition of this book we ended with a discussion of translation studies as a discipline, interdiscipline or sub-discipline, and saw the future in interdiscipli-narity. We discussed the nature of interdisciplines, referring to Willard McCarty's paper 'Humanities computing as interdiscipline' (1999),[10] which gives the following description of the role of an interdiscipline in academic society:

> A true interdiscipline is ... not easily understood, funded or managed in a world already divided along disciplinary lines, despite the standard pieties ... Rather it is an entity that exists in the interstices of the existing fields, dealing with some, many or all of them. It is the Phoenician trader among the settled nations. Its existence is enigmatic in such a world; the enigma challenges us to rethink how we organise and institutionalise knowledge.
>
> (McCarty 1999)

An interdiscipline therefore challenges the current conventional way of thinking by promoting and responding to new links between different types of knowledge and technologies. Viewing the hierarchy of disciplines as a systemic order, McCarty sees the 'conventional' disciplines having either a 'primary' or a 'secondary' relationship to a new interdiscipline. For us, translation studies would itself be the Phoenician trader among longer-established disciplines. It has the potential for a primary relationship with disciplines such as:

- linguistics (especially semantics, pragmatics, applied and contrastive linguis-tics, cognitive linguistics);
- modern languages and language studies;
- comparative literature;
- cultural studies (including gender studies and postcolonial studies);
- philosophy (of language and meaning, including hermeneutics and deconstruction and ethics);

and, in recent years, with sociology, history and creative writing. Some current projects are also **multidisciplinary**, involving the participation of researchers from various disciplines, including translation studies.

It is important to point out that the relationship of translation studies to other disciplines is not fixed. This explains the changes over the years, from a strong link to contrastive linguistics in the 1960s to the present focus on more cultural studies perspectives and even the recent shift towards areas such as computing and multi-media. Other, secondary, relationships come to the fore when dealing with the area of applied translation studies, such as translator training. For instance, specialized translation courses should have an element of instruction in the disciplines in which the trainees are planning to translate – such as law, politics, medicine, finance, science – as well as an ever-increasing input from information technology to cover computer-assisted translation.

While the discussion has continued on interdisciplinarity (e.g. Ferreira Duarte et al. 2006) and multidisciplinarity (House 2014), some, like Daniel Gile, have seen it as a threat:

> [P]artnerships established with other disciplines are almost always unbalanced: the status, power, financial means and actual research competence generally lie mostly with the partner discipline. Moreover, interdisciplinarity adds to the spread of paradigms and may, therefore, weaken further the status of [translation research] and [interpreting research] as autonomous disciplines.
>
> (Gile 2004: 29)

It is also true that translation studies has in some places been colonized by language departments driven by the perceived attractiveness of academic teaching programmes centred on the practice of translation but harbouring their own academic prejudices. Ironically, this has also worsened the **artificial gap between practice and theory**. For example, research assessments in the UK (formal external audits and evaluations of individuals' and departments' research output) have valued academic articles higher than translations, even translations of whole books. This ignores the fact that the practice of translation is an invaluable, not to say essential, experience for the translation theorist and trainer.

Yet the most fascinating developments have been the continued emergence of new perspectives, each seeking to establish a new 'paradigm' in translation studies. This provoked debate, highlighted by Chesterman and Arrojo (2000) and pursued in subsequent issues of *Target*, as to what **'shared ground'** there actually was in this potentially fragmenting subject area. The volume *New Tendencies in Translation Studies* (Aijmer and Alvstad 2005), deriving from a workshop at Göteborg University, Sweden in 2003, set out a concerted attempt to bring together and evaluate research methodologies. As the editors, with some understatement, pointed out in the introduction (ibid.: 1), there has been 'a movement away from a prescriptive approach to translation to studying what translation actually looks like. Within this framework the choice of theory and methodology becomes important.' Such choice is crucial and it depends on the goals of the research and the researchers. As we shall see as this book progresses, methodology has evolved and become more sophisticated (see Saldanha and O'Brien 2013). At the same time, there is considerable divergence on methodology, as translation studies has moved from the study of words to text to sociocultural context to the working practices of the translators themselves. An illustration of the diversity of current research can be gauged by the 19 panels at the 5th IATIS conference held in Belo Horizonte, Brazil, in July 2015.

1.4 Exploration: Translator studies

Read the online article by Chesterman (2010) for a discussion of some developments in Holmes' map. See also the bibliometric study by Zanettin et al. (2015), available through the ITS website, for a discussion of sub-fields in translation studies.

Even the object of study, therefore, has shifted over time, from translation as primarily connected to language teaching and learning to the study of the circumstances in which translation and translators operate.

Summary

Translation studies is an academic research area that has expanded massively over the years. Translation was formerly studied as a language-learning methodology or as part of comparative literature, translation 'workshops' and contrastive linguistics courses. The discipline as we now know it owes much to the work of James S. Holmes, who proposed both a name and a structure for the field, but the context has now advanced. The interrelated branches of theoretical, descriptive and applied translation studies initially structured research. Over time the interdisciplinarity and specialization of the subject have become more evident and theories and models have continued to be imported from other disciplines but also forged from within translation studies itself.

Discussion and research points

1   Investigate the use of other translation-related terms, such as 'adaptation', 'version' and 'transcreation'. In what contexts are they used? How easy is it to define these terms? In the light of your findings, try to write a definition of 'translation'.

2   Investigate how research-based translation studies fits into the university system in your country. How many universities offer 'translation studies' (or similar) MA or doctoral programmes? In which university departments/faculties are they housed? What are the 'primary' and 'secondary' relationships to other disciplines? What do you conclude is the status of translation studies in your country?

3   As you read each of the following chapters, try and locate each topic or concept within the Holmes/Toury 'map' (Figures 1.1 and 1.2). Carry out the same exercise with the van Doorslaer schema and compare the results.

The ITS website at www.routledge.com/cw/munday contains:

■   a video summary of the chapter;
■   a recap multiple-choice test;
■   customizable PowerPoint slides;
■   further reading links and extra journal articles;
■   more research project questions.

CHAPTER 2

Translation theory before the twentieth century

Key concepts

- **The 'word-for-word' ('literal') vs. 'sense-for-sense' ('free') debate.**
- **The importance of the translation of sacred texts.**
- **The vitalization of the vernacular: Luther and the German Bible.**
- **The influence of Dryden and the triad of metaphrase, paraphrase, imitation.**
- **Attempts at a more systematic prescriptive approach from Dolet and Tytler.**
- **Schleiermacher: a separate language of translation and respect for the foreign.**
- **The vagueness of the early terms used to describe translation.**

Key texts

Baker, Mona and Gabriela Saldanha (eds) (2009) *The Routledge Encyclopedia of Translation Studies,* 2nd edition, Abingdon and New York: Routledge, Part II: History and Traditions.

Bassnett, Susan (1980, revised edition 2013) *Translation Studies*, London and New York: Routledge, Chapter 2.

Cheung, Martha (ed.) (2006) *An Anthology of Chinese Discourse on Translation: From Earliest Times to the Buddhist Project,* Manchester: St Jerome.

Gutas, Dimitri (1998) *Greek Thought, Arabic Culture: The Graeco-Arabic Translation Movement in Baghdad and Early 'Abbāsid Society (2nd–4th/8th–10th Centuries)*, London and New York: Routledge.

Robinson, Douglas (1997b) *Western Translation Theory from Herodotus to Nietzsche*, Manchester: St Jerome. For fuller extracts from Cicero, St Jerome, Dolet, Bruni, Luther, Dryden and Tytler, among many others.

Schleiermacher, Friedrich (1813/2012) 'On the different methods of translating', in Lawrence Venuti (ed.) (2012) *The Translation Studies Reader*, 3rd edition, London and New York: Routledge, pp. 43–63.

2.0 Introduction

Watch the introductory video on the companion website.

The aim of this chapter is not to attempt a comprehensive history of translation or translators through the ages; this would be beyond the scope of any book. Instead, the main focus is the central recurring theme of 'word-for-word' and 'sense-for-sense' translation, a debate that dominated much of translation theory in what Newmark (1981: 4) called the **'pre-linguistics period of translation'**. It is a theme which Susan Bassnett sees as 'emerging again and again with different degrees of emphasis in accordance with differing concepts of language and communication' (2013: 53). In this chapter, we focus on a select few of the readily available writings based on the criterion of the influence they have exerted on the history of translation theory and research. The list of further reading will note some of the others that have a justifiable claim for inclusion or that provide a more detailed account. Historically, there has also been a very strong tendency to concentrate on western European writing on translation, starting with the Roman tradition, although over the past decades there has been an ever-growing list of publications in English addressing the wider geographic framework and for a wider audience.

2.1 Exploration: Timeline

The theory timeline on the ITS companion website locates the theorists who are discussed in this chapter.

2.1 'Word-for-word' or 'sense-for-sense'?

Up until the second half of the twentieth century, western translation theory seemed locked in what George Steiner (1998: 319) calls a 'sterile' debate over the 'triadic model' of 'literalism', 'paraphrase' and 'free imitation'. The distinction between 'word-for-word' (i.e. 'literal') and 'sense-for-sense' (i.e. 'free') translation goes back to Cicero (106–43 @AC) and St Jerome (347–420 AC). In the west, where the status of the Classical authors of ancient Greece and Rome remained pre-eminent, it formed the basis of key writings on translation for nearly two thousand years.

The Roman rhetorician and politician **Marcus Tullius Cicero** outlined his approach to translation in *De optimo genere oratorum* (46 @AC/1960 AC), introducing his own translation from the Greek of speeches of the fourth-century @AC Attic orators Aeschines and Demosthenes:

> And I did not translate them as an interpreter, but as an orator, keeping the same ideas and forms, or as one might say, the 'figures' of thought, but in language which conforms to our usage. And in so doing, I did not hold it necessary to render word for word, but I preserved the general style and force of the language.[1]

> (Cicero 46 @AC/1960 AC: 364)

The 'interpreter' of the first line is often read by translation studies as being the literal ('word-for-word') translator, while the 'orator' tried to produce a speech that moved the listeners. However, McElduff (2009: 136) points out that in ancient Rome it was the low social status of the 'interpreter' – a mediator of various kinds – that was disparaged because of a lack of education. This then led to 'limited and pedantic understanding' and to an inelegant, 'word for word', Latin style.

The disparagement of word-for-word translation came from others as well, such as the poet **Horace**, who, in a short but famous passage from his *Ars Poetica* (c.20 @AC),[2] underlines the goal of producing an aesthetically pleasing and creative poetic text in the TL. This attitude had great influence on the succeeding centuries. Thus, **St Jerome**, the most famous of all western translators, cites the authority of Cicero's approach to justify his own Latin revision and translation of the Christian Bible, later to become known as the Latin Vulgate. At a time when different and competing versions of the Bible were being produced, this was commissioned by Pope Damasus in 382 AC and aimed at establishing an official and standardized Latin translation for use in churches. Jerome revised and corrected earlier Latin translations of the Greek New Testament, the account of Jesus's life. For the Old Testament, he decided to return to the original Hebrew. This was a decision that was controversial to those who maintained the divine inspiration of the Greek Septuagint, the commonly accepted translation of the older texts, in use among Christians (Rebenich 2002: 53–4). The Septuagint was a Greek translation of the Hebrew Bible, undertaken over a long period beginning in the third century @AC in what has been described as 'the first major translation in western culture' (Rajak

2009: 1). By comparing the Greek Septuagint translation with the Hebrew original, Jerome noted points where the two versions differed. His overall translation strategy is formulated in *De optimo genere interpretandi*, a letter addressed to his friend, the senator Pammachius, in 395 AC.[3] In it, Jerome responds specifically to public criticisms of his originally private translation of a letter from Pope Epiphenius to John, the Bishop of Jerusalem. In perhaps the most famous statement ever made on the translation process, St Jerome defends himself against accusations of 'incorrect' translation and describes his strategy in the following terms:

> Now I not only admit but freely announce that in translating from the Greek – except of course in the case of the Holy Scripture, where even the syntax contains a mystery – I render not word-for-word, but sense-for-sense.[4]
>
> (St Jerome 395 AC/1997: 25)

Although some scholars (e.g. Vermeer 1994: 7) argue that these terms have been misinterpreted,[5] Jerome's statement is now usually taken to refer to what came to be known as **'literal'** (word-for-word) and **'free'** (sense-for-sense) translation. Jerome rejected the **word-for-word** approach because, by following so closely the form of the ST, it produced an absurd translation, cloaking the sense of the original. The **sense-for-sense** approach, on the other hand, allowed the sense or content of the ST to be translated. In these poles can be seen the origin of both the 'literal vs. free' and 'form vs. content' debate that has continued until modern times. To illustrate the concept of the TL taking over the sense of the ST, Jerome uses the military image of the original text being marched into the TL like a prisoner by its conqueror (Robinson 1997b: 26). As part of his defence St Jerome stresses the special 'mystery' of both the meaning and syntax of the Bible, for to be seen to be altering the sense of a sacred text was liable to bring a charge of heresy. Indeed, Jerome is explicitly making some distinction between different text types. While he translated Epiphenius's letter idiomatically ('sense for sense'), the Bible, he says, necessitated a literal method that paid closer attention to the words, syntax and ideas of the original.

2.2 Exploration: Cicero and St Jerome

Follow the links on the ITS website to a longer version of Cicero's and St Jerome's statements. Summarize their suggestions for a 'good' translation.

2.2 Early Chinese and Arabic discourse on translation

St Jerome's statement is usually taken to be the clearest expression of the 'literal' and 'free' poles in translation. The same concerns have been represented in other rich and ancient translation traditions such as in China and the Arab world. For instance, Hung and Pollard used similar terms when describing the history of **Chinese translation of Buddhist sutras** from Sanskrit (see Box 2.1).

Box 2.1

Sutra translation provided a fertile ground for the practice and discussion of different translation approaches. Generally speaking, translations produced in the first phase [Eastern Han Dynasty and the Three Kingdoms Period (c.148–265)] were **word-for-word** renderings adhering closely to source-language syntax. This was probably due not only to the lack of bilingual ability among the [translation] forum participants, but also to a belief that the sacred words of the enlightened should not be tampered with. In addition to contorted target-language syntax, transliteration was used very liberally, with the result that the translations were fairly incomprehensible to anyone without a theological grounding. The second phase [Jin Dynasty and the Northern and Southern Dynasties (c.265–589)] saw an obvious swing towards what many contemporary Chinese scholars call *yiyi* (**free translation**, for lack of a better term). Syntactic inversions were smoothed out according to target language usage, and the drafts were polished to give them a high literary quality. Kumārajīva was credited as a pioneer of this approach. In extreme cases, the polishing might have gone too far, and there are extant discussions of how this affected the original message. During the third phase [Sui Dynasty, Tang Dynasty and Northern Song Dynasty (c.589–1100)], the approach to translation was to a great extent dominated by Xuan Zang, who had an excellent command of both Sanskrit and Chinese, and who advocated that attention should be paid to the style of the original text: literary polishing was not to be applied to simple and plain source texts. He also set down rules governing the use of transliteration, and these were adopted by many of his successors.

(Hung and Pollard 2009: 372)

The vocabulary of Hung and Pollard's description (such as the gloss on *yiyi*) shows the influence of modern western translation terminology, the general thrust of the argument being similar to the Cicero/St Jerome poles described above. This is especially so because there are alternative translations for the terms – literally, *yìyì* is 'the translation of meaning' (see Chan 2001, below). Aesthetic and stylistic considerations are again noted, and there appear to be the first steps towards a rudimentary differentiation of text types, with non-literary STs being treated differently from literary TTs. Some of the issues, such as transliteration, relate most clearly to the problem of translation of foreign elements and names into a non-phonetic language (Chinese). However, it should be stressed that Hung and Pollard (2009) later revised and extended their discussion, emphasizing the changing context in which these translations were made. For example, the third phase was marked by increased linguistic competence and theological expertise on the part of the monks and officials involved and by stricter regulation on participation in the translation forums.

Translation choices were expounded in the prefaces to these texts, perhaps the most influential being by the religious leader **Dào'ān** (道安, 312–385 AC), who directed an extensive translation 'programme' of Buddhist sutras. These prefaces considered 'the dilemma which ever faced Buddhist translators: whether to make a free, polished and shortened version adapted to the taste of the Chinese public, or a faithful, literal, repetitious and therefore unreadable translation' (Zürcher 2007: 203). In the third preface to the translation of the *Prajnaparamita* (382 AC), Dào'ān lists five elements, called *shiben* ('losses'), where meaning was subject to change in translation (Box 2.2):

Box 2.2

In translating from foreign languages into Chinese, there are five losses to the original:

(1) The foreign words are entirely reversed, and to make them follow the Chinese [word order] is the first loss to the original.

(2) The foreign sutras esteem raw material [i.e. plain style], whereas the Chinese are fond of [elegant] style; if the transmission is to fit the feelings of the many [i.e. the Chinese *sangha*], it will have to match [elegant] style. This is the second loss to the original.

(3) The foreign sutras are minutely detailed, and regarding their recita-
tive exclamations and repeated exhortations, they do not shy away
from reiterating them three or four times. Now, cutting them off is
the third loss to the original.

(4) In the foreign sutras there are commentaries which elucidate
meaning that truly seem like disorderly phrases. Examining these
commentaries with regard to the words [of the main text?], one finds
that the text shows no difference. Removing about 1,500 [of the
words? of the commentaries?] entails the fourth loss to the original.

(5) After one subject is completed, it is approached once more from
[another] side, and [the authors] jump back to previous sentences
[or: take up previous sentences]; and what once was previous, now
becomes the new discourse, which has been completely omitted,
and that is the fifth loss to the original.

(translation, with parenthetical comments, in Lackner 2001: 362–3)

To summarize, these changes involve:

(1)   coping with the flexibility of Sanskrit syntax by reversing to a standard
Chinese order;

(2)   the enhancement of the literariness of the ST to adapt to an elegant
Chinese style;

(3)   the omission of repetitive exclamations;

(4)   the reduction in the paratextual commentaries that accompany the TTs; and

(5)   reduction or restructuring to ensure more logical and linear discourse.

Dào'ān also lists three factors (*buyi*, 'difficulties' or 'not deviating from the
text') that necessitated special care:

(1)   the directing of the message to a new audience;

(2)   the sanctity of the ST words; and

(3)   the special status of the STs themselves as the cumulative work of so many
followers.[6]

These points were to influence the work of the great Kuchan translator and
commentator **Kumārajīva** (344–413 AC) and those who followed him, until the

sixth century AC. Certainly, Dào'ān seems to have been one of the first to have highlighted the importance of both contrastive linguistic features (e.g. word order, syntax differences between SL and TL) and the social and historical context (audience, ST status) that affect translation. How far this was a concerted attempt to regulate the strategy to be employed in translating other texts, as Zürcher contends, is open to some debate (see Lackner 2001: 361–2).

Over recent years, there has been increased interest from the west in Chinese and other writing on translation and this has highlighted some important theoretical points. With specific reference to sutra transmission, Eva Hung (2005: 84–5) notes the problematization even of concepts such as 'original text' and 'source language', since these teachings were originally recited orally, leading to many variant STs, and there may have been 'half a dozen or more' Central Asian source languages involved before Sanskrit achieved its dominant position. In many cases the Sanskrit version has been lost but the Chinese has survived, which of course means that there is no longer any way of checking against any supposed ST. It also means that the Chinese for many has 'become' the source. Usually, the TTs were a collaborative effort, the draft translation of the spoken source being produced orally by a bilingual and written down by assistants before revision; explanations added by the Master also sometimes found their way into the TTs (Zürcher 2007: 31). Chan (2001: 199–204) discusses the problems of English equivalents for Chinese terms such as *yìyì*, which he claims has been used too liberally and in reality most closely matches sense-for-sense translation or even semantic correspondence (see Chapter 3); the opposite of *yìyì* is *zhìyì*, which has been translated as 'straightforward' or 'direct' translation, closely corresponding to the ST in the interests of 'faithfulness'.[7]

The 'literal' and 'free' poles surface once again in the rich translation tradition of the Arab world, which created the great centre of translation in Baghdad. There was intense translation activity in the 'Abbāsid period (750–1250 AC), encompassing a range of languages and topics. These were centred on the translation into Arabic of Greek scientific and philosophical material, often with Syriac as an intermediary language (Delisle and Woodsworth 1995: 112). Baker and Hanna (2009: 330), following Rosenthal (1965/1994), describe the two translation methods that were adopted during that period:

> The first [method], associated with Yuhanna Ibn al-Batrīq and Ibn Nā'ima al-Himsi, was highly literal and consisted of translating each Greek word with an equivalent Arabic word and, where none existed, borrowing the Greek word into Arabic.

According to Baker and Hanna (ibid.), this word-for-word method proved to be unsuccessful and was later revised using the second, sense-for-sense method:

> The second method, associated with Ibn Ishāq and al-Jawahari, consisted of translating sense-for-sense, creating fluent target texts which conveyed the meaning of the original without distorting the target language.

Once again, the terminology of this description is strongly influenced by the Classical western European discourse on translation. Although this does not negate the applicability of the two poles of translation to the Arabic tradition, there are of course other ways of considering the question. Salama-Carr (1995: 112–15) concentrates more on the way translation strategies 'helped establish a new system of thought that was to become the foundation of Arabic–Islamic culture – both on the conceptual and terminological levels'. Over the years, this saw the increased use of Arabic neologisms rather than the transliteration of Greek terms. Arab translators also became very creative in supplying instructive and explanatory commentaries and notes. However, Gutas, writing from a historical perspective, rejects a simplistic chronological explanation for the shifts in translation style in the 'Abbāsids' organized translation programme. Instead, he emphasizes the social, political and ideological factors involved. He contends (Gutas 1998: 138–50) that the wealth of texts increased the demand for translators which in turn led to their greater professionalization and improved knowledge of Greek. For Gutas, the divergences of style should be explained not as an evolution but as arising from different 'translation complexes' (groupings of translators and patrons) which operated independently on different texts. These included the translations of the medical writings of Hippocrates (c.460–c.370 @AC) and Galen (179–c.217 AC), of philosophical works, of Aristotle (384–322 @AC) on logic and the mathematics of Euclid (fourth–third century @AC), each with different goals.

2.3 Exploration: Different traditions

See the articles in *The Routledge Encyclopedia of Translation Studies* (Baker and Saldanha 2009, Part II) for a discussion of the early history of translation and translation theory in other cultures. Read the article by Krishnamurthy (2009), available through the ITS website, for a discussion of the Indian tradition.

2.3 Humanism and the Protestant Reformation

Within western society, issues of free and literal translation were for over a thousand years after St Jerome bound up with the translation of the Bible and other religious and philosophical texts. Before the arrival of the printing press (in China in the eleventh century AC and in Europe in the fifteenth century AC), texts were laboriously copied by hand, which led to numerous errors or variant readings. A sensitive religious text such as Jerome's Latin Vulgate, which was not actually accepted as official by the Roman Catholic Church until 1546, was also unstable because of constant attempts to 'correct' it with alternative readings, the addition of glosses and so on (Barnstone 1993: 194).

Language and translation became the sites of a huge power struggle. Latin, controlled by the Church in Rome, had a stranglehold over knowledge and religion until challenged by the **European Humanist movement** of the fourteenth and fifteenth centuries. The Humanists sought liberation from the power of the Church by recovering the refinement of Classical Latin and Greek and their secular writers, free from the changes wrought by the Middle Ages (Casanova 1999/2004: 48–9). Then, in the early fifteenth century, the **Protestant Reformation** of northern Europe, which was to lead to a huge schism within Christianity, began to challenge Latin through the translation of the Bible into vernacular languages. In such circumstances, the translation of any book which diverged from the Church's interpretation ran the risk of being deemed heretical and of being censured or banned. Even the mere act of translation could be considered a threat to the established order – for instance, the 1551 Index of the Spanish Inquisition prohibited the publication of the Bible in any vernacular language (Barnstone 1993: 195). An even worse fate lay in store for some of the translators who sought to make such texts available to a wider public. The most famous examples are the English theologian-translator **William Tyndale** (c.1490–1536) and the French humanist **Étienne Dolet** (1509–1546). Tyndale was a formidable linguist who was said to have mastered ten languages, including Hebrew. His extraordinary English Bible, produced in exile, was later used as the basis for the Geneva Bible (1560) and King James version (1611). It was banned and copies confiscated on the orders of King Henry VIII. Tyndale was abducted, tried for heresy and executed in the Netherlands in 1536 (Bobrick 2003, Chapter 2). Dolet was condemned by the theological faculty of the Sorbonne in 1546, apparently for adding, in his translation of one of Plato's dialogues, the phrase *rien du tout* ('nothing at all') in a passage about what existed after death. The addition led to the charge of blasphemy, the assertion being that Dolet did not believe in immortality. For such a translation 'error', he was burned at the stake.

The revolution in Bible translation practice in Europe was galvanized by Humanist advances in the study and knowledge of Greek and Hebrew and of Classical scholarship. Its culmination was Erasmus's edition of a parallel Greek-Latin New Testament in 1516 that was used by both Tyndale and Luther. The general climate of the Reformation and the new technology of the printing press meant that Bible translations dominated book production (Bobrick 2003: 81). Non-literal or non-accepted translation came to be seen and used as a weapon against the Church. The most notable example is **Martin Luther**'s crucially influential translation into East Central German of the New Testament (1522) and later the Old Testament (1534). Luther played a pivotal role in the Reformation while, linguistically, his use of a regional yet socially broad dialect went a long way to reinforcing that variety of the German language as standard. In response to accusations that he had altered the Holy Scriptures in his translations, Luther defended himself in his famous *Sendbrief vom Dolmetschen* ('Circular Letter on Translation') of 1530 (Luther 1530/1963).[8] One particularly notorious criticism levelled at Luther echoes that of Dolet. It centres around Luther's translation of Paul's words in Romans 3:28:

λογιζόμεθα γὰρ δικαιοῦσθαι πίστει ἄνθρωπον χωρὶς ἔργων νόμου.
[logizometha gar dikaiousthai pistei anthrōpon chōris ergōn nomou]

So halten wir nun dafür, daß der Mensch gerecht werde ohne des Gesetzes Werke, allein durch den Glauben.[9]
[Therefore, we hold that man is justified without the works of the law, only through faith.]

Luther had been heavily criticized by the Church for the addition of the word *allein* ('alone'/'only'), because there was no equivalent Greek word in the ST. The charge was that the German implies that the individual's belief is sufficient for a good life, making 'the works of the law' (i.e. religious law) redundant. Luther counters by saying that he was translating into 'pure, clear German',[10] where *allein* would be used for emphasis.

Luther follows St Jerome in rejecting a word-for-word translation strategy since it would be unable to convey the same meaning as the ST and would sometimes be incomprehensible. An example he gives is from Matthew 12:34:

ἐκ γὰρ τοῦ περισσεύματος τῆς καρδίας τὸ στόμα λαλεῖ
[ek gar tou perisseumatos tēs kardias to stoma lalei]

The English King James version translates this literally as:

> Out of the abundance of the heart the mouth speaketh.

Luther translates this with a common German proverb:

> Wes das Herz voll ist, des geht der Mund über.
> [With what the heart is full, the mouth overflows.]

This idiom means 'to speak straight from the heart'.

While Luther's treatment of the free and literal debate does not show great theoretical advance on what St Jerome had written over a thousand years before, his infusion of the Bible with the language of ordinary people and his consideration of translation in terms that focused on the TL and the TT reader were crucial. Typical of this is his famous quote extolling the language of the people:

> You must ask the mother at home, the children in the street, the ordinary man [sic] in the market and look at their mouths, how they speak, and translate that way; then they'll understand and see that you're speaking to them in German.[11]

From that time onwards, the language of the ordinary German speaks clear and strong, thanks to Luther's translation.

2.4 Fidelity, spirit and truth

In her *Early Theories of Translation*, Flora Amos sees the history of the theory of translation as 'by no means a record of easily distinguishable, orderly progression' (Amos 1920/1973: x). For her, theory was generally unconnected and amounted to a broad series of prefaces and comments by practitioners who often ignored, or were ignorant of, earlier discourse. As a result:

> [t]his lack of consecutiveness in criticism is probably partially accountable for the slowness with which translators attained the power to put into words, clearly and unmistakably, their aims and methods.
>
> (Amos 1920/1973: x)

For instance, Amos notes (ibid.: xi) that early translators often differed considerably in the meaning they gave to terms such as 'faithfulness', 'accuracy' and even the word 'translation' itself.

Such concepts are investigated by Louis Kelly in *The True Interpreter* (1979). Kelly looks in detail at the history of western translation theory, starting with the teachings of the Greek and Latin writers of Classical Antiquity and tracing the history of what he calls (ibid.: 205) the 'inextricably tangled' terms 'fidelity', 'spirit' and 'truth'. These were sites for contestation, depending to a large degree on historical context and on societal conceptualizations of translation. So, the concept of **fidelity** (or at least the translator who was *fidus interpres*, i.e. the 'faithful interpreter') had initially been dismissed as literal, word-for-word translation by Horace. Indeed, it was not until the end of the seventeenth century that fidelity had come to be generally identified with faithfulness to the meaning rather than the words of the author. Kelly (ibid.: 206) describes **spirit** as similarly having two meanings: the Latin word *spiritus* denotes creative energy or inspiration, proper to literature, but St Augustine (354–430 AC) used it to mean the Holy Spirit of God, and his contemporary St Jerome employed it in both senses. Much later, spirit lost the religious sense it originally possessed and was thenceforth used in the sense of the creative energy of a text or language. For St Augustine, spirit and **truth** (Latin *veritas*) were intertwined, with truth having the sense of 'content'; for St Jerome, truth meant the authentic Hebrew Biblical text to which he returned in his Latin Vulgate translation. Kelly considers that it was not until the twelfth century that truth became fully equated with 'content'. It is easy to see how in the translation of sacred texts, where 'the Word of God' is paramount, there has been such an interconnection of fidelity (to both the words and the perceived sense), spirit (the energy of the words and the Holy Spirit) and truth (the 'content').

In contrast to Amos, Rener (1989) makes a persuasive case for continuity in the early translation prefaces in the west. This continuity derived from a common theoretical conceptualization of language, dominant since the writings of Cicero and Quintilian (35–96/100 AC, see Robinson 1997b: 19) in ancient Rome. The study of language was divided into grammar (the 'correct' use of words and sentences) and rhetoric (their use as communication, notably to persuade). **Grammar** privileged words that exhibited the values of *proprietas* (acceptability), *puritas* (purity) and *perspecuitas* (clarity); a word should be accepted as an integral part of the language and commonly understood, it should have a long history and be employed in the texts of high-status writers. **Rhetoric** valued *elegantia* (elegance) and *dignitas* (dignity), which were stylistic considerations that covered structure, rhythm and musicality. The influence of this thinking persisted. A keen example of the importance of rhetoric can be seen in the Italian humanist **Leonardo Bruni** (1369–1444), who translated philosophical works of the Classical Greek and Latin authors and occupied high ecclesiastical office. Bruni was particularly concerned to retain the style of the original author, which he saw as an amalgam of the order and rhythm of the words and the 'polish and elegance' of the original (Robinson 1997b: 59–60). Indeed, Bruni felt that this was the only 'correct' way to translate. For him, such stylistic demands could only be met through the learnedness and literariness of the translator, who needed to possess excellent knowledge of the original language and considerable literary ability in his own language.

2.4 Exploration: Literalism and rhetoric

Read the online lecture by Hermans (n.d.) on Étienne Dolet, available at https://www.ucl.ac.uk/translation-studies/translation-in-history/documents/Hermans_pdf. Note his description of the move in translation from Early Modern literalism to Humanist style and rhetoric. See also Hermans (1997).

2.5 Early attempts at systematic translation theory: Dryden, Dolet, Tytler and Yán Fù

For Amos (ibid.: 137), the England of the seventeenth century – with Denham, Cowley and Dryden – marked an important step forward in translation theory with 'deliberate, reasoned statements, unmistakable in their purpose and meaning'. At that time, apart from the Bible, translation into English was almost exclusively confined to verse renderings of Greek and Latin Classics. Because at that time translation had come to be valued as an exercise in creativity and novelty, some of these renderings were extremely free. Abraham Cowley (1618–1667), in his preface to *Pindaric Odes* (1640), attacks poetry that is 'converted faithfully and word for word into French or Italian prose' (Cowley 1640, in Robinson 1997b: 161, also cited in Amos 1920/1973: 149). His approach is also to counter the inevitable loss of beauty in translation by using 'our wit or invention' to create new beauty. In doing this, Cowley admits he has 'taken, left out and added what I please' to the *Odes* (Robinson 1997b: 162, Amos 1920/1973: 150). Cowley even proposes the term 'imitation' for this very free method of translating (Robinson ibid.: 161, Amos ibid.: 151). The idea was not, as in the Roman period, that such a free method would enable the translator to surpass the original; rather that this was the method that permitted the 'spirit' of the ST to be best reproduced (Amos ibid.: 157).

Such a very free approach to translation produced a reaction, notably from another English poet and translator, **John Dryden** (1631–1700), whose brief description of the translation process would have enormous impact on subsequent translation theory and practice. In the preface to his translation of Ovid's *Epistles* in 1680, Dryden (1680/1992: 25) reduces all translation to three categories:

(1) **'metaphrase'**: 'word by word and line by line' translation, which corresponds to literal translation;

(2) **'paraphrase'**: 'translation with latitude, where the author is kept in view by the translator, so as never to be lost, but his words are not so strictly followed as his sense'; this involves changing whole phrases and more or less corresponds to faithful or sense-for-sense translation;

(3) **'imitation'**: 'forsaking' both words and sense; this corresponds to Cowley's very free translation and is more or less what today might be understood as adaptation.

Graphically, we might represent this as follows:

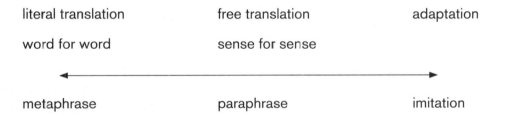

| literal translation | free translation | adaptation |
| word for word | sense for sense | |

metaphrase   paraphrase   imitation

Dryden criticizes translators such as Ben Jonson (1572–1637), who adopts metaphrase, as being a 'verbal copier' (ibid.). Such 'servile, literal' translation is dismissed with a now famous simile: ' 'Tis much like dancing on ropes with fettered legs – a foolish task.' Similarly, Dryden rejects imitation, where the translator uses the ST 'as a pattern to write as he supposes that author would have done, had he lived in our age and in our country' (ibid.). Imitation, in Dryden's view, allows the translator to become more visible, but does 'the greatest wrong . . . to the memory and reputation of the dead' (ibid.: 20). Dryden thus prefers paraphrase, advising that metaphrase and imitation be avoided.

This three-part, or 'triadic', model proposed by Dryden was to exert considerable influence on later writings on translation. Yet it is also true that Dryden himself changes his stance, with the dedication in his translation of Virgil's *Aeneid* (1697) showing a shift to a point between paraphrase and literal translation:

> I thought fit to steer betwixt the two extremes of paraphrase and literal translation; to keep as near my author as I could, without losing all his graces, the most eminent of which are in the beauty of his words.
>
> (Dryden 1697/1997: 174)

The description of his own translation approach in fact bears resemblance to his definition of imitation above: 'I may presume to say ... I have endeavoured to make Virgil speak such English as he would himself have spoken, if he had been born in England, and in this present age' (ibid.).

2.5 Exploration: Making Virgil speak English

How do you imagine Dryden would have set about making Virgil speak English? Look at some examples of Dryden's translations on the companion website. What does this reveal about Dryden's conception of language and thought? See Venuti (2008: 52–3) for further discussion.

In general, Dryden and others writing on translation at the time are very prescriptive, setting out what in their opinion has to be done in order for successful translation to take place. Despite its subsequent importance for translation theory, Dryden's writing remains full of the language of his time: the 'genius', or special characteristics, of the ST author and language,[12] the 'force' and 'spirit' of the original, the need to 'perfectly comprehend' the sense of the original, and the 'art' of translation.

Other early writers on translation also began to state their principles in a similarly prescriptive fashion. One of the first had been **Étienne Dolet** (see above), whose objective was to disseminate Classical teachings through a Humanist lens and to contribute to the development of the French language. In his 1540 manuscript *La manière de bien traduire d'une langue en aultre* ('The way of translating well from one language into another'; Dolet 1540/1997), he set out **five principles** in order of importance as follows:[13]

(1)   The translator must perfectly understand the sense and material of the original author, although he [sic] should feel free to clarify obscurities.
(2)   The translator should have a perfect knowledge of both SL and TL, so as not to lessen the majesty of the language.
(3)   The translator should avoid word-for-word renderings.
(4)   The translator should avoid Latinate and unusual forms.
(5)   The translator should assemble and liaise words eloquently to avoid clumsiness.

Here again, the concern is to reproduce the sense and to avoid word-for-word translation. But the stress on producing an eloquent and natural TL form was rooted in a Humanist enthusiasm for the rediscovered Classics and a political desire to reinforce the structure and independence of the new vernacular French language.

In English, the first comprehensive and systematic study of translation is **Alexander Fraser Tytler**'s 'Essay on the **principles of translation**', published in 1790. Rather than Dryden's author-oriented description ('write as the original author would have written had he known the target language'), Tytler (1747–1813) defines a 'good translation' as being oriented towards the target language reader:

> That in which the merit of the original work is so completely transfused into another language as to be as distinctly apprehended, and as strongly felt, by a native of the country to which that language belongs as it is by those who speak the language of the original work.
>
> (Tytler 1797/1997: 209)

And, where Dolet has five 'principles', Tytler (ibid.) has **three general 'laws'** or 'rules'.

(1)   The translation should give a complete transcript of the ideas of the original work.
(2)   The style and manner of writing should be of the same character with that of the original.
(3)   The translation should have all the ease of the original composition.

Tytler's first law ties in with Dolet's first two principles in that it refers to the translator having a 'perfect knowledge' of the original (ibid.: 210), being competent in the subject and giving 'a faithful transfusion of the sense and meaning' of the author. Tytler's second law, like Dolet's fifth principle, deals with the style of the author and involves the translator's both identifying 'the true character' (ibid.: 113) of this style and having the ability and 'correct taste' to recreate it in the TL. The third law (ibid.: 211–12) talks of having 'all the ease of composition' of the ST. Tytler regards this as the most difficult task and likens it, in a traditional metaphor, to an artist producing a copy of a painting. Thus, 'scrupulous imitation' should be avoided, since it loses the 'ease and spirit of the original'. Tytler's solution (ibid.: 211) is for the translator to 'adopt the very soul of his author'. But it is unclear what that actually is.

Tytler himself recognizes that the first two laws represent the two widely different opinions about translation. They can be seen as the poles of faithfulness of content and faithfulness of form, reformulations of the sense-for-sense and word-for-word diad of Cicero and St Jerome. Importantly, however, just as Dolet had done with his principles, Tytler ranks his three laws in order of comparative importance. Such hierarchical categorization gains force in more modern translation theory. For instance, the discussion of translation 'loss' and 'gain', which continues even to the present, is in some ways presaged by Tytler's suggestion that the rank order of the laws should be a means of determining decisions when a 'sacrifice' has to be made (ibid.: 212). Thus, ease of composition would be sacrificed if necessary for manner, and manner could be sacrificed in the interests of sense.

Tytler's laws are said by some (see Chan 2004: 68) to have influenced the work of the renowned Chinese thinker and translator **Yán Fù** (1854–1921). In his short preface[14] to his translation of Thomas Huxley's *Evolution and Ethics* (published in 1901), Yán Fù states his three translation principles as *xìn* (fidelity/faithfulness/trueness), *dá* (fluency/expressiveness/intelligibility/comprehensibility) and *yǎ* (elegance/gracefulness). These concepts became central to twentieth-century Chinese translation practice and theory. Hermans (2003, online) usefully discusses the range of meanings inherent in the three principles as well as the disagreements as to how these concepts align with western translation theory. Yán Fù himself generally placed *xìn* above *dá* (Chan 2004: 4–5), although he did not always abide by the hierarchy, often privileging *yǎ*. According to Sinn (1995), Yán Fù's translation practice promoted his own ideology through the selection of philosophical texts and the textual manipulation to which he subjected them. Modern-day Chinese linguists have also criticized his principles for being vague and difficult to apply (Chan 2004). A more positive view is taken by Huang (2003) and Wright (2001), situating Yán Fù in the historical context of his work and emphasizing his unprecedented role in the transmission of political thought from the west. Spira (2015: 101–11) discusses Yán Fù's central problem that arose from choosing an erudite and archaic Chinese literary style to render modern concepts that originated in a foreign language.

2.6 Exploration: Yán Fù's principles

Read the article by Luo Xuanmin and Hong Lei (2004) on Chinese translation theory and practice, available through the ITS website. Note their discussion of the influence of Yán Fù.

2.6 Schleiermacher and the valorization of the foreign

In Germany, the work of philosopher Johann Gottfried Herder (1744–1803) on language and thought was to have an important influence over the German Romantics of the early nineteenth century, including monumental figures such as Goethe, Wilhelm von Humboldt, Schlegel and Schleiermacher (Forster 2010). One of the Romantics' interest was in how translation could be a means for improving German literature and culture; they centred on the issues of translatability or untranslatability and the mythical nature of translation (see Lefevere 1977; Snell-Hornby 2006, Chapter 1). Most famously, in 1813, **Friedrich Schleiermacher** (1768–1834), recognized as a founder of modern Protestant theology and modern hermeneutics, delivered his seminal lecture *Über die verschiedenen Methoden des Übersetzens* ['On the different methods of translating'].[15] His **hermeneutics** expounded a Romantic approach to interpretation based not on absolute truth but on the individual's inner feeling and understanding (see Chapter 10).

Distinct from other translation theorists we have discussed so far in this chapter, Schleiermacher first distinguishes two different types of translator working on two different types of text. These are:

(1) the **'Dolmetscher'**, who translates commercial texts;
(2) the **'Übersetzer'**, who works on scholarly and artistic texts.

It is this second type that Schleiermacher sees as being on a higher creative plane, breathing new life into the language (1813/2012: 44). Although it may seem impossible to translate scholarly and artistic texts, since the ST meaning is couched in language that is very culture-bound and to which the TL can never fully correspond, the real question, according to Schleiermacher, is how to bring the ST writer and the TT reader together. He moves beyond the strict issues of word-for-word and sense-for-sense, literal, faithful and free translation, and considers there to be only two paths open for the 'true' translator:

> Either the translator leaves the writer in peace as much as possible and moves the reader toward him, or he leaves the reader in peace as much as possible and moves the writer toward him.[16]
>
> (Schleiermacher 1813/2012: 49)

Schleiermacher's preferred strategy is to **move the reader towards the writer**. This does not entail writing as the author would have done had he written in German. That would be similar to Dryden's formula, a **'naturalizing'** method that brought the foreign text in line with the typical patterns of the TL. Instead, Schleiermacher's method is to 'give the reader, through the translation, the impression he would have received as a German reading the work in the original language' (ibid.: 50).[17] In this way, the translator, an expert in the TL, can help the less competent but intelligent German reader to appreciate the ST. To achieve this, the translator must adopt an **'alienating'**, 'foreignizing' method of translation. This emphasizes the value of the foreign, by 'bending' TL word-usage to try to ensure faithfulness to the ST. Thus can the TT be faithful to the sense and sound of the ST and can import the foreign concepts and culture into German (Forster 2010: 416).

There are several consequences of this approach, including:

(1) If the translator is to seek to communicate the same impression which he or she received from the ST, this impression will also depend on the level of education and understanding among the TT readership, and this is likely to differ from the translator's own understanding.

(2) A special language of translation may be necessary, for example compensating in one place with an imaginative word where elsewhere the translator has to make do with a hackneyed expression that cannot convey the impression of the foreign.

Schleiermacher's influence has been huge. Indeed, Kittel and Polterman (2009: 417) claim that 'practically every modern translation theory – at least in the German-language area – responds, in one way or another, to Schleiermacher's hypotheses.' Schleiermacher's consideration of different text types becomes more prominent in Reiss's text typology (see Chapter 5 of this volume). The 'alienating' and 'naturalizing' opposites are taken up by Venuti as 'foreignization' and 'domestication' (see Chapter 9). Additionally, the vision of a 'language of translation' is pursued by Walter Benjamin and the description of the hermeneutics of translation is prominent in George Steiner's 'hermeneutic motion' (see Chapter 10).

2.7 Exploration

See the ITS website for a summary of the Newman–Arnold polemic on translation method from Victorian Britain.

2.7 Towards contemporary translation theory

In his detailed, idiosyncratic classification of the early history of translation theory, George Steiner lists a small number of fourteen writers who represent 'very nearly the sum total of those who have said anything fundamental or new about translation' (Steiner 1998: 283). This list includes St Jerome, Luther, Dryden and Schleiermacher and also takes us into the twentieth century with Ezra Pound and Walter Benjamin, among others (see Chapter 10). Steiner in fact describes as 'very small' the range of theoretical ideas covered in this period:

> We have seen how much of the theory of translation – if there is one as distinct from idealized recipes – pivots monotonously around undefined alternatives: 'letter' or 'spirit', 'word' or 'sense'. The dichotomy is assumed to have analysable meaning. This is the central epistemological weakness and sleight of hand.
>
> (Steiner 1998: 290)

Other modern theoreticians concur that the main problem with the writings on translation in this period was that the criteria for judgements were vague and subjective (Bassnett 2013) and that the judgements themselves were highly normative (Wilss 1977/1982). As a reaction against such vagueness and contradictions, translation theory in the second half of the twentieth century made various attempts to redefine the concepts 'literal' and 'free' in operational terms, to describe 'meaning' in scientific terms, and to put together systematic taxono-mies of translation phenomena. These approaches form the core of the following chapters in this book.

Case studies

The following case studies look briefly at two areas where the vocabulary of the 'literal vs. free' debate continues to be used in contemporary writing on transla-tion. Case study 1 examines two examples of criteria for assessing translations. Case study 2 looks at modern translators' prefaces from English translations of Marcel Proust's *À la recherche du temps perdu*. In both cases the aim is to iden-tify how far the ideas and vocabulary of early theory held sway in later writing on translation.

Case study 1: Assessment criteria

The area of assessment criteria is one where a more expert writer (a marker of a translation examination or a reviser of a professional translation) addresses a less expert reader (usually a candidate for an examination or a junior professional translator). It is interesting to see how far the vocabulary used is the rather vague vocabulary of early translation theory.

The Chartered Institute of Linguists' (CIoL) Diploma in Translation is the most widely known initial qualification for translators in the UK. Late in the twentieth century, the organization's Notes for Candidates[18] gave the following criteria for assessing the translations:

(1) Accuracy: the correct transfer of information and evidence of complete comprehension;
(2) The appropriate choice of vocabulary, idiom, terminology and register;
(3) Cohesion, coherence and organization;
(4) Accuracy in technical aspects of punctuation, etc.

The question of 'accuracy' appears twice (criteria 1 and 4). 'Accuracy' is in some ways the modern linguistic equivalent of 'faithfulness' and 'truth'; in the

CloL document there is an attempt at closer definition of accuracy, comprising 'correct transfer of information' and 'complete comprehension'. As we discuss in Chapter 3, these terms are influenced by terminology suggested by Nida in the 1960s. Criterion 2's 'appropriate choice of vocabulary', etc. suggests a more TL approach, while criterion 3 (cohesion and coherence) leads us into the areas of text and discourse analysis (see Chapters 5 and 6).

Thus, these criteria make an attempt at formalizing clear rules for translation. However, examiners' reports on the candidates' performances, although containing detailed examples of errors and of good translations, tend to be sprinkled with the vaguer and controversial vocabulary of early translation theory. A typical CloL examiners' report of the time (French into English, paper 1, November 1997) explains many student errors in considerable detail, but still stresses the criterion of TL fluency. Thus, 'awkwardness' is a criticism levelled at four student translations; they are considered to be unnatural and therefore defective examples of the TL. By contrast, candidates are praised for altering sentence structure 'to give a more natural result in English'. Perhaps the most interesting point is the use of the term 'literal translation'. 'Literal' is used four times – and always as a criticism – concerning, for example, literal translations of false friends. Interestingly enough, however, 'literal' is also used as a relative term. For example, '*too* literal a style of translating' (my emphasis) produced TT expressions such as 'transmitting the budget to the Chamber' (rather than 'delivering the budget'), and a '*totally* literal translation' (my emphasis) of *déjeuner-débat* (presumably something like 'lunch-debate' rather than 'lunchtime talk/discussion') 'produced very unnatural English'. Nevertheless, the qualification of the adjective *literal* by the adverbs *too* and *totally* suggests that *literal* alone is not now being viewed as the extreme. Rather, as was suggested in section 2.1 earlier, 'literal' is being used to mean a close lexical translation. Only when this strategy is taken to an extreme (when it is 'too' or 'totally' literal) is the 'naturalness' of the TL infringed.

Similar criteria are repeated in UNESCO's *Guidelines for Translators* of the same period.[19] 'Accuracy' is again 'the very first requirement'. The description of the aim of translation is that, after reaching an understanding of what the ST writer 'was trying to say', the translator should put this meaning into (in this case) English 'which will, so far as possible, produce the same impression on the English-language reader as the original would have done on the appropriate foreign-language reader'. This bears quite close resemblance to the wording of Schleiermacher's suggestion for literary translation, of moving the reader towards the author. Yet the method suggested by UNESCO as appropriate for achieving this is not to follow an 'alienating' strategy but to find an intermediate way between something that 'sounds' like a translation and something which is so 'aggressively characteristic' of the translator's idiolect that it strikes the reader as 'unusual'.

There are several additional points of particular interest concerning the UNESCO criteria:

(1)   The balance between the two poles ('sounding like a translation' and being 'aggressively characteristic') is described using an image ('a perpetual feat of tightrope walking') which is very close to Dryden's famous simile of the clumsy literal translator as 'dancing on ropes with fettered legs'.
(2)   The UNESCO document makes allowance for the TT readers, who are sometimes non-native speakers of the TL.
(3)   The suggested solution varies according to text type: the style of articles translated for periodicals should be 'readable', while politically sensitive speeches require a 'very close translation' to avoid being misinterpreted.

The first of these points indicates the extent to which old metaphors of translation persisted even in quite modern writings. The second point touches on a more reader-oriented approach, although the document rejects the existence of a 'special' language of translation. The third point shows an awareness that different approaches may be valid for different texts. This was noted by Schleiermacher in his division of categories into business and philosophical texts but which, as we discuss in Chapter 5, has far more to do with the text-type approach of Reiss.

Case study 2: The translator's preface

Translators' prefaces are a source of extensive information on the translation methods. Sometimes their function is to justify the production of a new translation of a classic work. This was the case with the English-language translation of Marcel Proust's masterpiece À la recherche du temps perdu (1913–1927). Originally translated from French into English in the 1920s by the celebrated Charles Kenneth Scott Moncrieff (1889–1930), the English was revised in 1981 by Terence Kilmartin and in 1992 by D. J. Enright.[20] A new translation was published by Penguin in 2002. The language of the prefaces reflects the cultural values of the time in which the translations were created.

In the introduction of the 1981 translation (p. x), the reasons given by Kilmartin for the revision were that there had been later publications of revised and corrected editions of the French original, and that there was a need to correct 'mistakes and misinterpretations' in the translation. The 1981 translation also contained a four-page 'Note on the translation' by Kilmartin. One of the most interesting points about Kilmartin's comments is the vocabulary he uses to describe the revisions he has carried out:

> I have refrained from officious tinkering [with the translation] for its own sake, but a translator's loyalty is to the original author, and in trying to be faithful to Proust's meaning and tone of voice I have been obliged, here and there, to make extensive alterations.
>
> (Kilmartin in Proust 1996: ix)

The concept of 'loyalty' to the author and being 'faithful' to the meaning could almost have come straight from the writings of the seventeenth century. The division between 'meaning' and 'tone of voice' could also be taken to originate in the debate on form vs. content. The use of general terms such as 'tone' in the commentary also echoes the imprecision of earlier writing.

The perceived 'literal' translation of the ST is criticized. Kilmartin (ibid.: x), referring to the translation of the 1920s, describes Scott Moncrieff's 'tendency to translate French idioms and turns of phrase literally', which makes them 'sound weirder', and his 'sticking too closely' to the original syntax especially in long sentences packed with subordinate clauses which seem 'unEnglish' in the TT: 'a whiff of Gallicism clings to some of the longer periods, obscuring the sense and falsifying the tone', claims Kilmartin (ibid.). The negative connotation of 'whiff of Gallicism' seems quite surprising in this context. Kilmartin is criticizing the apparent foreignness of the structure of the translation of one of the great French writers and has a preference for a totally 'naturalizing' (to use Schleiermacher's term) English style in the translation.

The major new multi-volume translation of Proust's novel began to appear in 2002 with Penguin, each volume produced by a different translator in a project overseen by general editor Cambridge academic Christopher Prendergast. He emphasizes that this is a new translation, not a revision, benefitting from a corrected source text (the 1987 Pléiade edition) that had resulted from the advances of scholarship. In the first volume, called *The Way by Swann's*,[21] the prefaces by Prendergast and by translator Lydia Davis reveal a somewhat more sophisticated awareness of the theoretical issues. Thus, Prendergast, who notes Vladimir Nabokov's recommendation of literalness (Nabokov 1955/2004), rejects the Kilmartin/Enright approach, stating:

> How to manage Proust's extraordinary syntactic structures in English is a very difficult issue. They are often strange even to French ears, and there may well be a respectable argument to the effect that oddly unEnglish shapes are sometimes the best way of preserving their estranging force.
>
> (Prendergast in Proust 2003: xi)

Prendergast is concerned to avoid examples, such as the use of *Mamma*, which transpose Proust's world into 'an upper-class Victorian nursery' (ibid.: viii). At the same time, he shows an awareness of the possible choices between foreignizing and naturalizing translation (see Schleiermacher) and seeks a balance rather than modernizing the old TT.

Likewise, Davis insists that her aim was as far as possible to reproduce Proust's style,

> to stay as close as possible to Proust's original in every way, even to match his style as nearly as I could [. . .] to reproduce as nearly as possible Proust's word choice, word order, syntax, repetition of words, punctuation − even, when possible, his handling of sounds, the rhythms of a sentence and the alliteration and assonance within it.
>
> (Davis in Proust 2003: xxxi)

Discussion of case studies

These two brief case studies indicate that the vocabulary of early translation theory persisted widely to the end of the twentieth century and beyond. 'Literal', 'free', 'loyalty', 'faithfulness', 'accuracy', 'meaning', 'style' and 'tone' are words that reappear again and again, even in areas (such as assessment criteria) which draw on a more systematic theoretical background. The tendency in most of the comments noted above is for a privileging of a 'natural' TT, one which reads as if it were originally written in the TL. In those cases, one can say that 'literal' translation lost out, and also that the 'alienating' strategy promoted by Schleiermacher has not been followed. What remains is the 'natural', almost 'everyday' speech style proposed by Luther. Yet the new Penguin Proust translation suggests a possible change of approach and in the CloL texts the pre-modifications of the term 'literal' ('*too* literal', '*totally* literal') indicate the shift in use of this term over the centuries. 'Literal' now means 'sticking very closely to the original'. Translators who go further than this leave themselves open to criticism. The 'imaginative' and 'idiomatic' translation is still preferred. However, the texts examined in the case studies were written mainly for the general reader or novice translator. As we shall see in the next chapter, the direction of translation theory from the second half of the twentieth century was generally towards a systematization of different elements of the translation process.

Summary

The general trend of western translation theory from Cicero in Classical antiquity to the twentieth century centred on the recurring debate as to whether translations should be literal (word-for-word) or free (sense-for-sense), a diad that is famously discussed by St Jerome in his translation of the Bible into Latin. Controversy over the translation of the Bible was central to translation theory in the west for well over a thousand years. Early western theorists tended to be translators who presented a justification for their approach in a preface to the translation. They are often portrayed as paying little attention (or not having access) to what others before them had written. However, they reflected a faithfulness to the religious text, often manifested in Early Modern literalism, or a Classical view of language based on principles of clarity, logic and elegance that came to the fore with the advent of European Humanism. In the late seventeenth century, Dryden's proposed triad of metaphrase, paraphrase and imitation is said to mark the beginning of a more systematic and precise definition of translation. Later, Schleiermacher's respect for the foreign text was to have considerable influence over scholars in modern times. In recent decades, there has been increased interest in Chinese and other discourse on translation, centred on the early translation projects of the Buddhist sutras and on the position of Yán Fù in twentieth-century China.

Further reading

There are a large number of collections and histories of translation. English is particularly well-served with Classe (2000), France (2000), and the five-volume *Oxford History of Literary Translation in English* (Braden et al. 2010, Ellis 2008, Gillespie and Hopkins 2005, France and Haynes 2006, Venuti forthcoming). In addition to those works included in the list of key texts at the beginning of this chapter, the following are of special interest: Amos (1920/1973), Delisle and Woodsworth (1995), Kelly (1979), Steiner (1975/1998), Schulte and Biguenet (1992), Weissbort and Eysteinsson (2006) and, for German, Lefevere (1977, 1992b) and Störig (1963). Readers are recommended to follow their specific interests regarding country, period, cultures and languages. Delisle and Woodsworth (1995) and Baker and Saldanha (2009) are particularly useful in giving the background to translation in a wider range of cultures. Kelly (1979) is especially strong on the Latin tradition and Rener (1989) is a very detailed exploration on the concept of language and translation from Classical times to Tytler. Adams (2003) looks at Latin bilingualism in Antiquity and McElduff (2013) examines Roman translation theories. Louw (2007) and Rajak (2009) examine translation of the Septuagint. Bobrick (2003) outlines the history of English Bible translation and how it transformed the language; Barnstone (1993) does the same from a translation studies perspective. Chan (2004) and Cheung (2006) look at the influence of Yán Fù on twentieth-century writers on translation. This and other Asian traditions are discussed in Cheung (2009), Hung and Wakabayashi (2005), Wakabayashi and Kothari (2009) and Sato-Rossberg and Wakabayashi (2012). Selim (2009) contains articles on translation and the Arab world. The papers in Hermans (2006a, 2006b) cover a range of non-western thought on translation. Pym (1998) and Rundle (2014) are useful as a presentation of investigative methods in translation history.

2.8 Exploration: Other traditions

See the ITS website for a discussion of new works that have appeared on the history of translation and translation theory.

Discussion and research points

1   Find recent reviews of translations, either in the press or in online readers' reviews, in your own languages. What kinds of comments are made about the translation itself? How far is the vocabulary used similar to that described in this chapter?

2 Look at the updated handbook to the Chartered Institute of Linguist's *Diploma in Translation* (http://www.ciol.org.uk/images/Qualifications/ DipTrans/DipTransHandbook.pdf). How far are the criteria still centred on the theoretical concepts discussed in this chapter? Compare also some recent examiners' reports and preparation seminar handouts (http://www. ciol.org.uk/index.php?option=com_content&view=article&layout=coil:nor elated&id=205&Itemid=672) to see how these criteria are now applied.

3 Investigate early writing on translation in your own languages and cultures. How closely does it resemble the writings discussed in this chapter? Are there significant differences in early translation theory written in different languages? Compare the varied papers in Hermans (2006a, 2006b).

4 Compare Dáo'ān's losses and difficulties, Dolet's principles, Tytler's laws and Yán Fù's principles. What are the similarities and differences between them? Try and depict this comparison visually (see Table 3.2 on page 72 for an example). How useful do you consider these principles for guiding a translator?

The ITS website at www.routledge.com/cw/munday contains:

- a video summary of the chapter;
- a recap multiple-choice test;
- customizable PowerPoint slides;
- further reading links and extra journal articles;
- more research project questions.

CHAPTER 3

Equivalence and equivalent effect

Key concepts

- **The problem of translatability and equivalence in meaning, discussed by Jakobson (1959) and central to translation studies for the following decades.**

- **Nida's 'scientific' methods to analyse meaning in his work on Bible translating.**

- **Nida's concepts of formal equivalence and dynamic equivalence and the principle of equivalent effect: focus on the receptor.**

- **Newmark's semantic translation and communicative translation.**

- **Development of 'science of translating' in the Germanies of the 1970s and 1980s.**

- **Pym's 'natural' and 'directional' equivalence.**

Key texts

Bassnett, Susan (1980, revised edition 2013) *Translation Studies*, London and New York: Routledge, Chapter 1.

Jakobson, Roman (1959/2012) 'On linguistic aspects of translation', in Lawrence Venuti (ed.) (2012), *The Translation Studies Reader*, 3rd edition, London and New York: Routledge, pp. 126–31.

Koller, Werner (1995) 'The concept of equivalence and the object of translation studies', *Target* 7.2: 191–222.

Newmark, Peter (1981) *Approaches to Translation*, Oxford and New York: Pergamon, republished (2001) by Shanghai Foreign Language Education Press.

Nida, Eugene (1964a) *Toward a Science of Translating*, Leiden: E. J. Brill.

Nida, Eugene (1964b/2012) 'Principles of correspondence', in Lawrence Venuti (ed.) (2012), *The Translation Studies Reader*, 3rd edition, London and New York: Routledge, pp. 141–55.

Nida, Eugene and Charles Taber (1969) *The Theory and Practice of Translation*, Leiden: E. J. Brill.

Pym, Anthony (2007) 'Natural and directional equivalence in theories of translation', *Target* 19.2: 271–94.

3.0 Introduction

Watch the introductory video on the companion website.

In order to avoid the age-old opposition between literal and free translation (see Chapter 2), theoreticians in the 1950s and 1960s began to attempt more systematic analyses. The new debate revolved around certain key linguistic issues. The most prominent were those of 'meaning' and 'equivalence', discussed in Roman Jakobson's 1959 paper (see section 3.1). Over the following twenty years many further attempts were made to define the nature of equivalence. In this chapter we shall look at several major works of the time: Eugene Nida's seminal concepts of formal and dynamic equivalence and the principle of equivalent effect (section 3.2), Peter Newmark's semantic and communicative translation (section 3.3), and Werner Koller's *Korrespondenz* and *Äquivalenz* (section 3.4).

3.1 Roman Jakobson: the nature of linguistic meaning and equivalence

In Chapter 1 we saw how, in his paper 'On linguistic aspects of translation' (1959/2012), structuralist Roman Jakobson describes three kinds of translation: intralingual, interlingual and intersemiotic, with interlingual referring to translation between two different written sign systems. Jakobson goes on to examine key issues of this type of translation, notably **linguistic meaning** and **equivalence**.

Jakobson follows the theory of language proposed by the famous Swiss linguist Saussure (1857–1913). Saussure distinguished between the linguistic system (*langue*) and specific individual utterances (*parole*). Central to his theory of *langue*, he differentiated between the 'signifier' (the spoken and written signal) and the 'signified' (the concept), which together create the linguistic **'sign'**. Thus, in English the word *cheese* is the acoustic signifier which 'denotes' the concept 'food made of pressed curds' (the signified). Crucially, the sign is arbitrary or unmotivated (Saussure 1916/1983: 67–9). Instead of *cheese*, the signifier could easily have been *bread, soup, thingummyjig* or any other word. Jakobson also stresses that it is possible to understand what is signified by a word even if we have never seen or experienced the concept or thing in real life. Examples he gives are *ambrosia* and *nectar*, words which modern readers will have read in Greek myths even if they have never come across the substances in real life; this contrasts with *cheese*, which they almost certainly have encountered first-hand in some form.

Jakobson then moves on to consider the thorny problem of **equivalence in meaning** between words in different languages, part of Saussure's *parole*. He points out (1959/2012: 127) that 'there is ordinarily no full equivalence between code-units'. Thus, the Russian *syr* is not identical to the English *cheese* (or, for that matter, the Spanish *queso*, the German *Käse*, the Korean *chijeu*, etc.) since the Russian 'code-unit' does not include the concept of soft white curd cheese known in English as *cottage cheese*. In Russian, that would be *tvarog* and not *syr*. This general principle of interlinguistic difference between terms and semantic fields importantly also has to do with a basic issue of language and translation. On the one hand, **linguistic universalism** considers that, although languages may differ in the way they convey meaning and in the surface realizations of that meaning, there is a (more or less) shared way of thinking and experiencing the world. On the one hand, **linguistic relativity** or **determinism** in its strongest form claims that differences in languages shape different conceptualizations of the world. This is the famous Sapir-Whorf hypothesis that had its roots in the behaviourism of the 1920s and in the anthropological study of the native American Hopi language, which, according to Whorf (1956), had no words or grammatical categories to indicate time. Another claim that is often made is that Eskimos have more words for snow because they perceive or conceive of it differently. This claim, and indeed linguistic determinism itself, is firmly rejected, amongst others, by Pinker (1994: 57–65; 2007: 124–51), who points out that the vocabulary of a language simply reflects what speakers need for everyday life. The absence of a word in a language does not mean that a concept cannot be perceived – someone from a hot climate can be shown slush and snow and can notice the difference.

Full linguistic relativity would mean that translation was impossible, but of course translation does occur in all sorts of different contexts and language pairs. In Jakobson's description (ibid.), interlingual translation involves 'substitut[ing] messages in one language not for separate code-units but for entire messages in some other language'. Thus, a translation of *cottage cheese* would not be the TT unit for *cottage* plus the unit for *cheese*; the message *cottage cheese* would be considered and translated as a whole. For the message to be 'equivalent' in ST and TT, the code-units will necessarily be different since they belong to two different sign systems (languages) which partition reality differently (the *cheese/syr* example above). In Jakobson's discussion, the problem of meaning and equivalence focuses on differences in the structure and terminology of languages rather than on any inability of one language to render a message that has been written or uttered in another verbal language. Thus, Russian can still express the full semantic meaning of *cheese* even if it breaks it down into two separate concepts.[1] The question of **translatability** then becomes one of degree and adequacy (see Hermans 1999: 301).

For Jakobson (ibid.: 129), cross-linguistic differences, which underlie the concept of **equivalence**, centre around obligatory grammatical and lexical forms: 'Languages differ essentially in what they must convey and not in what they may convey'. Examples of **differences** are easy to find. They occur at:

- the level of gender: e.g. *house* is feminine in Romance languages, neuter in German and English; *honey* is masculine in French, German and Italian, feminine in Spanish, neuter in English, etc.;
- the level of aspect: in Russian, the verb morphology varies according to whether the action has been completed or not;
- the level of semantic fields, such as kinship terms: e.g. the German *Geschwister* is normally explicated in English as *brothers and sisters*, since *siblings* is rather formal. Similarly, in Chinese it would be 兄弟姐妹 ('xiōng dì jiě mèi', literally meaning 'elder brother, younger brother, elder sister, younger sister').

Even what for many languages is a basic relational concept such as *to be* (English), *être* (French) and *sein* (German) is broken down in Spanish to *ser* and *estar*, while Arabic, Russian and many others do not use such a verb explicitly in the present tense. These examples illustrate differences between languages, but they are still concepts that can be rendered interlingually. As Jakobson (ibid.) puts it, '[a]ll is conveyable in any existing language'. For him, only poetry, with its unity of form and sense and where 'phonemic similarity is sensed as semantic relationship', is considered 'untranslatable' and requires 'creative transposition' (ibid.: 131).

3.1 Exploration: Interlinguistic difference

Look again at Jakobson's comment that 'Languages differ essentially in what they *must* convey and not in what they *may* convey.' Find examples from your own languages that illustrate this. How are these dealt with in translation?

The questions of meaning, equivalence and translatability became a constant theme of translation studies in the 1960s and were tackled by a new 'scientific' approach followed by one of the most important figures in translation studies, the American Eugene Nida (1914–2011).

3.2 Nida and 'the science of translating'

Eugene Nida's theory of translation developed from his own practical work from the 1940s onwards when he was translating and organizing the translation of the Bible, training often inexperienced translators who worked in the field.[2] Nida's theory took concrete form in two major works in the 1960s: *Toward a Science of Translating* (Nida 1964a) and the co-authored *The Theory and Practice of Translation* (Nida and Taber 1969). The title of the first book is significant; Nida attempts to move Bible translation into a more scientific era by incorporating recent work in **linguistics**. His more systematic approach borrows theoretical concepts and terminology both from semantics and pragmatics and from Noam Chomsky's work on syntactic structure which formed the theory of a universal generative–transformational grammar (Chomsky 1957, 1965).

3.2.1 The influence of Chomsky

Chomsky's generative–transformational model analyses sentences into a series of related levels governed by rules. In very simplified form, the key features of this model can be summarized as follows:

(1)   Phrase-structure rules generate an underlying or **deep structure** which is
(2)   transformed by transformational rules relating one underlying structure to another (e.g. active to passive), to produce

(3) a final **surface structure**, which itself is subject to phonological and morphemic rules.

The structural relations described in this model are held by Chomsky to be a universal feature of human language. The most basic of such structures are **kernel sentences**, which are simple, active, declarative sentences that require the minimum of transformation (e.g. *the wolf attacked the deer*).

Nida incorporates key features of Chomsky's model into his **'science' of translation**. In particular, Nida sees that it provides the translator with a technique for decoding the ST and a procedure for encoding the TT (Nida 1964a: 60). Thus, the surface structure of the ST is analysed into the basic elements of the deep structure; these are 'transferred' in the translation process and then 'restructured' semantically and stylistically into the surface structure of the TT. This three-stage system of translation (analysis, transfer and restructuring) is presented in Figure 3.1:

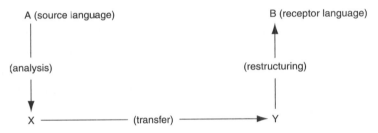

Figure 3.1   Nida's three-stage system of translation (from Nida and Taber 1969: 33)

Nida and Taber's own description of the process (1969: 63–9) emphasizes the 'scientific and practical' advantages of this method compared to any attempt to draw up a fully comprehensive list of equivalences between specific pairs of SL and TL systems. 'Kernel' is a key term in this model. Just as kernel sentences were the most basic structures of Chomsky's initial model, so, for Nida and Taber (ibid.: 39), **kernels** 'are the basic structural elements out of which language builds its elaborate surface structures'. Kernels are to be obtained from the ST surface structure by a reductive process of back transformation. This entails analysis using generative–transformational grammar's four types of functional class:

(1) events: often but not always performed by verbs (e.g. *run, fall, grow, think*);
(2) objects: often but not always performed by nouns (e.g. *man, horse, mountain, table*);
(3) abstracts: quantities and qualities, including adjectives and adverbs (e.g. *red, length, slowly*);

(4) relationals: including affixes, prepositions, conjunctions and copulas (e.g. *pre-*, *into*, *of*, *and*, *because*, *be*).

Examples of analysis (e.g. Nida 1964a: 64), designed to illustrate the different constructions with the preposition *of*, are:

> surface structure: *will of God*
>> back transformation: B (object, *God*) performs A (event, *wills*)

and   '

> surface structure: *creation of the world*
>> back transformation: B (object, *the world*) is performed by A (event, *creates*).

Nida and Taber (ibid.: 39) claim that all languages have between six and a dozen basic kernel structures and 'agree far more on the level of kernels than on the level of more elaborate structures' such as word order. Kernels are the level at which the message is transferred into the receptor language before being transformed into the surface structure in a process of: (1) 'literal transfer'; (2) 'minimal transfer'; and (3) 'literary transfer'. Box 3.1 displays an example of this transfer process in the translation of a verse from the New Testament story of John (John 1:6, cited in Nida 1964a: 185–7).

Box 3.1

- Greek ST:

1	2	3	4	5	6	7	8
egeneto	anthrōpos,	apestalmenos	para	theou,	onoma	autō	Iōannēs

- Literal transfer (stage 1):

1	2	3	4	5	6	7	8
became/happened	man,	sent	from	God,	name	to-him	John

- Minimal transfer (stage 2):

1	2	3	4	5	7	6	8
There CAME/WAS	a man,	sent	from	God,	WHOSE	name *was*	John

■   Literary transfer (stage 3, example taken from the *American Standard Version*, 1901[3]):

1	2	3	4	5	7	6	8
There	CAME	a man,	sent	from	God,	WHOSE	name *was* John

or (example taken from Phillips *New Testament in Modern English*, 1958[4]):

2	6	7	8	3	4	5
A man,	NAMED	*	John	WAS sent	BY	God

Notes: Adjustments from the ST are indicated as follows: changes in order are indicated by the numeral order, omissions by an asterisk (*), structural alterations by QK?JJ A? Nℝ?JQ and additions by *italics*.

The two examples of literary transfer are different stylistically, notably in syntax, the *American Standard Version* being more formal and archaic. The reason for this may be the kind of equivalence and effect that is intended, a crucial element of Nida's model (see section 3.2.3).

3.2.2 The nature of meaning: advances in semantics and pragmatics

When it comes to analysing individual words, Nida (1964a: 33ff) describes various 'scientific approaches to meaning' related to work that had been carried out by theorists in semantics and pragmatics. Central to Nida's work is the move away from the old idea that a word has a fixed meaning and towards a functional definition of meaning in which a word 'acquires' meaning through its context and can produce varying responses according to culture.

   Meaning is broken down into the following:

(1)   **Linguistic meaning:** the relationship between different linguistic structures, borrowing elements of Chomsky's model. Nida (ibid.: 59) provides examples to show how the meaning crucially differs even where similar classes of words are used. For instance, the following three expressions with the possessive pronoun *his* all have different meanings: *his house*

means 'he possesses a house', *his journey* equals 'he performs a journey' and *his kindness* is 'kindness is a quality of him'.

(2) **Referential meaning:** the denotative 'dictionary' meaning. Thus, *son* denotes a male child.

(3) **Emotive** or **connotative meaning:** the associations a word produces. So, in the phrase 'Don't worry about that, *son*', the word *son* is a term of endearment or may in some contexts be patronizing.

A series of techniques, adapted from linguistics, is presented as an aid for the translator in determining the meaning of different linguistic items. Techniques to determine referential and emotive meaning focus on analysing the structure of words and differentiating similar words in related lexical fields. These include **hierarchical structuring**, which differentiates series of words according to their level (for instance, the superordinate animal and its hyponyms *goat, dog, cow*, etc.) and techniques of **componential analysis**. The latter seek to identify and discriminate specific features of a range of related words. The results can be plotted visually to assist in making an overall comparison. For example, Table 3.1 plots family relationship terms (*grandmother, mother, cousin*, etc.) according to the values of sex (male, female), generation (the same, one, two or more apart) and lineality (direct ancestor/descendant or not).

Table 3.1 Example of componential analysis (adapted from Nida 1964a: 85)

	grand-father	grand-mother	father	mother	uncle	aunt	son	daughter	grand-son	grand-daughter
G1	+	+								
G2			+	+	+	+				
G3							+	+		
G4									+	+
Sex m	+		+		+		+		+	
Sex f		+		+		+		+		+
Lineality 1	+	+	+	+			+	+	+	+
Lineality 2					+	+				

For example, the first column, for *grandfather*, has the values of first generation, male sex and direct lineality. Such results are useful for a translator working with languages that have different kinship terms. Sometimes more values will need to be incorporated. For example, Chinese may distinguish lexically between the maternal and paternal grandfather.

Another technique is **semantic structure analysis** in which Nida (ibid.: 107) separates out visually the different meanings of *spirit* ('demons', 'angels', 'gods', 'ghost', 'ethos', 'alcohol', etc.) according to their characteristics (human vs. non-human, good vs. bad, etc.). The central idea of this analysis is to encourage the trainee translator to realize that the sense of a complex semantic term such as *spirit* (or, to take another example, *bachelor*) varies and most particularly is 'conditioned' by its context. *Spirit* thus does not always have a religious significance. Even (or perhaps especially) when it does, as in the term *Holy Spirit*, its emotive or connotative value varies according to the target culture (Nida ibid.: 36). The associations attached to the word are its connotative value, and these are considered to belong to the realm of pragmatics or 'language in use'. Above all, Nida (ibid.: 51) stresses the importance of context for communication when dealing with metaphorical meaning and with complex cultural idioms, for example, where the sense of the phrase often diverges from the sum of the individual elements. Thus, the Hebrew idiom *bene Chuppah* (lit. 'children of the bridechamber') refers to the wedding guests, especially the friends of the bridegroom (ibid.: 95).

In general, techniques of semantic structure analysis are proposed as a means of clarifying ambiguities, elucidating obscure passages and identifying cultural differences. They may serve as a point of comparison between different languages and cultures and are proposed by Nida especially for those working with widely differing languages.

3.2 Exploration: Componential analysis

Use Table 3.1 above to plot kinship terms for your L1 and L2. How far do these map onto the English terms? How helpful is this componential analysis for translation?

3.2.3 Formal and dynamic equivalence and the principle of equivalent effect

The old terms such as 'literal', 'free' and 'faithful' translation, which were examined in Chapter 2, are discarded by Nida in favour of 'two basic orientations' or 'types of equivalence' (Nida 1964a: 159): (1) formal equivalence; and (2) dynamic equivalence. These are defined by Nida as follows:

(1) **Formal equivalence:** Formal equivalence focuses attention on the message itself, in both form and content . . . One is concerned that the message in the receptor language should match as closely as possible the different elements in the source language.

(Nida 1964a: 159)

Formal equivalence, later called 'formal correspondence' (Nida and Taber 1969: 22–8), is thus keenly oriented towards the ST structure, which exerts strong influence in determining accuracy and correctness. Most typical of this kind of translation are 'gloss translations', with a close approximation to ST structure, often with scholarly footnotes. This type of translation will often be used in an academic or legal environment and allows the reader closer access to the language and customs of the source culture.

(2) **Dynamic equivalence:** Dynamic, later 'functional', equivalence is based on what Nida calls 'the principle of **equivalent effect**', where 'the relationship between receptor and message should be substantially the same as that which existed between the original receptors and the message'.

(Nida 1964a: 159).

The message has to be tailored to the receptor's linguistic needs and cultural expectation and 'aims at complete naturalness of expression'. 'Naturalness' is a key requirement for Nida. Indeed, he defines the goal of dynamic equivalence as seeking 'the closest natural equivalent to the source-language message' (Nida 1964a: 166, Nida and Taber 1969: 12). This receptor-oriented approach considers adjustments of grammar, of lexicon and of cultural references to be essential in order to achieve naturalness. The TT language should not show interference from the SL, and the 'foreignness' of the ST setting is minimized (Nida 1964a: 167–8) in a way that would be criticized by later culturally-oriented translation theorists (see Chapters 8 and 9).

For Nida, the success of the translation depends above all on achieving **equivalent effect** or **response**. It is one of the 'four basic requirements of a translation', which are (ibid.: 164):

(1) making sense;
(2) conveying the spirit and manner of the original;
(3) having a natural and easy form of expression;
(4) producing a similar response.

Although dynamic equivalence aims to meet all four requirements, it is also a graded concept since Nida accepts that the 'conflict' between the traditional notions of content and form cannot always be easily resolved. As a general rule for such conflicts, Nida considers that 'correspondence in meaning must have priority over correspondence in style' if equivalent effect is to be achieved. However, it is interesting to note the similarity with Tytler's principles of translation in one of the early attempts at systematizing translation theory at the end of the eighteenth century (see Chapter 2). This suggests that the scientific approach is still supported by the essential subjectivity of some of the language of the literal vs. free debate.

3.2.4 Discussion of the importance of Nida's work

The key role played by Nida is to develop the path away from strict word-for-word equivalence. His introduction of the concepts of formal and dynamic equivalence was crucial in introducing a receptor-based (or reader-based) orientation to translation theory. However, both the principle of equivalent effect and the concept of equivalence have come to be heavily criticized for a number of reasons: Lefevere (1993: 7) felt that equivalence was still overly concerned with the word level, while van den Broeck (1978: 40) and Larose (1989: 78) considered equivalent effect or response to be impossible. (How is the 'effect' to be measured and on whom? How can a text possibly have the same effect and elicit the same response in two different cultures and times?) Indeed, the whole question of equivalence inevitably entails subjective judgement from the translator or analyst.

It is interesting that the debate continued into the 1990s. In 1992 and 1993, for example, *Meta*, one of the leading international journals of translation studies, published a series of five papers by Qian Hu whose express aim was to demonstrate the **'implausibility' of equivalent response**. The focus in these papers[5] is notably on the impossibility of achieving equivalent effect when meaning is bound up in form, for example the effect of word order in Chinese and English, especially in literary works (Qian Hu 1993b: 455–6). Also, that 'the closest natural equivalent may stand in a contradictory relation with dynamic equivalents'. The example given (ibid.: 465) is of the English words *animal, vegetable, mineral* and *monster*. The closest Chinese equivalents are *dòng wù, zhí wù, kuàng wù* and *guài wù*. These all happen to contain the character *wù*, meaning 'object' (thus, *dòng wù* means 'moving object', hence *animal*). If these Chinese equivalents are chosen, such an unintended cohesive link would lead to what Qian Hu terms 'overtranslation'. Qian Hu also discusses cultural references, and the argument recalls the kind of criticism that has surrounded a notorious example where Nida (1964a: 160) considers that *give one another a hearty handshake all round* 'quite naturally translates' the early Christian *greet one another with a holy kiss*. While some may feel the loss of the source culture term/custom, such cultural adaptation is far from unusual. It is witnessed, for example, by Arabic translations of *Harry Potter* that translate *she kissed him on the cheek* by *she waved at him and said 'Good-bye, Harry'* (Dukmak 2012).

3.3 Exploration: Equivalent effect

Read the discussion of equivalent effect by Qian Hu in one or more of the papers in *Meta* available online (Qian Hu 1992a, 1992b, 1993a, 1993b, 1994). Note the criticisms made. Look also at the article by Miao Ju (2000) on the ITS companion website. How valid do you consider these criticisms to be?

The criticism that equivalent effect is subjective raises the question of whether Nida's theory of translation really is 'scientific'. The techniques for the analysis of meaning and for transforming kernels into TT surface structures are carried out in a systematic fashion, but it remains debatable whether a translator follows these procedures in practice. However, Nida's detailed description of real translation phenomena and situations in a wealth of varied languages is an important rejoinder to the vague writings on translation that had preceded it. Additionally, Nida showed he was aware of what he terms (ibid.: 3) 'the artistic sensitivity which is an indispensable ingredient in any first-rate translation of a literary work'.

One of Nida's fiercest critics is Edwin Gentzler, whose *Contemporary Translation Theories* (1993/2001) contains a chapter on 'the "science" of translation' (Gentzler's quotation marks). Working from within a deconstructionist perspective (see Chapter 10), Gentzler denigrates Nida's work for its theological and proselytizing standpoint. In Gentzler's view, dynamic equivalence is designed to convert the receptors, no matter what their culture, to the dominant discourse and ideas of Protestant Christianity. Ironically, Nida is also taken to task by certain religious groups who maintain that the Word of God is sacred and unalterable; the changes necessary to achieve dynamic equivalence would thus verge on the sacrilegious.

However, 'in the field' in the 1960s, dealing daily with real and practical translation problems and attempting to train translators for work in very different cultures, Nida achieved what few of his predecessors attempted: he went a long way to producing a systematic analytical procedure for translators working with all kinds of texts and he factored into the translation equation the receivers of the TT and their cultural expectations. Despite the heated debate it has provoked, Nida's systematic linguistic approach to translation exerted considerable influence on many subsequent and prominent translation scholars, among them Peter Newmark in the UK and Werner Koller in Germany.

3.3 Newmark: semantic and communicative translation

Peter Newmark (1916–2011)'s *Approaches to Translation* (1981) and *A Textbook of Translation* (1988) have been widely used on translator training courses and combine a wealth of practical examples of linguistic theories of meaning with practical applications for translation. Yet Newmark departs from Nida's receptor-oriented line. He feels that the success of equivalent effect is 'illusory' and that 'the conflict of loyalties, the gap between emphasis on source and target language, will always remain as the overriding problem in translation theory and practice' (Newmark 1981: 38). Newmark suggests narrowing the gap by replacing the old terms with those of 'semantic' and 'communicative' translation:

> Communicative translation attempts to produce on its readers an effect as close as possible to that obtained on the readers of the original. Semantic translation attempts to render, as closely as the semantic and syntactic structures of the second language allow, the exact contextual meaning of the original.
>
> (Newmark 1981: 39)

This description of **communicative translation** resembles Nida's dynamic equivalence in the effect it is trying to create on the TT reader, while **semantic translation** has similarities to Nida's formal equivalence. However, Newmark distances himself from the full principle of equivalent effect, since that effect 'is inoperant if the text is out of TL space and time' (1981: 69). An example would be a modern British English translation of Homer. No modern translator, irrespective of the TL, can possibly hope or expect to produce the same effect on the reader of the written TT as the oral ST had on its listeners in ancient Greece. Newmark (ibid.: 51) also raises further questions concerning the readers to whom Nida directs his dynamic equivalence, asking if they are 'to be handed everything on a plate', with everything explained for them.

Other differences are revealed by Newmark's definitions of his own terms (ibid.: 39–69), summarized in Table 3.2. Newmark (ibid.: 63) indicates that semantic translation differs from literal translation in that it 'respects context', interprets and even explains (metaphors, for instance). On the other hand, as we

Table 3.2 Comparison of Newmark's semantic and communicative translation

Parameter	Semantic translation	Communicative translation
Transmitter/ addressee focus	Focus on the thought processes of the transmitter as an individual; should only help TT reader with connotations if they are a crucial part of message	Subjective, TT reader focused, oriented towards a specific language and culture
Culture	Remains within the SL culture	Transfers foreign elements into the TL culture
Time and origin	Not fixed in any time or local space; translation needs to be done anew with every generation	Ephemeral and rooted in its own contemporary context
Relation to ST	Always 'inferior' to ST; 'loss' of meaning	May be 'better' than the ST; 'gain' of force and clarity even if loss of semantic content
Use of form of SL	If ST language norms deviate, then this must be replicated in TT; 'loyalty' to ST author	Respect for the form of the SL, but overriding 'loyalty' to TL norms
Form of TL	More complex, awkward, detailed, concentrated; tendency to overtranslate	Smoother, simpler, clearer, more direct, more conventional; tendency to undertranslate
Appropriateness	For serious literature, autobiography, 'personal effusion', any important political (or other) statement	For the vast majority of texts, e.g. non-literary writing, technical and informative texts, publicity, standardized types, popular fiction
Criterion for evaluation	Accuracy of reproduction of the significance of ST	Accuracy of communication of ST message in TT

saw in Chapter 2, literal translation means word-for-word in its extreme version and, even in its weaker form, sticks very closely to ST lexis and syntax.

Importantly, as long as equivalent effect is achieved, Newmark holds literal translation to be the best approach:

> In communicative as in semantic translation, provided that equivalent effect is secured, the literal word-for-word translation is not only the best, it is the only valid method of translation.
>
> (Newmark 1981: 39)

This assertion can be related to what other theorists (e.g. Levý 1967/2000, Toury 1995/2012) have said about the translator's work. Namely, that the constraints of time and working conditions often mean that the translator has to maximize the efficiency of the cognitive processes (see Chapter 4) by concentrating energy on especially difficult problems, by devoting less effort to those parts of the text where a reasonable translation is produced by the 'literal' procedure. However, if there is a conflict between the two forms of translation (if semantic translation would result in an 'abnormal' TT or would not secure equivalent effect in the TL) then communicative translation should be preferred. An example of this, provided by Newmark (ibid.: 39), is the common sign *bissiger Hund* and *chien méchant*. It would be translated communicatively as *beware of the dog!* in order to communicate the message, not semantically as *dog that bites!* and *bad dog!*

3.4 Exploration: Different terms

Look again at the above descriptions of Nida and Newmark's theories; refer also to the original writings. What are the main features of dynamic/formal equivalence and semantic/communicative translation?

3.3.1 Discussion of Newmark

Newmark's terms semantic translation and communicative translation have generally received far less discussion than Nida's formal and dynamic equivalence. This may be because, despite Newmark's relevant criticisms of equivalent effect, they raise some of the same points concerning the translation process and the importance of the TT reader. One of the difficulties encountered by translation studies in systematically following up advances in theory may indeed be partly attributable to the overabundance of terminology. Newmark himself, for instance, defines Juliane House's pair of 'overt' and 'covert' translation (see Chapter 6) in terms of his own semantic and communicative translation (Newmark 1981: 52) and considers communicative translation to be 'identical' to Nida's functional or dynamic equivalence (Newmark 2009: 30).[6]

Newmark has been criticized for his strong prescriptivism, and the language of his evaluations still bears traces of what he himself called the 'pre-linguistics era' of translation studies: translations are 'smooth' or 'awkward', while translation itself is an 'art' (if semantic) or a 'craft' (if communicative). Nonetheless, the large number of examples in Newmark's work provide ample guidance and advice for the trainee, and many of the questions he tackles are of important practical relevance to translation. It should also be noted that in his later discourse (e.g. Pedrola 1999, Newmark 2009: 34), he emphasized the aesthetic principles of writing, the difference between 'social, non-literary' and 'authoritative and serious' translation and an ethical and truth-seeking function for translation.

3.4 Koller: equivalence relations

Nida's move towards a science of translation proved to be especially influential in Germany, where the common term for translation studies is *Übersetzungswissenschaft* ('translation science'). Among the most prominent German scholars in the translation science field during the 1970s and 1980s were Wolfram Wilss, of Saarland University, and, from the then German Democratic Republic, the Leipzig School, including Otto Kade and Albrecht Neubert (Snell-Hornby 2006: 26–9, 2010).[7]

Important work to refine the concept of equivalence was carried out by Werner Koller in Heidelberg (West Germany) and Bergen (Norway). Koller's *Einführung in die Übersetzungswissenschaft* ([Research into the science of translation] 1979a; see also Koller 1979b/1989 and 1995) examines the concept of equivalence more closely along with its linked term 'correspondence' (Koller 1979a: 176–91). The two can be differentiated as follows:

(1) **Correspondence** falls within the field of contrastive linguistics, which compares two language systems and describes differences and similarities contrastively. Its parameters are those of Saussure's *langue* (Saussure 1916/1983). This would include the identification of false friends (e.g.

German *aktuel* means *current* and not English *actual)* and of signs of lexical, morphological and syntactic interference.

(2) **Equivalence**, on the other hand, relates to equivalent items in specific ST–TT pairs and contexts. The parameter is that of Saussure's *parole*. The following two examples show specific equivalences of *aktuel* in real texts:

> *Aktuel sind 7 Besucher online = There are* currently *7 guests online*

> *Wir bemühen diese Information so* aktuel *wie möglich zu halten = We shall try to keep this information* up-to-date.

Importantly, Koller (1979a: 185) points out that, while knowledge of correspondences is indicative of competence in the foreign language, it is knowledge and ability in equivalences that are indicative of competence in translation. However, the question still remains as to what exactly has to be equivalent.

In an attempt to answer this question, Koller (1979a: 186–91; see also Koller 1979b/1989: 99–104, Koller 1995 and Hatim and Munday 2004: 170–4) differentiates **five types of equivalence relations**, constrained, in what is known as **double linkage**, by the ST on the one hand and by the communicative conditions of the receiver on the other. These equivalence types are listed below:

(1) **Denotative equivalence**, related to equivalence of the extralinguistic content of a text. Other literature, says Koller, calls this 'content invariance'.

(2) **Connotative equivalence**, related to lexical choices, especially between near-synonyms. Koller considers this type of equivalence to be referred to by others as 'stylistic equivalence'.

(3) **Text-normative equivalence**, related to text types, with different kinds of texts behaving in different ways. This is closely linked to work by Katharina Reiss (see Chapter 5).

(4) **Pragmatic equivalence**, or 'communicative equivalence', is oriented towards the receiver of the text or message. This is Nida's dynamic equivalence.

(5) **Formal equivalence**, which is related to the form and aesthetics of the text, includes wordplays and the individual stylistic features of the ST. It is referred to by others as 'expressive equivalence' and should not be confused with Nida's term 'formal equivalence'.

Koller describes the different types of equivalence in terms of their research foci. These are summarized in Table 3.3.

Table 3.3   Characteristics of research foci for different equivalence types (following Koller 1979a: 187–91)

Type of equivalence	How attainable	Research focus
Denotative	By analysis of correspondences and their interaction with textual factors	Lexis
Connotative	'One of the most difficult problems of translation, and in practice is often only approximate' (Koller 1979b/ 1989: 189); theory needs to identify the connotative dimensions in different languages	Additional dimensions: formality (poetic, slang, etc.), social usage, geographical origin, stylistic effect (archaic, 'plain', etc.), frequency, range (general, technical, etc.), evaluation, emotion
Text-normative	Description and correlation of patterns of usage between languages using functional text analysis	Look at usage in different communicative situations
Pragmatic	Translate the text for a particular readership, overriding the requirements of other equivalences	Analyse the communicative conditions valid for different receiver groups in different language pairs and texts
Formal	An analogy of form in the TL, using the possibilities of the TL and even creating new ones	Analyse the potential of equivalence in rhyme, metaphor and other stylistic forms

The crucial point again is that, in order to assist the translator, the equivalences are hierarchically ordered according to the needs of the communicative situation. So, the translator first tries denotative equivalence and, if this is inadequate, will need to seek equivalence at a higher level – connotative, text-normative, etc. How the appropriate level is to be decided is open to debate, but an example (from Hatim and Munday 2004: 50–1) may help to explain:

'I had wanted for years to get Mrs Thatcher in front of my camera. As she got more powerful she got sort of sexier.'[8]

The quote is from photographer Helmut Newton, recalling his wish to capture on film the former British Prime Minister Margaret Thatcher. The problem is with the term *sexier* if we think of a potential translation into, say, Arabic. If we try denotative equivalence (i.e. translating it by *sexy*) this might convey the sense of 'pornographic'. Connotative equivalence (e.g. *attractiveness*) would be better but it may be too direct for the communicative purpose of this type of text (i.e. it would not achieve text-normative equivalence). Taking into account the needs of the TT readers (i.e. in order to achieve pragmatic equivalence), the translator may prefer *attractive femininity* or *attractive and full of life*, or add an expression such as *so to speak* to make it less direct. Full formal equivalence, in Koller's terms, would require creativity in the use of stylistic forms appropriate to the TL that may well not be feasible.

3.5 Exploration: Hierarchies of equivalence

Look at Koller's hierarchy of different types of equivalence (Koller 1995; Fawcett 1997: Chapter 5). Find examples from texts in your own languages to illustrate each type. Is this model more or less workable than Nida/Newmark's?

3.5 Later developments in equivalence

The notion of equivalence has held sway as a key issue in translation studies. Thus, for instance, Bassnett (1980/2013) devotes a section to 'problems of equivalence' in the chapter entitled 'central issues' of translation studies and Mona Baker's *In Other Words* (1992/2011) structures chapters around different types of equivalence – at the levels of the word, phrase, grammar, text, pragmatics, etc. (see Chapter 6), but with the proviso that equivalence 'is influenced by a variety of linguistic and cultural factors and is therefore always relative' (Baker 2011: 6).

Equivalence therefore continues to be a central, if criticized, concept. Kenny (2009: 96) summarizes criticism that has targeted the 'circularity' of the definitions of equivalence: 'equivalence is supposed to define translation, and translation, in turn, defines equivalence'. As might be imagined, scholars working in non-linguistic translation studies have been especially critical of the concept. Bassnett summarizes the major problem as she sees it:

> Translation involves far more than replacement of lexical and grammatical items between languages ... Once the translator moves away from close linguistic equivalence, the problems of determining the exact nature of the level of equivalence aimed for begin to emerge.
>
> (Bassnett 2013: 35)

Analysing existing theories, Pym (2007) defines two types of equivalence and describes how the rise of Computer-Assisted Translation (CAT) tools (see Chapter 11) has given a new twist to these types:

(i) **'natural' equivalence**, where the focus is on identifying naturally-occurring terms or stretches of language in the SL and TL. Translation glossaries and term bases, for example, routinely seek to plot 'natural' equivalents in the relevant languages;

(ii) **'directional' equivalence**, where the focus is on analysing and rendering the ST meaning in an equivalent form in the TT. Translation memories, working on a corpus of already translated material, impose existing 'directional' equivalents on the translator through the flagging up of exact and fuzzy matches with stretches of language in the database.

In descriptive studies, perhaps the biggest bone of contention in the comparison of a ST and a TT is the so-called *tertium comparationis* ('the third comparator'), an invariant against which two text segments can be measured to gauge variation from a core meaning. Take the following example of a Hausa proverb:

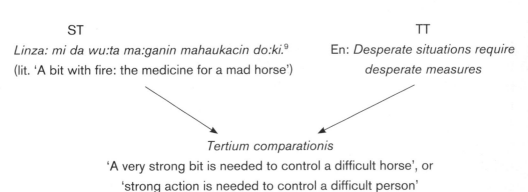

ST
Linza: mi da wu:ta ma:ganin mahaukacin do:ki.[9]
(lit. 'A bit with fire: the medicine for a mad horse')

TT
En: *Desperate situations require desperate measures*

Tertium comparationis
'A very strong bit is needed to control a difficult horse', or
'strong action is needed to control a difficult person'

Whether the suggested target segment is an appropriate equivalent would depend on circumstances, audience and the type of equivalence envisaged. On a racecourse, the ST phrase might well not be so metaphorical and might require more formal equivalence in translation.

The problem of the inevitable subjectivity that the invariant entails has been tackled by many scholars. In Chapter 4, we discuss taxonomic linguistic approaches that have attempted to produce a comprehensive model of translation shift analysis. Chapter 7 considers modern descriptive translation studies. Its leading proponent, Gideon Toury, shuns a prescriptive definition of equivalence and, accepting as given that a TT is 'equivalent' to its ST, instead seeks to identify the web of relations between the two. Yet there is still a great deal of practically oriented writing on translation that continues a prescriptive discussion of equivalence. Translator training courses also, perhaps inevitably, tend to have this focus: errors by the trainee translators tend to be corrected prescriptively according to a notion of equivalence held by the tutor.

Case study

The following case study considers two series of translations from the point of view of Nida's formal and dynamic equivalence. The three extracts in Box 3.2 are from English translations from the Hebrew of the opening of Genesis, the first book of the Old Testament of the Christian Bible.[10]

Box 3.2

1 *King James version* (KJV, originally published 1611)
   1:1 In the beginning God created the heaven and the earth.
   1:2 And the earth was without form, and void; and darkness was upon the face of the deep. And the Spirit of God moved upon the face of the waters.
   1:3 And God said, 'Let there be light': And there was light.

2 *New English Bible* (NEB, originally published 1970)
   1:1 In the beginning God created the heavens and the earth.
   1:2 Now the earth was without shape and empty, and darkness was over the surface of the watery deep, but the Spirit of God was moving over the surface of the water.

> 1:3 And God said, 'Let there be light': And there was light.
>
> 3   *New American Bible* (NAB, originally published 1970)
>   1:1 In the beginning, when God created the heavens and the earth,
>   1:2 the earth was a formless wasteland, and darkness covered the abyss, while a mighty wind swept over the waters.
>   1:3 And God said, 'Let there be light': And there was light.

Much theological debate has centred on the relation of verse 1:2 to verse 1:1 – namely whether *in the beginning* refers to the act of creation of the earth on the first day, or whether the first verse is a summary of the chapter. If the latter is the case, it would mean that a formless and empty earth existed before the creation of light in verse three. Both the NEB and NAB texts are also published with an extensive exegetical commentary to guide the reader's understanding.

Of equal interest linguistically is verse 1:2, especially as it may serve to demonstrate the usefulness of Nida's form of analysis of meaning and equivalence. Here, there are a number of differences between the TTs. The translations *deep* (KJV), *watery deep* (NEB) and *abyss* (NAB) refer to what is traditionally understood to be the lifeless salt ocean (*thwm* in Hebrew). In this case, it is the NEB which goes furthest to explaining the concept in terms the modern reader would immediately understand. Similarly, the NEB uses the term *surface* in place of the metaphorical *face* of KJV, a metaphor to be found in the original Hebrew (*paneem*). The NAB omits *face/surface* altogether, incorporating the sense instead into the verbs *covered* and *swept over*. Finally, the translation *Spirit of God* (KJV, NEB) is a *mighty wind* in NAB. The Hebrew original (*rwh*) refers to 'wind' or 'breath', and metaphorically to 'spirit'. The NAB retains the element of wind, but sees God as simply representing a superlative force, hence the interpretation *mighty*. Other possible translations are *wind from God* or *breath of God*, preserving both elements. The KJV's *Spirit of God* is firmly entrenched as the traditional rendering. On some occasions, for example in John 3 from the New Testament, the ST (in that case Greek) makes a play on the word *pneuma*, translated by KJV first as *spirit* and then *wind*.

It is with such words that Nida's techniques of semantic structure analysis (see section 3.2.2 above) can help the translator decide on the appropriate TL term. Yet the brief analysis in this case study suggests that the translation will vary according both to the interpretation of the translator (e.g. what does *in the beginning* actually refer to?) and the degree to which the translator feels that the message requires adaptation in order to be understood by the TT reader (e.g. *deep/abyss/watery deep, face/surface, Spirit of God/mighty wind*). While all the translations quoted seek dynamic equivalence in the sense of creating a response in the audience similar to that of the original text, the 'naturalness' of expression inevitably alters across time: today the KJV has come to be considered a canonized and formal archaic form in English, while the NEB is written in modern British English and the NAB's more narrative version is in modern American English.

The means by which the TTs attempt to achieve equivalent effect also differ: the NEB makes clear the links, including the choice of *now* at the start of verse 1:2. It also explicates with *surface, watery deep*, and *Spirit of God*. On the other hand, the NAB maintains a focus on the desolate wilderness, with *formless wasteland* and *mighty wind*, even if cohesive links are added with the conjunctions *when* and *while*. The KJV maintains the imagery of the ST closely with *face of the deep* and *face of the waters*. It also retains the threefold literal repetition of the conjunction *and* in verse 1:2. This is a formal syntactic device used throughout the Hebrew and Greek of the Bible and which Nida (1964a: 224) views as requiring 'certain adjustments' to avoid 'babyish' English. This suggests that the KJV is most concerned with formal equivalence with the original, whereas the NEB and NAB are more oriented towards dynamic equivalence, making important adjustments for the receivers.

There is little room for such adjustments or interpretation in some legal documents, where the translation technique may be one of formal equivalence. An example is given in Box 3.3, taken from common provisions Article 1 of the crucial international Treaty of Maastricht on European Union (7 February 1992).

Box 3.3

1   English
    By this Treaty, the HIGH CONTRACTING PARTIES establish among themselves a EUROPEAN UNION, hereinafter called 'the Union'.

    This Treaty marks a new stage in the process of creating an ever closer union among the peoples of Europe, in which decisions are taken as openly as possible and as closely as possible to the citizen.

> 2   Portuguese
> Pelo presente Tratado, as ALTAS PARTES CONTRATANTES instituem
> entre si uma UNIÃO EUROPEIA, adiante designada por «União».
>   O presente Tratado assinala uma nova etapa no processo de criaçao
> de uma união cada vez mais estrita entre os povos da Europa, em que
> as decisões serão tomadas de uma forma tão aberta quanto possível e
> ao nível mais próximo possível dos cidadãos.

In law, all versions of the treaty stand as equally valid. As a legal document, they have a high degree of formal equivalence, for example, the English and Portuguese read:

| By | this | Treaty, | the | HIGH | CONTRACTING PARTIES |
| Pelo | presente | Tratado, as | | ALTAS | PARTES CONTRATANTES |

| establish | | among themselves | | a EUROPEAN UNION, | hereinafter |
| instituem | | entre si | | uma UNIÃO EUROPEIA, | adiante |

| called | | 'the Union'. | |
| designada por | | «União». | |

Adjustments are minimal and systemic, such as the Portuguese cohesive *presente* for the English demonstrative pronoun *this*, the addition of the preposition 'desig-nada *por*' in Portuguese and the English definite article '*the* Union'. Although the formal structures of the two texts are very close in these examples, they still follow Nida's recipe of choosing the 'closest natural equivalent'. In both cases the language conforms to the conventions of legal terminology and the syntax is 'natural'.

   However, the goal of equivalent effect is also crucial in a legal text such as this. In order to function correctly, each text must stand for the same idea in each language and produce the same response. Otherwise, varied interpretations would give rise to legal confusion and potential loopholes. In this respect it is perhaps surprising that the French version of the treaty should contain a slightly different perspective. While, in the English, the treaty significantly 'marks a new stage in the process of creating an ever closer union' (suggesting an ongoing process, which tallies with the Portuguese), the relevant passage in the French is 'Le présent traité marque une nouvelle étape créant une union sans cesse plus étroite' ['The present treaty marks a new stage creating an ever closer union']. Here, the present participle *créant* ['creating'] suggests that, rather than a contin-uing process, the goal of closer union is in fact being achieved by the treaty.

3.6 Exploration

Look at the European Commission report 'Language and Translation in International Law and EU Law' (find it at http://bookshop.europa.eu, or see the ITS companion website), where the different language versions of legal texts, equally valid, are often authored simultaneously. Note the consequence of this practice for traditional views of equivalence and some of the problems which result.

Discussion of case study

Nida's model enables a more detailed analysis of meaning than was possible with earlier theories and points to the kind of effect the texts may have on their receivers. However, it is still not possible to measure that effect 'scientifically' and questions persist as to the precise identity of the receiver. With the Treaty on European Union, it may be a legal expert within the TT culture. How does the translator ensure that the effect will be the same on a Portuguese or British legal expert as it is on a French expert? When it comes to the translation of a religious text, such as the Bible, these questions multiply.

Finally, it is well to remember that Nida's work is aimed above all at training translators who do not have expertise in linguistics but who have to deal with very different cultures. It may, therefore, be more helpful to adopt his model not for the analysis of existing translations (where the focus is on identifying what the translator has done and what the effect is on the known audience) but for the analysis of a ST that is to be translated.

Summary

This chapter has examined important questions of translation raised by linguistics in the 1950s and 1960s. The key terms are 'meaning' and 'equivalence'. These were discussed by Roman Jakobson in 1959 and crucially developed by Nida, whose books analyse meaning systematically and propose that a translation should aim for 'equivalent effect' (the same effect on the TL audience as the ST had on the SL audience). Despite the subsequent questioning of the feasibility of that goal, Nida's great achievement is to have drawn translation theory away from the stagnant 'literal vs. free' debate and into the modern era. His concepts of **formal** and **dynamic equivalence** place the receiver in the centre of the equation and have exerted huge influence over subsequent theoreticians, especially in Germany. In the next chapter, we look at other scholars who have incorporated systematic linguistic models into the study of translation.

Further reading

Nida's work has been discussed in a large range of publications. Extensive criticism is to be found in Qian Hu (1992a, 1992b, 1993a, 1993b, 1994) and Snell-Hornby (1995). See also Nida's own writing on context (Nida 2002) and an appraisal of Nida's work (Dimitriu and Shlesinger 2009). For analyses of meaning, see Osgood et al. (1957), Lyons (1977), Leech (1983), Carter (1998), and, on translation, Larson (1998) and Malmkjær (2005). For equivalence and correspondence, see Catford (1965 and 2000; see also Chapter 4), Koller (1995), Fawcett (1997: Chapter 5), Kenny (2009) and Pym (2014: Chapters 2–3). For German *Übersetzungswissenschaft*, see Wilss (1977, 1982, 1996) and Snell-Hornby (2006).

Discussion and research points

1   Examine the layout of multilingual term bases such as the European Union's IATE (iate.europa.eu). What information is provided to ensure equivalence between terms? See Cabré (2010) and Bowker (2015) for a discussion on terminology practice.
2   Examine closely some of the different language versions of the Treaty of Lisbon (http://europa.eu/lisbon_treaty/full_text/index_en.htm), which amended the Maastricht Treaty on European Union and came into force in 2009. Can it be said that the versions have achieved dynamic or formal equivalence? What *tertium comparationis* are you using in making your judgements? Look also at equivalence relations in other international

documents (e.g. the Universal Declaration of Human Rights, http://www.ohchr.org/en/udhr/pages/introduction.aspx).

3   Investigate what other academics working in non-European languages say about the issue of equivalence. How far do their concepts differ from the western concept?

The ITS website at www.routledge.com/cw/munday contains:

- a video summary of the chapter;
- a recap multiple-choice test;
- customizable PowerPoint slides;
- further reading links and extra journal articles;
- more research project questions.

CHAPTER 4

Studying translation product and process

Key concepts

- **Overall translation strategies and specific translation procedures.**
- **Vinay and Darbelnet (1958): classic taxonomy of linguistic changes in translation.**
- **Catford (1965/2000) uses the term 'translation shift' in his linguistic approach to translation.**
- **Translational stylistics (Malmkjær 2003) attempts to identify and analyse translator style.**
- **Cognitive models seek to explain the processes of translation through theory and observation.**
- **Think-aloud protocols and other experimental methods for analysing the translation process.**

Key texts

Catford, John (1965/2000) 'Translation shifts', in Lawrence Venuti (ed.) (2000) *The Translation Studies Reader*, 1st edition, London and New York: Routledge, pp. 141–7. From Catford's *A Linguistic Theory of Translation*, London: Oxford University Press (1965).

Fawcett, Peter (1997) *Translation and Language: Linguistic Approaches Explained*, Manchester: St Jerome, Chapters 4 and 5.

Gutt, Ernst-August (1991/2000) *Translation and Relevance: Cognition and Context*, Manchester: St Jerome.

Hurtado Albir, Amparo and Fabio Alves (2009) 'Cognitive translation models', in Jeremy Munday (ed.) *The Routledge Companion to Translation Studies*, Abingdon and New York: Routledge, pp. 54–73.

Jääskeläinen, Rita (2009) 'Think-aloud protocols', in Mona Baker and Gabriela Saldanha (eds) *Routledge Encyclopedia of Translation Studies,* Abingdon and New York: Routledge, pp. 290–3.

Pym, Anthony (2016) *Translation Solutions for Many Languages: History of a Flawed Dream*, London and New York: Bloomsbury.

Vinay, Jean-Paul and Jean Darbelnet (1958/1995) *Comparative Stylistics of French and English: A Methodology for Translation*, translated and edited by Juan Sager, and Marie-Jo Hamel, Amsterdam and Philadelphia: John Benjamins. (See also the extract 'A methodology for translation', in Lawrence Venuti (ed.) (2004), *The Translation Studies Reader*, 2nd edition, London and New York: Routledge, pp. 128–37.)

Zhang, Meifang and Pan Li (2009) 'Introducing a Chinese Perspective on Translation Shifts: A Comparative Study of Shift Models by Loh and Vinay and Darbelnet', *The Translator* 15.2: 351–74.

4.0 Introduction

Watch the introductory video on the companion website.

This chapter looks at ways of analysing translation, first as a linguistic product (sections 4.1–4.3) and then as a cognitive process (4.4–4.5).

Since the 1950s, a variety of linguistic approaches to the analysis of translation have proposed detailed lists or taxonomies in an effort to categorize what happens in translation. The scope of this book necessarily restricts us initially to describing a small number of the best-known and most representative models, though we shall expand the discussion to include more recent developments. Thus, the focus in this first part of the chapter is on the following two linguistic models:

(1) Vinay and Darbelnet's taxonomy in *Comparative Stylistics of French and English* (1958/1995), which is the classic model and one which has had a very wide impact; and

(2) Catford's (1965) linguistic approach, which saw the introduction of the term 'translation shift'.[1]

4.1 Vinay and Darbelnet's model

Influenced by earlier work by the Russian theorist and translator Andrei Fedorov (1953), as described by Mossop (2013) and Pym (2016), Vinay and Darbelnet carried out a comparative stylistic analysis of French and English. They looked at texts in both languages, noting differences between the languages and identifying different translation 'strategies' and 'procedures'. These terms are sometimes confused in writing about translation. As we saw in Chapter 1 (pp. 23–4), in the technical sense a **strategy** is an overall orientation of the translator (e.g. towards 'free' or 'literal' translation, towards the TT or ST, towards domestication or foreignization) whereas a **procedure** is a specific technique or method used by the translator at a certain point in a text (e.g. the borrowing of a word from the SL, the addition of an explanation or a footnote in the TT).

4.1 Exploration: Metalanguage of strategies and procedures

See the article by Gil Bardají (2009) on the ITS website for a further discussion of terms.

Although the model proposed in *Stylistique comparée* ... centres solely on the French–English pair, its influence has been much wider. It built on work on French–German translation (Malblanc 1944/1963) and inspired two similar books on English–Spanish translation: Vázquez-Ayora's *Introducción a la traductología* ['Introduction to traductology'] (1977) and García Yebra's *Teoría y práctica de la traducción* ['Theory and practice of translation'] (1982). A later French response to the work was Chuquet and Paillard's *Approche linguistique des problèmes de traduction* ['Linguistic approach to problems of translation'] (1987). Vinay and Darbelnet's model came to wider prominence in 1995 when it was published in revised form in English translation, thirty-seven years after the original.[2]

4.1.1 Two strategies and seven procedures

The two general translation strategies identified by Vinay and Darbelnet (1995/2004: 128–37) are (i) **direct translation** and (ii) **oblique translation**, which hark back to the 'literal vs. free' division discussed in Chapter 2. Indeed, 'literal' is given by the authors as a synonym for direct translation (1995: 31; 2004: 128). The two strategies comprise **seven procedures**, of which **direct translation** covers three:

(1) **Borrowing:** The SL word is transferred directly to the TL. This category (1995: 31–2; 2004: 129) covers words such as the Russian *rouble, datcha,* the later *glasnost* and *perestroika,* that are used in English and other languages to fill a semantic gap in the TL. Sometimes borrowings may be employed to add local colour (*sushi, kimono, Oshōgatsu* . . . in a tourist brochure about Japan, for instance). Of course, in some technical fields there is much borrowing of terms (e.g. *computer, internet,* from English to Malay). In languages with differing scripts, borrowing entails an additional need for transcription, as in the borrowings of mathematical, scientific and other terms from Arabic into Latin and, later, other languages (e.g. الجبر [*al-jabr*] to *algebra*).

(2) **Calque:** This is 'a special kind of borrowing' (1995: 32–3; 2004: 129–30) where the SL expression or structure is transferred in a literal translation. For example, the French calque *science-fiction* for the English.

Vinay and Darbelnet note that both borrowings and calques often become fully integrated into the TL, although sometimes with some semantic change, which can turn them into false friends. An example is the German *Handy* for a *mobile* (cell) *phone.*

(3) **Literal translation** (1995: 33–5; 2004: 130–2): This is 'word-for-word' translation, which Vinay and Darbelnet describe as being most common between languages of the same family and culture. Their example is:

| English ST: | I | left | my spectacles | on the table | downstairs. |
| French TT: | J' | ai laissé | mes lunettes | sur la table | en bas. |

Literal translation is the authors' prescription for good translation: 'literalness should only be sacrificed because of structural and metalinguistic requirements and only after checking that the meaning is fully preserved' (1995: 288).[3] But, say Vinay and Darbelnet (ibid.: 34–5), the translator may judge literal translation to be 'unacceptable' for what are grammatical, syntactic or pragmatic reasons.

In those cases where literal translation is not possible, Vinay and Darbelnet say that the strategy of **oblique translation** must be used. This covers a further four procedures:

(4)   **Transposition:** This is a change of one part of speech for another (e.g. noun for verb) without changing the sense. Transposition can be:

-   **obligatory:** French *dès son lever* ['upon her rising'] in a past context would be translated by *as soon as she got up*; or
-   **optional:** in the reverse direction, the English *as soon as she got up* could be translated into French literally as *dès qu'elle s'est levée* or as a verb-to-noun transposition in *dès son lever* ['upon her rising'].

Vinay and Darbelnet (1995: 94) see transposition as 'probably the most common structural change undertaken by translators'. They list at least ten different categories, such as:

> verb → noun: *they have pioneered* → *they have been the first*;
> adverb → verb: *He will soon be back* → *He will hurry to be back.*

(5)   **Modulation:** This changes the semantics and point of view of the SL. It can be:

-   **obligatory**: e.g. *the time when* translates as *le moment où* [lit. 'the moment where'];
-   **optional**, though linked to preferred structures of the two languages: e.g. the reversal of point of view in *it is not difficult to show* > *il est facile de démontrer* [lit. 'it is easy to show'].

Modulation is a procedure that is justified 'when, although a literal, or even transposed, translation results in a grammatically correct utterance, it is considered unsuitable, unidiomatic or awkward in the TL' (2004: 133).

Vinay and Darbelnet place much store by modulation as 'the touchstone of a good translator', whereas transposition 'simply shows a very good command of the target language' (ibid.: 246). Modulation at the level of message is subdivided (ibid.: 246–55) along the following lines:

> **abstract<>concrete**, or **particular<>general:** *She can do no other* > *She cannot act differently*; *Give a pint of blood* > *Give a little blood*

> **explicative modulation**, or **effect<>cause:** *You're quite a stranger* > *We don't see you any more.*

> **whole<>part:** *He shut the door in my face* > *He shut the door in my nose*

part<>another part: *He cleared his throat > He cleared his voice*

reversal of terms: *You can have it > I'll give it to you*

negation of opposite: *It does not seem unusual > It is very normal*

active< >passive: *We are not allowed to access the internet > they don't allow us to access the internet*

rethinking of intervals and limits in space and time: *No parking between signs > Limit of parking*

change of symbol (including fixed and new metaphors): Fr. *La moutarde lui monta au nez* ['The mustard rose up to his nose'] > En. *He saw red* ['he became very angry'].

Modulation therefore covers a wide range of phenomena. There is also often a process of originally free modulations becoming fixed expressions. One example given by Vinay and Darbelnet (1995: 254) is *Vous l'avez échappé belle* [lit. 'You have escaped beautifully'] > *You've had a narrow escape.*

(6)   **Équivalence**, or **idiomatic translation:**[4] Vinay and Darbelnet use this term (1995: 38–9; 2004: 134) to refer to cases where languages describe the same situation by different stylistic or structural means. Équivalence is particularly useful in translating idioms and proverbs: the sense, though not the image, of *comme un chien dans un jeu de quilles* [lit. 'like a dog in a game of skittles'] can be rendered as *like a bull in a china shop*. The use of équivalence in this restricted sense should not be confused with the more common theoretical use discussed in Chapter 3 of this book.

(7)   **Adaptation** (1995: 39–40; 2004: 134–6): This involves changing the cultural reference when a situation in the source culture does not exist in the target culture. For example, Vinay and Darbelnet suggest that the cultural connotation of a reference to the game of cricket in an English text might be best translated into French by a reference to the Tour de France. The authors claim that a refusal to use such adaptation in an otherwise 'perfectly correct' TT 'may still be noticeable by an undefinable tone, something that does not sound quite right' (1995: 53). However, whereas their solution may work for some restricted metaphorical uses, it would make little sense to change the domain cricket to that of cycling in phrases such as *that isn't cricket* ('that isn't fair') or 'a sleepy Wednesday morning county match at Lords [cricket ground in London]'.

> ### 4.2 Exploration: Procedures
>
> Read Vinay and Darbelnet's own description of their model and try to find examples of the seven main procedures from ST–TT pairs in your own languages. Make a list of phenomena that are easy and difficult to categorize using their model.

4.1.2 Supplementary translation procedures

There are a large number of other techniques exemplified by Vinay and Darbelnet. Among those that have maintained currency in translation theory are the following:

- **Amplification:** The TL uses more words, often because of syntactic expansion, e.g. *the charge against him* > *the charge brought against him*. The opposite of amplification is **economy**.
- **False friend:** A structurally similar term in SL and TL which deceives the user into thinking the meaning is the same, e.g. French *librarie* means not English *library* but *bookstore*.
- **Loss, gain** and **compensation:** 'Lost in translation' has become a popular cliché, partly thanks to the film. Translation does inevitably involve some loss, since it is impossible to preserve all the ST nuances of meaning and structure in the TL. However, importantly a TT may make up for ('compensate') this by introducing a gain at the same or another point in the text. One example is the translation of dialogue: if the SL is a t/v language and shows a switch from formal to informal address (so, French *vous* to *tu*), English will need to find a compensatory way of rendering this, perhaps by switching from the use of the character's given name (e.g. *Professor Newmark* > *Peter*).
- **Explicitation:** Implicit information in the ST is rendered explicit in the TT. This may occur on the level of grammar (e.g. English ST *the doctor* explicated as masculine or feminine in a TL where indication of gender is essential), semantics (e.g. the explanation of a ST cultural item or event, such as US *Thanksgiving* or UK *April Fool's joke*), pragmatics (e.g. the opaque and culturally located US English idiom *it's easy to be a Monday morning quarterback*) or discourse (such as increased cohesion in the TT, see section 6.3.2). Non-obligatory explicitation has often been suggested as a characteristic of translated language (see the discussion in Chapter 7 on 'universals of translation').

- **Generalization**: The use of a more general word in the TT. Examples would be ST *computer* > TT *machine*, or ST *ecstatic* > TT *happy*. Again, generalization has been suggested as another characteristic of translation (see Toury's 'law of increasing standardization', Chapter 7).

4.1.3 Levels of translation

The seven main translation procedures are described (1995: 27–30) as operating on three levels. These three levels reflect the main structural elements of the book. They are:

(1) the **lexicon**;
(2) **syntactic structures**;
(3) the **message**; in this case, 'message' is used to mean approximately the utterance and its metalinguistic situation or context.

Two further terms are introduced which look above word level. These are:

(1) **word order and thematic structure** (1995: 211–31, called *démarche* in the French original);
(2) **connectors** (ibid.: 231–46, called *charnières* in the original). These are cohesive links (*also, and, but*, and parallel structures), discourse markers (*however, first* . . .), deixis (pronouns and demonstrative pronouns such as *she, it, this, that*) and punctuation marks.

Such levels of analysis begin to point to the text-based and discourse-based analysis considered in Chapters 5 and 6 of this book, so we shall not consider them further here. However, one further important parameter described by Vinay and Darbelnet does need to be stressed. This is the difference between servitude and option:

- **Servitude** refers to obligatory transpositions and modulations due to a difference between the two language systems. Thus, a translator will normally have no choice but to translate the Spanish noun–adjective combination *agua fría* [lit. 'water cold'] by *cold water*. Similarly, adverbial structures in German and Japanese have a fixed order of time–manner–place, e.g. *Morgen mit dem*

Fahrrad auf Arbeit ['tomorrow with the bicycle to work']. German also requires the verb, or auxiliary, to be in second position: *Morgen **muss** ich mit dem Fahrrad auf Arbeit fahren* ['tomorrow **must** I by bicycle to work travel'].

■ **Option** refers to non-obligatory changes that may be due to the translator's own style and preferences, or to a change in emphasis. This could be the decision to amplify or explicate a general term (e.g. *this > this problem/ question/issue*) or to change word order when translating between languages that permit flexibility – so, English *my mother will phone at six o'clock >* Spanish *a las seis llamará mi madre* ['at six will phone my mother'].

Clearly, this is a crucial difference. Vinay and Darbelnet (1995: 16) stress that it is option, the realm of stylistics, that should be the translator's main concern. The role of the translator is then 'to choose from among the available options to express the nuances of the message'.

4.1.4 Analytical steps

Vinay and Darbelnet (ibid.: 30–1) list **five analytical steps** for the translator to follow in moving from ST to TT. These are as follows:

(1) Identify the units of translation.
(2) Examine the SL text, evaluating the descriptive, affective and intellectual content of the units.
(3) Reconstruct the metalinguistic context of the message.
(4) Evaluate the stylistic effects.
(5) Produce and revise the TT.

The first four steps are also followed by Vinay and Darbelnet in their analysis of published translations. As far as the key question of the **unit of translation** is concerned, the authors reject the individual word. They consider the unit of translation to be a combination of a 'lexicological unit' and a 'unit of thought' and define it (ibid.: 21) as 'the smallest segment of the utterance whose signs are linked in such a way that they should not be translated individually'. In the original French version (1958: 275–7), an example is given of the division of a short ST and TT into the units of translation. The divisions proposed include examples of individual words (e.g. *he, but*), grammatically linked groups (e.g. *the watch, to* *look*), fixed expressions (e.g. *from time to time*) and semantically linked groups (e.g. *to glance away*). In the later, English, version of the book, new analysis gives units that are rather longer: for example, the groupings *si nous songeons* > *if we speak of* and *en Grande Bretagne, au Japon* > *in Great Britain, Japan* are each given as a single unit (1995: 321).

To facilitate analysis where oblique translation is used, Vinay and Darbelnet suggest numbering the translation units in both the ST and TT (for an example, see Table 4.1 in the case study section at the end of this chapter). The units which have the same number in each text can then be compared to see which translation procedure has been adopted.

4.3 Exploration: A Chinese perspective

One criticism of Vinay and Darbelnet's model is that it can less easily be applied to non-European languages. Read the article by Zhang and Pan Li (2009) on the ITS companion website which considers Loh's (1958) model for Chinese<>English translation. Summarize the main differences between the two models.

4.2 Catford and translation 'shifts'

Translation shifts are linguistic changes occurring in translation of ST to TT. Although Vinay and Darbelnet do not use the term, that is in effect what they are describing. The term itself seems to originate in Catford's *A Linguistic Theory of Translation* (1965), where he devotes a chapter to the subject. Catford (1965: 20) follows the Firthian and Hallidayan linguistic model, which analyses language as communication, operating functionally in context and on a range of different levels (e.g. phonology, graphology, grammar, lexis) and ranks (sentence, clause, group, word, morpheme, etc.).[5]

As far as translation is concerned, Catford makes an important distinction between formal correspondence and textual equivalence, which was later to be developed by Koller (see Chapter 3):

■ A **formal correspondent** is 'any TL category (unit, class, element of structure, etc.) which can be said to occupy, as nearly as possible, the "same"

place in the "economy" of the TL as the given SL category occupies in the SL' (Catford 1965: 27).

■ A **textual equivalent** is 'any TL text or portion of text which is observed on a particular occasion . . . to be the equivalent of a given SL text or portion of text' (ibid.).

Thus, formal correspondence is a more general system-based concept between a pair of languages (e.g. the noun *belongings* and the Spanish *efectos personales* ['personal effects']) while textual equivalence is tied to a particular ST–TT pair (e.g. *he searched through my belongings* translated as *examinó mi bolso* ['he examined my bag']). When the two concepts diverge (as in *efectos personales* and *bolso*), a **translation shift** is deemed to have occurred. In Catford's own words (1965: 73; 2000: 141), translation shifts are thus 'departures from formal correspondence in the process of going from the SL to the TL'.

Catford considers two kinds of shift: (1) shift of level and (2) shift of category.

(1)   A **level shift** (1965: 73–5; 2000: 141–3) would be something which is expressed by grammar in one language and lexis in another. This could, for example, be:

■ aspect in Russian being translated by a lexical verb in English: e.g. *igrat'* (*to play*) and *sigrat'* (*to finish playing*); or

■ cases where the French conditional corresponds to a lexical item in English: e.g. *trois touristes auraient été tués* [lit. 'three tourists would have been killed'] = *three tourists have been reported killed*.

(2)   Most of Catford's analysis is given over to **category shifts** (1965: 75–82; 2000: 143–7). These are subdivided into four kinds:

(a) **Structural shifts:** These are said by Catford to be the most common and to involve mostly a shift in grammatical structure. For example, the subject pronoun + verb + direct object structures of *I like jazz* and *j'aime le jazz* in English and French are translated by an indirect object pronoun + verb + subject structure in Spanish (*me gusta el jazz*) and in Italian (*mi piace il jazz*).

(b) **Class shifts:** These comprise shifts from one part of speech to another. An example given by Catford is the English *a medical student* and the French *un étudiant en médecine*. Here, the English pre-modifying adjective *medical* is translated by the adverbial qualifying phrase *en médecine*.

(c) **Unit shifts** or **rank shifts:** These are shifts where the translation equivalent in the TL is at a different rank to the SL. 'Rank' here refers to the hierarchical linguistic units of sertence, clause, group, word and morpheme.

(d) **Intra-system shifts:** These are shifts that take place when the SL and TL possess approximately corresponding systems but where 'the translation involves selection of a non-corresponding term in the TL system' (1965: 80; 2000: 146). Examples given between French and English are number and article systems – although similar systems operate in the two languages, they do not always correspond. Thus, *advice* (uncountable) in English becomes *des conseils* (plural) in French, and the French definite article *la* in *Il a la jambe cassée* ['he has the leg broken'] corresponds to the English indefinite article *a* in *He has a broken leg.*

Catford's book is an important attempt to systematically apply advances in linguistics to translation. However, his analysis of intra-system shifts betrays some of the weaknesses of his approach. From his comparison of the use of French and English article systems in short parallel texts, Catford concludes (1965: 81–2) that French *le/la/les* 'will have English *the* as its translation equivalent with probability .65', supporting his statement that 'translation equivalence does not entirely match formal correspondence'. This kind of statement of probability, which characterizes Catford's whole approach and was linked to the growing interest in machine translation at the time, was later heavily criticized by, among others, Delisle (1982) for its static contrastive linguistic basis. Revisiting Catford's book twenty years after publication, Henry (1984: 157) considers the work to be 'by and large of historical academic interest' only. He does, however, (ibid.: 155) point out the usefulness of Catford's final chapter, on the limits of translatability. Of particular interest is Catford's assertion that translation equivalence depends on communicative features such as function, relevance, situation and culture rather than just on formal linguistic criteria. However, as Catford himself notes (1965: 94), deciding what is 'functionally relevant' in a given situation is inevitably 'a matter of opinion'.

Despite the steps taken by Catford to consider the communicative function of the SL item and despite the basis of his terminology being founded on a functional approach to language, the main criticism of Catford's book is that his examples are almost all idealized (i.e. invented and not taken from actual translations) and decontextualized. He does not look at whole texts, nor even above the level of the sentence.

4.3 Option, markedness and stylistic shifts in translation

Other writing on translation shifts in the 1960s and 1970s from the then Czechoslovakia introduced a literary aspect, that of the '**expressive function**' or style of a text. Among these, Jiří Levý (1926–1967)'s groundbreaking work on literary translation (*Umění překladu*, 1963) links into the tradition of the Prague School of structural linguistics. It was mainly known in western Europe through its German translation *Die literarische Übersetzung: Theorie einer Kunstgattung* (Levý 1969) and its continuing relevance can be gauged by its more recent translation into English (Levý 2011). Levý looks closely at the translation of the surface structure of the ST and TT, with particular attention to poetry translation, and sees literary translation as both a reproductive and a creative labour with the goal of **equivalent aesthetic effect** (2011: 65–9).

The question of **stylistic shifts** in translation has received greater attention in more recent translation theory. This has to do with: (1) interest in the intervention of the translator and his/her relationship to the ST author as exemplified through linguistic choices; and (2) the development of more sophisticated computerized tools to assist analysis. The first point is typified by two papers, by Giuliana Schiavi and Theo Hermans, that appeared together in *Target* in the mid-1990s. Schiavi (1996: 14) borrows a schema from narratology to discuss an inherent paradox of translation:

> [A] reader of translation will receive a sort of split message coming from two different addressers, both original although in two different senses: one originating from the author which is elaborated and mediated by the translator, and one (the language of the translation itself) originating directly from the translator.

The mix of authorial and translatorial message is the result of conscious and unconscious decision-making from the translator. This mix, and the translator's '**discursive presence**', as Hermans (1996) puts it, is conveyed in the linguistic choices that appear in the TT. Of course, for many TT readers the TT words not only represent but are the words of the ST author.

For the analyst, the question is how far the style and intentions of the translator, rather than the ST author, are recoverable from analysis of the TT choices. Such analysis has been termed '**translational stylistics**' by Kirsten Malmkjær (2003). It has also been advanced by the use of corpus-based methods. These have attempted to identify the 'linguistic fingerprint' of the translator by comparing ST and TT choices against large representative collections of electronic texts in the SL and TL. So, for example, Baker (2000) compares the frequency of the lemma (forms of the verb) *SAY* in literary translations from Spanish and Portuguese (by Peter Bush) and Arabic (by Peter Clark), and uses the British National Corpus of texts[6] as a reference to judge their relative importance. So, she finds that *SAY* occurs twice as often in the Clark TTs, and that the collocation *SAY that* is most common. But this could simply be because of the influence of the SL; the Arabic *qaal* is generally more frequent in the language than is English *SAY* because the repetition of the same reporting verb in English is frowned upon.[7]

The difficulty in distinguishing between those shifts that are effects of the SL and those that are the result of translator's linguistic preferences relates to the difference between Vinay and Darbelnet's *servitude* and *option*. Despite these problems, there are some important features that can be investigated by such studies. Most important, perhaps, is the analysis of the relative markedness of stylistic choices in TT and ST. **Markedness** relates to a choice or patterns of choices that stand out as unusual and may come to the reader's attention. So, in English a sequence such as *Challenging it is. Boring it isn't* is marked because of the unusual word order with the adjectives in first position. The key is to look for the reason behind the markedness. In this case, the wording is from a job advert (to recruit police in London), so the markedness functions to draw the reader's attention to the advert and to illustrate that it is an unusual and challenging job.

In translation, it may usually be expected that a marked item in the ST would be translated by a similarly marked item in the TT but this is not always so. Some work has investigated the possibility that translation may be less marked: Kenny (2001), for instance, looks at the translation of creative lexical items and neologisms from German literary texts, similar to Tirkkonen-Condit's (2004) 'unique items hypothesis'. On the other hand, Saldanha (2011) investigates features such as italicized borrowings that make a particular translation distinctive. Some of my own work (e.g. Munday 2008) has also examined the distinctiveness of a specific translator's work. So, comparing patterns in the work of the translator Harriet de Onís, I identify:

- the manipulation of paratextual features (prefaces, footnotes, glossaries);
- a standardization of dialectal choices in dialogue (many different Latin American dialects standardized into a less dynamic early twentieth-century American English);
- the choice of a rich literary lexicon (e.g. *night was sifting through the jungle*); and
- certain syntactic patterns typical of condensed English style (e.g. the use of compound pre-modifiers such as the unusual *tree-dense night* and *branch-arched passage*).

The interesting point is to hypothesize the **motivation** behind the selections. Most crucially, the question is how far the unconscious (as well as conscious) choices may in fact be due to factors in the translator's environment, including education and the sociocultural and political context in which they operate. May a translator's choice reveal a personal ideological orientation? Or one that is promoted by the society in which they live? Why, for example, when describing an indigenous Amerindian tribe, does Onís translate *indios bravíos* as *savage Indians*? Such questions will be taken up more fully in Chapters 6 (discourse analysis), 7 (descriptive studies), 8 (translation and ideology) and 9 (translator and ethics).

4.4 Exploration: Definitions of style

Look also at the publications referred to in section 4.3 above. What definitions do they give of 'style'? What does this tell us about the different phenomena they are investigating? Look at the ITS website for a discussion of work on style by other Czech theorists of the time, notably Anton Popovič and František Miko.

4.4 The cognitive process of translation

The analysis of translation shifts, including stylistic shifts, seeks to describe the phenomenon of translation, classifying the changes that can be observed from comparing ST–TT pairs. It is a means of describing what constitutes the translation product but there are limits to what it can (or even attempts to) tell us about the actual cognitive process of translation. Other models choose a different approach, based on the observation, analysis and/or explanation of the cognitive processes of the translators themselves (see Hurtado Albir and Alves 2009). As Roger Bell (1991: 43) puts it: 'focus on the description of the process and/or the translator . . . form the twin issues which translation theory must address: how the process takes place and what knowledge and skills the translator must possess in order to carry it out'. Thus, for example, the **'interpretive model'** of translation, championed in Paris from the 1960s onwards by Danica Seleskovitch and Marianne Lederer and initially applied to the study of conference interpreting, explains translation as an (overlapping) three-stage process involving the following:

(1) **Reading and understanding** (Lederer 1994; 2003: 23–35) using linguistic competence and 'world knowledge' to grasp the sense of the ST. The linguistic component needs to be understood by reference not only to explicit but also to implicit meaning in an attempt to recover the authorial intention. The world knowledge we have, according to Lederer, is deverbalized, theoretical, general, encyclopedic and cultural and activated differently in different translators and by different texts: 'Translators are privileged readers called on to understand the facts in a text and to feel its emotional connotations. That is why translators do not feel equally close to all texts' (Lederer 2003: 31).

(2) **Deverbalization** (ibid.: 115) is 'an essential intermediate phase if the translator is to avoid transcoding and calques'. This was an explanation developed to explain the cognitive processing of the interpreter, where transfer supposedly occurs through sense and not words. Deverbalization is claimed to be 'less obvious in translation' (ibid.: 13), since the translator may be constantly comparing the surface wording between the written ST and TT.

(3) **Re-expression** (ibid.: 35–42), where the TT is constituted and given form based on the deverbalized understanding of sense.

A fourth stage, **verification**, where the translator revisits and evaluates the TT, was added by Jean Delisle (1982/1988, see Lederer 2003: 38).

In some ways, this model might appear quite similar to Nida's model of analysis, transfer and restructuring (see Chapter 3). However, rather than placing the emphasis on a structural representation of semantics, the interpretive model stresses the deverbalized cognitive processing that takes place. Yet **deverbalization**, a key plank in the interpretive model, is really underdeveloped theoretically partly because of the problems of observing the process. If deverbalization occurs in a non-verbal state in the mind, how is the researcher going to gain access to it, apart from in the reconstituted form of the verbalized output after the re-expression stage?

From the perspective of **relevance theory** (Sperber and Wilson 1986/1995), the important work of Ernst-August Gutt (1991/2000) claims translation is an example of a communication based around a cause-and-effect model of **inferencing** and **interpretation**. Any successful communication is said to depend on the communicator's ensuring that his/her 'informative intention' is grasped by the receiver, and this is achieved by making the stimulus (words, gestures, etc.) optimally relevant to the extent that the receiver 'can expect to derive adequate contextual effects without spending unnecessary effort' (Gutt 2000: 32). That is, the communicator gives the hearer **communicative clues** that allow the inference to be made. Hatim and Munday (2004: 57) illustrate this with a discussion of the following example from the Canadian parliament:

> *A Canadian MP had to apologize to the House for humming the theme song from 'The Godfather' while Public Works Minister Alfonso Gagliano, who is of Italian descent, addressed the body.*

Here, there are many inferences at work:

- from the MP, whose humming makes and invites a particular inferencing, suggesting a link between the practices of the government Minister and the Italian mafia;
- from the audience, who need to interpret the relationship between the film and the Minister, who is of Italian descent;
- the need to apologize arises from the inference, made by others and apparently accepted by the MP, that his actions amount to a slur.

Translators, for their part, are faced with a similar situation and have several responsibilities (ibid.: 190–3). They need to decide (i) whether and how it is possible to communicate the informative intention, (ii) whether to translate **descriptively** or **interpretively**, (iii) what the degree of **resemblance** to the ST should be, and so on. These decisions are based on the translator's evaluation of the cognitive environment of the receiver. To succeed, the translator and receiver must share basic assumptions about the resemblance that is sought, and the translator's intentions must agree with the receiver's expectations. In the above example, a translator would need to decide how much information to add to ensure that sufficient communicative clues were present to allow a TT audience to retrieve the ST intention. On the other hand, as an instance of failed communication, Gutt (2000: 193–4, following Dooley 1989) notes a translation of the Christian New Testament into Gauraní, an indigenous language spoken in some parts of Brazil. There, the initial, idiomatic translation had to be completely rewritten because the Guaraní expectation was for a TT that more closely corresponded to the form of the high-prestige Portuguese that is the official language of Brazil.

By focusing on the communicative process and cognitive processing, Gutt rejects those translation models, such as Register analysis (see Chapter 6) and descriptive studies (see Chapter 7), that are based on a study of input–output. He even contends that translation as communication can be explained using relevance theoretic concepts alone. In that respect, he claims (2000: 235) 'there is no need for developing a separate theory of translation, with concepts and a theoretical framework of its own'. We shall discuss this further in Chapter 6.

4.5 Ways of investigating cognitive processing

Some theorists have sought to gather detailed observational data towards the explanation of the translator's decision-making processes. One method, particularly popular in the 1990s, is **think-aloud protocols (TAPs)**. In this type of study, the translator is asked to verbalize his/her thought processes while translating or immediately afterwards (the latter being known as **retrospective protocol**), often with no prompting on content. This is usually recorded by the researcher and later transcribed and analysed.

Think-aloud is an experimental method innovated by psychology (notably Ericsson and Simon 1984) and may provide more detailed information on the translation process than simply comparing the ST–TT pair. Well-known early TAP studies of translation (e.g. Krings 1986, Lörscher 1991) used language learners as subjects. However, as experimental methods have developed, more systematic and rigorous studies have been carried out on expert translators or involving the comparison of the performance of expert translators with proficient language speakers who have no translator training (see Tirkkonen-Condit and Jääskeläinen 2000; Englund-Dimitrova 2005).

Despite the advantages of TAPs, there are some well-known and debated limitations. These include (see Jääskeläinen 2010, 'Think-aloud protocol', in Y. Gambier and L. van Doorslaer (eds), pp. 371–4):

■ Do TAPs actually give us information on the mental processes at work? Are they not really a representation of an intermediate stage, in which the subject relates what he/she thinks is happening?

■ The effort involved in verbalizing slows down the translation process and may affect the way the translator segments the text (Jakobsen 2003).

■ The data gathered is therefore incomplete and does not give access to processes which the translator does automatically.

■ What tools should the subjects be allowed to use (dictionaries, notes, internet . . .?)

More recent methods have 'triangulated' think-aloud protocols with **technological innovations**. That is, they support or supplement think-aloud with other experimental methods. These include:

- the video recording and observation of the subjects;
- the use of pre- or post-test interviews and/or questionnaires;
- the use of Translog software at the Copenhagen Business School (Jakobsen and Schou 1999, Hansen 2006, Carl 2012), which records the key-strokes made by the translator on the computer keyboard;
- the use of eye-trackers (O'Brien 2011, Saldanha and O'Brien 2013: 136–45), which records the focus of the eye on the text. The length of such fixation points, and the dilation of the pupil, may indicate the mental effort being made by the translator.

Potentially fruitful as such developments are, Hurtado Albir and Alves (2009: 73) warn that 'the field needs to put more effort into refining experimental designs and fostering the replication of studies, thus allowing for validation or falsification of previous findings'. Nevertheless, this remains one of the most exciting and rapidly developing areas in translation studies, particularly in the use of mixed empirical methods (Saldanha and O'Brien 2013: Chapter 4).

Case study

Over the years Vinay and Darbelnet's model of translation shifts has exerted considerable influence on translation theorists. We use it as the basis for this case study, applying it to a short illustrative text. This text is a brief extract about the area of Greenwich in London, taken from a tourist brochure for boat tours on the River Thames. Boxes 4.1 and 4.2 are extracts from the English ST and the French TT respectively.[8]

Box 4.1

Greenwich (ST)

The ancient town of Greenwich has been a gateway to London for over a thousand years. Invaders from the continent passed either by ship or the Old Dover Road, built by the Romans, on their way to the capital.

In 1012, the Danes moored their longships at Greenwich and raided Canterbury, returning with Archbishop Alfege as hostage and later murdering him on the spot where the church named after him now stands.

Box 4.2

Greenwich (French TT)

Les envahisseurs venant du continent passaient par cette ancienne ville, par bateau ou par la Old Dover Road (construite par les Romains) pour se rendre à la capitale. En 1012, les Danois amarrèrent leurs drakkars à Greenwich avant de razzier Canterbury et de revenir avec l'archevêque Alphège, pris en otage puis assassiné là où se trouve désormais l'église portant son nom.

[Back translation]

The invaders coming from the continent passed through this ancient town, by boat or along the Old Dover Road (built by the Romans) to reach the capital. In 1012, the Danes moored their drakkars at Greenwich before raiding Canterbury and returning with archbishop Alphege, taken in hostage then murdered there where is found henceforth the church bearing his name.

Following the model outlined in section 4.1.3 above, we first divide the ST into the smallest units of translation and match those units with the TT segments. Table 4.1 shows this division.

The first problem arises when trying to decide on the boundaries of segmentation, defined by Vinay and Darbelnet as the 'smallest' segment that can be translated in isolation. Often there are simultaneous lexical correspondences of both small and longer segments. For instance, ST translation unit 13 (*built by the Romans*) could be considered as three separate, clearly understandable segments: *built*, *by* and *the Romans*. Similarly, ST units 23 (*with Archbishop Alfege*) and 24 (*as hostage*) could be considered as a single unit of thought. The French *par* ['by'] of TT unit 12 (*par la Old Dover Road*) could also be a separate unit, being an addition to the equivalent ST unit. This type of segmentation problem recurs constantly. Categorization of the translation procedures used for each of the ST units is shown in Box 4.3.

Table 4.1   Segmentation of text into units of translation

ST (English)		TT (French) [with back translation]
Greenwich	1	Greenwich
The ancient town of Greenwich	2	
has been	3	
a gateway	4	
to London	5	
for over a thousand years.	6	
Invaders from the continent	7	Les envahisseurs venant du continent
		[The invaders coming from the continent]
passed	8	passaient [passed]
	4	par [through]
	2	cette ancienne ville [this ancient town]
either	9	
by ship	10	par bateau [by boat]
or	11	ou [or]
the Old Dover Road,	12	par la Old Dover Road
		[along the Old Dover Road]
built by the Romans,	13	(construite par les Romans)
		[built by the Romans]
on their way	14	pour se rendre [to reach]
to the capital.	15	à la capitale. [to the capital]
In 1012,	16	En 1012, [In 1012,]
the Danes	17	les Danois [the Danes]
moored their longships	18	amarrèrent leurs drakkars
		[moored their drakkars]
at Greenwich	19	à Greenwich [at Greenwich]
and	20	avant de [before]
raided Canterbury,	21	razzier Canterbury [raiding Canterbury]
returning	22	et de revenir [and returning]
with Archbishop Alfege	23	avec l'archevêque Alphège,
		[with archbishop Alphege]
as hostage	24	pris en otage [taken in hostage]
and later	25	puis [then]
murdering him	26	assassiné [murdered]
on the spot where	27	là où [there where]
the church named after him	28	
now stands.	29	se trouve désormais [is found henceforth]
	28	l'église portant son nom.
		[the church bearing his name]

Box 4.3

1   The title is originally a borrowing from English to French of the name *Greenwich*, which has now become a standard literal translation.

2   The corresponding unit in the TT is *cette ancienne ville*, located after units 8 and 4 in the TT. There is thus word order shift. In addition, the change from ST repetition *of Greenwich* to the TT connector *cette* (*ancienne ville*) is an example of economy and of transposition (proper noun → demonstrative pronoun).

3   Omission.

4   *a gateway* is only hinted at in the French by the preposition *par* after unit 8; again this is economy and transposition (noun → preposition).

5   Omission.

6   Omission.

7   Transposition (preposition *from* → verb + preposition + article *venant du*). This is also amplification.

8   Literal translation.

9   Omission.

10   Literal translation.

11   Literal translation.

12   Supplementation (a specific kind of amplification) involving the addition of *par*. Borrowing of *Old Dover Road*, although with addition of article *la*.

13   Literal translation, although there is a change in punctuation.

14   Transposition, adverbial adjunct (*on their way*) → verbal phrase (*pour se rendre*). There is also modulation of the message here through a change of point of view.

15   Literal translation.

16   Literal translation.

17   Literal translation.

18   Literal translation. This could also be classed as fixed modulation (whole → part) in that the origin of *drakkar* is the dragon sculpture on the prow of the longboats.

19   Literal translation.

20   Change of connector, *and* → *avant de*.

21   Literal translation.

22 Amplification, addition of connector *et* indicating logical relationship.
23 Literal translation, including borrowing of name *Alfege* with change of graphology (*Alphège*).
24 Amplification (addition of *pris*).
25 Economy with omission of connector (*and later → puis*).
26 Change of point of view (cause → effect, *murdering him → assassiné*).
27 Economy, deictic transposition of noun by demonstrative (*on the spot where → là où*).
28 Units 28 and 29 show word order shift in TT. In addition, ST unit 28 shows cause → effect modulation (*named after him → portant son nom*) and transposition (prepositional phrase → noun phrase).
29 Word order shift and modulation, change of point of view involving different limit of time (*now → désormais*).

4.5 Exploration: Evaluation of the model

Look again at the analysis in the case study. Are there points where you disagree with the analysis? What does this tell us about the use of this kind of model? The analysis focuses on the seven procedures, but are there also examples here of the supplementary procedures of loss/gain, compensation, explicitation, etc.?

Discussion of case study

Analysis of this box shows around thirteen direct translations out of twenty-nine translation units. In other words, around 40 per cent of the translations might be termed direct. Furthermore, the more complex 'cultural' procedures such as équivalence and adaptation are absent. Most of the oblique translation procedures revealed affect the lexical or syntactic level, although there is some shift in prosody and structure. The figures can only be approximate because there is a crucial problem of determining the translation unit and the boundaries between the categories are vague. Some units (e.g. units 2 and 14) show more than one shift; others (e.g. units 4 and 18) pose particular problems of evaluation. Most importantly, however, although Vinay and Darbelnet purport to describe the translation process, their model in fact focuses on the translation product. There is little incorporation of higher-level discourse considerations nor a means of discussing the effect the changes might have on the reader.

Summary

The 1950s and 1960s saw the emergence of attempts at detailed taxonomies of small linguistic changes ('shifts') in ST–TT pairs. Vinay and Darbelnet's classic taxonomy continues to exert most influence today and was useful in bringing to light a wide range of different translation techniques. However, like Catford, who in the 1960s applied a systematic contrastive linguistic approach to translation, theirs is a rather static model. Fuzziness of category boundaries is a problem, while other models have been proposed for non-European languages (e.g. Loh 1958). Another approach to the analysis of shifts, particularly stylistic shifts, came from Czechoslovakia in the 1960s and 1970s. Stylistic analysis, and its link to the identity, intentions and ideology of the translator, have come to the fore in the 'translatorial stylistics' of the new millennium (Malmkjær 2003).

Meanwhile, a different approach to the examination and explanation of translation procedures has been afforded by cognitive theorists, starting with the Paris School of the 1960s and including Gutt (from relevance theory) and Bell (from psycholinguistics and systemic functional analysis). Increasingly, such research methods have made use of technological advances such as think-aloud protocols, key-stroke logging and eye-tracking, although methodological procedures remain to be standardized.

Further reading

See Fawcett (1997), Hermans (1999) and Pym (2016) for further discussion of models described here. As noted above, versions of Vinay and Darbelnet's model have been used for other language pairs; note especially Malblanc (1944/1963) for German and Vázquez-Ayora (1977) for Spanish. Mounin (1963) is an early linguistic model from France (see also Larose 1989), while the strong Russian tradition can be followed up in Fedorov (1968) and Švecjer (1987), as well as in

Pym (2016) and Mossop (2013). See Koster (2000) for the linguistic analysis of poetry in translation.

For more on style in translation, see Barnstone (1993), Boase-Beier (2006), Bosseaux (2007), Parks (2007), Munday (2008) and Saldanha (2011). For voice in retranslation, see Alvstad and Assis Rosa (2015). For a summary of cognitive models and experimental design, see Alves (2003), Hurtado Albir and Alves (2009), O'Brien (2011) and Saldanha and O'Brien (2013). For Gutt's later work on translation as a **higher order act of communication**, see Gutt (2005). See also the discussion of Gutt in Hatim and Munday (2004, Unit 8).

Discussion and research points

1   Boxes 4.4–4.6 are extracts from the German, Italian and Spanish TTs of the case study extract. If you have a reading knowledge of these languages, analyse the TTs into units of translation and the translation procedures that have been followed, using Vinay and Darbelnet's model. If you work with another language, produce and analyse a translation in that TL (see also the ITS website for TT examples in Arabic, Chinese, Korean and Malay). How does your analysis of other TTs differ from that of the French translation?

Box 4.4

Greenwich

Seit über 1000 Jahren ist die historische Stadt Greenwich ein Tor zu London. Vom Kontinent kommende Invasoren passierten sie auf ihrem Weg nach London entweder per Schiff oder über Strasse Old Dover Road.

1012 legten die Dänen mit ihren Wikingerbooten in Greenwich an und überfielen Canterbury. Sie kehrten mit dem Erzbischof Alfege als Geisel zurück und ermordeten ihn später an der Stelle, an der heute die nach ihm benannte Kirche steht.

Box 4.5

Greenwich

L'antica città di Greenwich è una via di ingresso per Londra da più di mille anni. Gli invasori provenienti dal continente passavano sulle navi o lungo la Old Dover Road, costruita dai Romani, mentre si dirigevano verso la capitale.

Nel 1012 i Danesi attraccarono le loro navi a Greenwich e fecero razzia a Canterbury, tornando con l'arcivescovo Alfege, come ostaggio e più tardi assassinandolo sul luogo dove sorge ora la chiesa che porta il suo nome.

Box 4.6

Greenwich

El antiguo pueblo de Greenwich ha sido la entrada a Londres durante miles de años. Los invasores del continente pasaban por barco o a través de la Vieja Carretera de Dover, construida por los romanos, en su camino hacia la capital.

En el año 1012, los daneses amarraron sus grandes barcos en Greenwich, regresando con el arzobispo Alfege como rehén y posteriormente le mataron en el lugar donde ahora se encuentra la iglesia con su nombre.

2 One area that Vinay and Darbelnet do not cover is the translation of culture-specific items (CSIs) such as names, items of food and clothing, local customs, etc. (see Aixelà 1996, Dickins 2013). Read the articles on CSIs on the ITS companion website and note the categories used. How might this type of analysis be incorporated into a model of translation shifts?

3   Beaugrande (1978: 11) gives the following dismissal of Catford's book: 'Catford's "theory of translation" stands as an allegory of the limitations of linguistics at that time.' However, have a closer look at Catford's theory (e.g. Catford 2000) and read Henry's (1984) critique. List its strengths and possible applications.

4   Read Gutt's application of relevance theory (Gutt 2000, 2005; see also Hatim and Munday 2004, Unit 8) and summarize his arguments. How far do you think that Gutt demonstrates that relevance theory is sufficient to explain translation processes?

The ITS website at www.routledge.com/cw/munday contains:

■   a video summary of the chapter;
■   a recap multiple-choice test;
■   customizable PowerPoint slides;
■   further reading links and extra journal articles;
■   more research project questions;
■   more case studies.

CHAPTER 5

Functional theories of translation

Key concepts

- **Functional theories from Germany in the 1970s–1980s mark a move away from linguistic typologies towards a consideration of culture.**
- **Reiss stresses equivalence at text level, linking language functions to text types and translation strategy.**
- **Snell-Hornby's 'integrated approach' to text type in translation.**
- **Holz-Mänttäri's theory of translatorial action: a communicative process involving a series of players.**
- **Vermeer's skopos theory: translation depends on the purpose of the TT.**
- **Nord's translation-oriented text analysis.**
- **Recent developments in multimodality and digital text genres.**

Key texts

Nord, Christiane (2005) *Text Analysis in Translation: Theory, Methodology and Didactic Application of a Model for Translation-Oriented Text Analysis*, translated by Christiane Nord and Penelope Sparrow, 2nd edition, Amsterdam: Rodopi.

Nord, Christiane (1997) *Translating as a Purposeful Activity: Functionalist Approaches Explained*, Manchester: St Jerome.

Reiss, Katharina (1971/2000) *Translation Criticism: Potential and Limitations*, translated by Erroll F. Rhodes, Manchester: St Jerome and American Bible Society.[1]

Reiss, Katharina (1981/2004) 'Type, kind and individuality of text: Decision making in translation', translated by Susan Kitron, in Lawrence Venuti (ed.) *The Translation Studies Reader*, 2nd edition (2004), London and New York: Routledge, pp. 168–79.

Reiss, Katharina and Hans Vermeer (1984/2013) *Towards a General Theory of Translational Action: Skopos Theory Explained*, translated by Christiane Nord, English reviewed by Marina Dudenhöfer. Manchester: St Jerome.

Snell-Hornby, Mary (1988/1995) *Translation Studies: An Integrated Approach*, Amsterdam and Philadelphia: John Benjamins.

Vermeer, Hans (1989/2012) 'Skopos and commission in translational action', in Lawrence Venuti (ed.) *The Translation Studies Reader*, 3rd edition (2012), London and New York: Routledge, pp. 191–202.

5.0 Introduction

Watch the introductory video on the companion website.

The 1970s and 1980s saw a move away from linguistic typologies of translation shifts, and the emergence and flourishing in Germany of a functionalist and communicative approach to the analysis of translation. This tied in with advances in linguistic studies of the complex parameters of text comprehension and generation. In this chapter, we look at:

(1)   Katharina Reiss's early work on text type and Mary Snell-Hornby's later 'integrated' approach;

(2)   Justa Holz-Mänttäri's theory of translatorial action;[2]

(3)   Hans J. Vermeer's skopos theory, which centred on the purpose of the TT;

(4)   Christiane Nord's more detailed text-analysis model which continued the functionalist tradition in the 1990s and beyond.

5.1 Text type

Katharina Reiss's work in the 1970s built on the concept of equivalence (see Chapter 3) but viewed the text, rather than the word or sentence, as the level at which communication is achieved and at which equivalence must be sought (Reiss 1977/1989: 113–14). Her functional approach aimed initially at systematizing the assessment of translations. It borrows from the (1934/1965) categorization of the three functions of language by German psychologist and linguist **Karl Bühler** (1879–1963):

(1) **informative function** (*Darstellungsfunktion*);
(2) **expressive function** (*Ausdrucksfunktion*);
(3) **appellative function** (*Appellfunktion*).

Reiss links the three functions to their corresponding language 'dimensions' and to the text types or communicative situations in which they are used. These links can be seen in Table 5.1.

Table 5.1   Functional characteristics of text types and links to translation methods (translated and adapted from Reiss 1971/2000)

Text type:	*Informative*	*Expressive*	*Operative*
Language function:	Informative (representing objects and facts)	Expressive (expressing sender's attitude)	Appellative (making an appeal to text receiver)
Language dimension:	Logical	Aesthetic	Dialogic
Text focus:	Content-focused	Form-focused	Appellative-focused
TT should ...	Transmit referential content	Transmit aesthetic form	Elicit desired response
Translation method:	'Plain prose', explicitation as required	'Identifying' method, adopt perspective of ST author	'Adaptive', equivalent effect

The main characteristics of each text type are summarized by Reiss (1977/1989: 108–9) as follows.

(1) **Informative text type**. 'Plain communication of facts': information, knowledge, opinions, etc. The language dimension used to transmit the information is logical or referential, the content or 'topic' is the main focus of the communication.
(2) **Expressive text type**. 'Creative composition': the author uses the aesthetic dimension of language. The author or 'sender' is foregrounded, as well as the form of the message.
(3) **Operative text type**. 'Inducing behavioural responses': the aim of the appellative function is to appeal to or persuade the reader or 'receiver' of the text to act in a certain way, for example to buy a product (if an advert), or to agree to an argument (if a political speech or a barrister's concluding statement). The form of language is dialogic and the focus is appellative.

(4)   **Audio-medial** texts, such as films and visual and spoken advertisements which supplement the other three functions with visual images, music, etc. This is Reiss's fourth type, which is not represented in Table 5.1, and which are now commonly called 'multimodal texts' (see section 5.1.3 below).

Text types are therefore categorized according to their main function. For each of these text types, Reiss (1976: 20) also gives examples of what she calls 'text varieties' (*Textsorte*), now more commonly known as **genres**, that are typically associated with them. These are presented visually in Figure 5.1.

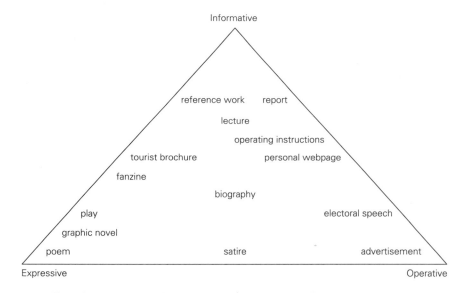

Figure 5.1   Reiss's text types and text varieties (adapted from Chesterman 1989: 105, based on a handout prepared by Roland Freihoff).

Following this diagram, a reference work (e.g. an encyclopedia, such as Wikipedia) would be the genre that is the most obviously informative text type; a poem is a highly expressive, form-focused type, and an advertisement is the clearest operative text type (attempting to persuade someone to buy or do something). Between these poles are positioned a host of **hybrid** types. Thus, a biography (e.g. of a major political figure such as Barack Obama) might be somewhere between the informative and expressive types, since it provides information about the subject while also partly performing the expressive function of a piece of literature. It may even have an operative function in convincing the reader of the correctness (or error) of the subject's actions. Similarly, a personal webpage gives facts about the individual but also often presents a flattering portrait. And a religious speech may give information about the religion while fulfilling the operative function by attempting to persuade the audience to behave in a certain way. It too may have an expressive function as a piece of rhetoric.

5.1 Exploration: Text types and genres

Look at translations that you yourself have done (either in a language class or in professional translation situations). How would you fit them into Katharina Reiss's text typology – both as text types and genres? How many are 'hybrids'?

Despite the existence of such hybrid types, Reiss (1977/1989: 109) states that 'the transmission of the predominant function of the ST is the determining factor by which the TT is judged'. She suggests 'specific translation methods according to text type' (Reiss 1976: 20). These methods occupy the last two rows of Table 5.1 and can be described as follows.

(1) The TT of an **informative text** should transmit the full referential or conceptual content of the ST. The translation should be in 'plain prose', without redundancy and with the use of explicitation when required. So, the translation of an encyclopedia entry of, say, the Tyrannosaurus Rex, should focus on transmitting the factual content and terminology and not worry about stylistic niceties.
(2) The TT of an **expressive text** should transmit the aesthetic and artistic form of the ST, in addition ensuring the accuracy of information. The translation should use the 'identifying' method, with the translator adopting the standpoint of the ST author. So, the translator of James Joyce would need to try to write from the perspective of the author. In literature, the style of the ST author is a priority.
(3) The TT of an **operative text** should produce the desired response in the TT receiver. The translation should employ the 'adaptive' method, creating an equivalent effect among TT readers. So, the TT of an advert needs to appeal to the target audience even if new words and images are needed.
(4) **Audio-medial texts** require what Reiss calls the 'supplementary' method, supplementing written words with visual images and music.

Reiss (1971/2000: 48–88) also lists a series of intralinguistic and extralinguistic **instruction criteria** (*Instruktionen*) by which the adequacy of a TT may be assessed. These are:

(1) **linguistic components:**
■   semantic equivalence

- lexical equivalence
- grammatical and stylistic features;

(2) **non-linguistic determinants:**

- situation
- subject field or domain
- time
- place (characteristics of country and culture)
- receiver
- sender
- 'affective implications' (humour, irony, emotion, etc.).

Although interrelated, the importance of these criteria varies according to text type and genre (Reiss 1971/2000: 58). For example, the translation of any content-focused text, such as our encyclopedia entry of the Tyrannosaurus Rex, should first aim at preserving semantic equivalence. The translation of the genre 'popular science book' would generally pay more attention to the accessibility and individual style of the ST author while the translation of a scientific article for experts would be expected to conform to the specialized conventions of the academic article. Similarly, Reiss (ibid.: 59) feels that it is more important for a metaphor to be retained in the translation of an expressive text than in an informative TT, where translation of its semantic value alone will be sufficient.

These adequacy criteria are valid as a measure of quality in those translation situations where the TT is to have the same function as the ST. There are, of course, occasions, as Reiss allows (1977/1989: 114), when the function of the TT may differ from that of the ST. An example she gives is Jonathan Swift's *Gulliver's Travels* (1726). Originally written as a satirical novel to attack the British government of the day (i.e. a mainly operative text), it is nowadays normally read and translated as 'ordinary entertaining fiction' (i.e. an expressive text). Alternatively, a TT may have a different communicative function from the ST: an operative election speech in one language may be translated for analysts in another country interested in finding out what policies have been presented and how (i.e. as an informative and expressive text).

5.1.1 Discussion of the text type model

Reiss's work is important because it moves translation theory beyond a consideration of lower linguistic levels, the mere words on the page, beyond even the effect they create, towards a consideration of the communicative function of translation. Indeed, recognition that the function of the TT may be different from the ST function was crucial in challenging the prevailing view of equivalence that saw the translator's goal as achieving equivalent effect (see Chapter 3). However, over the years there have been a number of criticisms of the text type model (see Fawcett 1997: 106–8). One of the **criticisms** is why there should only be three types of language function. Although she works in the same functionalist tradition as Reiss, Nord (1997: 44, see also section 5.4 below) perhaps implicitly accepts this criticism by feeling the need to add a fourth **'phatic'** function, taken from Roman Jakobson's typology, covering language that establishes or maintains contact between the parties involved in the communication.[3] A simple example would be a greeting or phrase such as 'Ladies and gentlemen' that is used to signal the start of a formal speech, or 'Hello' when someone answers the phone.

There are also question marks as to how Reiss's proposed translation methods are to be applied in the case of a specific text. Even the apparently logical 'plain-prose' method for the informative text can be questioned. Business and financial texts in English contain a large number of simple and complex metaphors: markets are *bullish* and *bearish*, profits *soar, peak, flatten, dive* and *plummet*, while *the credit crunch bites, hostile takeover bids* are launched and *fiscal haircuts* imposed.

5.2 Exploration: The translation of metaphors

Look for English source texts in the financial domain which contain the metaphors listed above. How would you translate them into your other language(s)? If possible, find out how they have been translated in target texts, for example for the United Nations, World Bank or European institutions.

Some of these have a fixed translation in another language, but the more complex and individualistic metaphors do not, and more recent work has also moved from the consideration of linguistic metaphor to conceptual metaphors (see Lakoff and Johnson 1980) that represent and structure perceptions of reality. One example given by Dickins (2005: 244) is the frequency of Arabic metaphors about information which feature verbs of motion (e.g. *There has reached to our programme . . . a question*) whereas English tends to prefer metaphors of giving and receiving (e.g. *Our programme has received a question*).

Another point is whether Reiss's preferred translation methods are reversible. For example, we might accept a plain-prose method for translating the English financial metaphors above into a language where such a metaphorical style was out of place – so, *profits soar* may be rendered as *profits increase considerably*. But what would we do when translating a financial text from that language into English? A translation of such a text *into* English (or other similar languages) surely requires not just attention to the informative value of the ST. It also requires the use of the lexical and conceptual metaphors that are common to that genre in English. Failure to do so would produce an English TT that was lacking in the expressive function of language.

This example contains an important implicit criticism for Reiss's whole theory – namely, **whether text types and genres can be differentiated on the basis of the primary function**. An annual business report, classed by Reiss as a strongly informative text, may also show a strongly expressive side. It may also have several functions in the source culture: as an informative text for the company's directors and as an operative text to persuade the shareholders and market analysts that the company is being run efficiently. In Figure 5.1, the biography could also easily have an appellative function, especially if it is an autobiography, such as Barack Obama's *Dreams from My Father* (Crown Publishers, 1995, 2004) or Tony Blair's *A Journey* (Cornerstone, 2010). An advertisement, while normally appellative, may have an artistic/expressive and/or informative function, such as many posters of the Spanish Civil War or of the Soviet Union. Co-existence of functions within the same ST and the use of the same ST for a variety of purposes are evidence of the fuzziness that fits uneasily into Reiss's clear divisions, which we shall look at in the next section. Finally, the translation method employed depends on far more than just text type. The translator's own role and purpose, as well as sociocultural pressures, also affect the kind of translation strategy that is adopted. This is a key question in the rest of this chapter and also in Chapter 6.

5.1.2 Mary Snell-Hornby's 'integrated approach'

In her book *Translation Studies: An Integrated Approach* (1988, revised 1995), the Vienna-based scholar, teacher and translator Mary Snell-Hornby reviews and attempts to include a wide variety of different linguistic and literary concepts in an overarching **'integrated'** approach to translation based on text types. Snell-Hornby comes from a predominantly German-theoretical background and notably borrows the notion of **prototypes** for categorizing text types. Depending on the text type under consideration, she incorporates cultural history, literary studies, sociocultural and area studies and, for legal, economic, medical and scientific translation, the study of the relevant specialized subject. Her view of the field is illustrated by Figure 5.2.

Snell-Hornby (1995: 31) explains that, horizontally, the diagram is to be read as a series of clines, from left to right, with no clear demarcations. This is complemented by a 'stratificational model' proceeding from the most general (A) to the most specialized (F).

In **level A**, she sets out to integrate 'literary', 'general language' and 'special language' translation into a single continuum, rather than isolating them according to separate areas of translation.

Level B indicates prototypical basic text types: so, for example, for literary translation there is Bible, stage/film, lyric poetry etc. On the right is light fiction, which begins to merge into the newspaper/general information types of general language.

Level C 'shows the non-linguistic disciplines . . . which are inseparably bound up with translation'. These include sociocultural knowledge for general language translation and special subject studies for specialized translation.

Level D then covers the translation process, including (i) understanding the function of the ST, (ii) the TT focus and (iii) the communicative function of the TT.

Level E covers areas of linguistics relevant to translation.

Level F, the lowest-order level, deals with phonological aspects, such as alliteration, rhythm and speakability of stage translation and film dubbing.

This is a very ambitious attempt to bring together diverse areas of translation and to bridge the gap between the commercial and artistic translations described by Schleiermacher in 1813 (see Chapter 2). Yet one must question whether an attempt to incorporate all genres and text types into such a detailed single overarching analytical framework is really viable. Inconsistencies are inevitably to be found. Here are some examples.

- On level B, can all 'newspaper texts' really be lumped together as 'general language translation'? Some may be quite specialized technical, scientific, financial, sporting, etc. texts. Should 'film' translation be treated as literary translation? Our discussion of the characteristics of audiovisual translation in Chapter 11 shows that it operates under very different constraints.
- Why is 'advertising' placed further from the literary than is 'general'? It may well have far more in common with the creative language of lyric poetry (see our discussion of 'transcreation', also in Chapter 11).

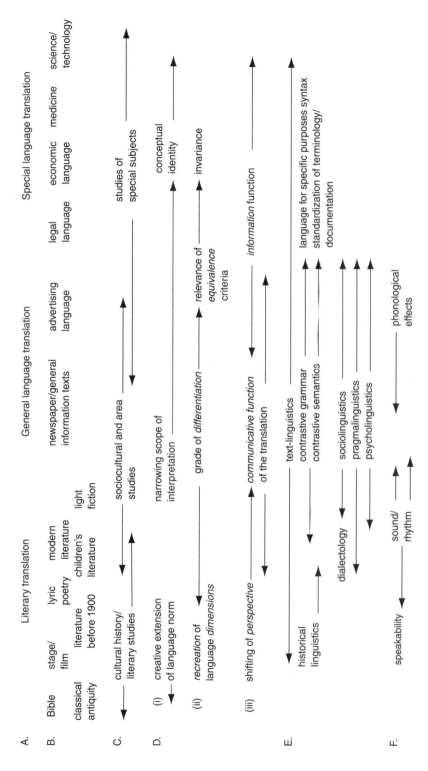

Figure 5.2 Text type and relevant criteria for translation (from Snell-Hornby 1995: 32)

■ On level C, 'cultural history' may be just as relevant to the translation of a medical text as to a literary one.

■ The 'studies of special subjects' may also be appropriate to the background of literary texts. For instance, it would be impossible to translate Tsao Hsueh-chin (1715–1763)'s *A Dream of Red Mansions* (红楼梦) without researching feudal society in the Qianlong era, and Thomas Mann's *Der Zauberberg* (*Magic Mountain*) requires knowledge of the regimes of Alpine sanatoria of the 1920s.

■ Similarly, 'speakability' need not be restricted to literary works. Translations of foreign news interviews may be designed to be read as a voice-over, while translations of written speeches may also need to retain, recreate or compensate for the rhythm or sound of the ST.

Even though we may quibble with Snell-Hornby's categorization, the removal of rigid divisions between different types of language is to be welcomed. There is no necessity for translation studies to focus solely on the literary or religious, as was so often the case in its early days. Nor, by contrast, should the focus be restricted solely to the technical. On the other hand, it would also be true to say that the consideration of all kinds of language in such an integrated continuum does not necessarily produce more useful results for the analysis of translations and for translator training. A student wishing to be a commercial translator is likely to need somewhat different training compared to one who would like to be a literary translator, even if each may benefit from studying the work of the other.

5.1.3 Web localization and digital genres

Technological developments in multilingual communication since the 1990s have stressed **domain specialization** and have seen new **multimodal genres** and **text types** emerge (emails, webpages, blogs, tweets, social media posts) that may demand instant translation, often provided by an automatic translate function. Jiménez-Crespo (2013: 97–9) provides a classification according to text type or 'supra-genres' (informational, advertising, instrumental, communication-interaction, entertainment), functions, participants, **web genres** (personal homepage, corporate website …) and subgenres (personal, professional, etc.). These are naturally hybrid and combine in different ways (ibid.: 100). A multilingual version is produced through a process known as **localization** (see section 11.2) in which, as well as linguistic transfer, adaptations are made in order to allow the 'product' (or text) to function satisfactorily in its target context or 'locale'.

5.3 Exploration: Web localization

Read the online article by Jiménez-Crespo (2011) on website localization and translation. Note the distinctive features of this type of process. How far do these fit with the Reiss and Snell-Hornby models described above?

5.2 Translatorial action

The translatorial action model proposed by Justa Holz-Mänttäri (*Translatorisches Handeln: Theorie und Methode*)[4] takes up concepts from communication theory and action theory. Her aim, among others, was to provide a model and produce guidelines that can be applied to a wide range of professional translation situations. Translatorial action views translation as purpose-driven, outcome-oriented human interaction. It construes the process of translation as 'message-transmitter compounds' [*Botschaftsträger im Verbund*] that involve intercultural transfer:

> [It] is not about translating words, sentences or texts but is in every case about guiding the intended co-operation over cultural barriers enabling functionally oriented communication.
>
> (Holz-Mänttäri 1984: 7–8)

Interlingual translation is described as 'translatorial action from a source text' and as a communicative process involving a series of **roles and players** (ibid.: 109–11), which are:

- **the initiator:** the company or individual who needs the translation;
- **the commissioner:** the individual or agency who contacts the translator;
- **the ST producer:** the individual(s) within the company who write(s) the ST, and who are not necessarily involved in the TT production;
- **the TT producer:** the translator(s) and the translation agency or department;
- **the TT user:** the person who uses the TT – for example, a teacher using a translated textbook or a rep using sales brochures;
- **the TT receiver:** the final recipient of the TT – for example, the students using the textbook in the teacher's class or clients reading the translated sales brochures.

These players each have their own specific primary and secondary goals. The text selected by Holz-Mänttäri for her detailed case study (ibid.: 129–48) present the instructions for installing a chemical toilet. The roles of the different participants in the translatorial action are analysed. In the case of the professional translator faced with such a text, the likely goals are primarily to earn money, and secondarily to fulfil the contract and to process the text message (ibid.: 138). According to the analysis given, the translator may be a non-expert both in the text type and specific subject area. Extra input of subject-area knowledge would need to come from the ST writer within the company or through careful research by the translator(s).

Translatorial action focuses very much on producing a TT that is **functionally communicative** for the receiver. This means, for example, that the form and genre of the TT must be guided by what is functionally suitable in the TT culture, rather than by merely copying the ST profile. What is functionally suitable has to be determined by the translator, who is the expert in translatorial action and whose role is to make sure that the intercultural transfer takes place satisfactorily. In the 'translatorial text operations' (the term Holz-Mänttäri uses for the production of the TT), the ST is analysed solely for its 'construction and function profile' (ibid.: 139–48). Relevant features are described according to the traditional split of 'content' and 'form' (ibid.: 126):

(1) **Content** is divided into (a) factual information and (b) overall communicative strategy.
(2) **Form** is divided into (a) terminology and (b) cohesive elements.

The needs of the receiver are the determining factors for the TT. Thus, as far as terminology is concerned, a technical term in a technical ST may require clarification for a non-technical TT user – e.g. a medical term such as *Thrombocytopenia* could be rephrased as *a reduced number of platelets in the blood*. Additionally, in order to maintain cohesion for the TT reader, a single term will normally need to be translated consistently (ibid.: 144).

5.2.1 Discussion of the model of translatorial action

The value of Holz-Mänttäri's work is the placing of translation (or at least the professional non-literary translation which she describes) within its sociocultural context, including the interplay between the translator and the initiator. Holz-Mänttäri (1986) later also describes the 'professional profile' of the translator. The inclusion of real-world commercial translation constraints is welcome in addressing some of the decisions faced by translators, and indeed the theory is flexible enough to incorporate the roles that have developed with new translation practices. These include work-flows and project management systems in larger international organizations and translation agencies as well as the informal 'user-generated content' (O'Hagan 2009) where non-professional translators provide translations (e.g. fansubs) and/or contribute to a mass-participant translation project (e.g. Facebook, Wikipedia).

However, the model can be criticized, not least for the complexity of its jargon (for example *message-transmitter compounds*), which does little to explain prac-tical translation situations for the individual translator. Also, since one of the aims of the model is to offer guidelines for intercultural transfer, it is disappointing that it fails to consider cultural difference in more detail or in the kinds of terms proposed by the culturally oriented and sociological models discussed in Chapters 8 and 9.

5.4 Exploration: Players in translatorial action

Imagine a situation in which you are working as a freelance translator. You contact a translation agency inquiring for work and, a while later, are offered half a 20,000-word translation from German into your first language. It is an online user manual for a lawnmower produced by a well-known company which sells the product worldwide. The agency asks you to do a sample translation of 500 words to prove your suitability for the task. This is assessed positively by an in-house translator. The project manager then sends you your allocated portion of the ST. You are asked to work on it using a CAT tool, through which the workflow is monitored and queries made and answered. Your work will be revised in-house. Look at the list of roles and players given by Holz-Mänttäri and match roles to the different participants in this translatorial action.
Read the online article by Babych et al. (2012) for an example of how the various roles and actions can be integrated into a collaborative training platform.

5.3 Skopos theory

Skopos is the Greek word for 'aim' or **'purpose'** and was introduced into transla-tion theory in the 1970s by Hans J. Vermeer (1930–2010) as a technical term for the purpose of a translation and of the action of translating. The major work on **skopos theory** (*Skopostheorie*) is Reiss and Vermeer's *Grundlegung einer* *allgemeinen Translationstheorie* (1984), translated as *Towards a General Theory of Translational Action* (2013). Although skopos theory pre-dates Holz-Mänttäri's theory of translatorial action, it may be considered to be part of that same theory because it deals with a translational action based on a ST – the action has to be negotiated and performed and has a purpose and a result (Vermeer 1989/2012). A TT, called the *Translatum* by Vermeer and *translational action* in Nord's translation, must be fit for purpose; that is, it must be **'functionally adequate'**. Therefore, knowing why a ST is to be translated and what the function of the TT will be is crucial for the translator.[5]

As the title of their 1984/2013 book suggests, Reiss and Vermeer aim for a general translation theory for all texts. The first part sets out a detailed explanation of Vermeer's skopos theory; the second part, 'specific theories', adapts Reiss's functional text-type model to the general theory. In this chapter, for reasons of space, we concentrate on the basic underlying 'rules' of the theory (Reiss and Vermeer 2013: 94ff). These are as follows:

(1) A translational action is determined by its skopos.
(2) It is an offer of information (*Informationsangebot*) in a target culture and TL concerning an offer of information in a source culture and SL.
(3) A TT does not initiate an offer of information in a clearly reversible way.
(4) A TT must be internally coherent.
(5) A TT must be coherent with the ST.
(6) The five rules above stand in hierarchical order, with the skopos rule predominating.

Some explanation is required here. Rule 1 is paramount: the TT is determined by its skopos. Rule 2 is important in that it relates the ST and TT to their function in their respective linguistic and cultural contexts. Here, the translator is once again the key player in a process of intercultural communication and production of the *Translatum*. The irreversibility in point 3 indicates that the function of a TT in the target culture is not necessarily the same as the ST in the source culture. For instance, a ST that provides detailed regulations about a University's degree structure might undergo a gist or partial translation to function as part of a TT that describes transfer between programmes in different education systems. Rules 4 and 5 touch on general skopos 'rules' concerning how the success of the action and information transfer is to be judged, on its **functional adequacy**: (a) the coherence rule, linked to internal textual coherence; and (b) the fidelity rule, linked to intertextual coherence with the ST. These are crucial.

(a)   The **coherence rule** states that the TT must be interpretable as coherent with the TT receiver's situation (Reiss and Vermeer 2013: 101). In other words, the TT must be translated in such a way that it makes sense for the TT receivers, given their circumstances, knowledge and needs. If the TT does not fit the needs of the TT receivers, it is simply not adequate for its purpose.

(b)   The **fidelity rule** merely states (ibid.: 102) that there must be coherence between the TT and the ST or, more specifically, between:

(i)   the ST information received by the translator;

(ii)   the interpretation the translator makes of this information;

(iii)   the information that is encoded for the TT receivers.

But the fidelity rule does not say what this coherence relationship should be. Importantly, the hierarchical order of the rules means that intertextual coherence between ST and TT (Rule 5) is of less importance than intratextual coherence within the TT (Rule 4). This, in turn, is subordinate to the skopos (Rule 1). In other words, the translator should first ensure that the TT fulfils its purpose, then make sure the TT is itself coherent and only then see that the TT demonstrates coherence with the ST. Even then, the type of match between ST and TT is not specified. This downplaying (or '**dethroning**', as Vermeer terms it) of the ST is a general fact of both skopos and translatorial action theory and one which has caused much controversy. Does it mean that 'anything goes' as long as the TT purpose is fulfilled?

Christiane Nord, another major functionalist, takes issue with this. She stresses that, while 'functionality is the most important criterion for a translation', this does not allow the translator absolute licence (Nord 2005: 31–2). There needs to be a relationship between ST and TT, and the nature of this relationship is determined by the purpose or skopos. This **'functionality plus loyalty' principle** underpins Nord's model. For Nord, **loyalty** is

> this responsibility translators have toward their partners in translational interaction. Loyalty commits the translator bilaterally to the source and the target sides. It must not be mixed up with fidelity or faithfulness, concepts that usually refer to a relationship holding between the source and target *texts*. Loyalty is an interpersonal category referring to a social relationship between *people*.
>
> (Nord 1997: 125)

Nord goes on to explain that this means that 'the target-text purpose should be compatible with the original author's intentions', while acknowledging that it is not always possible to be sure of those intentions. For her, loyalty plays the important role in that it 'limits the range of justifiable target-text functions for one particular source text and raises the need for a negotiation of the translation assignment between translators and their clients' (ibid.: 126).

In spite of criticisms, an important advantage of skopos theory is that it allows the possibility that the same text may be translated in different ways depending on the purpose of the TT and on the commission which is given to the translator. In Vermeer's words:

> What the skopos states is that one must translate, consciously and consistently, in accordance with some principle respecting the target text. The theory does not state what the principle is: this must be decided separately in each specific case.
>
> (Vermeer 1989/2012: 198)

So, if we use Vermeer's own example, an ambiguity in a will written in French would need to be translated literally, with a footnote or comment, for a foreign lawyer dealing with the case. On the other hand, if the will appeared in a novel, the translator might prefer to find a slightly different ambiguity that works in the TL without the need of a formal footnote. This would allow the TT to achieve functional equivalence through the creation of an unmarked ambiguity in the TT.

In order for the translatorial action to be appropriate for the specific case, the skopos needs to be stated explicitly or implicitly in the 'commission' (ibid.) or 'brief'. Vermeer describes the **commission** as comprising (1) a goal and (2) the conditions under which that goal should be achieved (including deadline and fee). Both should be negotiated between the commissioner and the translator. In this way, as the expert the translator should be able to advise the commissioner/ client on the feasibility of the goal. The nature of the TT 'is primarily determined by its skopos or commission' (ibid.: 200) and **adequacy** (*Adäquatheit*) comes to override equivalence as the measure of the translatorial action. In Reiss and Vermeer (2013: 127–8), adequacy describes the relations between ST and TT as a consequence of observing a skopos during the translation process. In other words, if the TT fulfils the skopos outlined by the commission, it is functionally and communicatively adequate. Equivalence is reduced to **functional constancy** between ST and TT (those cases where the function is the same for both ST and TT). However, full functional constancy is considered to be the exception.

> ### 5.5 Exploration: Skopos theory and audience design
>
> Skopos theory stresses the adaptation of the TT to fulfil the TT purpose and meet the TT audience's needs, but how are these intended uses and needs to be determined? Look at the article on audience design (Mason 2000) available through the ITS website. Note the types of receivers discussed and how these are addressed.

5.3.1 Discussion of skopos theory

Nord (1997: 109–22) and Schäffner (1998b: 237–8) discuss some of the criticisms that have been made of skopos theory. These include the following.

(1) What purports to be a 'general' theory is in fact only valid for non-literary texts. Literary texts are considered either to have no specific purpose and/or to be far more complex stylistically. Vermeer (1989/2012: 232–3) answers this by stressing that goals, purposes, functions and intentions are 'attributed to' actions. Thus, for a poet or his/her translator the goal may be to publish the resultant *Translatum* (poem) and to keep copyright over it so as to make money from its reproduction. He/she may also have the intention of creating something that exists for itself ('art for art's sake').

(2) Reiss's text type approach and Vermeer's skopos theory consider different phenomena and cannot be lumped together. The point at issue is the extent to which ST type determines translation method and the nature of the link between ST type and translation *skopos* (compare section 5.1 above).

(3) Jargon such as *Translatum* does little to further translation theory where workable terms (e.g. *target text*) already exist. However, as we have seen, in Nord's English translation the focus is firmly on the theory as 'translational action'.

(4) Skopos theory does not pay sufficient attention to the linguistic nature of the ST nor to the reproduction of micro-level features in the TT. Even if the skopos is adequately fulfilled, it may be inadequate at the stylistic or semantic levels of individual segments. This fourth criticism in particular is tackled by Christiane Nord with her model of translation-oriented text analysis, to which we shall now turn.

5.4 Translation-oriented text analysis

Christiane Nord's *Text Analysis in Translation* (1988/2005) presents a more detailed functional model incorporating elements of text analysis, which examines text organization at or above sentence level. Nord first makes a distinction between two basic types of translation product (and process), which are documentary translation and instrumental translation.[6]

Documentary translation 'serves as a document of a source culture communication between the author and the ST recipient' (Nord 2005: 80). Such is the case, for example, in literary translation, where the TT allows the TT receiver access to the ideas of the ST but where the reader is well aware that it is a translation. Other examples of documentary translation given by Nord are word-for-word and literal translation and 'exoticizing translation' that seeks to preserve local colour (ibid.: 81). In the latter, certain culture-specific lexical items in the ST are retained in the TT in order to maintain the local colour of the ST – for example, food items such as *Quark* (a kind of soft cheese), *Roggenbrot* (rye bread) and *Wurst* (a type of sausage) from a German ST.

An instrumental translation 'serves as an independent message transmitting instrument in a new communicative action in the target culture, and is intended to fulfil its communicative purpose without the recipient being conscious of reading or hearing a text which, in a different form, was used before in a different communicative situation' (ibid.). In other words, the TT receivers read the TT as though it were a ST written in their own language. The function may be the same for both ST and TT. For instance, a translated computer manual or software should fulfil the function of instructing the TT receiver in the same way as the ST does for the ST reader. Nord calls these **'function-preserving translations'**. However, she also gives examples of other kinds of translations where it is not possible to preserve the same function in translation. Such is the case with the translation of Swift's *Gulliver's Travels* for children, and with the translation of Homer into a novel for contemporary audiences.

Nord's *Text Analysis in Translation* is aimed primarily at providing translation students with a model of ST analysis which is applicable to all text types and translation situations. The model is based on a functional concept, enabling understanding of the function of ST features and the selection of translation strategies appropriate to the intended purpose of the translation. She thus shares many of the premises of Reiss and Vermeer's work, as well as Holz-Mänttäri's consideration of the other players in the translation action, but she pays more attention to features of the ST.[7] Nord's model involves analysing a complex series of interlinked extratextual factors and intratextual features in the ST. However, in her 1997 book, *Translating as a Purposeful Activity*, Nord proposes a more flexible version of the model, synthesizing many of the elements described in this chapter and highlighting three aspects of functionalist approaches that are of particular use for translator training (1997: 59). These are:

(1)   the importance of the translation commission (or 'translation brief', as Nord terms it);
(2)   the role of ST analysis;
(3)   the functional hierarchy of translation problems.

(1)   **The importance of the translation commission** (Nord 1997: 59–62): Before close textual analysis, the translator needs to compare the ST and TT profiles defined in the commission to see where the two texts may diverge. The translation commission should give the following information for both texts:
   ■   the **intended text functions**;
   ■   the **addressees** (sender and recipient);
   ■   the **time and place of text reception**;
   ■   the **medium** (speech or writing, and, we might now add, digital or hard copy);
   ■   the **motive** (why the ST was written and why it is being translated).

This information enables the translator to prioritize what information to include in the TT. Nord analyses a brochure for Heidelberg University. The motive is the celebration of the 600th anniversary of the university's founding and so clearly gives priority to events surrounding the anniversary.

(2)   **The role of ST analysis** (ibid.: 62–7): Once the above ST–TT profiles have been compared, the ST can be analysed to decide on: (a) the feasibility of translation: (b) the most relevant ST items that need to be taken into account to achieve functional translation; and (c) the translation strategy that will be necessary to fulfil the translation brief. Nord's model lists intratextual factors (2005: 87–142):
   ■   **subject matter:** including how culture-bound it is to the SL or TL context;
   ■   **content:** the 'meaning' of the text, including connotation and cohesion;
   ■   **presuppositions:** this has to do with the relative background knowledge of ST and TT receivers and with culture- and genre-specific

conventions. So, the ST may contain redundancies (explanations, repetitions, etc.) that may be omitted in the TT – e.g. a ST that explains that 10 Downing Street is the office of the British Prime Minister would be redundant in most TTs produced for a UK audience. On the other hand, there may be implicit meanings in the ST that need to be explained to the TT receiver – e.g. the owl that symbolizes wisdom in English-language cultures, red as a symbol of happiness in Chinese cultures, or the importance of the lotus flower in ancient Egypt, Buddhism, and other cultures;

- **text composition:** including microstructure (information units, stages of a plot, logical relations, thematic structure . . .) and macrostructure (beginning, end, footnotes, quotations . . .);
- **non-verbal elements:** illustrations, italics, font, etc.;
- **lexis:** including dialect, register and subject-specific terminology;
- **sentence structure:** including rhetorical features such as parenthesis and ellipsis;
- **suprasegmental features:** including stress, intonation, rhythm and 'stylistic punctuation'.

However, Nord stresses that this is only one model of analysis and that it does not really matter which text-linguistic model is used:

> What is important, though, is that [the model] include a pragmatic analysis of the communicative situations involved and that the same model be used for both source text and translation brief, thus making the results comparable.
>
> (Nord 1997: 62).

This provides some flexibility, although clearly the selection of analytical model is crucial in determining which features are prioritized in the translation.

(3) **The functional hierarchy of translation problems:** Nord (1997: 62ff; 2005: 189ff) establishes a functional hierarchy when undertaking a translation, working top-down from a pragmatic perspective and with the intended TT function paramount. This hierarchy is as follows:

(a) Comparison of the intended functions of the ST and the proposed TT helps to decide the functional type of translation to be produced (documentary or instrumental).

(b)   Analysis of the translation commission, as in (1) above, determines those functional elements that may be reproduced and those that will need to be adapted to the TT addressees' situation.

(c)   The translation type helps to decide the translation style. So, a documentary translation will be more source-culture oriented and an instrumental translation more target-culture oriented.

(d)   The problems of the text can then be tackled at a lower linguistic level, following the features of ST analysis in (2) above.

In many ways, this synthesized approach brings together strengths of the various functional and action theories:

■   The translation commission analysis incorporates Holz-Mänttäri's work on the players operative within the translatorial action.

■   The intended text functions pursue Reiss and Vermeer's concept of skopos, but without giving total dominance to the skopos.

■   The ST analysis, influenced by Reiss's work, gives due attention to the communicative function and genre features of the ST type and language, but without the rigidity of other taxonomies (see Chapter 4).

In our case study, we therefore apply this synthesized model to the translation of a specific ST.

Case study

This case study applies Christiane Nord's model of text analysis to a real-life translation commission. The ST in question is Usborne Cookery School's *Cooking for Beginners*,[8] an illustrated book of varied recipes to help British children aged 10+ years learn to cook. TTs were to be produced in a range of European languages for sale abroad. However, in order to keep costs down, the many illustrations were to be retained from the ST.

Using Nord's text analysis model above, it is clear that the kind of translation involved here is instrumental: the resulting TT is to function in the target culture as an independent message-transmitting text, with the TT receivers using it to learn how to cook.

The ST–TT profiles in the translation commission would be as follows:

- **The intended text functions:** The ST has an informative function, transmitting information about cookery and specific recipes. It also has an appellative function, since it is appealing to children to act on what they read (to make the recipes and become interested in food and in cooking). The TT will be function-preserving as far as is possible.
- **The addressees:** The ST addressees are probably both the British children aged 10 years and over mentioned earlier and their parents (or other older relatives, carers or friends), who are likely to be the purchasers of the book. Many of the recipes also presuppose some assistance from an adult. The TT addressees are the TL children aged 10+ and their parents or other adults.
- **The time and place of text reception:** The ST was published in the UK in 1998; the TTs appeared in Dutch, French, Italian and Spanish over the period 1999–2000. The time difference is, therefore, of little importance.
- **The medium:** The ST is a printed paperback book of forty-eight pages with many photographs and illustrations on each page. The TTs are to follow the same format, i.e. the words of the TL simply replace the SL words but the illustrations remain the same.
- **The motive:** The ST has the purpose of teaching British children the basics of cooking in an entertaining way using tools and ingredients that are readily available. The TT has the purpose of doing the same for the TT children.

The divergences in ST–TT profile therefore amount to the difference between the ST addressees and the TT addressees. However, this is a case not only of a difference in addressee language. Were that the only criterion, then the words on the page could simply be translated and transferred into the TL. There are also important differences of culture, especially regarding customs, experience and presuppositions. These become evident during ST analysis.

ST analysis

As noted earlier in section 5.4, any pragmatic-oriented analysis is acceptable as long as it allows comparability between ST and TT. For reasons of space, we do not undertake a detailed analysis here, but shall pick out three elements from Nord's list of intralinguistic factors that are of particular relevance in the analysis of the present ST:

(1)   non-verbal elements;
(2)   the register of the lexis;
(3)   presuppositions.

(1)   **Non-verbal elements:** The features of medium noted above are crucial for the translation process and product. The illustrations cannot be altered and the length of each TT caption/instruction must not exceed the length of the corresponding ST caption/instruction. Clearly these are severe limitations on the translator.

(2)   **The register of the lexis:** This is a factor that is difficult for the translator to decide. There are two main relevant factors. One, as noted in the intended text functions, is that we are dealing with a recipe book and, as is well known, recipes are a strictly organized text genre with conventions that vary interlingually. Thus, English prefers imperative forms ('cut the tomatoes', 'add the onion', etc.) whereas other languages (such as French, German, Spanish) use infinitive forms. The other factor is related to the appellative function and the fact that the addressees are children. The lexis in the ST is consequently slightly simplified and rather more interpersonal than in most cookery books. For example, the warning 'Take care that you don't touch anything hot' is unlikely to be given to an adult, while the caption 'Bring the milk to the boil, then turn the heat down low so that it is bubbling very gently' uses the explicitation *bubbling very gently* instead of the more complex and condensed word *simmer*.

The translator should normally aim to produce a similarly simplified TT that fulfils the same appellative function (as well as the informative function). Depending on the language, this may even mean going against the conventions of the recipe in the TL and not using infinitive forms, since they tend to distance the addressee.

(3)   **Presuppositions:** The real problem for the translator of this text results from the divergence in cultural background between the TT and ST addressees. This becomes evident in analysing the presuppositions implicit in the ST. A few examples are given in Box 5.1.

Box 5.1

The selection of dishes: Some dishes described may not exist in the target culture. This may be the case for *vegetable stir fry* and *prawn and pepper pilaff* or *fudgey fruit crumble*, among others. The presupposition in the ST is that the child will have seen these dishes, perhaps made by an adult, and understand what the final product is to look like. In target cultures where these dishes are unknown, the children and the adults may be unsure whether the recipe is turning out correctly. Changing the names of the recipes listed above (for example to *Chinese vegetables* and *exotic rice* or *hot fruit dessert*) may make them more accessible to the TT receivers, although not necessarily easier to cook.

Ingredients: Some ingredients, such as fresh ginger, pitta bread, or processed foods such as oven-bake chips and mini-croutons, may be unavailable in some target cultures. This means that either the whole recipe would be impossible to make, or the preparation of it would be different. In the TT some of these ingredients may be altered to ones that are more readily available in the target culture.

Cooking utensils: Utensils such as kettles, garlic presses and potato mashers are not used in all cultures. In a recipe for creamy fish pie (ST p. 12), a drawing of a potato masher is followed by the caption: 'Crush the potato by pressing a potato masher down, again and again, on the chunks. Do it until there are no lumps left.'

The translator has to find a translation for potato masher that matches the picture, the recipe instructions and the caption space. The Dutch and Italian translations give a single word: *puree-stamper* and *schiacciapatate* respectively. However, in the French and Spanish TTs the translators tried to overcome the problem that potato mashers do not exist in their cultures by suggesting a different utensil. In each case they orient the translation towards the target culture. The French caption tells the reader to crush the potatoes (*écraseles*) or to pass them through a blender (*passe-les à la moulinette*); in the Spanish, a fork is suggested or 'an instrument like the one in the picture' (*un utensilio como el de la ilustración*). Both translations are functionally adequate because they describe the picture, fit into the caption space and enable the TT readers to produce the mashed potatoes.

Discussion of case study

The text analysis approach followed in the case study allows important elements of the translation process to be identified. Nord's model places more emphasis on the ST than do other functionalists. This focus enables problematic features to be identified and classified. However, as we saw in Chapter 4, it would be wrong to think that all phenomena can be categorized easily. In the case of the recipe book, it is the difference in culture and experience of the ST and TT addressees which requires most attention. While functional theories may assist in translating *potato masher*, the link between culture and language is far more complex. The following chapter begins to explore this, and the concept of discourse, in more depth.

Summary

Functionalist and communicative translation theories advanced in Germany in the 1970s and 1980s moved translation from a mainly linguistic phenomenon to being considered as an act of intercultural communication. Reiss's initial work links language function, text type, genre and translation strategy. Reiss's approach was later coupled to Vermeer's highly influential skopos theory, where the translation strategy is decided by the purpose of the translation and the function of the TT in the target culture. Skopos theory is part of the model of translatorial action also proposed by Holz-Mänttäri, who places professional commercial translation within a sociocultural context, using the jargon of business and management. Translation is viewed as a communicative transaction involving initiator, commissioner, and the producers, users and receivers of the ST and TT. In this model, the ST is 'dethroned' and the translation is judged not by equivalence of meaning but by its adequacy to the functional goal of the TT situation as defined by the commission. Nord's model, designed for training translators, retains the functional context but includes a more detailed text-analysis model. More recent technological developments in digital text production have seen the focus shift to more multimodal texts, combining different semiotic modes, and to the creation of new and hybrid web genres. The players in the translatorial action itself now encompass on the one hand the management of industry-centred localization processes and on the other the user-generated content of fansubs and a range of volunteer translation practices.

Further reading

The key texts listed at the beginning of the chapter are fundamental for a greater understanding of the concepts. Nord's two major books (1997 and 2005) in particular provide a solid grounding in the ideas of the functionalists. Snell-Hornby (2006: 51–60), writing from a firmly German perspective, usefully discusses the theories described here. Jiménez-Crespo (2013) looks at digital genres. Like Trosberg (1997, 2000), he develops the analysis by incorporating functional linguistic categories, which will be discussed in Chapter 6.

Discussion and research points

1 Look at how translator training programmes in your country deal with the question of text domain in the teaching of specialized translation. How far do the categories they use correspond to those of Reiss?

2 Discuss how far ST genre determines TT method.

3 The theory of translatorial action was based on a conventional and hierarchical allocation of roles. Read the article by McDonough Dolmaya (2012), available through the ITS companion website, which discusses crowd-sourcing and 'user-generated' translation. Note the differences in roles in such scenarios.

4 Translate the same text to different skopoi. For example, online information about a tourist destination (1) for an audience of wealthy potential tourists and (2) to form part of an information pack for students who are going to spend a year studying there. What differences in translation strategy and procedures are there? How would the quality of the translation be evaluated?

5 How 'loyal' can a translator really be to the ST and to the ST author if functional adequacy is to be achieved (Nord 1997: 123–8)? Read the article (Nord 2002) on the ITS companion website.

6 Read the detailed description of Nord's text analysis model (Nord 1997, 2005). Apply it to the analysis of a range of STs and translation situations. How useful and practical is it for translator training?

The ITS website at www.routledge.com/cw/munday contains:

- a video summary of the chapter;
- a recap multiple-choice test;
- customizable PowerPoint slides;
- further reading links and extra journal articles;
- more research project questions.

CHAPTER 6

Discourse and Register analysis approaches

Key concepts

- **The 1970s onwards saw the growth of discourse analysis in applied linguistics. Building particularly on Halliday's systemic functional grammar, it has come to be used in translation analysis.**

- **House's model for the assessment of translation quality is based on Hallidayan-influenced Register analysis.**

- **Baker's influential coursebook presents discourse and pragmatic analysis for practising translators.**

- **Hatim and Mason add pragmatic and discourse levels to Register analysis.**

Key texts

Baker, Mona (1992/2011) *In Other Words: A Coursebook on Translation*, 2nd edition, London and New York: Routledge.

Blum-Kulka, Shoshona (1986/2004) 'Shifts of cohesion and coherence in translation', in Lawrence Venuti (ed.) (2004) *The Translation Studies Reader*, 2nd edition, London and New York: Routledge, pp. 290–305.

Fawcett, Peter (1997) *Translation and Language: Linguistic Approaches Explained*, Manchester: St Jerome, Chapters 7–11.

Hatim, Basil (2009) 'Translating text in context', in Jeremy Munday (ed.) (2009) *The Routledge Companion to Translation Studies*, Abingdon and New York: Routledge, pp. 36–53.

Hatim, Basil and Ian Mason (1997) *The Translator as Communicator*, London and New York: Routledge.

House, Juliane (1997) *Translation Quality Assessment: A Model Revisited*, Tübingen: Gunter Narr.

House, Juliane (2015) *Translation Quality Assessment: Past and Present*, London and New York: Routledge.

Munday, Jeremy (2012) *Evaluation in Translation: Critical Points of Translator Decision-Making*, London and New York: Routledge.

6.0 Introduction

Watch the introductory video on the companion website.

In the 1990s discourse analysis came to prominence in translation studies, drawing on developments in applied linguistics. There is a link with the text analysis model of Christiane Nord examined in the last chapter in that the organization of the text above sentence level is investigated. However, while text analysis normally concentrates on describing the way in which texts are organized (sentence structure, cohesion, etc.), discourse analysis looks at the way language communicates meaning and social and power relations. The model of discourse analysis that has had the greatest influence is Michael Halliday's systemic functional model, which is described in section 6.1. In the following sections we look at several key works on translation that have employed his model: Juliane House's (1997) *Translation Quality Assessment: A Model Revisited* and (2015) *Translation Quality Assessment: Past and Present* (section 6.2); Mona Baker's (1992/2011) *In Other Words* (section 6.3); and the work of Basil Hatim and Ian Mason, notably *Discourse and the Translator* (1990) and *The Translator as Communicator* (1997) (section 6.4). Hatim and Mason go beyond Register analysis to consider the pragmatic and semiotic dimensions of translation and the sociolinguistic implications of discourses and discourse communities. Munday (2012) focuses on the interpersonal function as a way of uncovering 'critical points' of translator decision-making.

6.1 The Hallidayan model of language and discourse

Halliday's model of discourse analysis, based on what he terms **systemic functional linguistics** (SFL), is geared to the study of language as communication. It sees meaning in the writer's linguistic choices and, through a detailed grammar, systematically relates these choices to the text's function in a wider sociocultural framework.[1] It borrows Bühler's tripartite division of language functions (informative, expressive, appellative) which we discussed in Chapter 5. In Halliday's model, importantly, there is a strong interrelation between the linguistic choices, the aims of the communication and the sociocultural framework.[2] This is illustrated in Figure 6.1.

The direction of influence is top down. Thus, the **sociocultural environment**[3] in which the text operates is the highest level. This will include the conventions operating at the time and place of text production. As well as social and cultural factors, it will reflect any political, historical or legal conditions. So, for example, the wave of translation of Latin American fiction in the United States from the 1960s onwards took place in the heightened political climate following the Cuban Revolution of 1959. At that time, various cultural, political and philanthropic organizations in the USA were seeking, for sometimes differing reasons, to build cultural ties with the South. In a different context, translation in the European Union is conditioned by the legal requirement to make available papers and information for

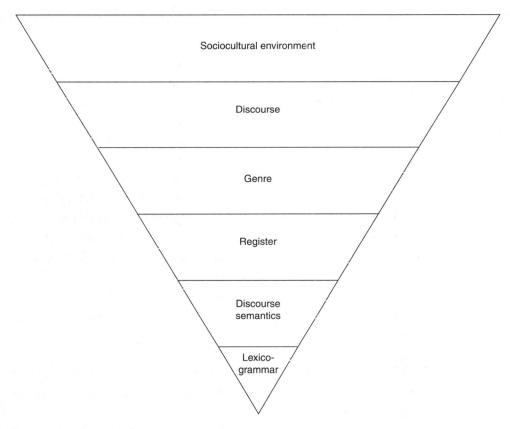

Figure 6.1   The Hallidayan model of language

the use of the political representatives and for access of the citizens in the twenty-four official languages of the Member States. That legal requirement is in part a statement of the identity and recognition of the different languages.[4]

The **sociocultural environment** therefore in part conditions the **genre**, understood in SFL as the conventional text type that is associated with a specific communicative function, for example an invoice sent by the accounts department of a company to a customer. Genre itself helps to determine other elements in the systemic framework. The first of these is **Register**. This should not be confused with the more standard sense of register as formal/informal. In SFL it is a technical term, richer and more complex. It links the variables of social context to language choice and comprises three elements:

(1) **Field:** what is being written about, e.g. the price for a delivery of goods;
(2) **Tenor:** who is communicating and to whom, e.g. a sales representative to a customer;
(3) **Mode:** the form of communication, e.g. written or spoken, formal or informal.

Each of the variables of Register is associated with a strand of meaning, or 'discourse semantics', in the text. These three strands, known as 'metafunctions', are:

(1) **ideational:** provides a representation of the world or an event;
(2) **interpersonal:** enacts social relationships;
(3) **textual:** makes a text hang together in a coherent way.

These strands of meaning are formed by the choices of lexis, grammar and syntax (**'lexicogrammar'**) made by the text producer (author, speaker, translator . . .). The links are broadly as in Table 6.1 (see also, Eggins 2004: 78).

Analysis of the lexicogrammatical patterns of transitivity, modality, thematic structure and cohesion can help reveal how the strands of meaning are constructed in a text (Eggins 2004: 84). For instance, Munday (2002) shows how the transitivity structures are changed in the translations of a political essay by García Márquez about a Cuban child who had been taken out of the country by a small boat to be with cousins in the USA. The centre of an international controversy, he had been visited in the USA by his Cuban grandmothers. Examples in the text include the shift from passive to active in the following:

- **ST:** las abuelas volvieron a Cuba escandalizadas de cuánto **lo habían cambiado** (lit. the grandmothers returned to Cuba outraged at how much **they had changed him**);
- **TT:** the grandmothers returned to Cuba outraged at how much **he had changed**.

Table 6.1   Register variables and their typical realizations

Register variable	Strand of meaning	Lexicogrammatical realization
Field (what the text is about and how this experience is represented)	Ideational	**Subject-specific terminology, transitivity** structures (verb types, selection of active/passive, selection of grammatical subject, use of nominalization instead of verb).*
Tenor (the relationship between participants)	Interpersonal	**Pronouns** ('I/we' exclusive or inclusive, 'you' formal or informal), **modality** (modal verbs and adverbs, e.g. *should, possibly, hopefully*) and **evaluative lexis** (e.g. *beautiful, dreadful*)
Mode (form of communication)	Textual	**Cohesion** (the way a text holds together lexically through lexical repetition, use of pronouns in place of nouns, collocation, etc.) and **thematic and information structures** (word order and placement of elements in the text)

* So, the choice of a nominalization and passive such as ***The decision made*** at the meeting was to reject your appeal may hide a reality that could otherwise be expressed by an active ***I and the other members of the Committee have decided that we are rejecting*** your appeal.

The effect of the TT is to disguise the fact that it is the boy's US relatives who are represented as being responsible for the change in his conduct. This type of analysis may be extremely useful for the translator in identifying important elements in a ST and seeing how they create meaning in a specific cultural and communicative context.

Although its functional focus makes it attractive for applied linguistic study, including the study of translation, Halliday's grammar is also extremely complex and, some might say, unwieldy. For that reason, those translation scholars whose work is described in the following sections have selected relevant elements for their purpose and, where necessary, simplified them. In the case of the first model, Juliane House's, the central concept is Register analysis.

6.2 House's model of translation quality assessment

House (1997: 159) herself considers that skopos and other approaches oriented towards the target audience are 'fundamentally misguided' because of their neglect of the ST. Instead, she bases her model on comparative ST–TT analysis

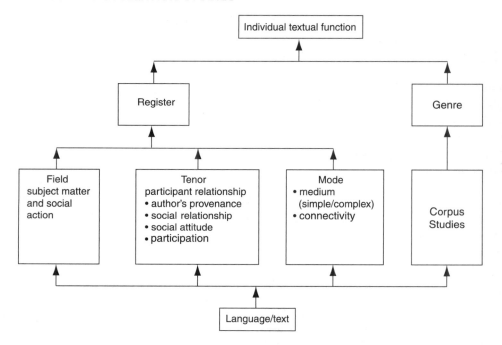

Figure 6.2   A revised scheme for analysing and comparing original and translated texts (House 2015: 127)

leading to the assessment of the quality of the translation, highlighting 'mismatches' or 'errors'. House's original model (1977, partly revised 1981) attracted criticisms (see section 6.5 below) that she tackled in a later major revision (1997: 101–4). This model has itself been revised in (House 2015).

The later models incorporate some of her earlier categories into an openly Hallidayan Register analysis of Field, Tenor and Mode. The model involves a systematic comparison of the textual 'profile' of the ST and of the TT. The schema for this comparison is shown in Figure 6.2.

This comparative model draws on various and sometimes complex taxonomies, but its central point is a Register analysis of both ST and TT. The model focuses on the **lexical**, **syntactic** and **textual** means used to construct Register. As is suggested in Figure 6.2, House's concept of **Register** covers a variety of elements, some of which are additional to those stated by Halliday.

- **Field** refers to the subject matter and social action, and covers the specificity of lexical items.
- **Tenor** includes 'the addresser's temporal, geographical and social provenance as well as his [or her] intellectual, emotional or affective stance (his [or her] "personal viewpoint")' (1997: 109; 2015: 64). 'Social attitude' refers

to formal, consultative or informal style. There is an element of **individuality** to this, as there is to stance.

■ **Mode** relates to 'channel' (spoken/written, etc.) and the degree of participation between addresser and addressee (monologue, dialogue, etc.).

The model is applied as follows:

(1) A profile is produced of the ST Register.

(2) To this is added a description of the ST genre realized by the Register.

(3) Together, this allows a 'statement of function' to be made for the ST, including the ideational and interpersonal component of that function (in other words, what information is being conveyed and what the relationship is between sender and receiver).

(4) The same descriptive process is then carried out for the TT.

(5) The TT profile is compared to the ST profile and a statement of 'mismatches' or errors is produced. These are categorized according to the situational dimensions of Register and genre. Such dimensional errors are referred to as 'covertly erroneous errors' (House 1997: 45) to distinguish them from 'overtly erroneous errors', which are denotative mismatches (which give an incorrect meaning compared to the ST) and target system errors (which do not conform to the formal grammatical or lexical requirements of the TL).

(6) A 'statement of quality' is then made of the translation.

(7) Finally, the translation can be categorized into one of two types: 'overt translation' or 'covert translation'.

In House's rather confusing definition (1997: 66; 2015: 54), 'an **overt translation** is one in which the addressees of the translation text are quite "overtly" not being directly addressed'. In other words, the TT does not pretend to be (and is not represented as being) an original and is clearly not directed at the TT audience. Such is the case with the translation after the event of a Second World War political speech by Winston Churchill. The ST speech was tied to a particular source culture, time and historical context; all these factors are different for the TT. Another example is the translations of literary texts, which are tied to their source culture.

With such translations, House (1997: 112; 2015: 55) believes that equivalence cannot be sought at the level of the individual text function since the discourse worlds in which ST and TT operate are different. Instead, House suggests a 'second-level functional equivalence' should be sought, at the level of language, Register and genre. The TT can provide access to the function of the ST, allowing the TT receivers to 'eavesdrop' on the ST. For example, Korean-language readers can use a Korean TT of Churchill's speech to gain access to the ST. But they know they are reading a translation and the individual function of the two texts cannot be the same.

A **covert translation** 'is a translation which enjoys the status of an original source text in the target culture' (1997: 69; 2015: 56). The ST is not linked particularly to the ST culture or audience; both ST and TT address their respective receivers directly. Examples given by House are a tourist information booklet, a letter from a company chairman to the shareholders and an article in the magazine *The UNESCO Courier*. The function of a covert translation is 'to recreate, reproduce or represent in the translated text the function the original has in its discourse world' (2015: 67). It does this without taking the TT reader into the discourse world of the ST. Instead, equivalence is necessary at the level of genre and the individual text function. To achieve this, what House calls a **'cultural filter'** needs to be applied by the translator, modifying cultural elements and thus giving the impression that the TT is an original. This may involve changes at the levels of language and Register. The meaning of cultural filter is discussed by House in the context of German–English comparative pragmatic studies. She gives examples of different practices in the two cultures that need to be reflected in translation. For instance, she finds that at that time German business communication tended to prefer a more direct content focus, whereas English was more interpersonal. This would need to be reflected in covert translation, the letter from the company chairman being more interpersonal in English, for instance.

House is at pains to point out the fact that the 'overt'–'covert' translation distinction is a cline rather than a pair of binary opposites. A text can be more, or less, covert/overt. Furthermore, if functional equivalence is desired but the ST genre does not exist in the same form in the target culture, the aim should be to produce a **version** rather than a 'translation'. Such would be the case, for instance, in the manufacturer's instructions for playing a board game, such as chess: imagine a ST which is directed at a ten-year old child and is written in correspondingly appropriate language (e.g. *The castle moves sideways or up/down. Try moving it as far as you want!*). If the TL genre conventions called for a more formal text, directed at adults (or, at least, treating children like adults), the instructions would need to be altered in the TL version (e.g. *The rook moves horizontally or vertically with no limit on the number of squares it may travel*).

'Version' is also the term used to describe apparently unforced changes in genre. For example, among the texts analysed by House is an extract (1997: 147–57) from a polemical history text about civilian Germans' involvement in the holocaust (ST English, TT German). A pattern of differences is identified in the dimensions of Field and Tenor. In Field, the frequency of the word *German*, which serves to highlight German civilian responsibility in the events, is reduced in the TT. In Tenor, there is a reduction in intensifiers, superlatives and other emotive lexis. This makes the author's critical stance less obvious in the TT, and House even suggests (ibid.: 155) that it has an effect on the genre. Whereas the ST is a controversial popular history book (even though it is based on the author's doctoral thesis), the German TT is a more formal academic treatise. House goes on to suggest possible reasons for these changes, notably pressure from the German publishers for political and marketing reasons. The linking of the linguistic analysis to real-world translation conditions is a move that owes something to the theory of translatorial action which was discussed in Chapter 5.

6.1 Exploration: Register shifts in the translation of museum texts

Read the article on Register shifts by Jiang Chengzhi (2009) available through the ITS website. Note those areas of House's model that are illustrated in the article.

6.3 Baker's text and pragmatic level analysis: a coursebook for translators

House's 1977 book was the first major translation studies work to use Halliday's now popular model. Another that later had some considerable influence on translation training is Mona Baker's *In Other Words: A Coursebook on Translation* (1992/2011). Baker looks at equivalence at a series of levels: at word, above-word, grammar, thematic structure, cohesion and pragmatic levels. Of particular interest in the present chapter is her application of the systemic approach to thematic structure and cohesion and the incorporation of the pragmatic level, of language in use.

6.3.1 Thematic and information structures

Baker is typical of many translation scholars who make detailed use of the terminology of functional grammar and discourse analysis in that she devotes the most attention to the textual function. Explicit analyses of the ideational and interpersonal functions are fewer (though see section 6.4 later). Baker focuses more on thematic considerations, comparing nominalization and verbal forms in theme position in a scientific report in Brazilian Portuguese and English (Baker 2011: 178–9). Thus, for example, the ST begins with a pronominal verbal form (my emphasis):

> **Analisou-se** as relações da dopamina cerebral com as funções motoras.
> [Analysed-one the relations of dopamine with the motor functions.]

The published English translation presents a normalized word order with the selection of an English passive form in final position (my emphasis):

> The relations between dopamine and motor functions **were analysed**.

However, for this example Baker recommends a different order of elements (i.e. a different thematic structure) so as to meet the **genre** conventions of English abstracts. This involves the use of the nominalization *analysis* in first position as the 'theme' of the sentence, along with a different passive verbal form (*is carried out*):

> An analysis is carried out of the relations between dopamine and motor functions.

An inherent problem, illustrated by this example, is that thematic structure is realized differently in different languages. Baker gives a number of examples from languages such as Portuguese, Spanish and Arabic. These are verb-inflected languages which may place the verb in first or 'theme' position, as in the Brazilian Portuguese example above. This inevitably creates a different thematic pattern in ST and TT.[5]

The most important point for ST thematic analysis is that the translator should be aware of the **relative markedness** of the thematic and information structures (see the discussion in our section 4.3 and also Hatim 2009). Baker points out (Baker 2011: 141) that this 'can help to heighten our awareness of meaningful choices made by speakers and writers in the course of communication' and, therefore, help decide whether it is appropriate to translate using a marked form. Again, what is marked varies across languages. Problems in copying the ST pattern into the TT have been treated by many scholars over the years. Thus, Vázquez-Ayora (1977: 217) emphasizes that calquing a rigid English word order when translating into a more flexible language such as Spanish would produce a monotonous translation. Gerzymisch-Arbogast (1986), in her detailed study of German and English, considers the German calquing of English pseudo-cleft sentences (e.g. *What pleases the public is . . . What I meant to say was . . .*) to be clumsy. This illustrates the dilemma, pointed out by Enkvist (1978), of balancing concern for information dynamics with the sometimes incompatible concern for other areas such as basic syntactic patterns. Some languages may also mark theme differently; for instance, Japanese uses the particles *ga* and *wa*, rather than word order, to mark new or contrastive themes.

That it is the textual function, and most especially the thematic structure, which has most frequently been discussed in works on translation theory is perhaps because of the attention paid to this function by influential monolingual works in text linguistics. Notable early examples are Enkvist (1978) and Beaugrande and Dressler (1981). Cohesion, an element that encompasses the textual and other metafunctions, has also been the subject of a number of studies of translation.

6.3.2 Cohesion

Cohesion is produced by the grammatical and lexical links which help a text hold together. In their seminal study of cohesion in English, Halliday and Hasan (1976) classify five types, which are listed in Table 6.2 along with typical examples (known as '**cohesive ties**').

Cohesion within the text is closely linked to the coherence of the argument. Blum-Kulka's well-known study 'Shifts of cohesion and coherence in translation' (1986/2004) hypothesizes that increased explicitation of cohesive ties may even be a general strategy adopted by all translators, for example (ibid.: 293):

> ST She told them not to help each other
> TT Elle leur dit de ne pas s'áider **et de travailler tout seul**
> (lit. 'She told them not to help each other **and to work all alone**').

Here, the TT explicates what is only an implicit ellipsis in the ST.

Blum-Kulka (ibid.: 294–5) shows how changes in cohesion in translation may bring about functional shifts in texts. She uses the example of a Hebrew translation of a scene from Harold Pinter's play *Old Times* (1971). In English, the enigmatic opening statement, 'Fat or thin?', is an ellipsis that leaves the referent deliberately unclear (*fat man/woman/boy/girl/animal*? etc.). Because Hebrew is

Table 6.2   Forms of cohesion, from Halliday and Hasan (1976)

Type of cohesion	Description	Example
Reference	A semantic relation where meaning needs to be interpreted through reference to something else, linked using a pronoun (*I, you, it . . .*), demonstrative (*this/that*), etc.	*I know Bill followed the match.* **He** *saw **it** on TV* – *he* refers to *Bill* and *it* to *the match*
Substitution	A grammatical substitution within the text	*Arctic foxes threatened by **red ones*** – *red ones* substitutes for *red foxes*
Ellipsis	A kind of zero substitution, where an element needs to be supplied	*For every dollar donated federally,* ***three more*** *are donated by the State* – the element *dollars* needs to be supplied
Conjunction	A semantic relation indicating how what follows is linked to what has gone before	Typical examples are additive (***and . . .***), adversative ***but, however . . .***) and temporal (***at first, then, finally . . .***)

Lexical cohesion	A lexical relation where cohesion is produced by the selection of vocabulary; these can be through reiteration (some form of **repetition** or linkage) and/or **collocation** (the typical co-occurrence of lexical items)	Reiteration, through:
		    – repetition of the same word (*lion . . . **lion***),
		    – synonym (*lion . . . **hunter***)
		    – superordinate (*lion . . . **cat***)
		    – general word (*lion . . . **creature***)
		Collocation, through:
		    – pairs of words (***inclement weather, quirk of fate, make a mistake***)
		    – words occurring in the same semantic field (***inclement weather . . . rain . . . wind . . . cold . . .***).

a gender-inflected language, the TT has to fill out at least part of this ellipsis by making the gender explicit and thus indicating whether the character referred to is a male or female. Similarly, literary translations from verb-inflected languages into English need to make explicit what are sometimes deliberately ambiguous grammatical subject referents. The first line of Argentine author Julio Cortázar's classic 1960s novel *Rayuela* (*Hopscotch*) begins with the question '¿*Encontraría a la Maga?*' In English the translator has to choose between potential grammatical subjects '*Would I/he/she/you find the Magus?*' and decide whether to specify that the Magus is female.

6.2 Exploration: Cohesive devices

Look at the categories and examples of cohesive devices listed in Table 6.2. Try to translate these examples into your L1 or L2. How many of them require a shift in cohesive device? How would you translate the gender-inflected examples above?

As with the thematic structure, it is in many ways the density and progression of cohesive ties throughout a text that are important. This web of relationships may have to differ between ST and TT, since the networks of lexical cohesion will not be identical across languages. As an illustration, Baker (2011: 195–6, 216) puts forward the idea, backed by short extracts and their translations, that Portuguese prefers lexical repetition to pronoun use and that Arabic prefers lexical repetition to variation. A TT should also normally be coherent. In other words, it should hang together logically in the mind of the TT receiver. This has to do with pragmatics, the subject of another of Baker's chapters.

6.3.3 Pragmatics and translation

Baker considers various aspects of pragmatic equivalence in translation, applying relevant linguistic concepts to interlinguistic transfer. Baker's definition of **pragmatics** is as follows:

> Pragmatics is the study of language in use. It is the study of meaning, not as generated by the linguistics system but as conveyed and manipulated by participants in a communicative situation.
>
> (Baker 2011: 230)

In this section, we briefly consider three major pragmatic concepts: **coherence, presupposition** and **implicature**.

The **coherence** of a text, related to cohesion (see above), 'depends on the hearer's or receiver's expectations and experience of the world' (ibid.: 232). Clearly this may not be the same for the ST and TT reader. Baker gives the example of a passage about the London department store Harrods. In order to make sense of the passage, the reader needs to know that *the flagship Harrods* and the description *the splendid Knightsbridge store* are synonyms. TT readers unfamiliar with London may not know this. The Arabic translation therefore makes the link explicit with the addition to the name of a gloss incorporating the repetition of the word *store* (*the main store Harrods*).

The area of **presupposition** is closely related to coherence. It is defined by Baker (ibid.: 259) as 'pragmatic inference'. Presupposition relates to the linguistic and extralinguistic knowledge the sender assumes the receiver to have or which are necessary in order to retrieve the sender's message. Thus, in the European Parliament in 1999, Commissioner Sir Leon Brittan's phrase *let me now turn to bananas* would presuppose that the receiver knows about the then current trade dispute between the European Union and the United States over banana imports.[6] Or at least it would presuppose that the receiver can access this information from the linguistic and extralinguistic contexts. This is most likely for the immediate receivers, since they were Members of the European Parliament and were aware of the issue. Similarly, the phrase *I discussed this issue in Washington* presupposes knowledge that Washington in this context refers to the seat of government of the United States and the venue for Sir Leon Brittan's talks. The problem for the translator occurs, of course, when the TT receivers cannot be assumed to possess the same background knowledge as the ST receivers, either because of cultural differences and/or because the text is being translated after a time gap when the original information is no longer activated by the reference. This is the kind of problem which Nida recognized with his concept of dynamic equivalence (see Chapter 3).

More emphasis is placed on presupposition by Fawcett (1997: 123–34), whose chapter on the subject contains many perceptive and interesting examples. Typical is the example of the metaphorical use of the place name *Mohács* in a Hungarian text. The name would mean little to most receivers in other cultures, so a translator would need to replace it with an explicitation of its historical significance as the site of a crushing defeat.

Baker gives more attention to **implicature**, another form of pragmatic inference, which she defines (Baker 2011: 223) as 'what the speaker means or implies rather than what s/he says'. The concept of implicature was developed by philosopher of language Paul Grice (1913–1988), who described a set of 'rules' or **'maxims'** that operate in normal co-operative conversation (Grice 1975). These are as follows:

(1) **Quantity:** Give the amount of information that is necessary. Do not give too much or too little.

(2) **Quality:** Say only what you know to be true or what you can support.

(3) **Relevance:** What you say should be relevant to the conversation.

(4) **Manner:** Say what you need to say in a way that is appropriate to the message you wish to convey and which (normally) will be understood by the receiver.

In addition, some theorists add the maxim of (5) **politeness:** Be polite in your comments (see Brown and Levinson 1987).

Participants in conversations assume the person to whom they are speaking is (subconsciously) following these maxims and they themselves co-operate by trying to make sense of what is being said. In turn, they also tend to be co-operative in what they say and the way they say it.

However, the maxims may be deliberately flouted, sometimes for a humorous effect. Such a flouting of the relevance maxim might have occurred, for instance, had Sir Leon Brittan, above, begun to discuss the value of eating bananas for breakfast. Particular problems are also posed for the translator when the TL culture operates with different maxims. An example is some of the translations from English into Arabic of the Harry Potter books, which delete references to alcohol and pork and tone down references to sorcery (Dukmak 2012). This shows a difference in the operation of the maxims of manner and politeness in the two cultures. This is also the case in an example (Gibney and Loveday, quoted in Baker 2011: 245) that occurred during negotiations between the USA and Japan in 1970. The Japanese Premier replies to American concerns on textile exports by saying *zensho shimasu* ('I'll handle it as well as I can'). This is understood by the US President as a literal promise to sort out a problem (i.e. it obeys the US-cultural quality and relevance maxims), whereas the Japanese phrase is really a polite formula for ending the conversation (i.e. it obeys the Japanese-cultural maxim of politeness). As Baker notes, this clearly shows that translators need to be fully aware of the different co-operative principles in operation in the respective languages and cultures (see also House 2002).

6.3 Exploration: Grice's maxims

Read House (1998) on the application of Grice's maxims to translation. Note cross-linguistic discrepancies in maxims.

6.4 Hatim and Mason: the levels of context and discourse

Two other works that developed out of the Hallidayan model of language have been especially influential for translation studies: Basil Hatim and Ian Mason's *Discourse and the Translator* (1990) and *The Translator as Communicator* (1997). They pay extra attention to the realization in translation of ideational and interpersonal functions (rather than just the textual function) and incorporate into their model the level of discourse.

An example of Hatim and Mason's analysis of functions is their examination (1997: 7–10) of a key passage from Albert Camus's novel *L'Étranger* [*The Outsider*] in which the main character, Meursault, shoots and kills an Arab on a beach near Algiers. Changes in the **transitivity structure** in the English transla-tion are seen to cause a shift in the **ideational function** of the text, affecting field. The passage in the French ST contains eight process verbs, of which four indicate intentional action by Meursault. These are:

> '*j'ai crispé* ma main', '*j'ai touché* le ventre poli de la crosse', '*j'ai tiré*', '*je frap-pais* sur la porte du malheur'
> [lit. '*I clenched* my hand', '*I touched* the polished belly of the [revolver] butt', '*I fired*' and '*I was striking* on the door of misfortune'].[7]

In translation, these become:

> 'my grip *closed*', 'the smooth underbelly of the butt *jogged* in my palm', '*I fired*' and 'another loud, fateful *rap* on the door of my undoing'.

In other words, the translation only shows one real action process (*I fired*); the others have become actions that occur *to* Meursault and over which it seems he has little control. Hatim and Mason's conclusion (ibid.: 10) is that the pattern of shifts in the TT has made Meursault more passive. However, they also make the point that the reason for these shifts may be the translator's overall reading of the novel, in which Meursault's passivity is a key feature of his character.

Hatim and Mason also consider shifts in **modality** (the **interpersonal** func-tion) with an example (ibid.: 73–6) of trainee interpreters' problems with the recog-nition and translation of a French conditional of allegation or rumour in a European Parliament debate. The phrase in question – 'un plan de restructuration qui *aurait été* ['would have been'] préparé par les administrateurs judiciaires' – calls for an indication of modality of possibility in English, such as 'a rescue plan which was *probably* prepared by the administrators' or 'a rescue plan which *it is rumoured* was prepared by the administrators'. The majority of the trainee interpreters in Hatim and Mason's sample incorrectly rendered the phrase by a factual statement such as '*had been* prepared'. This altered the truth value of the message in the TT.

Hatim and Mason's 'foundations of a model for analysing texts' (1997: 14–35) incorporate and go beyond House's Register analysis and Baker's pragmatic analysis. They combine the kind of bottom-up analysis discussed in the Camus example with some top-down consideration of the higher levels of discourse. Language and texts are considered to be realizations of sociocultural messages and power relations. They thus represent **discourse** in its wider sense, defined as:

> modes of speaking and writing which involve social groups in adopting a particular attitude towards areas of sociocultural activity (e.g. racist discourse, bureaucratese, etc.).
>
> (Hatim and Mason 1997: 216)

One example they give of the influence of the translator's discourse is the English TT of a Spanish ST about the history of the indigenous American peoples before the arrival of the Spaniards in Mexico. Hatim and Mason show (ibid.: 153–9) how lexical choices such as *pre-Colombian* and *Indian* in the TT impose a Eurocentric view on a ST that had been written from an indigenous perspective. The European translator is imposing a pro-western ideology and discourse on the recounting of the history of the Americas.

A semiotic function is also performed by idiolect and dialect. Hatim and Mason (ibid.: 97–110) consider idiolect within the analysis of Tenor and Register, examining the Cockney dialect of characters in George Bernard Shaw's play *Pygmalion*. The syntactic, lexical and phonetic features of the dialect are recognized by a British audience and associated with the way of speaking and the values of the uneducated London characters in the play. The systematic recurrence of this purposely functional feature of the speech of certain characters is identified by Hatim and Mason (ibid.: 103) as 'a noteworthy object of the translator's attention'. The peculiarities and connotations of the dialect are unlikely to be replicated easily in any TT culture. Furthermore, literary genre conventions may intervene. A translator into Arabic, for example, might be encouraged to adopt a formal classical style throughout since that is the only style felt to be appropriate for literature in Arab cultures (ibid.: 99).

Although Hatim and Mason propose 'foundations' for a model of analysing texts, they deal with a large number of concepts. It is not clear that their approach constitutes a model that can be 'applied' in the conventional sense of the term. Alternatively, the authors' proposals can be taken as a list of elements to be considered when examining translation. In particular, they concentrate (ibid.: 27–35) on identifying '**dynamic**' and '**stable**' elements in a text. These are presented as a continuum and linked to translation strategy: more 'stable' STs may require a 'fairly literal approach', while with more dynamic STs 'the translator is faced with more interesting challenges and literal translation may no longer be an option' (ibid.: 30–1).

More recent work both in SFL (e.g. the development of appraisal theory by Martin and White 2005) and translation theory (e.g. Munday 2012) has begun to examine in much more detail how dynamism operates in relation to the interpersonal function. Specifically, the interpersonal function constructs the subjectivity of the participants in the communication, for example with hedges in academic texts to indicate how strongly, or weakly, the writer holds a particular view.[8] Subjectivity is conveyed by what is called **evaluation** or attitude, that is, the choice of evaluative language. Prototypically these are epithets such as *brilliant*, or evaluative nouns such as *glory*, but all naming can be an expression of ideology or identity – Mossop (2007) gives the example of the shift from colonial *Bombay* to modern *Mumbai*, and the choice between the Anglophone *Montreal* and the Francophone *Montréal*. Also important, is the use of pronouns to locate the text producer in relation to the receiver.

For monolingual communication, this is all part of the writer–reader or speaker–hearer relationship. In translation, of course, there is a third participant, the translator, who **intervenes** in the process. An illuminating example (Munday 2012) is taken from translations of President Barack Obama's 2009 inauguration speech. Many translations of the speech downplay the degree of evaluation, for instance omitting a translation of the attitudinal adverb *even* in the following:

> *threats that demand* **even** *greater effort* [. . .] **even** *greater co-operation.*

Specific evaluative keywords that are not easily translatable may also be the site for sensitive translation decisions that may reveal the translator's subjective interpretation. Such is the case with the word *patchwork*. In the following, a key moment in the speech, it is not used with its frequent negative connotation:

> *our* **patchwork** *heritage is a strength . . . not a weakness. We are a nation of Christians and Muslims . . . Jews and Hindus . . . and non-believers.*

The term is omitted by some simultaneous interpreters working from a printed copy of the speech (i.e. producing what is known as **sight translation**), while some written translations generalize (e.g. *diverse heritage*) or explicate (*multi-ethnic heritage*). Finally, Obama's choice of pronouns constructs a relation around the concept of *we* (the American nation, the current American people or, sometimes, the US government). Translation into a language such as Indonesian or Thai would need to specify whether this *we* is inclusive (we and you) or exclusive (we, not including elements of the audience). The choice of translation of *you* would also need to indicate formality, informality and status, and would vary depending on the addressee. These are dynamic and very sensitive areas for translation.

6.4 Exploration: Translation of ideology

Read the article on textual approaches to the translation of ideology (Munday 2007) available online through the ITS companion website. Note the features of Register (Field, Tenor and Mode) and discourse that are identified in the analysis and the motivations for these uses.

6.5 Criticisms of discourse and Register analysis approaches to translation

Discourse analysis models have become extremely popular among many linguistics-oriented translation theorists and serve as a useful way of tackling the linguistic structure and meaning of a text. However, the basis of the Hallidayan model was famously attacked by literary theorist Stanley Fish (1981: 59–64) for being over-complicated in its categorization of grammar and for its apparently inflexible one-to-one matching of structure and meaning. This may cause it to struggle to cope with the variety of possible interpretations of literature, especially experimental literature. Some applications to literature (e.g. Fowler 1986/1996 and Simpson 1993) therefore adopted a more flexible 'toolkit' approach, employing those elements that appear most useful while also incorporating issues from literary criticism. In translation studies, others (e.g. Bosseaux 2007, Munday 2008, Saldanha 2011) have used the advances of **corpus stylistics** in order to reinforce objectivity.

As far as Juliane House's model is concerned, Gutt (2000: 47–54, see our Chapter 4), who writes from the perspective of relevance theory, raises the question as to whether it is possible to recover authorial intention and ST function from Register analysis. Even if it is possible, the basis of House's model is to discover 'mismatches' between ST and TT. Yet, while mismatches may indicate translation errors, they may also be caused by other translation strategies such as explicitation or compensation. It is less clear how House's model can interpret these.

The analytical frameworks of the translation theorists discussed in this chapter are also mainly English-language oriented. This becomes problematic with other languages, especially in the analysis of thematic and information structures. Other languages with a more flexible word order and subject-inflected verb forms need to be analysed differently. This type of problem becomes even more serious if attempts are made to impose such contrastive discourse analysis on **non-European languages** whose conceptual structure may differ crucially.

Linguistic differences are of course indicative of cultural differences, and Venuti (1998b: 21) is one critic who sees linguistics-oriented approaches as projecting 'a conservative model of translation that would unduly restrict [translation's] role in cultural innovation and change'. As an example, Venuti discusses Grice's maxims (see section 6.3.3 earlier) and criticizes them for the way in which they support a fluent and 'domesticating' translation strategy. Venuti considers the maxims suitable only for translation in closely defined fields, such as technical or legal documents. Baker herself is aware of the cultural bias of the maxims:

> Grice's maxims seem to reflect directly notions which are known to be valued in the English-speaking world, for instance sincerity, brevity, and relevance.
>
> (Baker 2011: 248)

It is Hatim and Mason who make a greater effort to incorporate a Hallidayan notion of culture and ideology into their analysis of translation, and they devote a chapter to ideology in *The Translator as Communicator* (Hatim and Mason 1997: 143–63). Their findings are illuminating, but, although they analyse a range of text types (written and spoken), their focus often remains linguistics-centred, both in its terminology and in the phenomena investigated ('lexical choice', 'cohesion', 'transitivity', 'style shifting', 'translator mediation', etc.). The case studies below follow this line by using the discourse analysis approaches presented in this chapter to examine two different films.

Case studies

Case study 1

This case study examines Werner Herzog's German film *The Enigma of Kaspar Hauser* (1974).[9] The film begins with a written introduction that scrolls down the screen (Box 6.1). A possible back translation in English is given in Box 6.2. The actual English translation, which appeared two lines at a time, occupied the bottom of the screen. This is given in Box 6.3.

Box 6.1: Written introduction to Kaspar Hauser

1   Am Pfingstsonntag des Jahres 1828 wurde in der Stadt N. ein verwahrloster Findling aufgegriffen, den man später Kaspar Hauser nannte.
2   Er konnte kaum gehen und sprach nur einen einzigen Satz.
3   Später, als er sprechen lernte, berichtete er, er sei zeit seines Lebens in einem dunklen Kellerloch eingesperrt gewesen, er habe keinerlei Begriff von der Welt gehabt und nicht gewußt, daß es außer ihm noch andere Menschen gäbe, weil man ihm das Essen hereinschob, während er schlief.
4   Er habe nicht gewußt, was ein Haus, ein Baum, was Sprache sei.
5   Erst ganz zuletzt sei ein Mann zu ihm hereingekommen. 6 Das Rätsel seiner Herkunft ist bis heute nicht gelöst.

Box 6.2: Back translation

1   On Whit Sunday in the year 1828 in the town of N. a ragged foundling was picked up whom one later called Kasper Hauser.
2   He could scarcely walk and spoke a single sentence.
3   Later, when he learnt to speak, he reported he had been locked up for his whole life in a dark cellar, he had not had any contact at all with the world and had not known that outside there were other people, because one slung food in to him, while he slept.

4   He did not know what a house, a tree, what language was.
5   Only right at the end did a man visit him.
6   The enigma of his origin has to this day not been solved.

Box 6.3: Subtitled version

1   One Sunday in 1828 a ragged boy was found abandoned in the town
    of N.
2   He could hardly walk and spoke but one sentence.
3   Later he told of being locked in a dark cellar from birth.
4   He had never seen another human being, a tree, a house before.
5   To this day no one knows where he came from – or who set him free.

House's model of quality assessment would show that, for the ST and TT, the
Field is similar. Both relate the story of a poor boy found in the town of N.
Nevertheless, there are mismatches in the amount of information that is given. In
the English, we are not told the boy's name, that he learnt to speak, that food
used to be shoved into the cellar while he slept, nor, precisely, that 'the enigma
of his origin' remains unsolved.

There is a similar story as far as **Mode** is concerned. In both cases the text is
written to be read, but the mode of presentation is different. The English is superimposed over part of the German, two lines at a time. To accommodate this crucial
visual constraint, the sentences have been shortened. Sentence 3 in the German
contains a complex of reported-speech subordinate clauses (starting 'he reported
he had been locked up . . .'). Its length gives a sense of formality befitting the early
nineteenth-century subject matter and speech patterns of the film. This sentence
is mostly omitted in the TT. The English sentences are therefore less varied
syntactically, although the thematic profile of the German sentences 1, 3 and 5,
where a time adjunct or adverbial is in first position, is effectively mirrored in the
English. Some higher-level cohesion is also lost in the immediate translation:
the omission of the name *Kaspar Hauser* is compensated for by its appearance in
the title of the film and in the early scenes, so one would imagine that the TT
reader would be able to retrieve it easily. The use of *Rätsel* ('enigma') in German
sentence 6 is lost in the translation; however, this is also compensated for since
the word *enigma* appears in the English title of the film. Moreover, TT sentence 5

(*To this day no one knows where he came from – or who set him free*) is far more informal than in the ST ('The enigma of his origin has to this day not been solved').

There are mismatches of **Tenor** arising from the non-translation of the German subjunctive in the reported speech after *berichtete er* ('he told of . . .'). The German subjunctives *sei, habe, gäbe* and so on, indicate the status of reported and not confirmed truth. These are either omitted or translated by a simple declarative statement of fact (*He had never seen another human being*). On the other hand, there are stronger interpersonal features in the final sentence in the English TT, with the two interrogatives (*where* and *who*) and the negative *no one*. These may be considered as another example of compensation (see section 4.1.2), with TT sentence 5 adding to the text an element of modality that was provided by the subjunctive in the German. House's concept of mismatches does not easily allow for compensation.

The result of the analysis points to the TT being what House calls an 'overt' translation. Subtitling is in fact an evident example of overt translation, since at all times during the film the TT reader is reminded visually of the translated words. However, because of the way the short written ST above has been reworked, it may be more correct to say that it is a summary translation or version.

Case study 2

This case study examines the English translation of the award-winning Mathieu Kassovitz French film *La haine* ('Hate') (1995) from the perspective of the discourse level of Halliday's grammar. The film is the stark story of three youths living in a poor area of Paris and of the violence and aggression that characterize and permeate their environment. Their idiolect (or sociolect, as it is mainly a class-based speech) is indicative of the identity they have constructed for themselves: it is aggressive, full of slang and obscenities, and often with little cohesion. This mirrors the poverty of their surroundings and their youth. It is thus a sociolect that has a purposeful semiotic function in the film. Its systematic recurrence among all three friends also fulfils the criteria presented by Hatim and Mason (1997: 103) for discourse that requires careful attention in translation.

The extra formality of the written subtitle tends to dictate against the repro-duction of very informal speech patterns. Nevertheless, the translators make an effort to reproduce some of the effect of the lexicogrammatical features, including the evaluative nominal forms *pigs* and *bastards* (for *police*) and *dickhead* and *wanker* (for *idiot*). However, there is a tendency for the TT to normalize the grammatical patterns in the TT, which produces increased cohesion and conventional thematic patterns. Thus, the ST *je lui aurais mis une balle ... BAAAAAAP!* ['I'd have put a bullet in him ... ZAAAAAAP!'] becomes the more formal and grammatically complex *If Hubert hadn't been there, I'd have shot him*. It is also difficult to imagine English-speaking youths using the polite imperative *Talk nicely!* for *Tu ne parles pas comme ça!* ['You don't talk like that!']. Or such a syntactically correct negative as *He didn't do anything* (rather than 'He ain't done nothing/ nuffin'/nowt').

The **dynamic** element of language noted by Hatim and Mason has been reduced in the subtitles, perhaps in part because of the intersemiotic shift from oral to written language. The increased cohesion of the TT and the reduction in some of the evaluative and interpersonal lexical items means that the identity constructed by the ST sociolect is less coherent. Also, the function it plays in binding the three main characters against the outside world is blurred.

Discussion of case studies

These brief case studies have suggested how discourse and Register analysis can begin to explain how texts construct meaning. Though it can be used to help a translator analyse a text prior to translation, House's model is perhaps designed more for the uncovering of 'errors' in a formal written TT. The analysis of the Kaspar Hauser example pointed out many such mismatches but not necessarily the reasons for the reworking. The reasons are likely to do with the on-screen constraints (see Chapter 11), such as the number of words that can fit on the screen, the need to keep the TT words legible when superimposed on the German text, and probably the commission's views on what was acceptable to the TT audience. Investigation into the specific translation commission for this text may uncover some interesting issues.

The brief case study of *La haine* indicates the potential of Hatim and Mason's flexible approach to analysis. An analysis of the lexicogrammar and discourse semantics of the characters' speech can explain the construction of their sociolect. The initial findings concerning the translation of informal grammatical patterns in the film would seem to corroborate Hatim and Mason's comments about the difficulties posed to translators by the dynamic element of communication. The characters' aggressive sociolect clearly reflects their sociocultural environment, yet it undergoes shifts in the TT. However, on many occasions the violence of the speech is communicated in the tone and level of the voice on the soundtrack, even if the TT receiver cannot understand the words. This is indicative of the complex nature of screen translation, with its audio and visual input, which a text-based discourse analysis may struggle to explain.

Summary

The discourse and Register analysis approaches described in this chapter are based on the model of Hallidayan systemic functional linguistics which links micro-level linguistic choices to the communicative function of a text and the sociocultural meaning behind it. House's (1977, 1997, 2015) model of Register analysis is designed to compare a ST–TT pair for situational variables, genre, function and language, and to identify both the translation method employed ('covert' or 'overt') and translation 'errors'. It has been criticized for its confusing and 'scientific' jargon; however, it provides a systematic means of uncovering some important considerations for the translator.

Works by Baker (1992/2011) and Hatim and Mason (1990, 1997) bring together a range of ideas from pragmatics and sociolinguistics that are relevant for translation and translation analysis. Baker's analysis is particularly useful in focusing on the thematic and cohesion structures of a text. Hatim and Mason, also working within the Hallidayan model, move beyond House's Register analysis and begin to consider the way social and power relations are negotiated and communicated in translation. This ideological level is further developed in the culturally oriented theories discussed in Chapters 8 and 9. First, in Chapter 7, we look at other theories that seek to place translation in its sociocultural context.

Further reading

See Hatim (2009) for a useful overview of discourse analysis in translation and its relation to functional theories, and also Baker et al. (2010) and Munday and Zhang (2015) for a range of recent studies. See Halliday and Hasan (1976) for cohesion, and Mason (2003/2012), Munday (2002) and Calzada (2007) for transitivity. See Munday (2009, 2010, 2012) for an analysis of the interpersonal function in translation. See Gutt (2000: 47–54) for criticisms of House's Register analysis and Fawcett (1997: 80–4) for a more balanced assessment.

Bell's *Translation and Translating* (1991) outlines the systemic functional model within a cognitive theory of translation. For a model of discourse analysis and text types, see Trosberg (1997, 2000). For analysis of thematic structure from a functional sentence perspective, see Enkvist (1978), Firbas (1986, 1992) and Rogers (2006). For work by House on the dynamic view of text and context, see House (2006). For pragmatics, see Leech (1983), Levinson (1983), Austin (1962) and Grice (1975). See Archer et al. (2012) for an introduction. See Morini (2013) for a pragmatic approach to literary translation.

For a more detailed introduction to the workings of systemic functional linguistics see Eggins (2004) and Thompson (2004). Leech and Short (1981) is a well-known application of the model for the analysis of literary prose. See also Simpson (1993) for a related model for the analysis of modality, transitivity and narrative point of view and Bosseaux (2007) and Munday (2008) for attempts to implement it (see also section 4.3 and the discussion of the translation of style).

Discussion and research points

1 Carry out a Register analysis on a ST–TT pair using House's model. What differences, if any, are there in text function? What 'mismatches' or errors are there? Is it a covert or overt translation? What might be motivating any differences you note? How useful is House's model for understanding the translation process that has produced the TT? Try analysing a technical and a literary pair of texts and compare results.

2 The text in Box 6.4 is part of a speech by Vice President of the European Commission Sir Leon Brittan to the European Parliament in Strasbourg on 3 May 1999. After following up some of the relevant recommended reading, carry out a Hallidayan analysis of this text focusing (a) on thematic and information structures (word order, placing of information, beginnings and endings of clauses and sentences, development of ideas) and (b) on cohesive patterns (lexical repetition, use of pronouns, collocation, etc.).

Box 6.4

Let me now turn to bananas. The Commission decided last week – with the consent of the Council of Ministers – not to appeal on either the substance of the issue or the so-called systemic question, but we do intend to pursue the latter issue, the systemic issue, in the panel which you brought against Section 301 of the US Trade Act. We also intend to pursue it in the dispute settlement understanding review and if necessary in the next trade round.

On the substance of the issue, our intention now is to change our regime in order to comply with the WTO [World Trade Organization] panel ruling. I believe that everybody has agreed that our objective has to be conformity with the WTO. But this will not be easy. We intend to consult extensively with all the main players with the objective of achieving a system which will not be threatened by further WTO challenges. I discussed this issue in Washington two weeks ago with the US agriculture secretary among others. My meetings were followed by discussions at official level. Subsequently, the Council asked the Commission to put forward proposals for amending the banana regime by the end of May in the light of further contracts with the US and other parties principally concerned.

How useful do you consider such an analysis to be for a translator? One of the criticisms of the Hallidayan model is that it is biased towards English. Try translating the text into your mother tongue or other foreign language. How applicable is the linguistic analysis to your TL?

3   'Grice's maxims seem to reflect directly notions which are known to be valued in the English-speaking world, for instance sincerity, brevity, and relevance' (Baker 2011: 248). Consider Grice's maxims with relation to the languages in which you work. What examples can you find of different maxims? How can a translator deal with any differences?

4   Follow up what Baker and Blum-Kulka say about cohesion and coherence. What examples can you find from your own languages to support the assertion that explicitation of cohesive ties is a universal feature of

translation? How do translators tend to deal with literary and other texts that are deliberately lacking in conventional cohesion or coherence? In some multimodal genres, such as adverts or websites, cohesion may be achieved visually, through layout, image and colour. Find examples of where this might be problematic in translation.

5   Find translations of Obama's inauguration speech in your own languages. How do the translators deal with questions of dynamic language, including the degree of evaluation, potentially contested key concepts and pronoun choice? What differences do you note between translations and interpretations of the speech? A transcription of the original speech can be found at http://www.whitehouse.gov/blog/inaugural-address/.

6   Case study 2 above is a discussion of *La haine*, in particular the problem of the semiotics of sociolect and the difficulties of translating it. How would or did your own TL deal with the translation of this film? Refer to Chapter 11 for a discussion of some of the constraints and characteristics of audiovisual translation.

The ITS website at www.routledge.com/cw/munday contains:

■   a video summary of the chapter;
■   a recap multiple-choice test;
■   customizable PowerPoint slides;
■   further reading links and extra journal articles;
■   more research project questions.

CHAPTER 7

Systems theories

Key concepts

- **Even-Zohar's polysystem theory (1970s) sees translated literature as part of the cultural, literary and historical system of the TL.**
- **Toury (1995/2012) puts forward a systematic methodology for descriptive translation studies (DTS) as a non-prescriptive means of understanding the 'norms' at work in the translation process and of discovering the general 'laws' of translation.**
- **Chesterman (1997) expands norms to include professional and ethical factors.**
- **Other models (e.g. Lambert and van Gorp 1985) propose different methodologies for TT description.**
- **Toury's 'laws' of translation are the law of standardization and the law of interference. Pym (2008) proposes resolving the contradiction between these by reference to the social conditions under which the TT is produced.**

Key texts

Chesterman, Andrew (1997) *Memes of Translation*, Amsterdam and Philadelphia: John Benjamins, Chapter 3.

Even-Zohar, Itamar (1978/2012) 'The position of translated literature within the literary polysystem', in Lawrence Venuti (ed.) (2012)*The Translation Studies Reader*, 3rd edition, London and New York: Routledge, pp. 162–7.

Hermans, Theo (ed.) (1985a) *The Manipulation of Literature: Studies in Literary Translation*, Beckenham: Croom Helm.

Hermans, Theo (1999) *Translation in Systems*, Manchester: St Jerome, Chapters 6 to 8.

Pym, Anthony, Miriam Shlesinger and **Daniel Simeoni** (eds) (2008) *Beyond Descriptive Translation Studies*, Amsterdam and Philadelphia: John Benjamins.

Toury, Gideon (1978/2012) 'The nature and role of norms in literary translation', in Lawrence Venuti (ed.) (2012), *The Translation Studies Reader*, 3rd edition, London and New York: Routledge, pp. 168–81.

Toury, Gideon (1995/2012) *Descriptive Translation Studies – And Beyond*, revised edition, Amsterdam and Philadelphia: John Benjamins.

7.0 Introduction

Watch the introductory video on the companion website.

In Chapters 5 and 6 we saw how linguistics broadened out from the models of the 1960s to an approach which incorporates first skopos theory and then Register and discourse analysis, relating language to its sociocultural function. In the 1970s, another reaction to the prescriptive models was polysystem theory (see section 7.1), which saw translated literature as a system operating in the larger social, literary and historical systems of the target culture. This was an important move, since translated literature had up to that point mostly been dismissed as a derivative, second-rate form. Polysystem theory fed into developments in descriptive translation studies (see section 7.2), a branch of translation studies that aims at identifying norms and laws of translation. Developments in the study of norms are discussed in section 7.3 (work by Chesterman), and work by systems theorists of the related Manipulation School is described in section 7.4.

7.1 Polysystem theory

Polysystem theory was developed in the 1970s by the Israeli scholar Itamar Even-Zohar borrowing ideas from the Russian Formalists of the 1920s and the Czech Structuralists of the 1930s and 1940s, who had worked on literary historiography and linguistics (see Further reading section). For the Formalists, a literary work was not studied in isolation but as part of a literary system, which itself is defined as 'a system of functions of the literary order which are in continual interrelationship with other orders' (Tynjanov 1927/1971: 72). Literature is thus part of the social, cultural, literary and historical framework and the key concept is that of the **system**, in which there is an ongoing dynamic of 'mutation' and struggle for the primary position in the literary canon.

Although building on work by the Formalists, Even-Zohar reacts against 'the fallacies of the traditional aesthetic approach' (Even-Zohar 1978: 22), which had focused on 'high' literature and had disregarded as unimportant literary systems or genres such as children's literature, thrillers and the whole system of translated literature. Even-Zohar (ibid.) emphasizes that translated literature operates as a system in itself:

(1)   in the way the TL culture selects works for translation;
(2)   in the way translation norms, behaviour and policies are influenced by other co-systems.

Even-Zohar focuses on the relations between all these systems in the overarching concept to which he gives a new term, the **polysystem**. This is defined by Even-Zohar as:

> a multiple system, a system of various systems which intersect with each other and partly overlap, using concurrently different options, yet functioning as one structured whole, whose members are interdependent.
>
> Even-Zohar (2005: 3)

Importantly, the interaction and positioning of these systems occurs in a **dynamic hierarchy**, changing according to the historical moment. If, at a given point, the highest position is occupied by an innovative literary type, then the lower strata are likely to be occupied by increasingly conservative types. On the other hand, if the conservative forms are at the top, innovation and renewal are likely to come from the lower strata. Otherwise a period of stagnation occurs (Even-Zohar 1978). This 'dynamic process of evolution' is vital to the polysystem, indicating that the relations between innovatory and conservative systems are in a constant state of flux and competition.

Because of this flux, the position of translated literature is not fixed either. It may occupy a **primary** or a **secondary position in the polysystem**. If it is primary, 'it participates actively in shaping the centre of the polysystem' (Even-Zohar 1978/2012: 163). It is likely to be innovatory and linked to major events of literary history as they are taking place. Often, leading writers produce the most important translations and translations are a leading factor in the formation of new models for the target culture, introducing new poetics, techniques and so on. Even-Zohar gives three major cases when translated literature occupies the **primary position** (see Figure 7.1):

(1) **When a 'young' literature is being established** and looks initially to more established literatures for ready-made models. Such would be the case in Toury's example of the Hebrew Enlightenment of the eighteenth and nineteenth centuries, which arose in Germany and used German models (Toury 1995/2012: 167). Another example is literature in Finnish, which developed in the nineteenth century using the models of realist novels from France and Britain.

(2) **When a literature is 'peripheral' or 'weak'** and it imports those literary types which it is lacking. This can happen when a smaller nation or language is dominated by the culture of a larger one. Even-Zohar sees that 'all sorts of peripheral literature may in such cases consist of translated literature' (1978/2012: 164). This happens at various levels. For instance, in modern Spain regions such as Galicia import many translations from the dominant Castilian Spanish, while Spain itself imports canonized and non-canonized literature from the English-speaking world. In Malaysia, local oral traditions were displaced by a written literature created from the Arabic models that had arrived with the introduction of Islam from the fifteenth century. When we think of other genres, the pervasive influence of English as the main international language for the dissemination of science is leading to the displacement of some local scientific traditions (e.g. in Scandinavian languages) even without translation.

(3) When there is a critical turning point in literary history at which established models are no longer considered sufficient, or when there is a **vacuum in the literature** of the country. Where no type holds sway, it is easier for foreign models to assume primacy. This can be domain specific, as occurred with the early twentieth-century translations of new German psychoanalytic work (Freud, Jung etc.) into languages such as English and French. And in India, the popularity of science-fiction writing began with the importation of models from English.

If translated literature assumes a **secondary position**, then it represents a peripheral system within the polysystem. It has no major influence over the central system and even becomes a conservative element, preserving conventional forms and conforming to the literary norms of the target system. Even-Zohar points out (ibid.: 165) that this secondary position is the 'normal' one for translated literatures.

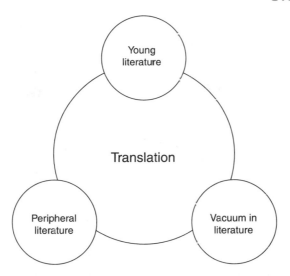

Figure 7.1   Conditions when translation is in primary position in polysystem

However, translated literature itself is stratified (ibid.: 164). Some translated literature may be secondary while others, translated from major source literatures, are
primary. An example Even-Zohar gives is of the Hebrew literary polysystem published
between the two world wars, when translations from Russian were primary but
translations from English, German and Polish were secondary.

Even-Zohar (ibid.: 166–74) suggests that the position occupied by translated
literature in the polysystem **conditions the translation strategy**. If it is primary,
translators do not feel constrained to follow target literature models and are more
prepared to break conventions. They thus often produce a TT that is a close match
in terms of adequacy, reproducing the textual relations of the ST. The influence of
the foreign language model may itself then lead to the production of new models
in the TL, for non-translated as well as translated languages. On the other hand, if
translated literature is secondary, translators tend to use existing target-culture
models for the TT and produce more 'non-adequate' translations. The technical
term 'adequate' is developed in the discussion of Toury's work in section 7.2.

Gentzler (2001: 118–20 and 123–5) stresses the way polysystem theory
represents an important advance for translation studies. The advantages of this
are several:

(1) literature itself is studied alongside the social, historical and cultural forces;
(2) Even-Zohar moves away from the isolated study of individual texts towards
     the study of translation within the cultural and literary systems in which it
     functions;

(3)   the non-prescriptive definition of equivalence and adequacy allows for vari-
       ation according to the social, historical and cultural situation of the text.

This last point offers translation theory an escape from the repeated arguments
that had begun to follow insistently the concept of equivalence in the 1960s and
1970s (see Chapter 3). Equivalence was no longer considered to be fixed – it
varied according to extratextual conditions.

However, Gentzler (ibid.: 120–3) also outlines **criticisms of polysystem
theory**. These include:

(1)   overgeneralization to 'universal laws' of translation based on relatively little
       evidence;
(2)   an over-reliance on an historically based Formalist model which, following
       Even-Zohar's own model of evolving trends, might be inappropriate for
       translated texts in the 1970s and beyond;
(3)   the tendency to focus on the abstract model rather than the 'real-life'
       constraints placed on texts and translators;
(4)   the question as to how far the supposed scientific model is really objective.

In addition, Even-Zohar restricts the application of the theory to literature. An
interesting question is how far it would be applicable to other text types, such as
the translation of scientific texts mentioned earlier.

Despite these objections, polysystem theory has had a profound influence on
translation studies, moving it forward into a less prescriptive observation of translation within its different contexts.

7.1 Exploration: Polysystem theory

The full article by Even-Zohar (2005) is available online.

7.2 Toury and descriptive translation studies

Working with Even-Zohar in Tel Aviv was Gideon Toury. After his early polysystem
work on the sociocultural conditions which determine the translation of foreign literature into Hebrew, Toury focused on developing a general theory of translation. In
Chapter 1, we considered Toury's diagrammatic representation of Holmes's 'map'

of translation studies. In his influential *Descriptive Translation Studies – And Beyond*, Toury calls for the development of a properly systematic descriptive branch of the discipline to replace isolated free-standing studies that are commonplace:

> What is missing is not isolated attempts reflecting excellent intuitions and supplying fine insights (which many existing studies certainly do), but a systematic branch proceeding from clear assumptions and armed with a methodology and research techniques made as explicit as possible and justified within translation studies itself. Only a branch of this kind can ensure that the findings of individual studies will be intersubjectively testable and comparable, and the studies themselves replicable.
>
> (Toury 2012: xiii)

Toury goes on to propose just such a methodology for the branch of **descriptive translation studies** (DTS).

For Toury, translations first and foremost occupy a position in the social and literary systems of the target culture; they are 'facts of target cultures: on occasion facts of a peculiar status, sometimes even constituting identifiable (sub)-systems of their own' (ibid.: 23). Their position determines the translation strategies that are employed. With this approach, Toury is continuing and building on the polysystem work of Even-Zohar and on earlier versions of his own work (Toury 1978, 1980, 1985, 1991). He (2012: 31–4 and 102) proposes the following **three-phase methodology for systematic DTS**, incorporating a description of the product and the wider role of the sociocultural system, as below:

(1) **Situate the text within the target culture system**, looking at its significance or acceptability.
(2) Undertake a **textual analysis** of the ST and the TT in order to identify relationships between corresponding segments in the two texts. Toury calls these segments 'coupled pairs'. This leads to the identification of translation shifts, both 'obligatory' and 'non-obligatory'.
(3) Attempt **generalizations** about the patterns identified in the two texts, which helps to reconstruct the process of translation for this ST–TT pair.

An important additional step is the repeating of these phases for other pairs of similar texts. This **replicability** allows the corpus to be extended and a descriptive profile of translations to be built up according to genre, period, author, etc. In this way, the norms pertaining to each kind of translation can be identified.

As more descriptive studies are performed, the ultimate aim is to state laws of behaviour for translation in general. The concepts of norms and laws are further discussed later in sections 7.2.1 and 7.2.2.

The second step of Toury's methodology is one of the most controversial areas. The decisions on which ST and TT segments to examine and what the relationships are between them is an apparatus which Toury (2012: 111) states should be supplied by translation theory. Yet, as we have seen in Chapters 4 and 5, linguistic translation theory is far from reaching a consensus as to what that apparatus should be. Most controversially, in earlier papers (1978/2012, 1985: 32), Toury still holds to the use of a hypothetical intermediate invariant or **_tertium comparationis_**[1] as an **'adequate translation'** against which to gauge translation shifts. However, at the same time he also admits that, in practice, no translation is ever fully 'adequate'. For this contradiction, and for considering the hypothetical invariant to be a universal given, he has been roundly criticized (see, e.g., Gentzler 2001: 130–1, Hermans 1999: 56–7).

In his 1995/2012 book, Toury drops the invariant concept. Instead, the model 'maps' the TT onto the ST, comparing the two to see where the two texts correspond and differ. This process involves 'a series of **(ad hoc) coupled pairs**' (Toury 2012: 103). In other words, the segments of the ST and TT that are analysed are not pre-determined and indeed will vary in different texts. Thus, in one study it is the addition of rhymes and omission of passages in the Hebrew translation of a German fairy tale; in another study it is two-part or 'conjoint' phrases in literature translated into Hebrew (see section 7.2.3 for an explanation of these). This is a type of comparison which Toury admits (ibid.: 105) is inevitably 'partial [and] indirect' and which will undergo 'continuous revision' during the very analytical process itself. The result has the advantage of being a flexible and non-prescriptive means of comparing ST and TT, but it is also one that lacks some consistency. Both flexibility and lack of consistency are revealed in the analysis contained in Toury's case studies.

7.2.1 The concept of norms of translation behaviour

The aim of Toury's case studies is to distinguish trends of translation behaviour, to make generalizations regarding the decision-making processes of the translator and then to 'reconstruct' the norms that have been in operation in the translation and make hypotheses that can be tested by future descriptive studies. The definition of **norms** used by Toury is:

the translation of general values or ideas shared by a community – as to what is right or wrong, adequate or inadequate – into performance instructions appropriate for and applicable to particular situations.

(Toury 2012: 63)

These norms are sociocultural constraints specific to a culture, society and time. An individual is said to acquire them from the general process of education and socialization, learning what kind of behaviour is expected in a given situation. Thus, university students may learn norms for translation from their tutors and these may even be set out formally in a handbook as a set of evaluation criteria. In terms of their 'potency' Toury places norms between rules and idiosyncrasies (ibid.: 65), which could be illustrated on a cline:

rules	norms	convertions	idiosyncrasies
	|	|	

STRONG   WEAK

<-->

Rules, supported by legislation, are the strongest constraints, since breaking a rule will normally incur a formal legal penalty or caution. In a professional translation context, this could be the breaking of a confidentiality agreement; or, in textual terms, committing a gross grammatical error in a translation test, where such accuracy is highly valued and which would usually lead to the loss of marks. **Norms**, as generally agreed forms of behaviour, are partly prescriptive in nature but weaker than rules. Violating them (for instance, writing a very informal translation commentary in an academic setting) might well lead to negative evaluation. **Conventions** (Nord 2003) are more informal and may be acquired by trial and error.

Toury considers translation to be an activity governed by norms, and these norms 'determine the (type and extent of) equivalence manifested in actual translations' (Toury 2012: 61). This suggests the potential **ambiguity of the term 'norm'**. Toury uses it first as a descriptive analytical category to be studied through regularity of behaviour – norms are 'options that translators in a given socio-historical context select on a regular bass' (Baker 2009: 190). So, the *belles infidèles* literary translations of eighteenth-century France generally privileged strategies that were free and conformed to the criterion of stylistic elegance. As we discussed above, norms also appear to exert pressure and to perform some kind of prescriptive function.

7.2 Exploration: Norms and rules

Look again at the rules-idiosyncrasies cline above. Add a definition or description to each of the terms to differentiate them.

Although Toury focuses initially on the analysis of the translation product, he emphasizes (Toury 2012: 5) that this is simply in order to identify the decision-making processes of the translator. His hypothesis is that the norms that have prevailed in the translation of a particular text can be reconstructed from two types of source:

(1)   from the **examination of texts**, the products of norm-governed activity (this will reveal 'regularities of behaviour' (ibid.: 64) – that is, the trends of relationships and correspondences between ST and TT segments; it will point to the processes adopted by the translator and, hence, the norms that have been in operation);

(2)   from the explicit **statements** made about norms by translators, publishers, reviewers and other participants in the translation act. However, Toury (ibid.: 88) warns that such explicit statements may be incomplete or biased in favour of the role played by the informants in the sociocultural system and are therefore best avoided.[2]

Toury (ibid.: 61ff) sees different kinds of norms operating at different stages of the translation process: (1) the initial norm; (2) preliminary norms; and (3) operational norms.

The basic **initial norm** refers to a general choice made by translators (Figure 7.2).

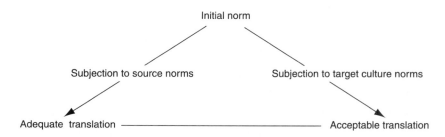

Figure 7.2   Toury's initial norm and the continuum of adequate and acceptable translation

Thus, translators can subject themselves to the norms realized in the ST or to the norms of the target culture or language. If it is towards the ST, then the TT will be **adequate**; if the target culture norms prevail, then the TT will be **acceptable**. For example, a translation of a scientific text from Portuguese to English may reproduce the complex sentence structure and argumentation patterns of the ST to give an 'adequate' translation, or alternatively rewrite the text to conform to the clarity of argumentation and standard SVO and passive structures of English scientific discourse (see Bennett 2011), an 'acceptable' translation. The poles of adequacy and acceptability are on a continuum since no translation is ever totally adequate or totally acceptable. Shifts are inevitable, norm-governed and 'a true universal of translation' (Toury 2012: 57). These may be obligatory (Vinay and Darbelnet's *servitude*), and non-obligatory (*option*), the latter being of greater interest since they reveal the choices made by the translator (see section 4.1.3, pp. 93–4).

Lower order norms described by Toury are **preliminary norms** and **operational norms** (ibid.: 58–9). Their relation to the initial norm is displayed in Figure 7.3.

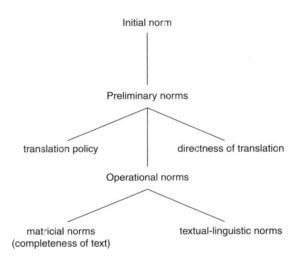

Figure 7.3   Initial, preliminary and operational norms

Preliminary norms are translation policy and directness of translation. **Translation policy** refers to factors determining the selection of texts for translation in a specific language, culture or time. Toury does not pursue this area in his case studies. **Directness of translation** relates to whether translation occurs through an intermediate language (e.g. Finnish to Greek via English). Questions for investigation include the tolerance of the TT culture to this practice, which languages are involved and whether the practice is camouflaged or not. **Operational norms** describe the presentation and linguistic matter of the TT. These are matricial norms and textual-linguistic norms. **Matricial norms** relate to the completeness of the TT. Phenomena include omission or relocation of passages, textual segmentation, and the addition of passages or footnotes. **Textual-linguistic norms** govern the selection of TT linguistic material: lexical items, phrases and stylistic features (compare Nord's list in Chapter 5).

The examination of the ST and TT should reveal shifts in the relations between the two that have taken place in translation (compare shift analysis in Chapter 4). It is here that Toury introduces the term **'translation equivalence'** (ibid.: 85), but he is at pains to emphasize that it is different from the traditional notion of equivalence, which we studied in Chapter 3. Toury's is a **'functional–relational concept'**, by which he means that equivalence is assumed between a TT and a ST. This is very important because analysis does not then focus prescriptively on whether a given TT or TT-expression is 'equivalent' to the ST or ST-expression. Instead it focuses on how the assumed equivalence has been realized and is a tool for uncovering 'the underlying concept of translation ... [the] derived notions of decision-making and the factors that have constrained it' (ibid.: 86).

As noted above, DTS aims to reconstruct the norms that have been in operation during the translation process. However, Toury stresses (ibid.: 67) that norms are a 'graded notion' since 'a translator's behaviour cannot be expected to be fully systematic' but will vary for a host of different reasons. In addition, these norms are of different intensity, ranging from behaviour that is mandatory (maximum intensity) to tendencies that are common but not mandatory and to behaviour that is tolerated only (minimum intensity) (ibid.: 67–9). We discuss this further in sections 7.2.4 and 7.3.

7.2.2 'Laws' of translation

Toury hopes that the cumulative identification of norms in descriptive studies will enable the formulation of probabilistic 'laws' of translation and thence of 'universals of translation'. The tentative laws he proposes are listed below:

(1)   The **law of growing standardization** (ibid.: 267–74), which states that 'in translation, textual relations obtaining in the original are often modified, sometimes to the point of being totally ignored, in favour of [more] habitual

options offered by a target repertoire' (ibid.: 268). This refers to the disruption of the ST patterns in translation and the selection of linguistic options that are more common in the TL. Thus, for example, there will be a tendency towards a general standardization and loss of variation in style in the TT, or at least towards an accommodation to target culture models. Examples would be the standardization of ST culture-specific items such as food terms that do not exist in the target culture (e.g. *pitta bread* translated as *flat bread*), or the translation of non-core forms into more general TL items (e.g. English *glisten* and *glint* translated as *shine*). Toury considers this to be especially the case if, as commonly occurs, translation assumes a weak and peripheral position in the target system.

(2)   The **law of interference** (ibid.: 274–9), which sees interference from ST to TT as 'a kind of default'. Interference refers to ST linguistic features (mainly lexical and syntactic patterning) that are copied in the TT. These may be **'negative'**, because they simply create non-normal TT patterns. For example, negative interference occurs when a new term (e.g. *benchmarking*) is borrowed into the TL or when a collocation is calqued from the ST and creates an unusual collocation in the TT (e.g. Vinay and Darbelnet's example of *Normal School* from the French élite *École Normale*). Or the interference may be **'positive'**. That is, the existence of features in the ST that will not be abnormal in the TL makes it more likely they will be used by the translator. For instance, subject–verb–object (SVO) order may tend to be selected by a translator working from English into a more flexible TL (e.g. Arabic, Hebrew, Spanish) where SVO is possible but where VSO order is more standard. In this way, the common SL patterns are reinforced in the TT. Toury (ibid.: 278) considers tolerance of interference to depend on sociocultural factors and the prestige of the different literary systems. Thus, there would be greater tolerance when translating from a prestigious language or culture, especially if the target language or culture is considered to be more 'minor'. An example would be translation from Arabic to Malay, where borrowing, especially of religious items, is very common. These laws are further discussed in section 7.2.4.

7.2.3 Toury's model in action

Toury (1995/2012) presents a series of case studies, including an 'exemplary' study of conjoint phrases in Hebrew TTs. Conjoint phrases or binomials are pairs of near-synonyms that function together as a single unit. Examples from English which Toury gives are *able and talented* and *law and order*; and, from German, *nie und nimmer* ('never ever'). He discusses (ibid.: 103–4) the significance of such phrases in Hebrew literature and indicates that their use is prevalent in old written Hebrew texts from the Bible onwards and in Hebrew texts from the end of the eighteenth century onwards, when the language was struggling to adapt to modern writing and was under the influence of imported literary models. However, the preference for conjoint phrases has declined over the past sixty years, as Hebrew has become a more confident and primary literature and has moved away from the imitation of imported models. Nevertheless, Toury (ibid.: 105) suggests that the number of such phrases in Hebrew translations of the same period tends to be higher than in Hebrew STs and that translations also contain more newly coined or 'free' combinations (rather than fixed phrases). He supports this with examples from Hebrew translations of children's literature, of Goethe and of a story by the German writer Heinrich Böll, 'Ansichten eines Clowns' ('Views of a clown'). In the latter case, the translator's very frequent use of conjoint phrases to translate single lexical items in German produces a Hebrew TT that is almost 30 per cent longer than the ST. The effect, in a translation published in 1971, is also to make the Hebrew seem very dated.

From these findings, Toury puts forward a possible generalization to be tested in future studies across languages and cultures. The claim (ibid.: 111) is that frequent use of conjoint phrases, particularly in place of single lexical items in the ST, 'may represent a universal of translation into systems which are young, or otherwise "weak" '. This consideration of translated literature as part of a hierarchical system of weak and strong literatures shows the way that DTS interlinks with polysystem theory.

Although DTS centres very much on description, the findings may also be applied (see the Holmes/Toury map in Chapter 1). An example is Toury's own translation of Mark Twain's *Connecticut Yankee in King Arthur's Court*, where Toury says he has deliberately used frequent conjoint phrases in Hebrew in order to create 'a parodistic air of "stylistic archaism" ' (ibid.: 112).

7.2.4 Discussion of Toury's work

It is now clear that Toury's methodology for DTS has been an important step towards setting firm foundations not only for future descriptive work but for the discipline as a whole. As early as 1993. Gentzler lists four aspects of Toury's theory that have had an important impact on translation studies:

(1) the abandonment of one-to-one notions of correspondence as well as the possibility of literary/linguistic equivalence (unless by accident);
(2) the involvement of literary tendencies within the target cultural system in the production of any translated text;
(3) the destabilization of the notion of an original message with a fixed identity;
(4) the integration of both the original text and the translated text in the semiotic web of intersecting cultural systems.

(Gentzler 1993/2001: 131)

Nevertheless, the ad hoc nature of the ST–TT mapping inevitably means that Toury's model is not fully objective or replicable. The alternative is Holmes's (1988a: 80) suggestion of an extensive 'repertory of features' approach. As we have seen in Chapter 4, this is potentially what Holmes called 'arduous and tedious', although this is certainly not a justification for not making an attempt. Other elements of the methodology are questioned by Hermans. These are Toury's ambivalence towards the notion of equivalence (Hermans 1999: 97) and the confusion inherent in the proposed terms 'adequate' and 'acceptable' because of their evaluative connotations in other contexts (ibid.: 77).[3] In a review of Toury's earlier (1980) book, Hermans (1995: 218) also queries Toury's exclusively TT-oriented position. Certainly, Toury's early stance risked overlooking, for example, some of the complex ideological and political factors such as:

- the **status of the ST** in its own culture. e.g. a 'classic' author such as Ernest Hemingway or a modern-day best-seller such as Stephen King's *The Dark Tower* series and its TV series and film tie-ins);
- the source culture's possible **promotion of translation** of its own literature, through grants from public or privately funded institutions, and online[4]; and
- the **effect** that translation might exert **back on the system of the source culture** (e.g. the success in translation of Nordic noir writers in the 2010s has considerably enhanced their reputation in their home countries).

These are areas which will benefit from employing concepts from studies of ideology in translation (see Chapter 8) and from reception theory, notably consideration of the way in which a new literary work influences its audience (see

Chapter 9). Toury's later work (e.g. 2004) in fact shows keener concern for **the relation of sociocultural factors to the linguistic choices** and, although it is worth noting that systems theorists in general have restricted their work to literary translation, the descriptive model does lend itself to the examination of the translation of non-fiction or technical texts or other modes such as audiovisual translation (Karamitroglou 2000, Pedersen 2011, see this volume, Chapter 11).

More recently, it is the 'norms' and particularly 'laws' of translation that have received closest attention. Criticisms which Gentzler makes of the earlier polysystem work (see section 7.1) have been levelled at Toury. In DTS, there is still a tendency to (over)generalize from case studies, and the 'laws' Toury tentatively proposes are in some ways simply reformulations of generally held, though not necessarily proven, beliefs about translation. It is also debatable to what extent a semi-scientific norm/law approach can be applied to a field such as translation. The norms described are, after all, abstract and only traceable in Toury's method by examining the results of the often subconscious behaviour that is supposedly governed by them. It is impossible to know or study all the variables relevant to translation and to find laws relevant to all translation (Hermans 1999: 92).

Toury's two laws themselves seem to some extent to be contradictory, or at least they appear to pull in different directions: the **law of growing standardization** depicts TL-oriented norms, while the **law of interference** is ST-oriented. We also suggest the need for modification of the law of interference, and even its replacement by more refined laws, such as that **the law of reduced control over linguistic realization in translation**. Such a law would take into account the constraining factors which affect the translation process and it would acknowledge that the concept of norms and laws in translation is more complex than is suggested by some of Toury's studies. These constraining factors include the effect of ST patterning, the preference for clarity and avoidance of ambiguity in TTs and real-life considerations for the translator, such as the need to maximize the efficiency of thought processes and the importance of decision-making under time pressure.

Toury answers some of these criticisms by stressing that these laws are probabilistic explanations at different levels of language. He defends the term 'law' rather than 'universals' because 'this notion [law] has the possibility of exception built into it [and] because it should always be possible to explain away (seeming) exceptions to a law with the help of another law, operating on another level' (Toury 2004: 29). As Toury argues, so-called **'universals' of translation** such as explicitation (see Chapter 4) should be understood to be common tendencies in translated texts and cannot cover every act of translation. No features of translation are ever 'universal' unless they are so general and bland as to be of little use (e.g. 'translation involves shifts'). In the same volume, Chesterman (2004) pursues this link between Toury's laws and different types of universals, suggesting a division into the following:

(1) **'S-universals'.** These relate to 'universal differences between translations and their source texts' (ibid.: 39). These patterns of shifts that occur in ST–TT pairs encompass Toury's two laws of interference and growing standardization as well as some of the trends of shifts identified by the models discussed in Chapters 4 to 6:
- TTs tend to be longer than STs;
- dialect tends to be normalized;
- explicitation is common;
- repetition is perhaps reduced;
- retranslation may lead to a TT that is closer to the ST.

(2) **'T-universals'.** These are features that characterize translated language as compared to naturally occurring language, irrespective of the source language. They are identified by examining TTs without reference to their STs. These might include:
- lexical simplification and conventionalization (including reduced variety in TTs);
- a contrary move towards non-typical patterns (e.g. unusual collocations such as *do a mistake* rather than *make a mistake*);
- under-representation of lexical items that are specific to the TL (e.g. the reduced use of culture-specific items such as *sophomore* or informal words such as *pester* which are associated with specific varieties of English).

Although S-universals are derived from a ST–TT pair comparison and T-universals are based on the study of TTs vs. non-translated TL texts, some of the features may overlap. So, some types of standardization discussed under S-universals derived from, say, Arabic>English and Russian>English text pairs may also be seen in lexical simplification as a T-universal in a corpus of English translations of promotional leaflets when compared to leaflets on similar topics written originally in English. Both types of universals also benefit from the study of large amounts of text. This is especially so for T-universals since subtler differences between translated language and naturally occurring language may well escape intuition and may only be identifiable using corpus-based techniques and the tools of corpus linguistics (see Chapter 11).

7.3 Exploration: Translation laws and universals

Look at the different laws and universals suggested above and see if you can find examples of them in translations involving your own language pairs. Read Chesterman (2010), available online, and note how these universals might be investigated.

In a volume which takes up the challenge of Toury's subtitle 'and beyond', Anthony Pym seeks to resolve the apparent contradiction in the two laws:

> The main point is that, thanks to these probabilistic formulations, it becomes quite reasonable to have contradictory tendencies on the level of linguistic variables. If social conditions A apply, then we might expect more standardization. If social conditions B are in evidence, expect interference. And there is no necessary contradiction involved.
>
> (Pym 2008: 321)

The link to social conditions is crucial, since it recognizes that they influence and to some extent determine the translation patterns. As an extreme example, in conditions of censorship where there is concern to filter out unwanted ideological elements of a ST, it might be expected that the TT would standardize or substitute culture-specific elements or even omit chunks that conflict with the accepted target culture ideology. This is what happened, for example, in the subtitling of Soviet Films in the Fascist Italy of the 1920s and 30s (Stephenson 2007). For Pym (2008: 323), it is the concept of risk and reward that is a possible means of unifying the two laws: 'Translators will tend to avoid risk by standardizing language and/or channelling interference, if and when there are no rewards for them to do otherwise.'

7.3 Chesterman's translation norms

Toury's concept of norms is focused mainly on their function as a descriptive category to identify translation patterns. However, as we noted in section 7.2.1, even such supposedly non-prescriptive norms attract approval or disapproval within society. Likewise, Chesterman (1997: 68) states that all norms 'exert a prescriptive pressure'.

Chesterman himself proposes another set of norms, covering the area of Toury's initial and operational norms (see Figures 7.1 and 7.3 earlier). These are (1) product or expectancy norms and (2) process or professional norms.

(1) **Product** or **expectancy norms** 'are established by the expectations of readers of a translation (of a given type) concerning what a translation (of this type) should be like' (ibid.: 64). Factors governing these norms include the predominant translation tradition in the target culture, the discourse conventions of the similar TL genre, and economic and ideological considerations. Chesterman makes two important points about these norms:

  (a) They allow evaluative judgements about translations since readers have a notion of what is an 'appropriate' or 'acceptable' translation of the specific genre and will approve of a translator who conforms to these expectations (ibid.: 65).

  (b) They are sometimes 'validated by a norm-authority of some kind' (ibid.: 66). For example, a teacher, literary critic and publisher's reader can confirm the prevalent norm by encouraging translations that conform with that norm. This may be, for instance, that a translation should meet TL criteria of readability and fluency (see Chapter 9). Alternatively, a literary critic may criticize a translation that offends the norm, and this criticism may damage the reception of that book among ordinary readers. Of course, as Chesterman notes, there may sometimes be a clash between the norm 'authorities' and society in general.

(2) **Professional norms** 'regulate the translation process itself' (ibid.: 67). They are subordinate to and determined by expectancy norms. Chesterman proposes three kinds of professional norm.

  (a) **The accountability norm** (ibid.: 68): This is an **ethical** norm, dealing with professional standards of integrity and thoroughness. The translator will accept responsibility for the work produced for the commissioner and reader.

  (b) **The communication norm** (ibid.: 69): This is a **social** norm. The translator, the communication 'expert', works to ensure maximum communication between the parties (compare Holz-Mänttäri's model of translatorial action in Chapter 5).

  (c) **The 'relation' norm** (ibid.: 69–70): This is a **linguistic** norm which deals with the relation between ST and TT. Again, in terms similar to those we discussed in Chapter 5, Chesterman rejects narrow equivalence relations and sees the appropriate relation being judged by the translator 'according to text-type, the wishes of the commissioner, the intentions of the original writer, and the assumed needs of the prospective readers'.

As with expectancy norms, these professional norms are validated partly by **norm authorities** such as other professionals and professional bodies but also partly by their very existence. They include social and ethical factors that are not covered by Toury, and therefore they may be useful in enhancing the description of the overall translation process and product. Table 7.1 provides a visual comparison of Toury and Chesterman's norms.

Table 7.1   Comparison of Toury's and Chesterman's norms

	Toury		*Chesterman*
Initial norm	TT's subjection to ST-oriented norms (**adequacy**) or TT-oriented norms (**acceptability**)	**Product or expectancy norms**	What the readers expect of the TT; they relate to translation tradition and prevailing genre and discourse conventions and give criteria for evaluation
Preliminary norms	**Translation policy** for selection of texts and **directness of translation** (sometimes via intermediate language)	**Professional norms**	**Accountability norm** is ethical; the translator accepts responsibility **Communication norm** is social; translator is expert
Operational norms	Relate to the choices in the text itself; **matricial norms** (is the text complete?) and **textual-linguistic norms** (the lexical and syntactic choices)		**Relation norm** is linguistic; judged according to text type, brief, ST author intentions and needs of TT readers

7.4 Exploration: Different norms and their applications

How might you investigate each of the norms presented in this chapter?

7.4 Other models of descriptive translation studies: Lambert and van Gorp and the Manipulation School

With the influence of Even-Zohar's and Toury's early work in polysystem theory, the International Comparative Literature Association held several meetings and conferences around the theme of translated literature. Particularly prominent centres were in Belgium, Israel and the Netherlands, and the first conferences were held at Leuven (1976), Tel Aviv (1978) and Antwerp (1980).

The key publication of this group of scholars, known as the **Manipulation School** or Group, was the collection of papers entitled *The Manipulation of Literature: Studies in Literary Translation*, edited by Theo Hermans (1985a). In his introduction, 'Translation studies and a new paradigm', Hermans summarizes the group's view of translated literature:

> What they have in common is a view of literature as a complex and dynamic system; a conviction that there should be a continual interplay between theoretical models and practical case studies; an approach to literary translation which is descriptive, target-organized, functional and systemic; and an interest in the norms and constraints that govern the production and reception of translations, in the relation between translation and other types of text processing, and in the place and role of translations both within a given literature and in the interaction between literatures.
>
> (Hermans 1985b: 10–11)

The link with polysystem theory and DTS can be seen to be strong and the Manipulation School proceeded on the basis of 'a continual interplay between theoretical models and practical case studies'.

A key point at that time was the exact methodology for the case studies. The paper by José Lambert and Hendrik van Gorp (1985/2006), '**On describing translations**', draws on Even-Zohar's and Toury's early work and proposes one such scheme for the comparison of the ST and TT literary systems and for the description of relations within them. Each system comprises a description of author, text and reader. Lambert and van Gorp divide the scheme into four sections (Lambert and van Gorp 1985/2006: 46–7):

(1) **preliminary data:** information on title page, metatexts (preface, etc.) and the general strategy (whether the translation is partial or complete); the results should lead to hypotheses concerning levels 2 and 3;

(2)   **macro-level:** the division of the text, titles and presentation of the chapters, the internal narrative structure and any overt authorial comment; this should generate hypotheses about the micro-level (level 3);

(3)   **micro-level:** the identification of shifts on different linguistic levels; these include the lexical level, the grammatical patterns, narrative point of view and modality (the results should interact with the macro-level (level 2) and lead to their 'consideration in terms of the broader systemic context';

(4)   **systemic context:** here micro- and macro-levels, text and theory are compared and norms identified; intertextual relations (relations with other texts including translations) and intersystemic relations (relations with other genres, codes) are also described.

Lambert and van Gorp (ibid.: 41) accept that 'it is impossible to summarize all relationships involved in the activity of translation' but suggest a systematic scheme that avoids superficial and intuitive commentaries and 'a priori judgments and convictions'. Like Hermans, they stress the link between the individual case study and the wider theoretical framework:

> It is not at all absurd to study a single translated text or a single translator, but it is absurd to disregard the fact that this translation or this translator has (positive or negative) connections with other translations and translators.
>
> (Lambert and van Gorp 1985/2006: 45)

This is still a crucial statement for those undertaking descriptive studies, even though DTS has moved on since that paper was written, not least with Toury's 1995/2012 work and later corpus-based studies. Scholars from the late André Lefevere onwards also rather marginalized polysystem theory as they began to consider more closely the role of ideology and patronage in the system of translated literature. In this respect, pointers for future work in the theory of descriptive studies were given by Hermans:

> The discipline generally, but the descriptive school in particular, urgently needs to take account of developments in some of the more vigorous intellectual and social movements of our time, including gender studies, poststructuralism, postcolonial and cultural studies, and the new interdisciplinarity of human sciences.
>
> (Hermans 1999: 159–60)

We shall examine the contribution to translation studies of some of these other movements in Chapters 8 and 9.

Case study

The text for this case study is the first in the hugely successful Harry Potter series: *Harry Potter and the Philosopher's Stone* by J. K. Rowling[5] and its translations into Italian (*Harry Potter e la pietra filosofale*[6]) and Spanish (*Harry Potter y la piedra filosofal*[7]). Following Toury's three-phase methodology, we shall:

(1)   place the TTs in their TT cultural systems;
(2)   'map' TT segments onto the ST equivalents;
(3)   attempt to draw some generalizations regarding the translation strategies employed and the norms at work.

Comparing two translations of the same ST, even though they are into different TLs, allows some triangulation of findings and helps to avoid jumping to conclusions based on a single isolated study, as Lambert and van Gorp warned.

(1)   Both the Italian and Spanish TTs are presented and accepted as translations, the translators' names and the original titles being published on the copyright pages. The Italian also has the translator's name on the title page. Both TTs are direct translations from English. Even though both target cultures have strong native children's literature traditions themselves, the decision to select this book for translation is not surprising given its huge success in the UK and the USA where it became the best-selling book in the country among both adults and children.

The fact that the Spanish and Italian books are translations is not stressed, however. The blurb on the back cover of the Spanish TT, for example, quotes comments from reviews in the UK and Italy and emphasizes the book's relevance to 'all children of all ages'. The Italian TT also incorporates illustrations by an Italian illustrator, Serena Riglietti, cited along with the translator on the title page, where the book is described as a *romanzo* (novel). The use of this word indicates the way in which the book is marketed as adult literature in Italy. There is a strong suggestion, therefore, that the Spanish and Italian publishers were prepared to make modifications, even perhaps including a modification of the genre, in order to ensure its full acceptability, including to more sophisticated adult readers.

(2)   The TTs are full translations of the ST with no major additions, omissions or footnotes. The choice of ST–TT segments to examine is *ad hoc* in Toury's model. In the case of *Harry Potter*, one of the most striking features of the book (and indeed of much children's literature) concerns the names of characters and elements related to the school of magic and sorcery of which Harry Potter is a pupil. The school itself has the sonorous and Anglo-Saxon sounding name of *Hogwarts*. Along the old English boarding school model, it is divided into houses with suggestive names such as *Slytherin, Gryffindor* and *Ravenclaw*. The names of the characters are similarly sonorous and suggestive: *Hagrid, Hedwig, Snape, Draco Malfoy, Argus Filch* and the headmaster *Albus Dumbledore*.

The two TTs deal with these names in very different ways. The Spanish TT, almost without exception, retains these names in the translation, although the first time Draco Malfoy appears, the translator adds an explanation of his name in brackets: 'Draco (dragón) Malfoy'. On the other hand, the Italian TT, although transferring some of the names such as *Hogwarts, Hagrid* and *Hedwig* directly into the TT, makes an attempt at translating the sense of others: *Slytherin* is *Serpeverde* ('green snake'), *Ravenclaw* is *Pecoranera* ('black sheep'), *Snape is Piton* ('python'), *Argus Filch* is *Argus Gazza* ('Argus Magpie'), and so on. Where the sound of the name is more important and where the original would be difficult for the TT readers to pronounce (as happens with *Gryffindor*) the Italian translator adapts (in this case to *Grifondoro*). She goes further with the headmaster's name: he becomes *Albus Silente*, and one of his titles, *Supreme Mugwamp*, is rendered by the colloquial and humorous *supremo Pezzo Grosso* ('Big Fish'). Even though this is not a neologism, it is markedly different from the neutral and formal Spanish *jefe supremo* ('supreme boss').

Names of crucial features of life in the school – such as the ball-game *Quidditch* and the term *Muggles* for non-magicians – are retained in Spanish, although italicized to emphasize their foreignness. In Italian, *Quidditch* is retained, but *Muggles* is replaced by the neologism *Babbani*. Some of the most playful names are those of the authors in the list of textbooks which the children receive before the start of term. Typical is *Magical Theory by Adalbert Waffling*. The Spanish does not change the author's name, while the Italian attempts to suggest the play on words with *Adalbert Incant*. Even more imaginatively, the Italian TT changes the author's name in *The Dark*

Forces by *Quentin Trimble* to *Dante Tremante*, using the rhyme of the Italian, the sense of *tremante* ('trembling') and, of course, the allusion to Dante and his inferno.

Interestingly, although the names are retained, there is intralingual translation between the UK and US versions, evident in the title (*The Sorcerer's Stone* in the US[9]) and in some lexical, cultural and syntactic selections – for instance, US *cookies* for UK *biscuits* and US *baseball* for UK *rounders*.

(3)   From these findings certain generalizations can be proposed concerning the translation norms that have been in operation:

    (a)   the Spanish adopts a more ST-oriented translation strategy, retaining the lexical items of the English original, even when this means that the TT reader will encounter pronunciation problems and/or not understand the allusion;

    (b)   the Italian adopts a more TT-oriented translation strategy, modifying many of the names to create new humorous sound patterns, plays on words and allusions.

This brief descriptive comparison of two translations suggests that different norms are at work in the two target cultures (or at least in these two translations). It also provides research questions that can be addressed in future studies in an attempt to refine the generalizations and contribute to knowledge of laws of translation. For example, were these same strategies followed in subsequent translations of the Harry Potter series in Spanish and Italian? Do translations of modern children's literature into Spanish generally tend to reinforce ST lexical patterns? How far does the translation strategy depend on the translator, the publisher, the SL, the social and historical conditions of production? What happens when names and cultural references are translated and transliterated into a language such as Arabic or Chinese? Do translations of this literature into Italian usually demonstrate a TL orientation? If so, does this suggest that Italian culture gives central position to its own culture, forcing imports to adapt to it? How has this varied over time? Do other genres show the same trend?

Discussion of case study

The advantages of Toury's methodology are that an attempt is made to place translation within its target-culture context, it is a relatively simple methodology to follow, and it is replicable. As other studies follow up the findings, a better picture can gradually be formed about the translation of the genre of modern children's literature, how this has varied over the years, the translation strategies into Italian and Spanish, their relation to what might have been assumed to be the more dominant English culture, and so on. A framework has thus been set up enabling researchers from almost any background to contribute in a meaningful way to our knowledge of translation. Nevertheless, some objections could be raised. So, the choice of ST–TT coupled pairs (segments that are analysed) is still far from systematic. Also, while the findings from the study of the translation of proper names are enlightening, names might be expected to be the most culturally bound items. It does not necessarily mean that the findings reflect the overall translation strategy. For this reason, it may well be preferable, as suggested by Holmes, to develop a checklist of features to examine, even if that list is not as comprehensive as some of the taxonomies we reviewed in Chapters 4 and 5. The location of such studies within the target-culture context is also inevitably limited in Toury's model. Focus could be shifted to look more deeply at the interaction between culture, ideology and text, and to look at the translators and publishing industry themselves. These topics are discussed in the next two chapters.

Summary

Even-Zohar's polysystem theory moves the study of translations out of a purely linguistic analysis of shifts and a one-to-one notion of equivalence and into an investigation of the position of translated literature as a whole in the historical and literary systems of the target culture. Toury then focuses attention on finding a methodology for descriptive translation studies. His TT-oriented theoretical framework combines linguistic comparison of ST and TT and consideration of the cultural framework of the TT. His aim is to identify the patterns of behaviour in the translation and thereby to 'reconstruct' the norms at work in the translation process. The ultimate aim of DTS is to discover probabilistic laws of translation, which may be used to aid future translators and researchers. The exact form of ST–TT comparison remains to be determined; scholars of the related Manipulation School led an interplay of theoretical models and case studies in the 1980s, among which was Lambert and van Gorp's systematic 'scheme' for describing translations. Chesterman has later developed the concept of norms.

Further reading

For a summary of the influence of the Russian Formalists on polysystem theory, read Gentzler (2001: 118–25). Selected Formalist writings in English translation are to be found in Matejka and Pomorska (1971). For further reading on polysystem theory, see Even-Zohar (1978, 1990, 2005) and, for a challenge to the theory, Fung Chang (2008, 2010). For further discussion on norms, see Komissarov (1993), Hermans (1996), Nord (1997), Pym (1998) and Schäffner (1999, 2010). For the Manipulation School and other descriptive approaches, see the collection of papers in Hermans (1985a). Related work by Lefevere is discussed in Chapter 8. For a later perspective on descriptive translation studies, including norms, see the papers in Pym et al. (2008). For translation universals, see Mauranen and Kujamäki (2004).

Discussion and research points

1 'Translation is no longer a phenomenon whose nature and borders are given once and for all, but an activity dependent on the relations within a certain cultural system' (Even-Zohar 1978/2012: 167). What are the implications of this comment for translation and translation studies? How far do you agree with it? How far do you agree that translations are 'facts of target cultures' alone?

2 How far do Chesterman's norms complement or advance Toury's concept of norms? Expand Figure 7.3 to account for Chesterman's norms. Are there other elements or norms which you feel they have omitted? Follow up the discussion of norms in the suggested further reading.

3 Using Toury's methodology, carry out a descriptive study of the translation of proper names in two of the Harry Potter books in another TL. Are your findings similar to those given in the case study in this chapter? What generalizations is it possible to then make about the translation process? What hypotheses can you propose and how would you seek to investigate them further? If you are working in a class, compare your findings with other members of the class. How replicable do the studies seem to be?

4 Carry out a study of the same texts using Lambert and van Gorp's model. What differences do you note compared to Toury's model? Which seems to be more rigorous? Is it possible to merge the two?

5 Systems theories have focused almost exclusively on literary translation. How far do you feel these theories may work for non-fiction, journalistic and technical texts?

The ITS website at www.routledge.com/cw/munday contains:

■ a video summary of the chapter;
■ a recap multiple-choice test;
■ customizable PowerPoint slides;
■ further reading links and extra journal articles;
■ more research project questions.

CHAPTER 8

Cultural and ideological turns

> ## Key concepts
>
> - **The 'cultural turn': The term used in translation studies for the move towards the analysis of translation from a cultural studies angle.**
> - **Rewriting: translation as a form of 'rewriting' and the ideological tensions around the text.**
> - **Gender and translation: the feminists' translation 'project', and the question of language and identity.**
> - **Postcolonial translation theories: Translation has played an active role in the colonization process and the image of the colonized.**
> - **Translation, ideology and intervention: Translation manipulates the image of the source culture.**
> - **'Committed' approaches: Theorists have various agendas of their own.**
> - **Multilingualism: Much translation takes place within superdiverse societies where language is a marker of power and identity.**

Key texts

Bassnett, Susan and André Lefevere (eds) (1990) *Translation, History and Culture*, London and New York: Pinter.

Bassnett, Susan and Harish Trivedi (eds) (1999) *Post-colonial Translation: Theory and Practice*, London and New York: Routledge.

Harvey, Keith (1998/2012) 'Translating camp talk: Gay identities and cultural transfer', in Lawrence Venuti (ed.) *The Translation Studies Reader*, 3rd edition, 2012, pp. 344–64.

Lee, Tong-King (2013) *Translating the Multilingual City: Cross-lingual Practices and Language Ideology*, Oxford: Peter Lang.

Lefevere, André (1992a) *Translation, Rewriting and the Manipulation of Literary Fame*, London and New York: Routledge.

Niranjana, Tejaswini (1992) *Siting Translation: History, Post-structuralism, and the Colonial Context*, Berkeley, CA: University of California Press.

Simon, Sherry (1996) *Gender in Translation: Cultural Identity and the Politics of Transmission*, London and New York: Routledge.

Spivak, Gayatri (1993/2012) 'The politics of translation', in Lawrence Venuti (ed.) *The Translation Studies Reader*, 3rd edition, 2012, pp. 312–30.

8.0 Introduction

Watch the introductory video on the companion website.

In their introduction to the collection of essays *Translation, History and Culture*, Susan Bassnett and André Lefevere dismiss the kinds of linguistic theories of translation we examined in Chapters 3 to 6, which, they say, 'have moved from word to text as a unit, but not beyond' (Bassnett and Lefevere 1990: 4). Also dismissed are 'painstaking comparisons between originals and translations' which do not consider the text in its cultural environment. Instead, Bassnett and Lefevere focus on the interaction between translation and culture, on the way in which culture impacts and constrains translation and on 'the larger issues of context, history and convention' (ibid.: 11). They examine the image of literature that is created by forms such as anthologies, commentaries, film adaptations and translations, and the institutions that are involved in that process. Thus, the move from translation as text to translation as culture and politics is what Mary Snell-Hornby (1990), in her paper in the same collection, terms **'the cultural turn'**. It is taken up by Bassnett and Lefevere as a metaphor for this cultural move and serves to bind together the range of case studies in their collection. These include studies of changing standards in translation over time, the power exercised in and on the publishing industry in pursuit of specific ideologies, feminist writing and translation, translation as 'appropriation', translation and colonization, and translation as rewriting, including film rewrites.

Translation, History and Culture constitutes an important collection and the beginning of a period in which the cultural turn held sway in translation studies.

In this chapter, we consider three areas where cultural studies has influenced translation studies: translation as rewriting, which is a development of systems theory studied in Chapter 7 (section 8.1); translation and gender (section 8.2), and translation and postcolonialism (section 8.3). The ideology of the theorists themselves is discussed in section 8.4 and other, more recent, work on translation, ideology and power in 8.5. It should be pointed out, however, that the chapter concentrates on studies that laid the foundation in this area; in order to give due representation to ongoing work from many other parts of the globe, the reader is referred to the ITS website at www.routledge.com/cw/munday for more case studies and research summaries.

8.1 Translation as rewriting

André Lefevere (1945–1996) worked in comparative literature departments in Leuven (Belgium) and then in the USA at the University of Texas, Austin. His work in translation studies developed out of his strong links with polysystem theory and the Manipulation School (see Chapter 7). Although some may argue that Lefevere sits more easily among the systems theorists, his later work on translation and culture in many ways represents a bridging point to the 'cultural turn'. His ideas are most fully developed in his book *Translation, Rewriting and the Manipulation of Literary Fame* (Lefevere 1992a).

Lefevere focuses particularly on the examination of 'very concrete factors' that systemically govern the reception, acceptance or rejection of literary texts; that is, 'issues such as power, ideology, institution and manipulation' (Lefevere 1992a: 2). The people involved in such power positions are the ones Lefevere sees as 'rewriting' literature and governing its consumption by the general public. The motivation for such rewriting can be **ideological** (conforming to or rebelling against the dominant ideology) or **poetological** (conforming to or rebelling against the dominant/preferred poetics). An example given by Lefevere (ibid.: 8) is of Edward Fitzgerald, the nineteenth-century translator (or 'rewriter') of the *Rubayait* by Persian poet, mathematician and astronomer Omar Khayyám (1048–1131). Fitzgerald considered Persians inferior and felt he should 'take liberties' in the translation in order to 'improve' on the original. He made it conform to the expected western literary conventions of his time and the work was a phenomenal commercial success (Davis 2000: 1020).

8.1 Exploration: Rewriting

Lefevere (1992a: 9) claims that 'the same basic process of rewriting is at work in translation, historiography, anthologization, criticism, and editing'. Find examples of each type of rewriting and describe what they have in common.

The bringing together of studies of 'original' writing and translations shows translation being incorporated into general literary criticism. However, it is translation that is central to Lefevere's book:

> Translation is the most obviously recognizable type of rewriting, and . . . it is potentially the most influential because it is able to project the image of an author and/or those works beyond the boundaries of their culture of origin.
>
> (Lefevere 1992a: 9)

For Lefevere, the literary system in which translation functions is controlled by two main factors, which are: (1) professionals within the literary system, who partly determine the dominant poetics; and (2) patronage outside the literary system, which partly determines the ideology. The interrelation is expressed in Figure 8.1.

The inner circle depicts the **professionals within the literary system**. These include critics and reviewers (whose comments affect the reception of a work), academics and teachers (who often decide whether a book is studied or not) and translators themselves, who decide on the poetics and at times influence the ideology of the translated text (as in the Fitzgerald example above).

The outer circle shows the **patronage outside the literary system**. These are 'the powers (persons, institutions) that can further or hinder the reading, writing, and rewriting of literature' (ibid.: 15). Patrons may be:

- influential and powerful individuals in a given historical era (e.g. Elizabeth I in Shakespeare's England, Hitler in 1930s Germany, etc.);
- groups of people (publishers, the media, a political class or party);
- institutions which regulate the distribution of literature and literary ideas (national academies, academic journals and, above all, the educational establishment).

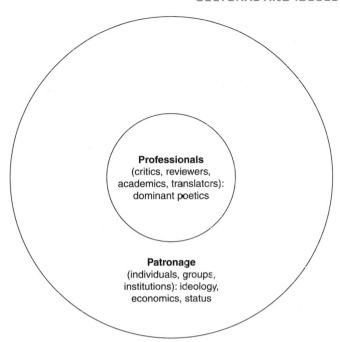

Figure 8.1 Control factors inside and outside the literary system

Lefevere (ibid.: 16) identifies three elements to this patronage:

(1) **The ideological component:** This constrains the choice of subject and the form of its presentation. Lefevere adopts a definition of ideology that is not restricted to the political. It is, more generally and perhaps less clearly, 'that grillwork of form, convention, and belief which orders our actions'.[1] He sees patronage as being mainly ideologically focused.

(2) **The economic component:** This concerns the payment of writers and rewriters. In the past, this was in the form of a pension or other regular payment from a benefactor. Nowadays, it is more likely to be translator's fees and in some cases royalty payments. Other professionals, such as critics and teachers, are, of course, also paid or funded by patrons (e.g. by newspaper publishers, universities and the State).

(3) **The status component:** This occurs in many forms. In return for economic payment from a benefactor or literary press, the beneficiary is often expected to conform to the patron's expectations. Similarly, membership of a group involves behaving in a way conducive to supporting that group: Lefevere gives the example of the Beat poets using the City Lights bookstore in San Francisco as a meeting point in the 1950s.

Patronage (ibid.: 17) is termed **undifferentiated** if all three components are provided by the same person or group. This might be the case with a totalitarian ruler whose efforts are directed at maintaining the stability of the system. Patronage is **differentiated** when the three components are not dependent on one another. Thus, a popular best-selling author may receive high economic rewards but accrue little status in the eyes of the hierarchy of the literary system.

Patronage wields most power in the operation of ideology, while the professionals have most influence in determining the poetics. As far as **the dominant poetics** is concerned, Lefevere (ibid.: 26) analyses two components:

(1) **Literary devices:** These include the range of genres, symbols, leitmotifs and narrative plot and characters, which may become formalized as in the case of European fairytales (e.g. princesses, princes, evil stepmothers) or Japanese *manga* comics.

(2) **The concept of the role of literature:** This is the relation of literature to the social system in which it exists. The struggle between different literary forms is a feature of polysystem theory (see section 7.1). Lefevere takes this idea further and looks at the role of institutions in determining the poetics:

> Institutions enforce or, at least, try to enforce the dominant poetics of a period by using it as the yardstick against which current production is measured. Accordingly, certain works of literature will be elevated to the level of 'classics' within a relatively short time after publication, while others are rejected, some to reach the exalted position of a classic later, when the dominant poetics has changed.
>
> (Lefevere 1992a: 19)

Classic status is enhanced by a book's inclusion in school or university reading lists, in anthologies or its use as a comparison in reviews (e.g. 'the new Hemingway'). With respect to an established canon, Lefevere sees 'clear indication of the conservative bias of the system itself and the power of rewriting' because such classics may never lose their status – they are reinterpreted or 'rewritten' to conform to changes in dominant poetics. This is the case, for example, with the Greek Classics, which continue to exert influence on western European literature. Thus, poetics may transcend languages and groups – Lefevere (ibid.: 31) claims that this occurs in the literary traditions shared by the four thousand languages and communities of sub-Saharan Africa (ibid.: 31). But, importantly, in the final instance and at the higher level, the dominant poetics tends to be determined by ideology: for instance, the early spread of Islam from Arabia led to the poetics of Arabic being adopted by other languages such as Persian, Turkish and Urdu.

8.1.1 Poetics, ideology and translation in Lefevere's work

The interaction between poetics, ideology and translation leads Lefevere to make a key claim:

> On every level of the translation process, it can be shown that, if linguistic considerations enter into conflict with considerations of an ideological and/or poetological nature, the latter tend to win out.
>
> (Lefevere 1992a: 39)

For Lefevere, therefore, **the most important consideration is the ideological one**. In this case, it refers to the translator's ideology or the ideology imposed upon the translator by patronage. The poetological consideration refers to the dominant poetics in the TL culture. Together, ideology and poetics dictate the translation strategy and the solution to specific problems. An example given by Lefevere is taken from the Classical Greek play *Lysistrata* (411 @AC), by Aristophanes; there, Lysistrata asks the allegorical female peace character to bring the Spartan emissary to her, adding *En mē dido tēn cheira, tēs sathēs age* [lit. 'If he doesn't give you his hand, take him by the penis'].

Lefevere lists English translations over the years that have rendered *penis* variously as *membrum virile, nose, leg, handle, life-line* and *anything else*, often accompanied by justificatory footnotes. According to Lefevere, such euphemistic translations are 'to no small extent indicative of the ideology dominant at a certain time in a certain society' (ibid.: 41)[2] and they 'quite literally become the play' for the TT audience that cannot read the ST (ibid.: 42).

This is very much the case in Lefevere's discussion of the diary of Anne Frank, a young Dutch Jewish schoolgirl in hiding with her family during the Second World War. Anne Frank had begun to rewrite the diary for possible later publication before her family was arrested and sent to a concentration camp, where Anne died. Lefevere describes how the 1947 Dutch edition of the diary

– prepared in conjunction with (and 'rewritten' by) Anne's father Otto – alters the image of the girl by, for example, omitting paragraphs relating to her sexuality. 'Unflattering' descriptions of friends and family are also cut as are sentences referring to several people who collaborated with the Germans, the latter omissions made at the request of the individuals named.

Lefevere then examines the German translation published in 1950. This translation was done by Anneliese Schütz, a friend of Otto Frank, and contains both errors of comprehension and alterations to the image of Germans and Germany. Lefevere lists many of these discrepancies, including instances where derogatory remarks about Germans are omitted or toned down. References to the Germans' treatment of the Jews are also altered. The following is a clear example:

> Dutch ST: er bestaat geen groter vijandschap op de wereld dan tussen Duitsers en Joden
> [lit. there is no greater enmity in the world than between Germans and Jews]
> German TT: eine grössere Feindschaft als zwischen diesen Deutschen und den Juden gibt es nicht auf der Welt
> [lit. there is no greater enmity in the world than between these Germans and the Jews]
>
> (Lefevere 1992a: 66)

According to Lefevere, the decision to translate *Duitsers* ('Germans') by *diesen Deutschen* ('these Germans') rather than by simply *den Deutschen* ('the Germans') was taken by Schütz in conjunction with Otto Frank because they felt that this is what Anne 'meant' to say and also so as not to risk sales in postwar Germany by insulting all Germans. Such rewriting, before and during translation, is, in Lefevere's eyes, due to ideological pressures.

8.2 Exploration: Control factors

Read the online article by Aksoy (2010) on the role of translation and ideology in the establishment of a national literature in Turkey. Make a list of examples of Lefevere's 'control factors' that affected this process.

8.2 Translation and gender

The interest of cultural studies in translation inevitably took translation studies away from purely linguistic analysis and brought it into contact with other disciplines. Yet this 'process of disciplinary hybridization' (Simon 1996: ix) has not always been straightforward. Sherry Simon, in her *Gender in Translation: Cultural Identity and the Politics of Transmission* (1996), criticizes translation studies for often using the term culture 'as if it referred to an obvious and unproblematic reality' (ibid.: ix). Lefevere (1985: 226), for example, had defined it as simply 'the environment of a literary system'.

Simon approaches translation from a gender-studies angle. She sees a language of sexism in translation studies, with its images of dominance, fidelity, faithfulness and betrayal. Typical is the seventeenth-century image of *les belles infidèles*, translations into French that were artistically beautiful but unfaithful (Mounin 1955), or George Steiner's male-oriented image of translation as penetration in *After Babel* (see Chapter 10). Feminist theorists also see a parallel between the status of translation, which is often considered to be derivative and inferior to original writing, and that of women, so often repressed in society and literature. This is the core of feminist translation theory, which seeks to 'identify and critique the tangle of concepts which relegates both women and translation to the bottom of the social and literary ladder' (Simon 1996: 1). But Simon takes this further:

> For feminist translation, fidelity is to be directed toward neither the author nor the reader, but toward the writing project – a project in which both writer and translator participate.
>
> (Simon 1996: 2)

Simon gives the example of the committed '**translation project**' in which, in politically active 1980s Canada, feminist translators set out to emphasize their identity and ideological position that was part of the cultural dialogue between Quebec and Anglophone Canada. One of these, Barbara Godard, theorist and translator, is openly assertive about the manipulation this involved:

> The feminist translator, affirming her critical difference, her delight in interminable rereading and re-writing, flaunts the signs of her manipulation of the text.
>
> (Godard 1990: 91)

Simon also quotes the introduction to a translation of Lise Gauvin's *Lettres d'une autre* (1984) by another committed feminist translator, Susanne de Lotbinière-Harwood. The latter explains her translation strategy in political terms:

> My translation practice is a political activity aimed at making language speak for women. So my signature on a translation means: this translation has used every translation strategy to make the feminine visible in language.
>
> (de Lotbinière-Harwood, quoted in Gauvin 1989: 9;
> also cited in Simon 1996: 15)

One such strategy discussed by Simon is the treatment of linguistic markers of gender. Examples quoted from de Lotbinière-Harwood's translations include using a bold 'e' in the word *one* to emphasize the feminine, capitalization of *M* in *HuMan Rights* to show the implicit sexism, the neologism *auther* (as opposed to *author*) to translate the French neologism *auteure*, and the female personification of nouns such as *aube* (*dawn*) with the English pronoun *she* (Simon 1996: 21).

8.3 Exploration: The feminist translation project

What linguistic strategies are available for such a feminist translation project in translations into your languages? See the article by Wallmach (2006) available through the ITS website.

Other chapters in Simon's book revalue the contribution women translators have made to translation throughout history, discuss the distortion in the translation of French feminist theory and look at feminist translations of the Bible. Among the case studies are summaries of the key literary translation work carried out by women in the first half of the twentieth century. Simon points out that the great classics of Russian literature were initially made available in English in translations produced mainly by one woman, Constance Garnett. Her sixty volumes of translation include almost the entire work of Turgenev, Tolstoy, Dostoevsky, Chekov and Gogol. Similarly, key works of literature in German were translated by women translators: Jean Starr Untermeyer, Willa Muir (in conjunction with her husband Edwin) and Helen Lowe-Porter.[3]

The important role played by women translators up to the present is emphasized by Simon's reference to the feminist Suzanne Jill Levine, the translator of Guillermo Cabrera Infante's *Tres tristes tigres*. In contrast to the self-effacing work of some of the earlier translators mentioned above, Levine collaborated closely with Infante in creating a 'new' work, as we discuss in Chapter 9. From the feminist perspective, however, it is not only Levine's self-confidence but also her awareness of a certain 'betrayal' – translating a male discourse that speaks of the woman betrayed – that fascinates Simon. She hints (ibid.: 82) at the possible ways Levine may have rewritten, manipulated and 'betrayed' Infante's work in her own feminist project.

8.2.1 Language and identity

Other research in translation and gender has problematized the issue of **language and identity**. One example, in queer translation, is Keith Harvey's study 'Translating camp talk' (Harvey 1998/2012), which involved combining linguistic methods of analysis of literature with a cultural-theory angle, enabling study of the social and ideological environment that conditions the exchange. Harvey draws on the theory of contact in language practice and on politeness to examine the homosexual discourse of camp in English and French texts and in translations. Contact theory[4] is used by Harvey to examine the way 'gay men and lesbians work within appropriate prevailing straight (and homophobic) discourses' (ibid.: 346), often appropriating language patterns from a range of communities. Thus, he describes (ibid.: 347–9) the use of girl talk and Southern Belle accents (*Oh, my!, adorable*, etc.), French expressions (*ma bébé, comme ça*) and a mix of formal and informal register by gay characters in Tony Kushner's *Angels in America*.[5] Such characteristics are typical of camp talk in English. Harvey points out that French camp interestingly tends to use English words and phrases in a similar language 'game'. Importantly, Harvey links the linguistic characteristics of camp to cultural identity via **queer theory** (ibid.: 351–4). Camp then not only exposes the hostile values and thinking of 'straight' institutions, but also, by its performative aspect, makes the gay community visible and manifests its identity.

Harvey brings together the various linguistic and cultural strands in his analysis of the translation of camp talk in extracts from two novels. The first (ibid.: 354–9) is the French translation of Gore Vidal's *The City and the Pillar*.[6] There are significant lexical and textual changes in the French translation:

- The same pejorative word, *tante/s* ('aunt/s'), is used for both the pejorative *pansies* and the more positive *queen*.
- The phrase *to be gay* is translated by the pejorative *en être* ('to be of it/them'), concealing the gay identity.
- Hyperbolic gay camp collocations such as *perfect weakness* and *screaming pansies* are either not translated or else rendered by a negative collocation.

In general, therefore, markers of gay identity either disappear or are made pejorative in the TT. Harvey links these findings to issues of the target culture. He discusses how the suppression of the label *gay* in the translation 'reflects a more general reluctance in France to recognize the usefulness of identity categories as the springboard for political action' (ibid.: 358) and shows a 'relative absence of radical gay (male) theorizing in contemporary France' (ibid.: 359).

The second extract analysed by Harvey is from the translation into American English of a novel by the Frenchman Tony Duvert.[7] Here, he shows (ibid.: 360–4) how the translator's additions and lexical choices have intensified and made more visible some of the camp language, thus turning a playful scene into one of seduction. Harvey suggests that the reason for such a translation strategy may be due to commercial pressures from the US publishers, who were supporting gay writing, and the general (sub)cultural environment in the USA which assured the book a better reception than it had enjoyed in France.

8.3 Postcolonial translation theory

In *Translation and Gender*, Sherry Simon's focus centres on underlining the importance of the cultural turn in translation. In the conclusion, she insists on how 'contemporary feminist translation has made gender the site of a consciously transformative project, one which reframes conditions of textual authority' (1996: 167) and summarizes the contribution of cultural studies to translation as follows:

> Cultural studies brings to translation an understanding of the complexities of gender and culture. It allows us to situate linguistic transfer within the multiple 'post' realities of today: poststructuralism, postcolonialism and postmodernism.
>
> (Simon 1996: 136)

In subsequent years it is in fact **postcolonialism** that has attracted the attention of many translation studies researchers. Though its specific scope is sometimes undefined, postcolonialism is generally used to cover studies of the history of the former colonies, studies of powerful European empires, resistance to the colonialist powers and, more broadly, studies of the effect of the imbalance of power relations between colonized and colonizer. The consequent crossover between different contemporary disciplines can be seen by the fact that essays by Simon and by Lefevere appear in collections of postcolonial writings on translation, and Simon herself makes extensive reference to the postcolonialist Spivak. In particular, Simon highlights (ibid.: 145–7) Spivak's concerns about the ideological consequences of the translation of 'Third World' literature into English and the distortion this entails. Spivak has addressed these questions in her seminal essay 'The politics of translation' (1993/2012), which brings together feminist, postcolonialist and poststructuralist approaches. Tensions between the different approaches are highlighted, with Spivak speaking out against western feminists who expect feminist writing from outside Europe to be translated into the language of power, English. In Spivak's view, such translation is often expressed in '**translatese**',[8] which eliminates the identity of individuals and cultures that are politically less powerful and leads to a standardization of very different voices:

> In the act of wholesale translation into English there can be a betrayal of the democratic ideal into the law of the strongest. This happens when all the literature of the Third World gets translated into a sort of with-it translatese, so that the literature by a woman in Palestine begins to resemble, in the feel of its prose, something by a man in Taiwan.
>
> (Spivak: 1993/2012: 314–16)

Spivak's critique of western feminism and publishing is most biting when she suggests (ibid.: 322) that feminists from the hegemonic countries should show real solidarity with women in postcolonial contexts by learning the language in which those women speak and write. In Spivak's opinion, the 'politics of translation' currently gives prominence to English and the other 'hegemonic' languages of the ex-colonizers. Translations into these languages from Bengali too often fail to translate the difference of the Bengali view because the translator, although with good intentions, over-assimilates it to make it accessible to the western readers. Spivak's own translation strategy[9] necessitates the translator's intimate understanding of the language and situation of the original. It draws on poststructuralist concepts of rhetoric, logic and the social. This topic is further discussed in Chapter 10.

Spivak's work is indicative of how cultural studies, and especially postcolonialism, has focused on issues of translation, the transnational and colonization. The linking of colonization and translation is accompanied by the argument that translation has played an active role in the colonization process and in disseminating an ideologically motivated image of colonized peoples. Just as, in section 8.2, we saw a parallel which feminist theorists have drawn between the conventional male-driven depiction of translations and of women, so has the metaphor been used of the colony as an imitative and inferior translational copy whose suppressed identity has been overwritten by the colonizer. Translation's role in disseminating such ideological images has led Bassnett and Trivedi (1999: 5) to refer to the 'shameful history of translation'.

The central intersection of translation studies and postcolonial theory is that of **power relations**. Tejaswini Niranjana's *Siting Translation: History, Poststructuralism, and the Colonial Context* presents an image of the postcolonial as 'still scored through by an absentee colonialism' (Niranjana 1992: 8). She sees literary translation as one of the discourses (the others being education, theology, historiography and philosophy) which 'inform the hegemonic apparatuses that belong to the ideological structure of colonial rule' (ibid.: 33). Niranjana's focus is on the way translation into English has generally been used by the colonial power to construct a rewritten image of the 'East' that has then come to stand for the truth. She gives other examples of the colonizer's imposition of ideological values. These vary from missionaries who ran schools for the colonized and who also performed a role as linguists and translators, to ethnographers who recorded grammars of native languages. Niranjana sees all these groups as 'participating in the enormous project of collection and codification on which colonial power was based' (ibid.: 34). She specifically attacks translation's role within this power structure:

> Translation as a practice shapes, and takes shape within, the asymmetrical relations of power that operate under colonialism.
>
> (Niranjana 1992: 2)

Furthermore, she goes on to criticize translation studies itself for its largely western orientation and for three main failings that she sees resulting from this (ibid.: 48–9):

(1) that translation studies has until recently not considered the question of power imbalance between different languages;

(2)   that the concepts underlying much of western translation theory are flawed ('its notions of text, author, and meaning are based on an unproblematic, naively representational theory of language');

(3)   that the 'humanistic enterprise' of translation needs to be questioned, since translation in the colonial context builds a conceptual image of colonial domination into the discourse of western philosophy.

Niranjana writes from an avowedly poststructuralist perspective. The latter forms the basis of Chapter 10 where we consider the influence of the deconstructionists such as Derrida. This overlapping is indicative of the interaction of different aspects of cultural studies and of the way in which they interface with translation studies. It also informs Niranjana's recommendations for action, which are:

(1)   In general, the postcolonial translator must call into question every aspect of colonialism and liberal nationalism (ibid.: 167). For Niranjana, this is not just a question of avoiding western metaphysical representations. It is a case of 'dismantl[ing] the hegemonic west from within…', deconstructing and identifying the means by which the west represses the non-west and marginalizes its own otherness' (ibid.: 171). By identifying and highlighting the process, such repression can then be countered.

(2)   Specifically, Niranjana calls for an 'interventionist' approach from the translator. 'I initiate here a practice of translation that is speculative, provisional and interventionist', she proclaims (ibid.: 173) in her analysis of translations of a spiritual vacana poem from Southern India. She attacks existing translations (including one by the celebrated A. K. Ramanujan) as 'attempting to assimilate Śaivite poetry to the discourses of Christianity or of a post-Romantic New Criticism' (ibid.: 180), analogous to nineteenth-century native responses to colonialism. Her own suggested translation, she claims, resists the 'containment' of colonial discourse by, amongst other things, restoring the name of the poet's god Guhēśvara and the *linga* representation of light, and by avoiding similes that would tone down the native form of metaphorization (ibid.: 182–6).

Asymmetrical power relationships in a postcolonial context also form the thread of the important collection of essays entitled *Post-colonial Translation: Theory and Practice*, edited by Susan Bassnett and Harish Trivedi (1999). In their introduction (ibid.: 13) they see these power relationships being played out in the unequal struggle of various local languages against 'the one master-language of our postcolonial world, English'. Translation is thus seen as the battleground and exemplification of the postcolonial context. There is a close linkage of **transla-tional** to **transnational**. 'Transnational' refers both to those postcolonials living 'between' nations as emigrants (as in the example of Salman Rushdie, discussed in Bhabha 1994) and, more widely, as the 'locational disrupture' that describes the situation of those who remain in the melting pot of their native 'site':

> In current theoretical discourse, then, to speak of postcolonial translation is little short of tautology. In our age of (the valorization of) migrancy, exile and diaspora, the word 'translation' seems to have come full circle and reverted from its figurative literary meaning of an interlingual transaction to its etymo-logical physical meaning of locational disrupture; translation seems to have been translated back to its origins.
>
> (Bassnett and Trivedi 1999: 13)

Crucial, here, are the interrelated concepts of **'in-betweenness'**, **'the third space'**, and **'hybridity'** and **'cultural difference'**, which postcolonial theorist Homi Bhabha uses to theorize questions of identity, agency and belonging in the process of **'cultural translation'** (Bhabha 1994: 303–7).

8.4 Exploration: In-betweenness and the 'third space'

Read the journal article by Batchelor (2008) available through the ITS website and note how the above highlighted concepts have been related to translation. See also the discussion on **in-betweenness** in Tymoczko (2003) and Bennett (2012).

For Bhabha, the discourse of colonial power is sophisticated and often camouflaged. However, its authority may be subverted by the production of ambivalent cultural hybridity that allows space for the discourse of the colonized to interrelate with it and thus undermine it. The consequences for the translator are crucial. As Michaela Wolf (2000: 142) states, 'The translator is no longer a mediator between two different poles, but her/his activities are inscribed in cultural overlappings which imply difference.' Other work on colonial difference, by Sathya Rao (2006), challenges Bhabha's view that postcolonial translation is subversive. Rao proposes the term 'non-colonial translation theory', which 'considers the original as a radical immanence indifferent to the (colonial) world and therefore untranslatable into it' (ibid.: 89). This calls for a 'radically foreign performance' or non-translation.

The contributions contained in Bassnett and Trivedi's book show that postcolonial translation studies take many forms. Several chapters are based on the theory and practice of translation from an Indian perspective: 'Indian literary traditions are essentially traditions of translation', says Devy (1999: 187), and studies are included of the work of renowned translators B. M. Srikantaiah (Viswanatha and Simon 1999) and A. K. Ramanujan (Dharwadker 1999). In the latter case, Dharwadker reacts against Niranjana's attack on Ramanujan, stating that Ramanujan had worked from an earlier and different version of the poem, that Niranjana ignores the translator's commentary on the poem, and that the goal of the translation was to orient the western reader to cross-cultural similarities.

8.5 Exploration

See the ITS website for a discussion of postcolonial translation in the Irish context.

8.4 The ideologies of the theorists

One consequence of this widening of the scope of translation studies is that it has brought together scholars from a wide range of backgrounds. Yet it is important to remember that theorists themselves have their own ideologies and agendas that drive their own criticisms. These are what Brownlie (2009: 79–81) calls **'committed approaches'** to translation studies. Thus, the feminist translators of the Canadian project are very open about flaunting their manipulation of texts. Sherry Simon is also explicit in stating that the aim of her book on gender and translation is 'to cast the widest net around issues of gender in translation . . . and, through gender, to move translation studies closer to a cultural studies framework' (Simon 1996: ix).

To be sure, these new cultural approaches have widened the horizons of translation studies with a wealth of new insights, but there is also a strong element of conflict and competition between them. For example, Simon (1996: 95), writing from a gender-studies perspective, describes the distortion of the representation in translation of the French feminist Hélène Cixous, since many critics only have access to that portion of her work that is available in English. However, Rosemary Arrojo, writing from a postcolonial angle, claims that Cixous's own appropriation of the Brazilian author Clarice Lispector 'is in fact an exemplary illustration of an aggressively "masculine" approach to difference' (Arrojo 1999: 160).

Such differences of perspective are inevitable and even to be welcomed as translation and translation studies continue to increase their influence. In many ways, it is part of the rewriting process described by Lefevere. Furthermore, the anthologizing, canonizing process can be seen everywhere. The present book, for example, cannot avoid rewriting and to some extent manipulating other work in the field. The cultural turn might also be described as an attempt by cultural studies to colonize the less established field of translation studies.

Additionally, postcolonial writers have their own political agenda. Cronin, for instance, posits the potential for English-speaking Irish translators to 'make a distinctive contribution to world culture as a non-imperial English-speaking bridge for the European audiovisual industry' (Cronin 1996: 197). This, he feels, can be achieved 'using appropriate translation strategies', although he does not give details except for 'the need to protect diversity and heterogeneity'. The promotion of such translation policies, even though it is from the perspective of the 'minority' cultures, still involves a political act and a manipulation of translation for specific political or economic advantage.

8.5 Translation, ideology and power in other contexts

The question of power in postcolonial translation studies, and Lefevere's work on the ideological component of rewriting, has led to the examination of power and ideology in other contexts where translation is involved. Several volumes have been published featuring one or other of these terms: Venuti's (1992) *Rethinking Translation: Discourse, Subjectivity, Ideology*, Flotow's (2000) *Translation and Ideology*, Gentzler and Tymoczko's (2002) *Translation and Power*, Calzada Pérez's (2003) *Apropos of Ideology*, and Cunico and Munday's (2007) *Translation and Ideology: Encounters and Clashes*. The concept of ideology itself varies enormously, from its neutral coinage by Count Destutt de Tracy in 1796 to refer to a new science of ideas to the negative Marxian use as 'false consciousness', or misguided thinking and even manipulation. Much research from an ideological perspective is interested in uncovering manipulations in the TT that may be indicative of the translator's conscious 'ideology' or produced by 'ideological' elements of the translation environment, such as pressure from a commissioner, editor or institutional/governmental circles. This is particularly the case in the translation and adaptation of news translation. Linguistic models that have been employed for analysis include those from discourse analysis (Hatim and Mason 1990, 1997, see this volume, Chapter 6), critical discourse analysis (following Fairclough 2001, 2003, see Munday 2007a) and narrative theory (Baker 2006).

8.6 Exploration: Ideology

Consult some of the volumes mentioned in the paragraph above and compare the different definitions of 'ideology'. Note examples of forms of manipulation in translation.

The harsh, macro-contextual constraints of censorship that may exist in authoritarian regimes are perhaps the most obvious example of ideological manipulation. Kate Sturge (2004) looks at the ideology behind the selection of texts in Nazi Germany. Using material on book production and sales, Sturge shows that texts from cultures deemed to be kindred were encouraged, hence the promotion of Scandinavian and Flemish/Dutch texts. Reviews in the authorized press also supported the racist official policy of eliminating 'all elements alien to the German character' that were felt to be characteristic of foreign literature.

Other research has focused on the disparity of power between **languages**, most specifically on the growth of English as a lingua franca globally (see House 2014b) and what this asymmetry means in the translational context in non-literary genres. Karen Bennett (2006, 2007, 2011) writes on the 'epistemicide' caused by the dominance of English scientific and academic style, which effectively eliminates (or, at least, massively overshadows) more traditional, discursive Portuguese writing in those fields. To be accepted in the international academic community (including in translation studies) now increasingly means conforming not only to accepted English style for those genres and text types but also to the ways of formulating and expressing ideas which this entails.

To be sure, language imbalance (and the economic and political power behind it) has been a constant backdrop to translation through the ages. This has encompassed the hegemony and prestige of Classical languages such as Greek, Latin and Sanskrit which constrained translation of sacred scriptures and scientific texts into vernacular languages. More recent political developments include the creation of Bahasa Malaysia as a language distinct from Bahasa Indonesia to promote national unity in Malaysia, the promotion of 'lesser-spoken' languages such as Irish and Basque in Europe, and the division of Serbo-Croat into distinct languages (Serbian and Croatian) for political and identitary reasons.

Recent research has also begun to pay more attention to the fact that much translation takes place informally between co-existing linguistic communities in multilingual cities rather than between participants living in separate countries and speaking different national languages. In *Cities in Translation*, Sherry Simon (2012: 3) considers the cases of linguistically divided 'dual cities', where 'two historically rooted language communities ... feel a sense of entitlement to the same territory'. The cities she considers are Barcelona, Calcutta, Montreal and Trieste. A slightly different example is Singapore, which has four official languages (English, Malay, Mandarin and Tamil) but one (English) dominates in the public realm (law, government, etc.) even though Mandarin is the first language for half the population. Lee (2013) investigates the dynamics of translation for the Chinese community in Singapore and what this reveals about cultural identity and power relations. Such complex, 'superdiverse' societies are home to dynamic, multilingual forms of communication, including the phenomenon of 'translanguaging' (Garcia and Li Wei 2014) which values language diversity.

Case study

This case study concerns *The Last Flicker* (1991), the English translation of Gurdial Singh's Punjabi novel *Marhi Da Deeva* (1964).[10] Punjabi and English have shared an unequal and problematic power equation owing to a long history of British rule in India and the imposition of the English language during that time. In more recent years, the native literature of the Punjab has become more valued, and no writer more so than Gurdial Singh, joint winner of India's prestigious Jnanpith Literary Award in 1999.[11]

It is significant first of all that his novel should have been selected for translation, even twenty-seven years after the publication of the ST. This fact immediately raises the status of a novel in its source culture. Its enormous success in its other translations, in Hindi and Russian, may have assisted its publication in English, which coincided with the release in India of a film based on the novel. There may be other political and cultural reasons too: the publisher of the translation, Sahitya Akademi, is the national organization set up by the government of India 'to foster and co-ordinate literary activities in all the Indian languages and to promote through them the cultural unity of India'.[12] In this instance, therefore, English is being used as a tool both nationally and internationally.

The translation is by Ajmer S. Rode, a Punjabi settled in Canada. The fact that the book has been translated by a fellow countryman, but one who is settled in a western country, that it has been promoted by a central government organization and that it is written in the hegemonic language of English immediately raises a complex range of cultural issues concerning the power structures at play in and around the text and translator.

A further factor is added by the setting of the novel in an isolated village in the Malwa region of Punjab. The poorly educated characters converse with each other in the local Malwai dialect of Punjabi. Their colloquial dialogue constitutes a crucial element of the fictional discourse, with the third person narrator portraying characters and situations through the character's speech rhythms and the cultural environment they evoke.

In the English translation, the dialogue shows a mix of registers: there are archaic insults (*wretched dog!*) and others that combine slight archaism with the reference points of rural life (*that oaf, big-boned like a bullock*), alongside modern American (or mock-American) expletives (*asshole, Goddam dumb ox, fucking God, fucking piece of land, king shit!, bullshit, bloody big daddies*) and speech markers (*huh, yeah, right?*). Lexis such as *Goddam, bullshit, fucking God*, etc., clearly points to a cultural context very different from the one within which the novel was conceived, uprooting the characters from rural Punjab and giving them the speech accents of street-smart urban North America.

The mixing of registers in the translation also affects kinship markers. Culturally loaded as they often are, they are sometimes replaced by their nearest English equivalents and on other occasions are retained in their original form for emphasis. For instance, *Bapu*, a term used for father or an elder, is preserved in its original form while the overtly Americanized *mom* and Anglicized *aunty* replace *Maa* and *Chachi/Tayyi*.[13] Kinship culture in Punjab is inextricably bound up with notions of hierarchy and status-consciousness, as well as revealing the emotional bonds between characters. At times, the emotional bonds are indicated by Americanized terms of endearment, such as the use of *honey* by a father to refer to his daughter. This points to a disruption in translation of a central theme from the source culture.

Nevertheless, it is also true that this kind of text would pose problems for any translator. The translation of a Punjabi regional novel for the international audience will inevitably involve spatial and cultural dislocation. What the translator has done is to translate the regional and social dialect of a small village community with the sociolect of urban working-class North America, where he has lived for several years. This may prove problematic for those reading the text in English in India, since the indicators of the dislocation towards the hegemonic Anglo-Saxon culture – as Spivak or Niranjana might call it – would be very noticeable. Yet the mix of registers also serves to make apparent that we are reading a translation. The result is not exactly the 'with-it translatese' bemoaned by Spivak nor the dominant Anglo-American domesticating translations castigated by Venuti (1995/2008; see Chapter 9); it is rather a dislocationary translation practice that brings into sharp relief the clash of different cultures. The characters are dislodged from their source culture, but they are also made to come alive and challenge the English-language reader. This is the kind of complex interventionist approach the translator has carried out, but he leaves himself open to the criticism that he has chosen to superimpose the sociolect of the hegemonic power.

Interestingly enough, the translation of *Marhi Da Deeva* was followed by the translation of two other Singh novels: *Adh Chanani Raat* (*Night of the Half-Moon*, Madras: Macmillan, 1996) and *Parsa* (National Book Trust, 1999); these translations brought Singh to the attention of an even wider audience and are perhaps indicative of the success of the first translation.

Discussion of case study

This case study, which looks at the language of the TT and sees cultural implications in the choices made, has examined a novel from a minority language that has been translated into the hegemonic international language (English) under the patronage of a centralized national organization (the Sahitya Akademi). The language of the characters becomes mingled with that of the colonizer, and their identity – embedded in their Punjabi cultural milieu – is blurred. While postcolonial theories help to understand the power relations that operate around the translation process, it is also clear from this brief analysis of *The Last Flicker* that a whole range of interacting factors are at work. These include the perhaps inevitable dislocation of the source culture, the dislocation of the Punjabi translator in Canada and the location of the patronage within India itself. It would now be interesting to compare the translation strategies employed in the other novels. The aim would be to see how far this translation strategy is due to translation policy or to the way literary translators function in general. The latter is an issue that will be considered in the next chapter.

Summary

This chapter has focused on the varieties of cultural studies in translation studies. Linguistic theories of translation have been sidelined and attention has centred on translation as cultural transfer and the interface of translation with other growing disciplines within cultural studies. Those examined in this chapter have been:

- section 8.1: translation as rewriting, developed from systems theories and pioneered by André Lefevere, studying the power relations and ideologies existing in the patronage and poetics of literary and cultural systems that interface with literary translation;
- section 8.2: translation and gender, with the Canadian feminist translation project described by Sherry Simon, making the feminine visible in translation; it also encompasses work (Harvey) on the translation of gay texts where, again, language partly constructs identity;
- section 8.3: translation and postcolonialism, with examples from Spivak, Niranjana and Cronin comparing the 'dislocature' of texts and translators working in former colonies of the European powers or in their languages;
- sections 8.4 and 8.5: translation and ideology: a theory or an individual translation may be a site of ideological manipulation, but the struggle is also between asymmetric languages in international organizations and in multilingual societies.

The next chapter now turns to examine the role of translators themselves at the translation interface.

Further reading

For an introduction to cultural studies, read Longhurst et al. (2013) or During (2005). For translation as rewriting, and adaptations, read additionally Lefevere

(1985, 1993) and Raw (2012); see Abend-David (2014) for examples of adaptation in the dubbing and subtitling of films. For an introduction to gender issues, read Butler (1990) and Richardson and Robinson (2007). For translation and gender, read Godard (1990), Santaemilia (2005), Larkosh (2011) and von Flotow (2011); for an analysis of gender in audiovisual translation, see De Marco (2012); for a bibliography of queer translation, see https://queertranslation.univie.ac.at/bibliography/. For an introduction to postcolonialism, read Said (1978) and Young (2003). In addition, for translation and postcolonialism, see Cheyfitz (1991), Rafael (1993), Bhabha (1994), Robinson (1997a) and Simon and St-Pierre (2000). For the use of Bhabha's 'cultural translation', read Trivedi (2005).

For translation from Arabic, see Faiq (2004) and Selim (2009), and the translation studies portal (http://www.translationstudiesportal.org/home) for the Arab world, Turkey and Iran; from China and Japan, see Cheung (2009), St André and Peng (2012), Hung and Wakabayashi (2005) and Sato-Rossberg and Wakabayashi (2012); see also the range of studies in Hermans (2006a, 2006b). For Africa, see Bandia (2008, 2010), Batchelor (2009) and Inggs and Meintjes (2009). For India, see Kothari (2003), Wakabayashi and Kothari (2009) and Burger and Pozza (2010).

For translation, power and ideology, see Flotow (2000), Gentzler and Tymoczko (2002), Calzada Pérez (2003), Cunico and Munday (2007) and Lee (2013). For censorship, Billiani (2007), Seruya and Lin Moniz (2008), Rundle and Sturge (2010) and Woods (2012). For translation and nationalism see Bermann and Wood (2005). For translanguaging, see Garcia and Li Wei (2014) and the journal Translation and Translanguaging in Multilingual Contexts (ed. Laviosa).

Discussion and research points

1 Lefevere identifies two factors (the professionals and patronage), combined with poetics and ideology, which control the literary system. Examine how each functions in specific translations in your own culture. Which seems to be the more important? Are there other factors which you would add?

2 Should women writers ideally be translated by women only? What about male writers? Look at published translations and their prefaces to see how often this is considered.

3 Choose a 'classic' work from your own language and culture. What seems to have consolidated its position as a classic? Research details of its translations. Has it been translated more than once? How do such (re)translations express the dominant poetics of the time?

4 What research work has been carried out on postcolonialism and translation in your own context and language(s)? Do the results correspond to those discussed here?

5 How is power difference manifested or contested in large organizations such as the United Nations, the European Union, or multinational companies? See the European Commission report *Lingua franca: Chimera or reality*? (2010).

6 Think of further examples of 'dual cities' and of multilingual 'superdiversity'. Investigate how translation operates in one of these sites.

The ITS website at www.routledge.com/cw/munday contains:

■ a video summary of the chapter;
■ a recap multiple-choice test;
■ customizable PowerPoint slides;
■ further reading links and links to freely available journal articles;
■ more research project questions;
■ more case studies.

CHAPTER 9

The role of the translator
Visibility, ethics and sociology

Key concepts

- **Venuti: the 'invisibility' of the translator and the ethical consequences.**
- **'Foreignizing' vs. 'domesticating' translation.**
- **Berman: the 'negative analytic' and deformation of translation.**
- **The sociology of translation focuses on the role of the translator and the social nature of translation.**
- **The power network of the translation industry.**
- **The reception of translation – paratexts, reception theory and translation reviewing.**

Key texts

Berman, Antoine (1985b/2012) 'Translation and the trials of the foreign', translated by Lawrence Venuti, in Lawrence Venuti (ed.) (2012), *The Translation Studies Reader*, Routledge: London and New York, pp. 240–53.

Gouanvic, Jean-Marc (2005) 'A Bourdieusian theory of translation, or the coincidence of practical instances: Field, "habitus", capital and illusio', *The Translator* 11.2: 147–66.

Heilbron, Johan and Gisèle Sapiro (2007) 'Outline for a sociology of translation', in Michaela Wolf and Alexandra Fukari (eds) (2007), *Constructing a Sociology of Translation*, Amsterdam and Philadelphia: John Benjamins, pp. 93–107.

Maier, Carol (2007) 'The translator as an intervenient being', in J. Munday (ed.) *Translation as Intervention*, London: Continuum, pp. 1–17.

Milton, John and Paul Bandia (eds) (2009) *Agents of Translation*, Amsterdam and Philadelphia: John Benjamins.

Simeoni, Daniel (1998) 'The pivotal status of the translator's habitus', *Target* 10.1: 1–39.

Venuti, Lawrence (1995/2008) *The Translator's Invisibility: A History of Translation*, London and New York: Routledge.

Venuti, Lawrence (1998) *The Scandals of Translation: Towards an Ethics of Difference*, London and New York: Routledge.

9.0 Introduction

Watch the introductory video on the companion website.

Chapter 8 examined varieties of cultural studies that have focused on translation. In this chapter, we concentrate on other research that deals with the position and involvement of the translator and others involved in the translation process. We see how this is manifested in the methods and strategies of their translation practice. Section 9.1 looks at the influential work of Lawrence Venuti, notably the 'invisibility' of translation and the translator in Anglo-American culture (section 9.1.1) and the 'domesticating' and 'foreignizing' translation strategies which are available to the translator (section 9.1.2). Section 9.1.3 considers work by Antoine Berman that follows a similar line. Berman's 'negative analytic' attacking the homogenization of the translation of literary prose.

Section 9.2 focuses on the 'positionality' and ideology of the translator. Section 9.3 introduces recent and increasingly important work on the sociology of translation, and section 9.4 deals with crucial aspects of the powerful translation and publishing industry. Section 9.5 examines the reception of translations, notably the reviewing process, and what this reveals about cultural attitudes to translation in general. The case study illustrates one method of investigating these ideas by analysing the epitextual reviews of a translated text.

9.1 The cultural and political agenda of translation

Like the other cultural theorists discussed in Chapter 8, Venuti insists that the scope of translation studies needs to be broadened to take account of the value-driven nature of the sociocultural framework. Thus he contests Toury's 'scientific'

descriptive model with its aim of producing 'value-free' norms and laws of translation (see Chapter 7):

> Toury's method ... must still turn to cultural theory in order to assess the
> significance of the data, to analyse the norms. Norms may be in the first
> instance linguistic or literary, but they will also include a diverse range of
> domestic values, beliefs, and social representations which carry ideological
> force in serving the interests of specific groups. And they are always housed
> in the social institutions where translations are produced and enlisted in
> cultural and political agendas.
>
> (Venuti 1998: 29)

In addition to governments and other politically motivated institutions, which may
decide to censor or promote certain works (compare Lefevere's discussion of
control factors in section 8.1), the groups and social institutions to which Venuti
refers would include the various players in the publishing industry as a whole.
Above all, these would be the publishers and editors who choose the works and
commission the translations, pay the translators and often dictate the translation
method. They also include the literary agents, marketing and sales teams and
reviewers. The reviewers' comments indicate and to some extent determine how
translations are read and received in the target culture. Each of these players has
a particular position and role within the dominant cultural and political agendas of
their time and place. The translators themselves are part of that culture, which
they can either accept or rebel against.

9.1.1 Venuti and the 'invisibility' of the translator

The Translator's Invisibility (1995/2008) draws on Venuti's own experience as a
translator of experimental Italian poetry and fiction. **Invisibility** is a term he uses
'to describe the translator's situation and activity in contemporary British and
American cultures' (Venuti 2008: 1). Venuti sees this invisibility as typically being
produced:

(1)   by the way translators themselves tend to translate 'fluently' into English, to
      produce an idiomatic and 'readable' TT, thus creating an 'illusion of
      transparency';

(2)   by the way the translated texts are typically read in the target culture:

> A translated text, whether prose or poetry, fiction or nonfiction, is judged acceptable by most publishers, reviewers and readers when it reads fluently, when the absence of any linguistic or stylistic peculiarities makes it seem transparent, giving the appearance that it reflects the foreign writer's personality or intention or the essential meaning of the foreign text – the appearance, in other words, that the translation is not in fact a translation, but the 'original'.
>
> (Venuti 2008: 1)

Venuti (1998: 31) sees the most important factor for this as being 'the prevailing conception of authorship'. Translation is seen as derivative and of secondary quality and importance. Thus, English-language practice since Dryden has been to conceal the act of translation so that, even now, 'translations are rarely considered a form of literary scholarship' (Venuti 1998: 32).

9.1.2 Domestication and foreignization

Venuti discusses invisibility hand in hand with two types of translation: domestication and foreignization. These practices[1] concern both the choice of text to translate and the translation method. Their roots are traced back by Venuti to Schleiermacher and his 1813 essay 'Über die verschiedenen Methoden des Übersetzens' (Schleiermacher 1813/2012, see Chapter 2 of this book). Venuti sees **domestication** as dominating British and American translation culture. Just as the postcolonialists are alert to the cultural effects of the differential in power relations between colony and ex-colony, so Venuti (2008: 15) bemoans the phenomenon of domestication since it involves 'an ethnocentric reduction of the foreign text to receiving cultural values'. This entails translating in a transparent, fluent, 'invisible' style in order to minimize the foreignness of the TT. Venuti allies it with Schleiermacher's description of translation that 'leaves the reader in peace, as much as possible, and moves the author toward him'. Domestication further covers adherence to domestic literary canons by carefully selecting the texts that are likely to lend themselves to such a translation strategy (Venuti 1998: 241).

On the other hand, **foreignization** 'entails choosing a foreign text and developing a translation method along lines which are excluded by dominant cultural values in the target language' (ibid.: 242). It is the preferred choice of Schleiermacher, whose description is of a translation strategy where 'the translator leaves the writer in peace, as much as possible and moves the reader toward [the writer]' (Schleiermacher 1813/2012: 49). Venuti (2008: 15–16) follows this and considers foreignizing practices to be a 'highly desirable . . . strategic cultural intervention' which seek to 'send the reader abroad' by making the receiving culture aware of the linguistic and cultural difference inherent in the foreign text. This is to be achieved by a non-fluent, estranging or heterogeneous translation style designed to make visible the presence of the translator and to highlight the foreign identity of the ST. This is a way, Venuti says, to counter the unequal and 'violently' domesticating cultural values of the English-language world.

In *The Scandals of Translation*, Venuti links foreignization to **'minoritizing'** translation. One of the examples he gives of a minoritizing project is his own translation of works by the nineteenth-century Italian novelist Iginio Ugo Tarchetti (1839–1869) (Venuti 1998: 13–20). The very choice of works to translate is minoritizing: Tarchetti was a minor writer, a Milanese bohemian who confronted the literary establishment by using the standard Tuscan dialect to write experimental and Gothic novels that challenged the moral and political values of the day. As far as the language is concerned, the minoritizing or foreignizing practice of Venuti's translation comes through in the deliberate inclusion of foreignizing elements such as modern American slang. These aim to make the translator 'visible' and to make the readers realize they are reading a translation of a work from a foreign culture. Venuti (ibid.: 15) gives the extract shown in Box 9.1 as an example of what he means by this approach.

Box 9.1

Nel 1855, domiciliatomi a Pavia, m'era allo studio del disegno in una scuola privata di quella città; e dopo alcuni mesi di soggiorno aveva stretto relazione con certo Federico M. che era professore di patologia e di clinica per l'insegnamento universitario, e che morì di apoplessia fulminante pochi mesi dopo che lo aveva conosciuto. Era un uomo amantissimo delle scienze, della sua in particolare – aveva virtù e doti di mente non comuni – senonche, come tutti gli anatomisti ed i clinici in genere, era scettico profondamente e inguaribilmente – lo era per convinzione, ne io potei mai indurlo alle mie credenze, per quanto mi vi adoprassi nelle discussioni appassionate e calorose che avevamo ogni giorno a questo riguardo.

In 1855, having taken up residence at Pavia, I devoted myself to the study of drawing at a private school in that city; and several months into my sojourn, I developed a close friendship with a certain Federico M., a professor of pathology and clinical medicine who taught at the university and died of severe apoplexy a few months after I became acquainted with him. He was very fond of the sciences and of his own in particular – he was gifted with extraordinary mental powers – except that, like all anatomists and doctors generally, he was profoundly and incurably skeptical. He was so by conviction, nor could I ever induce him to accept my beliefs, no matter how much I endeavored in the impassioned, heated discussions we had every day on this point.[2]

(Venuti 1998: 15)

Among the elements of this extract which Venuti considers to be distinctive of **foreignization** are the close adherence to the ST structure and syntax (e.g. the adjunct positions in the first sentence), the calques *soggiorno* as *sojourn*, *indurlo* as *induce him* and the archaic structure *nor could I ever* instead of *and I could never*.

9.1 Exploration: Foreignization

Look at the extract in Box 9.1 and identify more foreignizing features in the English TT.

In other passages (see ibid.: 16–17), Venuti juxtaposes both archaisms (e.g. *scapegrace*) and modern colloquialisms (e.g. *con artist, funk*), and uses British spellings (e.g. *demeanour, offence*) to jar the reader with a 'heterogeneous discourse'. Venuti is happy to note (ibid.: 15) that some of the reviews of the translation were appreciative of this 'visibility'. However, other reviews attacked the translation for not following what, in Venuti's terms, would be a fluent translation practice.

Importantly, domestication and foreignization are considered to be not binary opposites but part of a continuum, and they relate to **ethical choices** made by the translator in order to expand the receiving culture's range:

The terms 'domestication' and 'foreignization' indicate fundamentally *ethical* attitudes towards a foreign text and culture, ethical effects produced by the choice of a text for translation and by the strategy devised to translate it, whereas the terms like 'fluency' and 'resistancy' indicate fundamentally *discursive* features of translation strategies in relation to the reader's cognitive processing.

(Venuti 2008: 19)

This relationship, operating on different levels, might be depicted as follows (Figure 9.1):

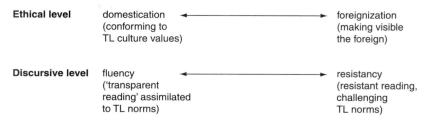

Figure 9.1   Domestication and foreignization: ethical and discursive levels

Although Venuti advocates foreignizing translation in this book, he is also aware of some of its contradictions. It is a subjective and relative term that still involves a degree of domestication since it translates a ST for a receiving culture. Indeed, foreignization depends on the dominant values of the receiving culture because it becomes visible precisely when it departs from those values. However, Venuti stoutly defends foreignizing translations. They 'are equally partial [as are domesticating translations] in their interpretation of the foreign text, but they tend to flaunt their partiality instead of concealing it' (2008: 28). In addition, Venuti (ibid.: 19) emphasizes the 'culturally variable and historically contingent' nature of the domestication and foreignization. Just as we saw with the discussion of descriptive studies (Chapter 7), the values associated with these terms, reconstructed from close textual analysis or archival research, vary according to external sociocultural and historical factors.

Venuti's general premises about foreignizing and domesticating translation practices, and about the invisibility of the translator and the relative power of the publisher and the translator, can be investigated in a variety of ways by:

- comparing ST and TT linguistically for signs of foreignizing and domesticating practices;
- interviewing the translators about their strategies and/or researching what the translators say they are doing, their correspondence with the authors and the different drafts of a translation if available;
- interviewing the publishers, editors and agents to see what their aims are in publishing translations, how they choose which books to translate and what instructions they give to translators;
- looking at how many books are translated and sold, which ones are chosen and into which languages, and how trends vary over time;
- looking at the kind of translation contracts that are made and how 'visible' the translator is in the final product;
- seeing how literally 'visible' the fact of translation is, looking at the packaging of the text, the appearance or otherwise of the translator's name on the title page, the copyright assignation, translators' prefaces, correspondence, etc.;
- analysing the reviews of a translation, author or period. The aim would be to see what mentions are made of the translators (are they 'visible'?) and by what criteria reviewers (and the literary 'élite') judge translations at a given time and in a given culture.

9.2 Exploration

See the ITS website for further discussion of Venuti's work on invisibility.

9.1.3 Antoine Berman: the 'negative analytic' of translation

Questions of how much a translation assimilates a foreign text and how far it signals difference had already attracted the attention of the noted French theorist, the late Antoine Berman (1942–1991). Berman's *L'épreuve de l'étranger: Culture et traduction dans l'Allemagne romantique* (1984), translated into English as *The Experience of the Foreign: Culture and Translation in Romantic Germany* (1992), preceded and influenced Venuti. The latter himself produced an English translation of the prominent article 'La traduction comme épreuve de l'étranger' (Berman 1985), in English entitled 'Translation and the trials of the foreign' (Berman 1985b/2012). In it, Berman (ibid.: 240) describes translation as an *épreuve* ('experience'/'trial') in two senses:

(1)   for the target culture in experiencing the strangeness of the foreign text and word;
(2)   for the foreign text in being uprooted from its original language context.

Berman deplores the general tendency to negate the foreign in translation by the translation strategy of 'naturalization', which would equate with Venuti's later 'domestication'. 'The properly ethical aim of the translating act', says Berman (ibid.: 241), is 'receiving the Foreign as Foreign', which would seem to have influenced Venuti's 'foreignizing' translation strategy at the time. However, Berman considers that there is generally a 'system of textual deformation' in TTs that prevents the foreign from coming through. His examination of the forms of deformation is termed **'negative analytic'**:

> The negative analytic is primarily concerned with ethnocentric, annexationist translations and hypertextual translations (pastiche, imitation, adaptation, free writing), where the play of deforming forces is freely exercised.
>
> (Berman 1985b/2012: 242)

Berman, who translated Latin American fiction and German philosophy, sees every translator as being inevitably and inherently exposed to these ethnocentric forces, which determine the 'desire to translate' as well as the form of the TT. He feels that it is only by psychoanalytic analysis of the translator's work, and by making the translator aware of the forces at work, that such tendencies can be neutralized. His main attention is centred on the translation of fiction:

> The principal problem of translating the novel is to respect its shapeless polylogic and avoid an arbitrary homogenization.
>
> (Berman 1985b/2012: 243)

By this, Berman is referring to the linguistic variety and creativity of the novel and the way translation tends to reduce variation. He identifies twelve **'deforming tendencies'** (ibid.: 244), listed below:

(1)   **Rationalization:** This mainly entails the modification of syntactic structures including punctuation and sentence structure and order. An example

would be translations of Dostoevsky which remove some of the repetition and simplify complex sentence structures. Berman also refers to the abstractness of rationalization and the tendency to generalization.

(2) **Clarification:** This includes explicitation (compare section 4.1.2), which 'aims to render "clear" what does not wish to be clear in the original' (ibid.: 245).

(3) **Expansion:** Like other theorists (for example, Vinay and Darbelnet, see Chapter 4), Berman says that TTs tend to be longer than STs. This is due to 'empty' explicitation that unshapes its rhythm, to 'overtranslation' and to 'flattening'. These additions only serve to reduce the clarity of the work's 'voice'.

(4) **Ennoblement:** This refers to the tendency on the part of certain translators to 'improve' on the original by rewriting it in a more elegant style. The result, according to Berman (ibid.: 246), is an annihilation of the oral rhetoric and formless polylogic of the ST. Equally destructive is the opposite – a TT that is too 'popular' in its use of colloquialisms.

(5) **Qualitative impoverishment:** This is the replacement of words and expressions with TT equivalents 'that lack their sonorous richness or, correspondingly, their signifying or "iconic" features' (ibid.: 247). By 'iconic', Berman means terms whose form and sound are in some way associated with their sense. An example he gives is the word *butterfly* and its corresponding terms in other languages.

(6) **Quantitative impoverishment:** This is loss of lexical variation in translation. Berman gives the example of a Spanish ST that uses three different synonyms for *face* (*semblante, rostro and cara*); rendering them all as *face* would involve loss.

(7) **The destruction of rhythms:** Although more common in poetry, rhythm is still important to the novel and can be 'destroyed' by deformation of word order and punctuation.

(8) **The destruction of underlying networks of signification:** The translator needs to be aware of the network of words that is formed throughout the text. Individually, these words may not be significant, but they add an underlying uniformity and sense to the text. Examples are augmentative suffixes in a Latin American text – *jaulón* ('large cage'), *portón* ('large door', etc.).

(9) **The destruction of linguistic patternings:** While the ST may be systematic in its sentence constructions and patternings, translation tends to be 'asystematic' (ibid.: 249). The translator often adopts a range of techniques,

such as rationalization, clarification and expansion, all of which standardize the TT. This is actually a form of incoherence since standardization destroys the linguistic patterns and variations of the original.

(10) **The destruction of vernacular networks or their exoticization:** This relates especially to local speech and language patterns which play an important role in establishing the setting of a novel. Examples would include the use of diminutives in Spanish, Portuguese, German and Russian or of Australian English terms and cultural items (*outback, bush, dingo, wombat*). There is severe loss if these are erased, yet the traditional solution of exoticizing some of these terms by, for example, placing them in italics, isolates them from the co-text. Alternatively, seeking a TL vernacular or slang equivalent to the SL is a ridiculous exoticization of the foreign. Such would be the case if an Australian farmer were made to speak Bavarian in a German translation (compare also the case study of translation from Punjabi in Chapter 8).

(11) **The destruction of expressions and idioms:** Berman considers the replacement of an idiom or proverb by its TL 'equivalent' to be an 'ethnocentrism': 'to play with "equivalence" is to attack the discourse of the foreign work', he says (ibid.: 251). Thus, an English idiom from Joseph Conrad containing the name of the well-known London mental health hospital *Bedlam*,[3] should not be translated by *Charenton*, a similar French institution, since this would result in a TT that produces a new network of French cultural references.

(12) **The effacement of the superimposition of languages:** By this, Berman means the way translation tends to erase traces of different forms of language that co-exist in the ST. These may be the mix of American English and varieties of Latin American Spanish in the work of new Latino/a writers, the blends of Anglo-Indian writing, the proliferation of language influences in Joyce's *Finnegan's Wake*, different sociolects and idiolects, and so on. Berman (ibid.: 251) considers this to be the 'central problem' in the translation of novels.

Counterbalancing the 'universals' of this negative analytic is Berman's **'positive analytic'**, his proposal for the type of translation required to render the foreign in the TT. This he calls **'literal translation'**:

Here 'literal' means: attached to the letter (of works). Labor on the letter in translation, on the one hand, restores the particular signifying process of works (which is more than their meaning) and, on the other hand, transforms the translating language.

(Berman 1985b/2012: 252–3)

Berman's term is markedly different and more specific compared to the conventional use of 'literal translation' discussed in Chapter 2; his use of 'literal' and 'letter' and his reference to the 'signifying process' point to a Saussurean perspective and to a positive transformation of the TL. How exactly this is to be done, however, depends on the creativity and innovation of the translator in his search for truth. This is pursued in Berman's posthumous work (1995), published in English in Françoise Massardier-Kenney's translation as *Toward a Translation Criticism* (Berman 2009).

9.3 Exploration: Negative analytic

The article by Marilyn Booth (2008) on the ITS website discusses the ethical issues behind the domesticating translation of the *Girls of Riyadh* novel by Egyptian author Alaa al-Aswany. Note what could be called forms of 'negative analytic'.

Berman's work is important in linking philosophical ideas to translation strategies with many examples drawn from existing translations. His discussion of the **ethics of translation** as witnessed in linguistic 'deformation' of TTs is of especial relevance and a notable counterpoint to earlier writing on literary translation. But ethics also encompasses the context of translation and those professionals (translators, publishers, reviewers ...) whom Lefevere described (see section 8.1). The following sections consider various aspects of the sociocultural context, including observations that come from the participants themselves, beginning with the translators.

9.2 The position and positionality of the translator

Toury (2012: 88; see also this volume, Chapter 7) warns that explicit comments from participants in the translation process need to be treated with circumspection since they may be biased. However, more recent work in translation studies has given greater value to such comments. At best they are a significant indication of the subject's working practices; at worst they still reveal what a subject feels he/she ought to be doing. This section limits itself to English-language translators of Latin American fiction, but the ideas and arguments that are presented are representative of the writing of many other translators.

Venuti's 'call to action' (2008: 265–77), for translators to adopt 'visible' and 'foreignizing' practices, is perhaps a reaction to those contemporary translators who seem to debate their work along lines appropriate to the age-old and vague terms which we discussed in Chapter 2 – for example, Gregory Rabassa (2005) discusses the relative exigencies of 'accuracy' and 'flow' in literary translation. Translators also often consider that their work is intuitive, that they must be 'led' by language and listen to their **'ear'** (Rabassa 1984: 35, Felstiner 1980: 81, Grossman 2010: 10). In similar vein, Margaret Sayers Peden, the translator of Latin American authors Sábato, Fuentes, Allende and Esquivel, listens to the **'voice'** of the ST. She defines this as 'the way something is communicated: the way the tale is told; the way the poem is sung' and it determines 'all choices of cadence and tone and lexicon and syntax' (1987: 9). John Felstiner, who translated Pablo Neruda's classic poem about Machu Picchu, went as far as to listen to Neruda reading his poems so as to see the stresses and the emphases (Felstiner 1980: 51). In her American retranslation of the classic *Don Quixote*, Gabriel García Márquez's translator Edith Grossman also declares that 'the essential challenge of translation [is] hearing, in the most profound way I can, the text in Spanish and discovering the voice to say (I mean, to write) the text again in English' (Grossman 2003/2005: xix).

The 'invisibility' of translators has been such that relatively few of them have written in detail about their practice. However, this has changed more recently with the publication of Norman Thomas di Giovanni's (2003) account of his collaboration with Borges, of Grossman's (2010) volume *Why Translation Matters* and of the memoirs of perhaps the most celebrated translator of all, Gregory Rabassa (2005), not to mention translator blogs and online interviews with translators. Two other full-length works of import by contemporary literary translators of Latin American Spanish are Felstiner's *Translating Neruda: The Way to Machu Picchu* (1980) and Levine's *The Subversive Scribe: Translating Latin American Fiction* (1991). Felstiner (1980: 1) makes the important point that much of the work that goes into producing a translation 'becomes invisible once the new poem stands intact'. This includes the translator's own background and research as well as the process of composition. Felstiner describes his immersion in the work and culture of the ST author, including visits to Machu Picchu itself and his reading of Neruda's poem in that environment. However, he still uses age-old terms to describe 'the twofold requirement of translation', namely, 'the original must come through essentially, in language that itself rings true' (Felstiner 1980: 24). Phrases such as *come through essentially* and *ring true* are typical of the approaches of early translation theory discussed in Chapter 2 and suggest that there is a mystique about the 'art' of translation.

On the other hand, Levine sees herself (1991: xi) as a 'translator–collaborator' with the Cuban author Cabrera Infante, and as a 'subversive scribe', 'destroying' the form of the original but reproducing the meaning in a new form (ibid.: 7). Levine sometimes creates a completely different passage in translation in order to give free rein to the English language's propensity to punning, surprising the reader with a mixture of the Latin American and the Anglo-Saxon. One example, from Cabrera Infante's *Tres tristes tigres*, is the translation of the first line of the song Guantanamera ('Yo soy un hombre sincero') as 'I'm a man without a zero', playing on the sound of the words (*sincero* meaning 'sincere', but phonetically identical to *sin cero*, meaning 'without a zero') (ibid.: 15). Levine also (ibid.: 23) invents humorous names of books and authors (such as *I. P. Daley's Yellow River* and *Off the Cliff by (H)ugo First*) to replace a list in the Spanish ST. This would appear to be a very domesticating approach, altering whole passages to filter out the foreign and to fit in with the target culture expectations. Yet the 'jarring' linguistic result in English, juxtaposed to a Latin American context, goes some way to creating what would be a 'foreignizing' reading. For Levine, adopting a feminist and poststructuralist view of the translator's work, the language of translation also plays an ideological role:

> A translation should be a critical act . . . creating doubt, posing questions to the reader, recontextualising the ideology of the original text.
>
> (Levine 1991: 3)

The stance and **positionality** of the translator have become much more central in translation studies. Chapter 8 described some of the forms in which translation is manipulated by the ideology of the sociocultural context. Such an ideological effect has its counterpart in the stance of the translator him or herself. Maria Tymoczko, in an article entitled 'Ideology and the position of the translator: In what sense is a translator "in between"?', echoing Homi Bhabha's 'third space' (see Chapter 8), takes issue with those who see the translator as a neutral mediator in the act of communication:

[T]he ideology of a translation resides not simply in the text translated, but in the voicing and stance of the translator, and in the relevance to the receiving audience. These latter features are affected by the place of enunciation of the translator: indeed they are part of what we mean by the 'place' of enunciation, for that 'place' is an **ideological positioning** as well as a geographical or temporal one. These aspects of a translation are motivated and determined by the translator's cultural and ideological affiliations as much as or even more than by the temporal and spatial location that the translator speaks from.

(Tymoczko 2003: 183)

Tymoczko (ibid.: 199) rejects the 'Romantic' and 'élitest' western notion of uncommitted, individual translators working away on their own and concludes (ibid.: 201) that 'effective calls for translators to act as ethical agents of social change must intersect with models of engagement and collective action'. Carol Maier (2007), herself both translator of Latin American literature and a translation studies theorist, names this positioning 'intervenience' and the translator **'an intervenient being'**. That this extends beyond the literary to include technical, volunteer and other forms of translation is also evident from the volume devoted to **translator activism**, co-edited by Boéri and Maier (2010), part of what Wolf (2012) sees as the 'activist turn' in sociological approaches to translation.

9.4 Exploration: The translator's turn

Two areas where the role of the translator has become visible are in the study of translator drafts (e.g. Munday 2013, 2014) and the translator as a character in fiction (e.g. Kaindl and Spitzl 2014).

9.3 The sociology and historiography of translation

Since the turn of the millennium, the study of translators and the social nature of translation have become centre stage in translation studies research. This includes the dramatic increase in works of translation historiography, as we suggested in Chapter 2, but most strikingly encompasses the simultaneous development of a 'sociology' of translation (cf. Pym 2006, Wolf and Fukari 2007, Heilbron and Sapiro 2007, Milton and Bandia 2009, Vorderobermeier 2014, Angelelli 2014, Tyulenev 2014).

Many studies have drawn on the work of French ethnographer and sociologist **Pierre Bourdieu** (1977, 1991) and his concepts of:

- **field** of social activity, which is the site of a power struggle between participants or agents − for us, this field is translation and the participants potentially include the author, commissioner, publisher, editor, translator, and reader;
- **habitus**, which is the broad social, identitary and cognitive make-up or **'disposition'** of the individual, which is heavily influenced by family and education; habitus is particularly linked to field and to cultural capital and has been central to recent sociological work in translation studies (see below);[4]
- the different types of **capital** which an individual may acquire or be given − these comprise the more tangible **economic capital** (money and other material assets) and the more intangible: **social capital** (such as networks of contacts), **cultural capital** (education, knowledge) and **symbolic capital** (status); and
- **illusio**, which may be understood as the cultural limits of awareness.

Bourdieu's work has been adopted by some scholars as a less deterministic alternative to the polysystem framework (see Chapter 7), especially as a means of theorizing the role of the translator, which seemed worryingly absent from earlier theories. An early but still seminal article in this vein is by the late Daniel Simeoni (1948–2007). In 'The pivotal status of the translator's habitus' (Simeoni 1998), he overtly seeks a better conceptualization of what drives the translator's disposition and decision-making and how this comes to be. Simeoni stresses that the study of the **'translatorial habitus'** complements and improves on Toury's norm-based descriptive translation studies (see Chapter 7) by focusing on how the translator's own behaviour and agency contribute to the establishment of norms. In his study of the modern-day translator, Simeoni rather depressingly concludes that translation is a poorly structured activity where 'most translating agents exert their activity in fields where their degree of control is nil or negligible' (ibid.: 14) and that their habitus is generally one of **'voluntary servitude'**.

In her introduction to the special issue of *The Translator* devoted to Bourdieusian concepts, Inghilleri (2005b) more positively considers that research employing Bourdieu's theorization can help us understand how translators and interpreters are 'both implicated in and able to transform the forms of practice in which they engage'. Jean-Marc Gouanvic's work is important in this context. His monograph *Sociologie de la traduction* (Gouanvic 1999, 'Sociology of translation') examines French translations of American science-fiction, and his article in the Inghilleri collection (Gouanvic 2005) investigates the habitus of three major French translators of American literature, Maurice-Edgar Coindreau, Marcel Duhamel and Boris Vian. Here, the **habitus** as an integral part of the individual translator's history, education and experiences is emphasized:

> the **habitus**, which is the generative principle of responses more or less well adapted to the demands of a certain field, is the product of an individual history, but also, through the formative experiences of earliest infancy, of the whole collective history of family and class.
>
> (Bourdieu 1991: 91, in Gouanvic 2005: 158–9)

Although Gouanvic claims that lexical and prosodic choices revealing the 'voice' of the translator are 'not a conscious strategic choice but an effect of his or her specific habitus, as acquired in the target literary field' (ibid.: 158), the relation between these choices in the text and the translator's 'disposition' is far from evident. What exactly causes a translator to act in a given way in a given situation, and why does one translator act differently from another?

Sociology was the main 'new perspective' in translation studies treated in Ferreira Duarte et al. (2006). Andrew Chesterman's paper, 'Questions in the sociology of translation', stresses that the importance of this approach lies in emphasizing **translation practice**, how the translator, and other agents, act as they carry out their tasks in the translation process or 'event' and what the interrelation is between these agents – what Pym (2006: 4) terms 'causation'. As well as specific questions, Chesterman briefly describes the application of Bruno Latour's **actor-network theory**. Buzelin (2005: 215) sees the advantages of this, analysing the roles of each agent, participant or mediator in the network and 'provid[ing] solid bases for testing interpretative hypotheses relating to the nature of the translation process'. In translation studies, the theory has been applied to the translation of poetry (Jones 2011) amongst others. A third approach draws on the social systems work of German sociologist Niklas Luhmann and features strongly in the work of Hermans (2007) and Tyulenev (2012). In contrast to Latour, Luhmann views society as a complex of closed **functional systems** that operate beyond the immediate influence of humans.

9.5 Exploration: Sociological models

Read Inghilleri (2009), available through the ITS website, for a summary of the three approaches (Bourdieu, Latour, Luhmann) presented here.

9.4 The power network of the translation industry

In presenting their 'Outline for a sociology of translation', Heilbron and Sapiro (2007: 95) assert the elements that must be covered by this approach: 'firstly, the structure of the field of international cultural exchanges: secondly, the type of constraints – political and economic – that influenced these exchanges; and thirdly, the agents of intermediation and the processes of importing and receiving in the recipient country'.

As far as the economics is concerned, the translator's lot may be miserable. Venuti (1992: 1–3, 1998: 31–66) has already described and lamented how the literary translator works from contract to contract often for a usually modest flat fee, with the publishers (rather than translators) initiating most translations and generally seeking to minimize the translation cost. Publishers, as Venuti shows, are very often reluctant to grant copyright or a share of the royalties to the translator. Venuti deplores this as another form of repression exercised by the publishing industry, but it is a repression that is far from uncommon because of the weakness of the translator's role in the network. Fawcett (1995: 189) describes this complex network as amounting to a **'power play'**, with the final product considerably shaped by editors and copy-editors. This most often results in a domesticating translation. Interviews with publishers confirm that it is often the case that the editor is not fluent in the foreign language and that the main concern is that the translation should 'read well' in the TL (Munday 2008).

In some cases, the power play may result in the ST author's omission from the translation process altogether: Kuhiwczak (1990) reports the dramatic fate of Milan Kundera's *The Joke*, whose first English translator and editor, working jointly, decided to unravel the ST's intentionally distorted chronology in an attempt to clarify the story for the readers. Kundera was sufficiently shocked and used his dominant position to demand a new translation. Venuti (1998: 6) questions Kundera's role, including the use of the previous translator's work without acknowledgement, claiming that 'Kundera doesn't want to recognize the linguistic and cultural differences that a translation must negotiate'. Such conflict of course does not normally materialize when the author is long dead, or unknown, as is the case for Stephen Mitchell's new poetic 'version' of the Mesopotamian epic *Gilgamesh*. In the preface, Mitchell openly recognizes his omission of what he calls 'some of the quirks of Akkadian style', such as repetitions and enumerations. He also adds links between passages as well as occasionally altering their order to create what he defends as a more coherent poem 'faithful to the original Akkadian text' (Mitchell 2005: 66).

There is a range of other **agents** playing key roles in the preparation, dissemination and fashioning of translations. These include commissioners, mediators, literary agents, text producers, translators, revisers and editors. The volume edited by Milton and Bandia (2009) provides detailed examples of such cultural **'gate-keepers'**, to use Bourdieu's term, whose work has been innovative either stylistically or politically. In similar vein, Haddadian-Moghaddam's book on literary translation in modern Iran presents an innovative, three-tier model for the study of agency at the levels of decision-making, motivation and contextual constraints (2014: 27).

For many authors writing in other languages, the benchmark of success is to be translated into English. In fact, the decision whether or not to translate a work is the greatest power wielded by the editor and publisher. According to Venuti (1998: 48), publishers in the UK and USA tend to choose works that are easily assimilated into the target culture. The percentage of books translated in both countries is extremely low, comprising only between two and four per cent of the total number of books published (Venuti 2008: 11). On the other hand, not only is the percentage of books translated in many other countries much higher, but the majority of those translations are also from English (ibid.). Venuti sees the imbalance as yet another example of the cultural hegemony of British and American publishing and culture. It is very insular and refuses to accept the foreign yet is happy for its own works to maintain a strong hold in other countries. Venuti had expressed this in damning terms in the introduction to *Rethinking Translation: Discourse, Subjectivity, Ideology*:

> It can be said that Anglo-American publishing has been instrumental in producing readers who are aggressively monolingual and culturally parochial while reaping the economic benefits of successfully imposing Anglo-American cultural values on a sizeable foreign readership.
>
> (Venuti 1992: 6)

9.6 Exploration: Translation flows and statistics

'Translation flows', the number of books translated into and out of a language, are indicators of the direction of cultural exchange (see Casanova 2002/2010, Heilbron 1999/2010). Read the reports on the European literary translation sector available online (http://www.ceatl.eu/current-situation/translation-statistics). How far do these statistics support the claims made by Venuti? Look for similar statistics regarding your own languages.

9.5 The reception and reviewing of translations

The link between the workings of the publishing industry and the reception of a given translation is clearly made in Meg Brown's in-depth study of Latin American novels published in West Germany in the 1980s. She stresses (Brown 1994: 58) the role of reviews in informing the public about recently published books and in preparing the readership for the work. Brown adopts ideas from **reception theory**, including examining the way a work conforms to, challenges or disappoints the readers' aesthetic **'horizon of expectation'**. This is a term employed by Jauss (1982: 24) to refer to readers' general expectations (of the style, form, content, etc.) of the genre or series to which the new work belongs.

One way of examining the reception is by looking at the reviews of a work, since they represent a 'body of reactions' to the author and the text (Brown 1994: 7) and form part of the sub-area of translation criticism in Holmes's 'map' (see Chapter 1). Reviews are also a useful source of information concerning that culture's view of translation itself, as we saw in section 9.1.2, where Venuti (1998: 18–20) uses literary reviews as a means of assessing the reception of his foreignizing translation of Tarchetti. Venuti quotes reviews that criticize the translation specifically because of its 'jarring' effect. This links in with Venuti's observations (2008: 2–3) that most English-language reviews prefer 'fluent' translations written in modern, general, standard English that is 'natural' and 'idiomatic'.

Venuti considers such a concentration on fluency and the lack of discussion of translation as prime indicators of the relegation of the translator's role to the point of 'invisibility'. The TT is normally read as if the work had originally been written in the TL, the translator's contribution being almost completely overlooked. There are several reasons for the lack of focus in reviews on the process of translation. One of these, noted by the American reviewer Robert Coover (in Ronald Christ 1982: 17), is that 'whenever cuts are requested by the publishers of a review, the first to go are usually the remarks about the translation'. Many reviewers are also not able to compare the ST with the TT (ibid.: 21) and restrict themselves to often critical comments on individual words. Ronald Christ's article is one of the few relatively detailed discussions of issues related to translation reviews. Another, by Carol Maier (1990), looks at reviews of Latin American literature in general. Maier goes a step further by noting how North American reviewers diminish the foreignness of a translation 'by focusing almost exclusively on [its] potential role in English, comparing it to "similar" works in North American literature and evaluating the ease with which it can be read' (ibid.: 19). She sees translation reviewing as being 'largely undeveloped' (ibid.: 20) and makes a series of suggestions, among which is the need 'to incorporate the contributions of translation theory and translation criticism into the practice of reviewing'.

There is no set model for the analysis of reviews in translation, although the whole gamut of **paratexts** (devices appended to the text) is the subject of the cultural theorist Gérard Genette's *Paratexts* (1997).[5] Genette considers two kinds of paratextual elements: (1) **peritexts**; and (2) **epitexts**.

(1)   **Peritexts** appear in the same location as the text and are provided by the author or publisher. Examples given by Genette (ibid.: 12) are titles, subtitles, pseudonyms, forewords, dedications, prefaces, epilogues and framing elements such as the cover and blurb.

(2)   An **epitext** 'is any paratextual element not materially appended to the text within the same volume but circulating, as it were, freely, in a virtually limitless physical and social space' (ibid.: 344). Examples are marketing and promotional material, which may be provided by the publisher, correspondence on the text by the author, and also reviews and academic and critical discourse on the author and text which are written by others. The paratext is 'subordinate' to the text (ibid.: 12) but it is crucial in guiding the reading process. For example, a reader who first encounters a review of a book will approach the text itself with certain preconceptions based on that epitext. If we additionally adopt the analytical approach of reception theory (Jauss 1982), we can analyse reviews **synchronically** or **diachronically**. An example of a synchronic analysis would be an examination of a range of reviews of a single work; examples of a diachronic analysis would be an examination of reviews of books of an author or newspaper over a longer time period.

9.7 Exploration: Reception

Read the article, available through the ITS website, on reviews of the work of Roberto Bolaño by Esperança Bielsa (2013). Note the different peritextual and epitextual elements discussed and how Bolaño's image differs in Spain and the UK.

Case study

This case study investigates many of the areas discussed in this chapter by focusing on the epitexts and peritexts of a single book in English translation. This is a collection of short stories (*Doce cuentos peregrinos*) by the Colombian Nobel Prize winner García Márquez (1927–2014) which was published in Spanish by Mondadori España (Madrid) and Oveja Negra (Bogotá) in 1992. Its English translation, *Strange Pilgrims*, by Edith Grossman, appeared in hardback in 1993, published by Alfred Knopf (New York) and Jonathan Cape (London), both imprints of Random House. Pertinent research questions in this case study are:

- How 'visible' is the translator in the reviews?
- How is the translation judged by English-language reviewers?
- Do their comments suggest that García Márquez's success is due to what Venuti might term 'ethnocentric domestication' and 'violence'?

Reviews of the translation show a marked difference in the reception in the USA and in the UK. In the USA, reviews adopt an adulatory tone. In some instances, they might have been motivated by a self-interest in promoting the book. Thus, an advance review in the publishing industry's *Booklist*[6] raves that 'every story here is marvelous'. The daily and weekly press are similarly enthusiastic: *Time Magazine*[7] sees 'the enchanting density of García Márquez at his best'; *The New York Review of Books*[8] considers most of the stories to be 'undoubted masterpieces'.

The book is almost overlooked as a work of translation, and this supports Venuti's claim about the invisibility of translators. *Booklist, The Atlantic Monthly*[9] and *Time* give no mention that the book has even been translated. *The New York Review of Books* includes a short accolade: 'the quality of the tales is greatly enhanced by Edith Grossman's admirable translation'. This last review is more detailed and incorporates a summary of García Márquez's standing. It also makes an attempt to analyse his style and it is here that the crucial point that it is a translation is most glaringly absent. The example selected by the reviewer (Bayley) as 'a characteristic Márquez sentence' is the first sentence from the story 'Miss Forbes's summer of happiness': 'When we came back to the house in the afternoon, we found an enormous sea serpent nailed by the neck to the door frame.' This is not, in fact, a complete Márquez sentence at all, since the longer ST sentence had been divided by the translator and the circumstantial adjuncts reordered. The reviewer's reaction to this sentence is a clear indication that, while the translator's identity may be obscured, her words are definitely interpreted as the ST author's own.

Bayley also endeavours to incorporate García Márquez into the accepted literary culture of the European and US world, comparing his 'sense of detail' to Kafka and to Kundera, 'which suggests not only that magic realism has spread throughout Europe, but that something very like it was, or has become, a part of the literary spirit of our age, in Europe and America'. The suggestion is that García Márquez and the Latin Americans have had a recent profound influence on Europe and the USA, but that magic realism may have been at the core of the contemporary 'literary spirit', rendering Latin America's contribution less vital.

An appropriation of Latin America's success can also be seen in one peritextual feature – the cover of the US Penguin paperback. The predictably upbeat blurb on the back cover ends with the following conclusion: 'Strange Pilgrims is a triumph of narrative sorcery by one of our foremost magicians of the written word.' The choice of the possessive pronoun shows that García Márquez's nationality and identity have been subsumed into the *our* of general literary heritage. The passivity of Latin America is also suggested by the theme of the stories, summarized as 'Latin American characters adrift in Europe'. The cover for the British paperback edition, on the other hand, makes the characters more active: 'the surreal haunting "journeys" of Latin Americans in Europe'.

British reviews of the translation were not as adulatory as those in the US. In the *Times Literary Supplement*,[10] García Márquez is criticized for 'crowd-pleasing' since 'these are for the most part facile stories, too easy on the mind, soft-centred and poorly focused'. *The Independent*[11] considers them on the whole as 'slight', 'laboured', 'portentous' and 'disappointing'.

Janette Turner Hospital, the reviewer in *The Independent*, launches an attack on both the author, for his 'leaden prose', and on the translator, for 'occasional ambiguous welters of pronouns'. The immediate question is how qualified the reviewer is to make such judgements about language. She talks about the 'metaphor and off-kilter lyricism of the novels', presumably referring to the English of the translations she has read. The 'off-kilter lyricism' may also suggest that the reviewer herself has a stereotype of García Márquez the magic realist and is disappointed not to find this in *Strange Pilgrims*. Her horizon of expectation has been disappointed. The criticism of the ambiguous pronouns appears rather strange since the effect of the pronouns is to increase cohesion and to avoid potential ambiguity. This is a further indication that translator and reviewer are on different wavelengths in a 'discussion' which the translator can hardly win.

The reviews show that the translator's role, while not 'invisible', is rarely highlighted. The generally brief, superficial comments on the translator mirror the observations of Christ and Maier and the examples quoted by Venuti. The translation is indeed mostly read as if it had originally been written in English (compare the recommendations for good translation given by translators such as Dryden in Chapter 2). This impression is fostered by other epitexts, notably the sales pitch of the book, which seek to guide the reception in English. There is also a strong hint that García Márquez's whole image, as well as his language, may have undergone some form of cultural appropriation or domestication, especially in the US context.

Discussion of the case study

The case study looked at one area of the sociocultural systems around the translator. It has shown that a study of a wide range of reviews is both reasonably straightforward methodologically and informative about one literary 'élite's' reaction to translation. Venuti's comments about the invisibility of the translator and about the cultural hegemony of the British and American publishing world seem to be borne out in the study. However, this kind of study needs to be developed, incorporating other ideas described in the last two chapters. Thus, close analysis of the ST and TT would tell more about the translation strategy adopted by Edith Grossman. The publishers and other players can be interviewed and the results of the study compared with reviews of other books. Finally, the reception of a text is also obviously much wider than that of reviewers, encompassing a wide range of readers in a variety of different institutions and cultural settings. Moreover, as we saw in the last chapter, the cultural aspect of translation goes far beyond an analysis of the literary reception of a text and is entangled in an intricate web of political and ideological relations.

Summary

This chapter has focused on the role of the (mainly literary) translator. The key term in the first part of the chapter has been Venuti's 'invisibility'. This refers to how, in Anglo-American cultures, the foreign is made invisible both by publishing strategies and by the preference for a 'fluent' TT that erases traces of the foreign. Venuti discusses two strategies, 'domesticating' and 'foreignizing', favouring the latter in a policy of 'resistance' to the dominant 'ethnocentrically violent' values of publishers and literary reviewers. Berman, an important influence on Venuti, also discusses the need for translation strategies that allow the 'foreign' to be experienced in the target culture.

The second part of the chapter sites the agents or participants in the translation process in a network which plays out power struggles over text, culture and 'symbolic capital': practising translators, who often view their work in vague terms; publishers, who drive and are driven by market forces worldwide; and reviewers, who represent one form of the reception of the TT. The translator as agent has become central to work in these areas. In order to understand the interaction in a more sophisticated or operational form than was possible with polysystem theory, translation studies has imported what are sometimes competing concepts from sociology (Bourdieu, Latour, Luhmann, etc.).

Meanwhile, the work of Venuti and of Berman has links both to those cultural studies theorists discussed in Chapter 8 and the philosophical approaches examined in the next chapter, where the concept of the foreign and its linguistic, hermeneutic and ethical relationship to the source is paramount. Indeed, Venuti (2013: 3) discusses how he later developed what he describes as 'a more rigorously conceived hermeneutic model that views translation as an interpretive act, as the inscription of one interpretive possibility among others'.

Further reading

For influences on Venuti's work, see Schleiermacher (1813/2004, see also section 2.5 in this volume) and the references in Chapter 10 on translation and philosophy. For more on Berman, see Berman (1984/1992, 1985a/1999, and particularly 1995/2009). For some translators' accounts of their own work, as well as online interviews, see Frawley (1984), Warren (1989), Weaver (1989), Orero and Sager

(1997), di Giovanni (2003), Qvale (2003), Rabassa (2005), Bassnett and Bush (2006) and the very useful collection of short articles by Balderston and Schwartz (2002). For translation and creativity, Loffredo and Perteghella (2006). For more on translator activism, see Tymoczko (2010). For methods of historical research see Pym (1998) and Bastin and Bandia (2006). For reception theory see Jauss (1982) and Holub (1984), and for the reception of translation, including reviews, see Brown (1994) and Gaddis Rose (1997) and Brems and Ramos Pinto (2013). See Kang (2015) for online reviews. For book covers, read Harvey (2003). For translation and ethics, read Pym (2001), Bermann and Wood (2005), Maier (2007) and Tymoczko (2003). For sociology, read Simeoni (1998), Inghilleri (2005a), Buzelin (2005), Wolf and Fukari (2007), Hermans (1999, 2007), Angelelli (2014), Vorderobermeier (2014) and Tyulenev (2012, 2014).

Discussion and research points

1 Read and summarize Venuti's own descriptions of foreignizing and domesticating practices, fluency and resistancy. How do 'foreignization' and 'domestication' differ from terms such as 'literal' and 'free' (see Chapter 2)? How useful are the terms as 'heuristic research tools', as Venuti has suggested? Note the later developments in Venuti's position (Venuti 2013: 3–4).

2 Translate a short literary text into your TL. Translate it first using a domesticating and then a foreignizing orientation. In what areas do differences occur in your translations? How does this affect the image of the source culture? Try doing the same using a travelogue or tourist brochure as a ST.

3 How far do you agree with Venuti's statement (1992: 10) that 'any attempt to make translation visible today is necessarily a political gesture'? What kinds of ethical decisions does a translator have to make?

4 Read in detail Berman's account of his negative analytic. How far do the points match the phenomena discussed in the linguistic theories of Chapter 4? Analyse a literary text and its TT using Berman's categories. Which categories seem to be the most prominent in your analysis? Are there other related phenomena which you feel need to be accounted for? Discuss how it would be possible to introduce a 'positive analytic' into the TT.

5 What do you understand by the terms 'ear' and 'voice'? Is it possible, or even desirable, to look at literary translation in the more precise theoretical terms we have seen in Chapters 3 to 6? Read the collection of articles in Alvstad and Assis Rosa (2015) for more in this area.

6 How far are the concepts of domestication/foreignization, visibility, positive/negative analytics, ethics, habitus and gatekeepers, etc., relevant for non-literary translation?

The ITS website at www.routledge.com/cw/munday contains:

- a video summary of the chapter;
- a recap multiple-choice test;
- customizable PowerPoint slides;
- further reading links and extra journal articles;
- more research project questions.

CHAPTER 10

Philosophical approaches to translation

Key concepts

- **Hermeneutics (the theory of interpretation of meaning), linked to the German Romantics.**
- **Steiner's hermeneutic motion, the four moves of translation.**
- **Pound: the energy of language, using archaism to overturn the literary poetics of the time, an early foreignization.**
- **Benjamin: the 'pure' language of interlinear translation.**
- **Derrida: deconstruction and the undermining of basic premises of linguistic translation theory.**
- **Lewis's 'abusive fidelity': an experimental translation strategy that overturns normal usage.**

Key texts

Benjamin, Walter (1923/2012) 'The translator's task', translated by Steven Rendall, in Lawrence Venuti (ed.) (2012), *The Translation Studies Reader*, 3rd edition, London and New York: Routledge, pp. 75–83.

Derrida, Jacques (1985) 'Des tours de Babel', in Joseph F. Graham (ed.), *Difference in Translation*, Ithaca, NY: Cornell University Press, French original pp. 209–48; English translation by Joseph F. Graham in the same volume, pp. 165–207.

Lewis, Philip E. (1985/2012) 'The measure of translation effects', in Lawrence Venuti (ed.) *The Translation Studies Reader*, 3rd edition, London and New York, Routledge, pp. 220–39.

Pound, Ezra (1918/2012) 'Guido's relations', in Lawrence Venuti (ed.) (2012), *The Translation Studies Reader*, 3rd edition, London and New York: Routledge, pp. 84–91.

Ricœur, Paul (2004/2006) *On Translation*, translated by Eileen Brennan, London and New York: Routledge.

Steiner, George (1975/1998) *After Babel: Aspects of Language and Translation*, 3rd edition, London, Oxford and New York: Oxford University Press.

10.0 Introduction

Watch the introductory video on the companion website.

This book has so far considered literary, linguistic and cultural theories of translation. The present chapter moves on to look at philosophical approaches that have sought out the essence of (generally literary) translation. The writings contained in this chapter have been selected for their considerable influence on translation studies and for their questioning of some of the fundamental tenets of translation theory, notably the stability of meaning, the interpretation of the source text and the retrieval of intended meaning, the role of language and its relation to thought, the role of the translator and his/her relation to the text; indeed, the very question of translatability.

This chapter examines George Steiner's hermeneutic motion (section 10.1), Ezra Pound's energizing of language (section 10.2), Walter Benjamin's 'pure' language of translation (section 10.3), and Derrida and the deconstruction movement's questioning of translation (section 10.4). The Exploration box suggestions are designed to link to ideas, such as equivalence, discussed in previous chapters, while the further reading section expands on concepts described here.

10.1 Steiner's hermeneutic motion

Although hermeneutics as a theory of the interpretation of meaning dates back at least to ancient Greece, the modern hermeneutic movement owes its origins to the eighteenth and nineteenth century German Romantics. Drawing on the work of Herder (1744–1803), they included Schleiermacher (1768–1834, see Chapter 2), Goethe (1749–1832), Schlegel (1772–1829), Wilhelm von Humboldt (1767–1835), Hölderlin (1770–1843) and Novalis (1772–1801). In the twentieth century, leading figures included Heidegger (1889–1976) and Gadamer (1900–2002).[1] However, it is George Steiner's hugely influential *After Babel* which was the key modern reference for the hermeneutics of translation. Steiner (1975/1998: 249) defines the **hermeneutic approach** as 'the investigation of what it means to "understand" a piece of oral or written speech, and the attempt to diagnose this process in terms of a general model of meaning'.

Originally published in 1975, with subsequent editions in 1992 and 1998, *After Babel* claims to be 'the first systematic investigation of the theory and processes of translation since the eighteenth century'. Steiner's initial focus is on the psychological and intellectual functioning of the mind of the translator, and he goes on to discuss the process of meaning and understanding underlying the translation process. When he returns to considering the 'theory' (always in inverted commas) of translation, it is to posit his own hermeneutically oriented and **'totalizing' model**. This model, following Roman Jakobson (see Chapter 1), conceives of translation in a wide compass in which it shares features with acts of communication that are not limited to the interlingual:

> A 'theory' of translation, a 'theory' of semantic transfer, must mean one of two things. It is either an intentionally sharpened, hermeneutically oriented way of designating a working mode of all meaningful exchanges, of the totality of semantic communication (including Jakobson's intersemiotic translation or 'transmutation'). Or it is a subsection of such a model with specific reference to interlingual exchanges, to the emission and reception of significant messages between different languages ... The 'totalizing' designation is the more instructive because it argues the fact that all procedures of expressive articulation and interpretative reception are translational, whether intra- or interlingually.
>
> (Steiner 1998: 293–4)

Steiner's description of the hermeneutics of translation, 'the act of elicitation and appropriative transfer of meaning' (ibid.: 312), is based on a conception of translation not as a science but as 'an exact art', with precisions that are 'intense but unsystematic' (ibid.: 311). The **hermeneutic motion** which forms the core of Steiner's description (ibid.: 312–435) consists of four moves, as in Figure 10.1.

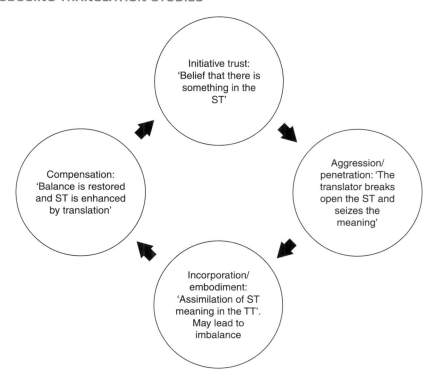

Figure 10.1 Steiner's hermeneutic motion

The main points of each move are as follows:

(1) **Initiative trust** (ibid.: 312–13): The translator's first move is 'an investment of belief', a belief and trust that there is something there in the ST that can be understood. Steiner sees this as a concentration of the human way of viewing the world symbolically. In the case of translation, the translator considers the ST to stand for something in the world, a coherent 'something' that can be translated even if the meaning might not be apparent immediately. This position entails two risks described by Steiner:

■ The 'something' may turn out to be 'everything'. This was the case of medieval translators and exegetists of the Bible (and, one might add, for translators of sacred works from other traditions) who were overwhelmed by the all-embracing divine message.

■ It may be 'nothing'. This may be either because they are deliberately non-communicative (e.g. nonsense rhymes) or because meaning and form are inextricably interwoven and cannot be separated and translated.

(2) **Aggression** (ibid.: 313–14): This is an 'incursive ... extractive ... invasive'
     move. Steiner looks to Heidegger for a basis of this view of comprehension
     as 'appropriative' and 'violent'. Noting St Jerome's use of the metaphor of
     meaning made captive by the translator, Steiner graphically depicts the
     translator's seizure of the ST: 'The translator invades, extracts, and brings
     home. The simile is that of the open-cast mine left an empty scar in the land-
     scape' (ibid.: 314). Steiner considers that some texts and genres 'have
     been exhausted by translation' and that others have been translated so well
     they are now only read in translation – for the latter, Steiner gives the
     example of Rilke (1875–1926)'s German translations of the sonnets of
     French Renaissance poet Louise Labé (c.1520–1566).

     At times, Steiner describes the aggression involved as **'penetration'**
     (ibid.: 314, 319). As we shall discuss in section 10.1.1, this metaphor has
     been strongly criticized by feminists for its violent male-centric sexual imagery.

(3) **Incorporation** (ibid.: 314–16): The third movement in Steiner's herme-
     neutics refers to how the ST meaning, extracted by the translator in the
     second movement, is brought into the TL which is already full of its own
     words and meanings. Different types of **assimilation** can occur: Steiner
     considers the two poles to be **'complete domestication'**, where the TT
     takes its full place in the TL canon, such as Luther's German Bible (see
     Chapter 2); or **'permanent strangeness** and marginality', such as
     Nabokov's 1964 English rendering of Pushkin (1825–1832)'s Russian
     verse novel *Eugene Onegin*, which consisted of a literal translation with
     more footnotes than text (see Nabokov 1955/2012).

     The crucial point Steiner makes (1998: 315) is that the importing of the
     meaning of the foreign text 'can potentially dislocate or relocate the whole
     of the native structure'. With further metaphors, he suggests the two ways
     in which this process functions:

(a) as **'sacramental intake'**: the target culture ingests and becomes
     enriched by the foreign text; or
(b) as **'infection'**: the target culture is infected by the source text and
     ultimately rejects it. Steiner gives the example of French seventeenth-
     century neoclassical literary models (e.g. the plays of Corneille, Racine
     and Molière) which complied with the strict technical artistic principles
     of ancient Greece and Rome. Initially, these were poorly imitated in
     Russian and German, among others, but were ultimately rejected by
     the more fluid ideas of European Romanticism (see Chapter 2).

The struggle for supremacy between literary systems is similar to the concepts described by the polysystem theorists such as Even-Zohar (see Chapter 7). This struggle, 'the dialectic of embodiment', also takes place within the individual translator:

> The **dialectic of embodiment** entails the possibility that we may be consumed. This dialectic can be seen at the level of individual sensibility. Acts of translation add to our means; we come to incarnate alternative energies and resources of feeling. But we may be mastered and made lame by what we have imported.
>
> (Steiner 1998: 315)

Thus, just as a culture can be unbalanced by the importation of certain translated texts, so too can a translator's energies be enhanced or, on the other hand, consumed by translation that saps the creative powers necessary for the production of his or her own works. Steiner sees such **imbalance** as stemming from a 'dangerously incomplete' hermeneutic motion (ibid.: 316). Balance can only be restored by the act of compensation, the fourth movement.

(4)   **Compensation** (ibid.: 316–19) or the 'enactment of reciprocity' is 'the crux of the métier and morals of translation'. Steiner describes the aggressive appropriation and incorporation of the meaning of the ST which 'leaves the original with a dialectically enigmatic residue'. In other words, although there has been a loss for the ST the 'residue' is positive. Steiner considers the ST to be 'enhanced' by the act of translation. **Enhancement** occurs immediately a ST is deemed worthy of translation, and the subsequent transfer to another culture broadens and enlarges the original. The ST enters into a range of diverse relationships with its resultant TT or TTs, metaphorized as the 'echo' and the 'mirror' (ibid.: 317), all of which enrich the ST. For example, even if a TT is 'only partly adequate' ('adequate' here is used in a non-technical sense), the ST is still enhanced since its own 'resistant vitalities' and 'opaque centres of specific genius' are highlighted in contrast to the TT.

Imbalance is caused by the energy which flows out of the ST and into the TT, 'altering both and altering the harmonics of the whole system' (ibid.: 317–18). Such imbalance needs to be compensated. At those points where the TT is lesser than the original, the TT makes the original's virtues 'more precisely visible'; where the TT is greater than the original, it nevertheless identifies points in the ST that have the potential for enhancement and for the realization of its 'elemental reserves'. In this way, balance and equity are restored. Steiner sees this requirement of equity between the texts as providing real and 'ethical' meaning to the concept of faithfulness:

> The translator, the exegetist, the reader is *faithful* to his [sic] text, makes his response responsible, only when he endeavours to restore the balance of forces, of integral presence, which his appropriative comprehension has disrupted.
>
> (Steiner 1998: 318; author's emphasis)

Steiner was confident that this fluid, moral, balanced 'hermeneutic of trust' (ibid.: 319) would allow translation theory to escape the 'sterile triadic model' (literal, free and faithful) which had marked theory up to and into the twentieth century (see this volume, section 2.1).[2]

10.1 Exploration: The hermeneutic of trust

Read Steiner's description of the hermeneutic of trust. How does it differ from the literal/free/faithful model we discussed in Chapter 2? Compare Steiner's position with Ricœur's extended hermeneutic theory as described in online articles by Kearney (2007) and Kharmandar (2015).

10.1.1 Elective affinity and resistant difference

The rest of Steiner's chapter on the hermeneutic motion is devoted to detailed analysis of examples of literary translation within that context. Steiner points out particularly successful translations, such as Jean Starr Untermeyer's collaboration with Hermann Broch in her English translation of his *The Death of Virgil* (1945). In Steiner's view (ibid.: 337), the TT becomes 'in many ways indispensable to the original'. In the merging 'meta-syntax' of English and German, where the English follows the German so closely, Steiner sees a kind of 'interlinear' text, 'close to the poets' dream of an absolute idiolect' (ibid.: 338). Similarly, in Hölderlin's translations of the Greek Classics of Pindar and Sophocles in the first decade of the 1800s it is the 'verbal interlinear, a mid-zone between antique and modern, Greek and German', which attracts Steiner's praise (ibid.: 341). Here, too, Steiner differentiates himself from that earlier translation theory which had derided word-for-word or literal translation. Steiner's focus is on the word, 'which can be circumscribed and broken open to reveal its organic singularity' (ibid.: 347).

Steiner feels that real understanding and translation occur at the point where languages diffuse into each other. The ability to move outside the self is key: 'This insinuation of self into otherness is the final secret of the translator's craft', he says (ibid.: 378), speaking of Ezra Pound's translations (see section 10.2). Pound translated from Chinese and Japanese without knowing very much of the languages, and Steiner (ibid.: 379–80) considers this to be an advantage, since remoteness from the ST and culture allows the translator to work without preconceptions or the complications of mutual contact. Here is perhaps the crucial issue discussed by Steiner, and one that is related to the other philosophical writings on translation examined in this chapter:

> The relations of the translator to what is 'near' are inherently ambiguous and dialectical. The determining condition is simultaneously one of elective affinity and resistant difference.
>
> (Steiner 1998: 381)

For Steiner, the question of **resistant difference** occurs in two ways:

(1) the translator experiences the foreign language differently from his or her mother tongue; and
(2) the relation between each pair of languages, source and target, differs and imposes its vivid differences on the translator and society.

The resulting experience for the translator is all-encompassing and affects his or her very identity (ibid.: 381).

This linguistic and cultural effect of **resistant difference** may prevent the translator from penetrating and incorporating the original text. However, Steiner also sees this impermeability as being transcended by **'elective affinity'** (ibid.: 398), which occurs when the translator has been drawn to that text as a kindred spirit and recognizes him- or herself in it. When resistant difference and elective affinity are both present at the same time, the text both rejects and attracts the translator. This creates a creative tension that then expresses itself in good translation:

Good translation ... can be defined as that in which the dialectic of impen-
etrability and ingress, of intractable alienness and felt 'at-homeness' remains
unresolved, but expressive. Out of the tension of resistance and affinity, a
tension directly proportional to the proximity of the two languages and historical communities, grows the elucidative strangeness of the great translation.

(Steiner 1998: 413)

In Steiner's view, the closer the two languages and cultures, the higher the potential for unresolved tension and therefore 'great' translation. Paradoxically, therefore, translation between two distant cultures and languages is deemed to be
'trivial' (ibid.) because tension is reduced.

10.1.2 Discussion of Steiner

The status of Steiner's work as a classic can be gauged by its three editions over
the course of the last three decades of the twentieth century. It is certainly a
monumental work in the breadth of its literary references. It has introduced many
non-specialists to translation theory, even if it is more marginal to contemporary
translation studies. However, its influence can be seen on more modern theorists
such as Berman and Venuti (see Chapter 9). Both emphasize the importing of
the foreign into the target culture and, like Steiner, do not equate good translation
with fluent domestication. Steiner's 'resistant difference' and 'elective affinity' are
in an unresolved state of tension, mirrored by the pull of Venuti's domesticating
and foreignizing practices.

But in many ways *After Babel* is a book that is stuck in a past time. Steiner's
extensive references to Chomsky's generative–transformational grammar as a
support for a universalist view of language, and thus an all-embracing theory of
translation, now seem dated. So too is the male-dominated language of the
metaphor, for which he has been severely criticized by feminist translation theorists. Chamberlain (1988/2012: 260–1) particularly takes Steiner to task for his
metaphors of 'erotic possession', notably the second 'penetrative' step of the
hermeneutic motion. In addition, she criticizes him for basing his model for the
restitutive step on Claude Lévi-Strauss's *Anthropologie structurale* (1958,
Structural Anthropology 1963) 'which regards social structures as attempts
at dynamic equilibrium achieved through an exchange of words, women and
material goods' (Steiner 1998: 319).

Nevertheless, despite these criticisms, Steiner's book remains an important contribution to hermeneutics and to the theory of the language of literary translation. We shall now look at two other main influences, both of whom are considered in some detail by Steiner and both of whom question the role of language. These are Ezra Pound and Walter Benjamin.

10.2 Exploration: Applying Steiner to a case study

Case Study 1 at the end of this chapter and shows how Seamus Heaney's modern translation of *Beowulf* exhibits features of Steiner's hermeneutic motion.

10.2 Ezra Pound and the energy of language

Steiner (1998: 249) refers to both Pound and Benjamin as belonging to the age of 'philosophic–poetic theory and definition' and to having made an important contribution to developing theories of relations between languages. In the case of the twentieth-century American modernist poet Ezra Pound (1885–1972), this was done through both the practice and criticism of translation.

Although Pound's focus may have altered throughout his long active years, he was always experimental, looking at the expressive qualities of language, seeking to energize language by clarity, rhythm, sound and form, rather than sense. His 'reading' of Chinese ideograms, based on the notes of Ernest Fenollosa (1853–1908), is typical of his imagist approach (see *Cathay* 1915). It privileged the creative form of the sign, capturing the energy of the thing or event pictured.

Pound's whole work was very much influenced by his reading of the literature of the past, including Greek and Latin, Anglo-Saxon, Provençal and Italian poetry. In his translations (e.g. Pound 1963), he sought to escape from the rigid straitjacket of the Victorian/Edwardian English tradition by experimenting with an archaicizing (and not necessarily clear) style which Venuti (2008: 34) links to his own foreignizing strategy. Venuti notes Pound's deliberately close translation of the Anglo-Saxon text *The Seafarer* (1917), where Pound sets out to imitate the original metre and calques ST words such as *bitre breostceare / bitter breast-cares* and *corna caldast / corn of the coldest*. This technique is also adopted by Heaney in his translation of *Beowulf* (see case study 1).

Pound's own writing about translation is idiosyncratic in its informality, a counterpoint to the archaicizing of his translations. A major example is 'Guido's relations' (Pound 1918/2012), an essay related to Pound's own translation of Guido Cavalcanti, an Italian poet from the thirteenth century who wrote in the *dolce stil nuovo* ('sweet new style'). Pound discards the possibility of translating into a Victorian or even a thirteenth-century English idiom:

> The ultimate Britons were at that date unbreeched, painted in woad, and grunting in an idiom far more difficult for us to master than the Langue d'Oc of the Plantagenets or the Lingua di Si.
>
> (Pound 1918/2012: 90)

Instead, Pound advocates an innovative solution, using what he terms 'pre-Elizabethan English', because of its 'clarity and explicitness' in bringing out the difference of the Italian text. His own translation in that mode is inevitably permeated by what is the now archaic language and spelling of that era (*makying, clearnesse*, etc.). Pound himself (ibid.: 93) puts forward objections to this strategy, namely that a serious poem may in this way be rendered merely 'quaint', that thirteenth-century Italian is to a modern Italian reader much less archaic in 'feel' than is fourteenth- or fifteenth-century English, and that it is doubtful whether such a solution is any more 'faithful' than his earlier attempts.

Pound's **experimentalism** and challenging of the poetic doctrine of his time continue to provide inspiration for many later translators and theorists who read his ideas into their own work. Thus, his use of translation is described as 'a tool in the cultural struggle' (Gentzler 2001: 28) even though his conscious archaicizing and foreignizing in translation leads to his 'marginalization' (Venuti 2008: Chapter 5). His view of translation as criticism and his own form of 'creative' translation also heavily influenced Brazilian poets including Haroldo de Campos (1929–2003), whose role in the Brazilian 'cannibalist' movement was paramount. Else Vieira describes the link between Pound and the ideas of de Campos:

> The translation of creative texts, de Campos argues, is always recreation, the opposite of a literal translation, but always reciprocal; an operation in which it is not only the meaning that is translated but the sign itself in all its corporeality (sound properties, visual imagetics, all that makes up the iconicity of the aesthetic sign) . . . With Pound, translation is seen as criticism, insofar as it attempts theoretically to anticipate creation, it chooses, it eliminates

repetitions, it organizes knowledge in such a way that the next generation may find only the still living part. Pound's well-known 'Make it new' is thus recast by de Campos as the revitalization of the past via translation.

(Vieira 1999: 105)

For the Brazilian translation scholars, this revitalization is to be found in the taking of the life energies of the ST and their re-emergence in a nourished TT. It is part of what de Campos called **'transcreation'**.

10.3 Exploration: Transcreation

Just as Pound continues to be 'reborn' or 'regested' in many guises, so too has 'transcreation' come to be reused as a central term in the translation of new technologies, notably video games and advertising (see section 11.1.8). The online article by Miguel Bernal (2006) and the book by O'Hagan and Mangiron (2013: 199ff) note features of transcreation in practice.

10.3 The task of the translator: Walter Benjamin

Walter Benjamin (1892–1940)'s 1923 essay 'Die Aufgabe des Übersetzers', translated into English as 'The task of the translator' by Harry Zohn in 1969 and retranslated in 2012 as 'The translator's task' by Steven Rendall (Benjamin 1923/2012), originally formed an introduction to Benjamin's own German translation of Baudelaire's *Tableaux Parisiens*.[3] It has become one of the seminal philosophical texts on literary translation.

Language, and a philosophy of language, was central to Benjamin's criticism and essays, from his 1916 work 'On language as such and on the language of Man' (see Hanssen 2004). Benjamin rejected the modern rationalistic and instrumentalist view of language; influenced by the mystical Kabbala tradition of Judaism and by the early German Romanticists, he saw **language as magical** and its mission was to reveal spiritual content. This inspires his 'Task of the translator' essay, where the translated text does not exist to give readers an understanding of the 'meaning' or information content of the original. Instead, it exists separately but in conjunction with the original, coming after it, emerging from its 'afterlife' but also giving the original 'continued life'. This recreation assures survival of the original work once it is already out in the world, in 'the age of its fame' (Benjamin 1923/2012: 77).

According to Benjamin, the purpose of translation is 'the expression of the most intimate relationships among languages' (ibid.). It reveals inherent relationships which are present but which remain hidden without translation. It does this not by seeking to be the same as the original but by 'harmonizing' or bringing together the two different languages. In this expansive and creative way, translation both contributes to the growth of its own language (by the appearance in the TL of the new text) and pursues the goal of a 'pure' and higher language. This **'pure language'** is released by the co-existence and complementation of the translation with the original. The strategy to achieve this is through a 'word-for-word rendering' which allows the 'pure language' to shine through:

> True translation is transparent; it does not obscure the original, does not stand in its light, but rather allows pure language, as if strengthened by its own medium, to shine even more fully on the original. This is made possible primarily by conveying the syntax word-for-word; and this demonstrates that the word, not the sentence, is translation's original element.
>
> (Benjamin 1923/2012: 81)

The capacity to release this 'pure' language is singular to translation:

> To set free in his own language the **pure language** spellbound in the foreign language, to liberate the language imprisoned in the work by rewriting it, is the translator's task.
>
> (Benjamin 1923/2012: 82)

The metaphors of liberation from imprisonment are the very opposite of the kind of images we saw used by earlier translators such as St Jerome, who sought to march the ST meaning into captivity (see above and Chapter 2). For Benjamin (ibid.: 82), liberation only occurs if the translator allows the TL to be 'put powerfully in movement by the foreign language'. Literalness of syntax and the freedom of pure language come together in interlinear translation. That is, a word-for-word TL gloss inserted above the words of the original. The **'prototype'** or **'ideal' translation**, in Benjamin's opinion (ibid.: 83), is an interlinear version of the Bible which allows the divine Word to appear (see Britt 2003, Hanssen 2004).

10.4 Exploration: Benjamin's ideal language

In Box 3.1 in Chapter 3, we described equivalence with the help of literal transfer, which is a type of interlinear translation. Look at an online example of an interlinear translation of a sacred text. What features might be said to 'liberate' the language? In what ways does this differ from formal equivalence/correspondence?

Benjamin's stress on allowing the foreign to enter the TL harks back to Schleiermacher's concept of 'foreignization' and of bringing the reader to the foreign text (see Chapter 2) and, more explicitly, to Hölderlin's 1804 German translations of the Greek dramatist Sophocles (compare section 10.1.1 above). His philosophical idea of harmoniously creating a 'pure' language from source and target is a search for a **higher truth** through the form of language rather than the fidelity to 'meaning'. It is an ideal, abstract concept that has been challenged by **Paul Ricœur** (1913–2005), who rejects the possibility of the 'perfect translation'. For Ricœur (2006: 23), Benjamin's pure language does not offer a practical translation solution. Translation, for Ricœur (ibid.), poses an **ethical** problem – it risks betraying author and reader but it operates its practice of **'linguistic hospitality'**, allowing the two texts to live side by side. In such dialogues Benjamin's preface has continued to exert influence on translation studies and on later postmodernists and deconstructionists such as Derrida.

10.4 Deconstruction

Deconstruction has sought to dismantle some of the key premises of linguistics, starting with Saussure's clear division of signified and signifier. It has also challenged the capacity to define, capture or stabilize meaning. Saussure's sign stood for the concept (see Chapter 3), and his linguistics was based on language as a differential system. By contrast, deconstruction's concept of *différance* (see below) suggests a location at some uncertain point in space and time between 'differ' and 'defer'. Clearly, such questioning of basic concepts of signifying and meaning has exceptional consequences for translation.

Allied to the postmodern and poststructuralist movements, deconstruction involves an interrogation of language and the very terms, systems and concepts which are constructed by that language. Deconstruction rejects the primacy of meaning fixed in the word and instead foregrounds or 'deconstructs' the ways in which a text undermines its own assumptions and reveals its internal contradictions (Norris 2002).

The movement has its origins in France in the 1960s. Its leading figure was the French philosopher Jacques Derrida (1930–2004). The terminology employed by Derrida is complex and shifting, like the meaning it dismantles. The term *différance* is perhaps the most significant; it plays on the two meanings of the French verb *différer* ('defer' and 'differ'), neither of which totally encompasses its meaning, and its spelling shift (from the standard *différence* to *différance*) is a silent, visual indication of a blurring of the signifier and the dislocation or deferral of meaning. This is emphasized in Norris's concise description of the importance of Derrida's term:

> Where Derrida breaks new ground . . . is n the extent to which 'differ' shades into 'defer'. This involves the idea that meaning is always deferred, perhaps to the point of an endless supplementarity, by the play of signification. Différance not only designates this theme but offers in its own unstable meaning a graphic example of the process at work.
>
> (Norris 2002: 32)

10.4.1 Readings of Benjamin

Deconstructionists have approached translation through their reading and commentary of Benjamin's 'The task of the translator' (see section 10.3). Prime among these is Jacques Derrida's 'Des tours de Babel' (1985), published in both French and English. The very title of the paper is a play on words, the French *tours* potentially having the sense of 'turns', 'turns of phrase', 'towers' (of Babel). In French, *des tours* ('of/some turns/towers') additionally has the same sound as *détour(s)* (with the sense of the English 'detour(s)'). Thus, from the very beginning there is a questioning of the basis of the language of the translation, rejecting the theories of meaning and translation that are based on a stable linguistic identity. Derrida interrogates Jakobson's division of interlingual, intralingual and intersemiotic translation (see section 1.1), pointing out the illogicality of Jakobson's definition of 'interlingual translation or translation proper', with the word translation being used as a translation of itself.

Derrida then embarks on a complex rereading and commentary on Benjamin's text. By this act, which he terms 'translating [and] the translation of another text on translation' (ibid.: 175), he calls into question many of the other premises on which translation theory has been based. These include the possibility of fully describing and explaining the translation process by written or spoken language. In addition, and most importantly, Derrida redefines Benjamin's 'pure language' as *différance* (see Venuti 1992: 7) and deconstructs the distinction between source and target texts. In Derrida's opinion, a commentary is a translation (in the broad sense of the term) of a translation (that is, TT). Furthermore, original and translated text owe a debt to each other; they also owe a mutual dependence and survival, once the translation act or Babelian performance has taken place.

10.4.2 Abusive fidelity

> **10.5 Exploration: Deconstruction and abusive fidelity**
>
> See the companion website for a discussion of Derrida's essay 'What is a relevant translation?' and of Venuti's translation of it as an example of 'abusive fidelity'.

Abusive fidelity is a translation strategy advocated by Philip Lewis in his own essay on the translation of Derrida, 'The measure of translation effects' (Lewis 1985/2012), which appears in the same volume as Derrida's 'Des tours de Babel'. Lewis makes use of contrastive stylistics and applied discourse analysis in the discussion of translation from French into English and identifies a trend in English towards 'more explicit, precise, concrete determinations, for fuller more cohesive delineations' (ibid.: 223). Like Venuti, Lewis notes that translators have traditionally tended to conform to fluent patterns or 'use-values' in the TL. He argues for a different translation strategy, which he calls **'abusive fidelity'**. This involves risk-taking and experimentation with the expressive and rhetorical patterns of language, supplementing the ST, giving it renewed energy: this is 'the strong, forceful translation that values experimentation, tampers with usage, seeks to match the polyvalencies or plurivocities or expressive stresses of the original by producing its own' (ibid.: 226). To translate Derrida, where the signifier–signified distinction is deconstructed, requires 'a new axiomatics of fidelity, one that requires attention to the chain of signifiers, to syntactic processes, to discursive structures, to the incidence of language mechanisms on thought and reality formation' (ibid.).

Lewis sees the need for the translator to **compensate** for the inevitable losses in translation, the loss of the 'abuse' that is present in the original. The abuse that is needed in the translation, says Lewis (ibid.: 227), is not just any abuse, but needs to 'bear upon the key operator or a decisive textual knot' in the text and to 'resist' the domesticating 'use-values'. Based on the kinds of features identified as characterizing French–English translation, and on the tensions between abuse and use, the original and the translation, Lewis analyses the shifts, or 'differences' as he calls them, that occur in the earlier English translation of Derrida's essay 'White mythology' (Derrida 1974). These include (Lewis 1985/2012: 229–35):

- typographical changes: omitting italics, adding parentheses and inverted commas around important technical terms;
- the dropping of suffixes: French *métaphorique* becomes *metaphor* rather than *metaphorics*;
- the loss of precision in the translation of linguistic and philosophical terms: French *effet* ('effect'), *valeur* ('value') and *articulation* are rendered as *phenomenon, notion* and *joint*;
- changes to syntactic and discursive order;
- the failure to recreate the play on the word *tour*: the translation given is *metaphor* rather than *turn*.

For these reasons, Lewis considers that the English translation of 'White mythology' fails to achieve abusive fidelity because the 'abuses' of the French text disappear. The 'performative dimension' (ibid.: 239) of Derrida's language, which deconstructs the ideas of the text, is not present in the English. For Lewis, a different strategy is required: the **experimental translation strategy** he proposes may be especially relevant in tackling some of the difficulties of the translation of philosophical texts of this kind where the language plays such a role in deconstructing the premises upon which language stands. His approach is also of special interest because it borrows elements from contrastive discourse analysis to examine philosophical translation from an interdisciplinary perspective. It has also influenced writing in other fields of translation studies. For example, Nornes (1999/2004) draws on Lewis's idea to recommend an **abusive approach to subtitling** to experiment with language and the visual aspect of the screen. He discusses approvingly the practice of fansubbing of Japanese *animé* films (ibid.: 466–7). The amateur subtitlers experiment with font colour and size to represent aspects of voice and dialect, they use borrowings of foreign words and populate the screen with notes and unusually placed titles. Such practices flout the norms and conventions of mainstream subtitling.

In such fashion the deconstructionists have brought new ways of reading to translation and have interrogated some long-held beliefs, such as the primacy and stability of meaning and the sign.

10.6 Exploration: Abusive translation practices

Further examples of 'abusive fidelity' can be seen in Case study 2 (below). Nornes (2007: Chapter 5) gives specific examples of abusive subtitling. Look at a fansubbed *animé* film. What 'abusive' subtitling methods are used and why? How successful do you consider them to be?

Case studies

Case study 1

The first case study attempts to see how far the translation strategy of a celebrated poet and translator might be explained by Steiner's model of the hermeneutic process. The text in question is the Irish poet Seamus Heaney's modern verse translation of the Anglo-Saxon epic poem *Beowulf*.[4] On publication in the UK in 1999, it was greeted with much critical acclaim and was soon the winner of the prestigious Whitbread Award. An important section of the book is Heaney's preface, relating the process of translation and his construction of a modern language for an old epic whose origins lie more than a thousand years before.

Heaney (1999: x) describes the strange relation the poem holds for present-day students of English, who struggle to grasp the meaning or to gain a sufficiently rudimentary understanding of the Anglo-Saxon language and of the Scandinavian culture it depicts. The temporal and cultural displacement felt by a modern reader of the translation is described by Heaney (ibid.: xii) in terms derived from his immersion in the Anglo-Saxon language:

In spite of the sensation of being caught between a 'shield-wall' of opaque references and a 'word-hoard' that is old and strange, such readers are also bound to feel a certain 'shock of the new'. This is because the poem possesses a mythic potency. Like Shield Sheafson (as *Scyld Scēfing* is known in this translation), it arrives from somewhere beyond the known bourne of experience, and having fulfilled its purpose (again like Shield) it passes once more into the beyond.

(Heaney 1999: xii)

The terms *shield-wall* and *word-hoard* derive from the language used in the TT, itself modelled on the Anglo-Saxon rather than the Latin. And the 'mythic potency' referred to could also relate to the language. Although the name of Scyld Scēfing is modernized, it retains the strangeness of another time and place. Furthermore, Heaney's mystical image of the travelling force of the poem, from beyond the 'bourne of experience', indicates that there is more to this poem than verses sung and words on a page.

Nevertheless, in the extract above Heaney's language reveals that he has trust that there is meaning in the original poem, the first step in Steiner's hermeneutic motion. Despite the temporal and cultural displacement, despite the poem's arriving from 'beyond the known bourne of experience', despite, that is, its 'resistant difference', Heaney is taken up by its power and is willing to attempt a translation. We might say that Heaney's enthusiasm for the Anglo-Saxon text demonstrates elective affinity. The tension that is caused by the resistant difference of languages and cultures that are so close (in location and tradition if not time) leads to the creation of a great translation.

The strangeness of the poem, the tension of heathen past and modern reader, is highlighted by Heaney's metaphors for bringing the foreign to the present. Thus, he tells (ibid.: xiii) of bringing the poem from the misty landscape of Anglo-Saxon England to the 'global village of the third millennium'; also, he equates the intercalated stories in the poem with modern-day TV channel-surfing. Such metaphors are rather different, modern versions of Steiner's 'open-cast mine', yet the idea of extracting and transporting remains. This can be equated to the act of aggression that is Steiner's second movement.

The temporal and spatial dislocation in the preface is paralleled by the dislocation of the language. Heaney (ibid.: xvi) notes the contrast in the original poem between the Christian English of the time and the earlier heathen vernacular culture. This contrast problematizes the search for a suitable 'voice' in the translation. Heaney has here extracted the meaning from the text, but he is struggling to find a language with which to incorporate it into the target language, the third movement of the hermeneutic motion. Yet Heaney finds that voice in his own past: 'I consider Beowulf to be part of my voice-right,' he says, coining a new term and linking his own past to the language and culture of the poem. The link lies in Heaney's background as a Catholic in Northern Ireland, with his English scored through by the influence of the Irish language that he had to learn. As a student, he discovered that the word *lachtar*, which was still part of the English idiom of his older Irish relatives, was in fact derived from Irish. This was 'like a rapier point of consciousness pricking me with an awareness of language-loss and cultural dispossession, and tempting me into binary thinking about language' (ibid.: xxiv). This description of dispossession and suppression of language seems to resemble the postcolonialist arguments which we discussed in Chapter 8. There, for example, Cronin gives an account of the struggle between the dominant English language and culture and the native Irish. It also in many ways fits Steiner's account which describes how the meaning and words of the original come into the new language and cause dislocation.

However, Heaney goes beyond this level; he recounts (ibid.: xxv–vi) how he 'escaped' from this cultural determination by what he terms 'illumination by philology'. This happened when he came to translate and realized that the Old English word *þolian* ('to suffer') in *Beowulf* still existed, as *thole*, in the rural area of Ireland where Heaney grew up. For him this was his 'right of way' into the voice and music of the TT. He found a voice that was familiar to him – the heavy speech of the poor farm workers in the fields that fitted the Anglo-Saxon narrative. To this Heaney adds archaic words such as *bawn* ('fort'), used in Elizabethan English and deriving from the Irish *bó-dhún*, meaning 'a fort for cattle'. The result is a challenging and re-energizing of the language of the English translation with elements from the past and from an alternative culture. This very closely resembles Steiner's description of the fourth movement, that of compensation: the translation is being infused by the influence of another language so that it comes alive. It works in the new time frame and, by its strategies and success, it enhances the original Anglo-Saxon poem and provides balance to the interpretive process.

The translation strategy also fulfils a personal need. It underpins the translation with Heaney's own biography and language, which is 'one way for an Irish poet to come to terms with that complex history of conquest and colony, absorption and resistance, integrity and antagonism' (ibid.: xxx). The tension between the elective affinity Heaney feels for the poem and the temporal resistant distance is therefore resolved by elements of the translator's linguistic and cultural background that link the source and target culture.

Discussion of case study 1

The case study sets out to see how far philosophical approaches to translation are to be found in modern translation practice. Heaney's preface shows indications of the way that a search for language, and therefore a questioning of the language of earlier translations, plays an integral part in the construction of a modern *Beowulf*. The search imbues the language of that translation with conscious links both to the past culture (Anglo-Saxon and Scandinavian) and to a culture and language in conflict (Irish), the language of the translator. Heaney himself is caught between the past and present, as he transfers a myth into a dominant language which he then disrupts with the voice of his own past. This process bears strong relation to Steiner's hermeneutic motion. It also echoes some of the arguments of the postcolonial theorists discussed in Chapter 8. Steiner's model, based on a theory of interpretation, is able to explain quite closely the working practice of an acclaimed modern literary translator.

Case study 2

This second case study deals with a text whose very language seemed designed to resist translation. The text in question is a short story, *Níneve*,[5] by the late Argentine author and translator Héctor Libertella (1945–2006), which I originally translated for a collection of Latin American fiction in translation. It is based on the true story of the British archaeologist Sir Henry Rawlinson's excavation of the Assyrian city of Nineveh, where he discovered and recorded important inscriptions written on an almost inaccessible rockface. Libertella uses language to illustrate, question and undermine the various archaeologists' attempts to understand the inscriptions and also the deceit and mistrust between the competing groups. It is interesting to see how far the kind of approach to translation adopted by Derrida and Lewis in section 10.4 is 'relevant' in discussing such a text.

The central themes of the story are illusion and deceit, which are conveyed with an array of wordplays and word confusions – such as *efectivo demente* ('effective demented/effective of mind') for *efectivamente* ('effectively/indeed') – in the Spanish. When such wordplays did not function in English, one possibility was to seek compensation at other points, tying in the sense of the wordplays and dislocation with the very form of the words on the page. Since a central strand of the story is the piecing together of old texts and the deciphering of ancient hieroglyphs, this is not an infrequent occurrence. In the following passage, Sir Rawlinson – or 'Sir Henry' as he is known in English texts of the time – is feverishly examining the lines of one such inscription:

> prolongando por estas líneas su mirada Sir Rawlinson las releyó mil veces, hasta donde lo permitieron sus ojos distraídos, y por la pura repetición acabó agotándolas y agotando un punto más cuanto leía otra vez. Y otra vez.
>
> extending his gaze over these lines, Sir Henry reread them a thousand times, as far as his dis tracted eyes allowed him, and by dint of pure re petition petition he eventually ex hausted the lines and ex hausted one letter more every time he re read them. And re red them.

The central idea in this passage is of repetition and rereading, of exhausting the deceptive, partially deciphered text at each reading. *Re* is one of the prefixes that is on other occasions dislocated by Libertella (e.g. *re partimos, re pone*). In the above passage, I used this technique even when it was not in the Spanish, to give *re petition, re read* and so on. To stress this repetitive process on the page I added '*re petition* **petition**'. The disappearance of each *punto* ('dot') as Sir Henry reads can also be visually represented in the English text, translating *punto* as *letter* and the phrase *re read them* (past tense) losing one letter to become *re red them* the second time, preserving the sound but surprising the reader visually, just as the red clay tablets surprise and deceive the archaeologists. Plot, pun and image (real and metaphoric) coincide here.

Discussion of case study 2

Deceit is revealed in Libertella's ST by a language that twists and turns and dislocates itself. The translation strategy that I employed bears some resemblance to Lewis's 'abusive fidelity'. That is, it strives to recreate the energy of the ST by experimentation. This involves some risk-taking and refusal, in part, to accept the normal 'use-values' of the TL. Hence the dislocation of the *re* prefixes, the representation of the loss of the *punto* in the phrase *re red*, and so on. It is important that such a translation strategy should not be merely comic wordplays but should 'bear upon the key operator ... or decisive textual knots', as Lewis puts it. The focus of my translation, therefore, is on the way the inscription escapes deciphering, on the slipperiness of its meaning, on themes that run throughout the text. Libertella is illustrating these by his attack on the 'use-values' of Spanish, and the translator needs to be creative in constructing or deconstructing a similar attack in English.

Just as Derrida blurs the ST–TT distinction in his reading of Benjamin, so there are elements in the Libertella texts which merge. The very name of the archaeologist needs to be pieced together from the two texts: 'Sir Rawlinson' in the Spanish, 'Sir Henry' in the English. He is located somewhere between or across these two texts, texts which illustrate the deceit of the language more strongly, perhaps, when they are examined side by side. The translation highlights the deception. It 'abuses' the fidelity to the original in, for example, the shift from *read* to *red*. The reader is surprised by the introduction of the new element of colour, absent in the Spanish yet suggestive of the red clay tablets and of Sir Henry's tired, red and yet hungry eyes.

Nevertheless, such an experimental translation strategy demands a certain 'leap of faith' from the reader to accept that the experimentation is not just facile wordplay. This may be easier when the text in question is philosophical; however, I would argue, for Libertella's *Nineve*, that more conventional strategies cannot hope to recreate the energy of the original. It is perhaps significant that the translation of *Nineve* was not included in the final collection precisely because the UK publisher felt that its experimentation would prove indigestible to the target audience. This is further illustration of the ultimate power of the publisher which we saw in Chapter 9.

Summary

This chapter has considered a number of theorists whose work has questioned key pillars of translation theory. Steiner draws upon the German hermeneutic tradition in *After Babel* (1975/1998), his monumental description of literary translation, which re-interprets the role of the translator and at the time brought translation to the attention of many non-specialists. Ezra Pound's translations and criticisms emphasize the way that language can energize a text in translation, while Walter Benjamin's 'The task of the translator' talks poetically about the release of a 'pure' language through 'literal' translation. Derrida 'deconstructs' some of the long-held certainties of translation, including the opposition between source and target languages, the stability of the linguistic sign and the possibility of equivalence. This calling into question of the principles of linguistic translation theory raised issues of a new order for translation studies. Among the experimental translation techniques which have emerged are Haroldo de Campos's 'transcreation', which has echoes in contemporary videogame localization, and Lewis's 'abusive affinity', taken over to subtitling by Nornes. In this, the translator, in tune with and responding to the ST, openly flouts standard norms and conventions of translation in an attempt to produce a stronger, more energetic TT.

Further reading

Philosophical approaches to translation cover a wide field. For Pound's writing on translation, see Pound (1951, 1953, 1954); for the Brazilian cannibalists, influenced by Pound, see Vieira (1997, 1999). Venuti (1995/2008) examines Pound's work in considerable detail. Benjamin's essay has influenced a large number of other theorists, including Niranjana (1992, see Chapter 8). The latter discusses Benjamin and Derrida in some depth.

Norris (2002) is a readable introduction to deconstruction. Graham (1985) contains other significant papers besides Derrida's 'Des tours de Babel'. See also the introduction to Venuti (1992), Arrojo (1998) and Davis (2001) for a description of the poststructuralist reading of translation.

See Palmer (1969) and Forster (n.d.) for an introduction to hermeneutics and Hermans (2009) for a brief introduction to hermeneutics in translation theory; Eco (2003) for an entertaining discussion of translation as 'negotiation'. See also Schleiermacher (1813/2004) and Heidegger (1962, 1971); many of the German originals, including Benjamin's 'Die Aufgabe des Übersetzers', are to be found in Störig (1963). Guenthner and Guenthner-Reutter (1978) edited an interesting collection of papers on philosophy and meaning in translation, and Andrew Benjamin has an important volume entitled *Translation and the Nature of Philosophy* (1989). See Weissbrod (2009) for a discussion of Ricœur and Toury. For issues in translating philosophical texts, see Foran (2012) and Cassin (2015).

Discussion and research points

1   Steiner's hermeneutic motion proposes an analysis of the translator's interpretative act, while Derrida and other deconstructionists question

the very nature of meaning. How far is it possible to reconcile them with the more linguistically oriented writing on meaning and interpretation such as we discussed in Chapter 3?

2   Steiner claims that there is less tension in translation between languages and cultures that are more distant. Find examples to support or challenge this assessment.

3   Read some of Pound's own translations and poems (e.g. from *New Selected Poems and Translations*, 2010). Is it possible to identify an experimental translation style? Try to adopt some of these in your own translations of poetry. Comment on the results.

4   Read Benjamin's 'The translator's task' and summarize his view of translation. Why do you think the essay has had such an influence among some theorists? Carry out an online search for comments on the essay by translators. If possible, compare the two different translations (by Zohn and Randall). What do Randall's revisions tell us about the translation of philosophical texts?

5   Find examples of translations and/or translator prefaces in which Lewis's 'elective affinity' may have been a factor. For instance, translations made by established translators or authors who have specifically selected the source texts. How far do the resulting translations display experimental or risk-taking strategies?

6   What relevance do the theories in this chapter have for technical and other specialized translation practices? Read Foran (2012) for a discussion of the specialized translation of philosophical texts.

The ITS website at www.routledge.com/cw/munday contains:

- a video summary of the chapter;
- a recap multiple-choice test;
- customizable PowerPoint slides;
- further reading links and extra journal articles;
- more research project questions.

CHAPTER 11

New directions from the new media

Key concepts

- **The new media have transformed translation practice and caused theory to revisit and embrace new concepts.**
- **Audiovisual translation studies, especially subtitling but embracing all forms of multimodality, has become a sub-branch of translation studies.**
- **The concepts of 'vulnerable translation' and 'transcreation'.**
- **Localization and globalization: modern translation practice and environment alter notions of equivalence and of power.**
- **New technologies: the complex interaction between machine and translator.**
- **Corpus-based, and corpus-driven, translation studies: a means of investigating translated language.**

Key texts

Chiaro, Delia (2009) 'Issues in audiovisual translation', in Jeremy Munday (ed.) *The Routledge Companion to Translation Studies*, Abingdon and New York: Routledge, pp. 141–65.

Cronin, Michael (2003) *Translation and Globalization*, London and New York: Routledge.

Delabastita, Dirk (1989) 'Translation and mass-communication: Film and TV translation as evidence of cultural dynamics', *Babel* 35.4: 193–218.

Díaz Cintas, Jorge and **Aline Remael** (2007) *Audiovisual Translation: Subtitling*, Manchester: St Jerome.

Hartley, Anthony (2009) 'Technology and translation', in Jeremy Munday (ed.) *The Routledge Companion to Translation Studies*, Abingdon and New York: Routledge, pp. 106–27.

Jiménez-Crespo, Miguel (2013) *Translation and Web Localization*, London and New York: Routledge.

Olohan, Maeve (2004) *Introducing Corpora in Translation Studies*, London and New York: Routledge.

Pérez-González, Luis (2014) *Audiovisual Translation: Theories, Methods and Issues*, London and New York: Routledge.

Pym, Anthony (2004) *The Moving Text: Localization, Translation, and Distribution*, Amsterdam and Philadelphia: John Benjamins.

11.0 Introduction

Watch the introductory video on the companion website.

The emergence and proliferation of new technologies have transformed translation practice, as will be evident from some of the translation examples that feature throughout this fourth edition. Additionally, new technologies are exerting an impact on the theorization of translation. This chapter briefly looks at three examples: (11.1) audiovisual translation studies, (11.2) localization and globalization and (11.3) corpus-based translation studies.

11.1 Audiovisual translation

11.1.1 Early days: the 'virgin area of research'

Very dramatic developments in translation studies have occurred in the field of audiovisual translation, most notably subtitling. Initially audiovisual translation was more or less overlooked by translation theory. Katharina Reiss (1971/2000; see section 5.1, this volume) had included what she termed an **'audio-medial'** text type, but this was not developed and indeed her definition seemed to refer more to fields such as advertising rather than film and documentary translation. In James

S. Holmes's 'map' (Chapter 1) there is a category of 'medium-restricted' theories but no specific mention of audiovisual at all. Later, Snell-Hornby (1988/1995) links 'film' to 'literary translation' in her integrated theory (see Figure 5.2).

Early articles by Titford (1982) and Mayoral et al. (1988) coined the term **'constrained translation'**, focusing on the non-verbal elements that marked out audiovisual translation. Notwithstanding these publications, and despite a lengthy bibliography, Dirk Delabastita was justified in saying that the field was 'still a virgin area of research' at the time of his groundbreaking article 'Translation and mass-communication: Film and TV translation as evidence of cultural dynamics' (1989: 202). That article sought to identify some of the important characteristics of this type of translation, namely that 'film establishes a multi-channel and multi-code type of communication' (ibid.: 196). These codes include what Delabastita describes as:

- the verbal (with various stylistic and dialectal features)
- the literary and theatrical (plot, dialogue, etc., appropriate to the genre)
- the proxemic and kinetic (relating to a wide range of non-verbal behaviour)
- the cinematic (camera techniques, film genres and so on).

Delabastita avoids any simplistic verbal–non-verbal distinction by emphasizing that the visual channel sometimes conveys verbal signs (e.g. credits, letters, shop signs) and that the acoustic channel transmits some non-verbal signs (music, background noise, etc.). He maps this against five types of operative realizations drawn from Classical rhetoric (repetition, addition, reduction, transmutation and substitution) to give a large number of possible translation procedures (ibid.: 199–200).

It is noteworthy that Delabastita constantly compares film translation to other forms of translation, such as theatrical performance. In his view, the major difference is that, whereas drama is constituted slightly differently on each occasion it is performed, film is recorded and 'is perfectly producible in material terms'. That is, once recorded, the film is distributed and replayed to and by different audiences but, except on rare occasions, it remains unaltered.[1] There are also very particular **constraints** that normally govern the subtitling of film, namely the co-existence of the sound channel and the vision channel, which restrict the procedures open to the translator. One example from the theatre is Shakespeare's *Othello* (ibid.: 198). In place of a handkerchief in the ST, a material token of love which comes to symbolize infidelity, some French translators have given Desdemona a crucifix. In film, such a change would be impossible because the image cannot be altered and because of the requirement not to contradict the image.

Delabastita's article attempts to deal with both subtitling and dubbing but is 'only a first step towards the development of a competence model' (ibid.: 201) for this kind of translation. Importantly, Delabastita, based in Belgium (where dual subtitles – in Dutch and French – are common), was working from within a norm-based descriptive framework (see Chapter 7) that encompassed not only linguistic phenomena but also the sociocultural and historical environment. Delabastita raises another question that pertains to the status of the practice and theory and is reminiscent of discussions at the infancy of translation studies: the name for the phenomenon and whether it could really be classed as 'translation' rather than 'adaptation' (compare Chapter 1).

11.1.2 The name and nature of the field

Delabastita's article in many ways marked much early research into this medium. Certainly, the discussion of the name for the field and its relation to the umbrella term 'translation studies' has received much attention. Rather than 'film translation', Luyken et al. (1991) speak of **'audiovisual language transfer'**. Meanwhile, Gottlieb (1994) describes interlingual subtitling as a form of **'diagonal translation'**: not only is the SL rendered as a TL but speech is rendered by written text, in contrast to the more conventional 'horizontal' transfer that occurs in interpreting (speech by speech) and in interlingual translation (written text by written text). Relating this to Roman Jakobson's types of translation (see section 1.1), Gottlieb considers subtitling to be 'intrasemiotic':

> it operates within the confines of the film and TV media, and stays within the code of verbal language. The subtitler does not even alter the original; he or she adds an element, but does not delete anything from the audiovisual whole.
>
> (Gottlieb 1994: 105)

Gambier (2003), in his introduction to a special issue of *The Translator* devoted to the subject, discusses the competing terms **'audiovisual translation'**, **'screen translation'** and **'multimedia translation'**. Each has a slightly different bias, in part due to the rapid development of the technology that has seen subtitling, for instance, move from film to documentary to news to entertainment, from video to DVD to video games, from cinema to opera to computer screen and now portable media, and so on. Although Gambier himself proposed the term **'transadaptation'** ('tradaptation' in French, see Gambier 2004), within a few years Díaz Cintas and Remael (2007: 11–12) were concluding that '[the term] audiovisual translation (AVT) was fast becoming the standard referent'.

However, Gambier's article was timely because of its identification of the different types of audiovisual activity and the way in which these were causing a rethink of older, translation-based categories. Thus, among others, there is:

- **interlingual subtitling**, now in various forms for the cinema and video (where the subtitles are 'open', meaning that they are an integral part of the version of the film), and DVD (where they may be 'closed', meaning that the viewer can select whether to see them or not and in which language);
- **bilingual subtitling**, in countries such as Belgium, where subtitles are provided simultaneously in two languages;
- **intralingual subtitling** for the hard of hearing, increasingly a regulatory requirement;
- **dubbing**, which covers 'lip-synchronization' or 'lip-sync', where the SL voice-track is replaced by a TL voice-track;
- **voice-over**, used mainly for documentary or interview;
- **surtitling**, subtitles which are projected above the stage or on the seatbacks at the opera or theatre;
- **audio description**, a mainly intralingual audio commentary on the action on the stage or film, etc., for the visually impaired.

11.1 Exploration: Types of AVT

Read the extract of Chapter 1 of Luis Pérez-González's *Audiovisual Translation* (2014), available through the ITS companion website. Map Gambier's types onto Pérez-González's three 'transfer methods' of AVT: subtitling, revoicing and assistive. Which additional types does Pérez-González include? Try to find an example of each type.

AVT is a vast area and has grown rapidly in both teaching and research terms. To date, the bulk of the work has been carried out on interlingual subtitling and on the linguistic translation strategies and technical requirements and constraints. Linde and Kay (1999: 3) note the differences between interlingual subtitling and written translation, notably the **space and time constraints** (normally a maximum of two lines of text each of a maximum of around 38 Roman characters or 13–15 Chinese or Japanese characters, depending on the medium, and a duration of around six seconds for each caption) that lead to a necessary reduction in the number of words on the screen. They also emphasize the other obvious additional constraints of the **image** on the screen, which is normally inviolable, and the soundtrack in the source language, which is retained. The subtitler must therefore try to respect aspects of the cinematography such as camera cuts and match the duration of the subtitles to the rhythm of the dialogue. Note, however, that these constraints are altering: DVD subtitling is now typically more flexible and some films, notably the very successful *Slumdog Millionaire* (Danny Boyle, 2008), even play with the location of the English subtitles of the Hindi part of the soundtrack, placing them at different points on the screen. Others, such as *Man On Fire* (Tony Scott, 2004) and *Day Watch* (Timur Bekmambetov, 2007), flouted typographical conventions to convey the on-screen emotions.

11.1.3 The linguistic and prescriptivist nature of subtitling research

In their seminal study of subtitling, Díaz Cintas and Remael devote only a short chapter to semiotics but go into great detail about the intricate technical considerations and the stylistics and linguistics of the translation process. They sum up what they term **'subtitling guidelines'** as follows:

> Subtitling style will vary somewhat with genre, and customers will always have their say, but some subtitling guidelines are almost universal. Grammar and lexical items tend to be simplified and cleaned up, whereas interactional features and intonation are only maintained to some extent (e.g. through word order, rhetorical questions, occasional interjections, and incomplete sentences). In other words, not all the features of speech are lost, quite a few can be salvaged in writing, but rendering them all would lead to illegible and exceedingly long subtitles. [. . .] [S]ubtitling focuses on those items that are informationally most relevant.
>
> (Díaz Cintas and Remael 2007: 63–4)

Although the above are classified as 'guidelines', they are what in Toury's descriptive terms (see Chapter 7) would be 'generalizations'. They are made from the authors' own studies and experience, 'almost universal' features which, in another context, might go some way to determining descriptive 'laws' for audiovisual translation. Díaz Cintas and Remael are therefore drawing on a tradition of terminology and methodology from translation studies. This is also the case with the prominent 'translation issues' they note (ibid.: 184–236) which include 'marked speech' (style, register, dialect/sociolect/idiolect, taboo words), culture-bound references, songs and humour. As far as culture-specific references are concerned, Chiaro (2009: 154–65) gives many examples, including:

- institutions and systems (*Supreme Court, Grand Jury*);
- the school system of grades and assessments (*First grade, baccalauréat, a degree*);
- place names (*DC, LA, Time Square*);
- units of measurement (*pounds, ounces, gallons*);
- monetary system (*dollars, pounds, rupis, yuan, yen*);
- food and drink (*pancakes, sushi, dahl*);
- festivals (*Halloween, Thanksgiving, Chinese New Year, Eid*);
- nationally known names, personalities, pastimes (*The Knicks, snakes and ladders*).

In the case of marked speech, acceptability in oral and written production often varies. So, the appearance of a taboo term in a subtitle or piece of writing tends to have a stronger effect than hearing the same word.

Most of these are difficult translation problems in other genres and modes too, for example in translating the fictional dialogue of the Brontë sisters, D. H. Lawrence and John Steinbeck; also in drama scripts (see the discussion on Pirandello in Anderman 2005: 325–6) where the characters speak with a strong dialectal and/or sociolectal voice that has no equivalent in the TL and that can scarcely be indicated graphically. When attempts are made to replace a dialect, such as in *La haine*, where in places a semi-black American dialect replaces the non-standard French, it may attract criticism (Díaz Cintas and Remael 2007: 192; compare the contrasting standardization strategies in the film discussed in the case study in Chapter 6). There are also interesting divergences from the issues of traditional translation studies: punctuation, reduction and line breaks, for instance, feature very prominently (ibid.: 102–43, 145–71 and 172–80). These are rarely treated in such detail in other forms of translation.

11.1.4 Norms of audiovisual translation

Much has been written on the technical and linguistic aspects of subtitling, but less attention has so far been paid to the integration of subtitling and broader analytic models. Without such a move, audiovisual translation studies risks remaining the realm of a prescriptive, practice-based phenomenon rather than extending to embrace a theoretical branch of its own. This section will look at a sample of theoretical frameworks borrowed for the study of audiovisual translation and employed by Karamitroglou and Pedersen (norms), Taylor (transcription) and Chaume (codes).

Karamitroglou (2000) is an early study that draws on **polysystem theory** and the concept of **norms** to discuss dubbing and subtitling preferences in Greece. He emphasizes the need to consider the range of human agents involved in the process, as well as 'the catalytic role of the audience' and the importance of differentiating between different film types and genres (ibid.: 105). The list of the elements considered covers:

- the human agents;
- the products (TTs);
- the recipients (addressees and customers);
- the mode (characteristics of audiovisual translation);
- the institution (critics, distributors, TV channels, etc. which participate in the preparation and making of the film);
- the market (cinemas, film clubs, etc. which decide the screening of the TTs).

The **human agents** include the following: 'spotters, time-coders, adapters, dubbing director, dubbing actors, sound technicians, video experts, proof-reading post-editors, translation commissioners, film distributors and finally the translator him/herself' (ibid.: 71). Karamitroglou uses a questionnaire survey of the different professionals within the industry, a useful and wide-ranging ethnographic tool. However, the findings are rather restricted. More recently, Pedersen (2011) has carried out a detailed investigation of linguistic norms of subtitling for television using a corpus of 100 Anglophone films subtitled into Danish and Swedish in an attempt to circumvent the problem of individual case studies (compare the rationale for descriptive translation studies in Chapter 7). The model of analysis is centred on 'extralinguistic cultural references (ECRs)' (compare Díaz-Cintas' and Remael's 'translation issues' above) and the translation 'strategies' employed: retention, specification, direct translation, generalization, substitution, omission or the use of an official equivalent.

11.2 Exploration: Extralinguistic cultural references

Carefully read Pedersen's description of translation strategies for ECRs in Pedersen (2005), http://www.euroconferences.info/proceedings/2005_Proceedings/2005_Pedersen_Jan.pdf . Make a note of examples of each of the 'strategies' above.

11.1.5 Multimodal transcription

In contrast to Karamitroglou's macro-contextual research, Christopher Taylor (2003) tackles the key micro-contextual question of **multimodal transcription** – in other words, how to record and analyse a multimodal product in writing. Taylor borrows from Thibault's (2000) model for the analysis of film and TV advertising, which consists of breaking down a film sequence into individual frames/shots/phases and then producing a multi-layered multi-columned description as in Table 11.1.

Table 11.1 Multimodal transcription model (following Taylor 2003: 192–3)

Frames		Shots		Phases	
Duration of frame and order of presentation	**Presentation of the visual frames**	**Components of the visual image**	**'Kinesic action' of the characters**	**Dialogue and description of the soundtrack**	**Metafunctional interpretation of how the film creates meaning**
Frames numbered individually and duration indicated in seconds. Frames are selected according to the level required in the analysis	Still images from the source	Camera position, perspective, focus, distance, salient items, clothing, colours, etc.	Gestures, movements, etc.	Words uttered, tone, music, etc.	Ideational, interpersonal, textual, and visual grammar

The sixth element (metafunctional interpretation) is taken from Hallidayan linguistics (ideational, interpersonal, textual meaning, cf. Chapter 6) and from Kress and van Leeuwen's (1996/2006) visual grammar, which integrates the different semiotic modalities of visual texts. Taylor applies this form of transcription and analysis to a scene from Roberto Benigni's *La vita è bella* (1999), among others. Taylor contends that the findings will be useful for a subtitler in 'spotting' where to best locate subtitles and in deciding on where to omit verbal elements. However, the form of transcription, unwieldy for long sections, is probably of most use for theoretical descriptive studies of subtitles. The finding that 'the **interpersonal** component is extremely important and is carried largely by the voice prosodies and the kinesic action' (Taylor 2003: 197) is an interesting illustration of the role of non-verbal material. At the same time it begs the question whether, in a multimodal age and copyright permitting, it will become increasingly the norm in such studies for analysis to be presented visually anyway, or at least in a combination of the visual and written. Hence Díaz Cintas and Remael's decision to include a DVD of extracts to complement the discussion in their book.

11.3 Exploration: Multimodal transcription

Study Taylor's article on the ITS website (Taylor 2003) and try out the model of transcription on a short extract (2–3 minutes) from a subtitled film. Note any difficulties in using the model (e.g. how and where to punctuate and how to represent spoken language). What evidence can you find in the subtitles to support or challenge the 'guidelines' suggested by Díaz Cintas and Remael above?

11.1.6 Codes and narratives

Frederic Chaume proposes a combination of **translation studies and film studies** in an attempt to produce an 'integrated' model of analysis of 'rules' and norms designed for the analysis of 'the signifying codes of cinematographic language' (Chaume 2004: 13, 16). Focussing mainly on dubbing, Chaume identifies ten such codes (ibid.: 17–22). The first four concern the acoustic channel:

(1) **The linguistic code:** Here Chaume (ibid.: 17) makes the crucial point that problems such as wordplay, co-presence of multiple languages,

culture-specific elements, etc. 'are shared by other translation types (e.g. legal, scientific, technical, etc.) and should not be considered problems specific to audiovisual translation'. For him, the features of the linguistic code in audiovisual texts are that they are most often scripted but 'written to be spoken as if not written', which poses considerable demands on the translator to conform to a similar register.

(2)   **The paralinguistic code:** The preparation of dubbing scripts would involve the addition of symbols to indicate laughter, pauses, and so on, while in subtitling graphical signs (upper case, exclamation marks, suspension marks, etc.) indicate voice level, tone and pauses.

(3)   **The musical and special effects code:** The representation and adaptation of song lyrics and their function.

(4)   **The sound arrangement code:** There are differences depending on whether the speaker is on or off screen. This will necessitate orthographic variation in subtitling (an off-screen character's words may be indicated in italics) and will affect both the translation procedure and sound quality in dubbing (an on-screen speaker's words will need to be lip-synchronized).

The other six codes relate to the visual channel:

(5)   **The iconographic code:** Iconographic symbols unlikely to be recognized by the TT viewer (e.g. a picture or portrait of a figure famous in the SL culture but not in the TL culture) may need verbal explanation if it is important for the under-standing of the text. Coherence with the image needs to be maintained. Similarly, any wordplay with reference to an item that appears on screen creates a specific problem. Like Delabastita above, Chaume (ibid.: 19) makes the point that audiovisual translation is distinct since the presence of the image on screen restricts the range of free translation that would be open to written translation.

(6)   **Photographic codes:** Examples of the problems which arise are changes in lighting which necessitate a change of colour for subtitles and also the use of a culture-specific visual or colour feature which may confuse or be misunderstood by the TT audience. So, while in Asia white is often associ-ated with death (for example, a white carnation in a Japanese film), in the west it is more commonly the colour black. On the other hand, a red carna-tion may be the symbol of love.

(7)   **The planning code:** Relates to close-ups that require lip synchronization in dubbing and also the translation of important information on features that are not spoken (on posters, etc.).

(8) **The mobility code:** Concerns the positioning of the characters in a dubbed scene and the need to co-ordinate movement and words (e.g. a shake of the head and a negative phrase in most cultures).

(9) **Graphic codes:** The representation of intertitles, titles, text and subtitles that appear on screen in the ST. This is a particular problem for dubbing.

(10) **Syntactic codes:** Involve editing principles, such as the checking of the association of a verbal textual element to the image and other semiotic forms and also the start and end of sequences.

Chaume's codes are useful in drawing attention to the non-linguistic and particularly to the visual. Only one of the ten codes is linguistic, a huge departure from the norm in most translation studies work. The main focus is applied; that is, on a model that has pedagogical applications, for teaching the techniques to trainee subtitlers. However, in Chaume's paper, and perhaps due to space limitations, there is little indication of precisely how these codes are realized on screen. As far as the linguistic code is concerned, there seems to be quite general agreement on the relatively restricted number of such issues in audiovisual translation (reduction, omission, register variation, humour, punctuation, etc., see Gambier 2003: 153). It is quite possible that future progress in descriptive studies will come from the exploration of the other codes and from taking up Jorge Díaz Cintas's call for macro-level incorporation of those aspects of power, culture and ideology that for some time have been common in 'mainstream' translation studies (Díaz Cintas 2003: 32).

11.4 Exploration: Codes of cinematic language

Refer to the full version of Chaume's paper online (http://www.erudit.org/revue/meta/2004/v/n1/009016ar.html). Look for examples from products that are dubbed or voice-overed or are accompanied by audio description to illustrate each of Chaume's codes. You may find additional examples in Chaume's book *Audiovisual Translation: Dubbing* (2012).

11.1.7 Subtitles as 'vulnerable translation'

Gottlieb (1994) calls subtitling a form of House's 'overt translation' (see Chapter 6) since the visibility of the title is an inherent part of the activity. And the physical status of the medium is central because the TTs are 'modifications of originals' which retain the 'nonverbal elements' (Gottlieb 1997: 309). In fact, of course, they also retain the verbal elements of the ST, which makes them 'a written, additive, synchronous type of translation of a fleeting, polysemiotic text type' (ibid.: 312). This physical status provokes a paradoxical situation for the subtitler: on the one hand, the subtitles are visible to all, yet more often than not the individual translator is not credited with his/her work and remains in a state of 'forced invisibility' (Díaz Cintas and Remael 2007: 40). The co-existence of ST soundtrack and TT subtitles creates another tension, which is described by the concept of **'vulnerable translation'**: 'Not only must subtitles respect space and time constraints, they must also stand up to the scrutiny of an audience that may have some knowledge of the original language' (ibid.: 57). In other words, a viewer with some understanding of the ST will have an expectation of the subtitles which, when disappointed (e.g. if there is an omission, or reduction), may cast doubt on the quality of those titles. This vulnerability is less often present in other forms of translation and represents an additional pressure for the subtitler.

11.1.8 Fansubs and video games, a site for transcreation

The rapid development of technology has had important knock-on effects for audiovisual translation practice as well as bringing new challenges for translation studies. New forms of translation are being created, two of which are fansubs and video games. **Fansubs** (Díaz Cintas and Muñoz Sánchez 2006) is the (legally rather dubious) practice of amateur subtitling and distribution of films, TV series and other film extracts online. It was originally used for the translation of mainly Japanese *manga* and *animé* cartoons and the practice has now proliferated thanks to the greater access to free subtitling software such as Subtitle Workshop, Jubler or Open Subtitle Editor. Díaz Cintas (2005) points to the peculiar characteristics of the addition of glosses and metalinguistic information in the titles and the fact that little work has thus far been done in this area. The practice of amateur translation is not confined to subbing – the Harry Potter series appeared in unauthorized written translation in several languages including German, where a collective team of fans translated the fifth volume in less than forty-eight hours. A French translation led to the amateur translator being arrested for alleged breach of copyright.[2]

Video game translation is a blend of audiovisual translation and software localization. Indeed, Mangiron and O'Hagan (2006: 11) call this type of activity 'game localization' since the games may be subtitled or dubbed or both. The important defining feature is the 'creativity and originality' that is demanded of the translator in order to ensure that the game is entertaining (ibid.: 13). Such creativity includes the renaming of elements and characters, using neologisms, and the deliberate choice of non-standard dialects. Commenting on the American version of the game *Final Fantasy*, Mangiron and O'Hagan (ibid.: 17) give the example of the weapon *fūrinkazan* (comprising the Chinese characters for 'wind, forest, fire and mountain') that, due to space constraints and genre conventions, is translated by the more concise *Conqueror*; for humorous (and, we might say, stereotypical) effect, a Cockney London accent is also added to the speech of the merchant O'aka, even though he speaks with a standard accent in Japanese.

Bernal Merino (2006: 32–3) discusses the term **transcreation** 'used by a new wave of companies seeking to distance themselves from traditional translation firms'. Originally, this term was employed by the Indian translator and academic P. Lal (1964) for his domesticating English translations of Sanskrit plays (see also Holmstrom 2006) and later used by the Brazilian writer Haroldo de Campos and the Brazilian postcolonial theorist Else Vieira (1999) (see section 10.2). Transcreation is contrasted to other terms such as 'domestication', 'localisation' and 'skopos'. So, while 'transcreation' is used to stress the creative and transformative nature of the process, 'the skopos of game localisation is to produce a target version that keeps the "look and feel" of the original, yet passing itself off as the original' (Mangiron and O'Hagan 2006: 20). Here, the creativity behind the new term 'transcreation' is combined with the description 'look and feel', which comes straight from the discourse of localization and translation.

11.5 Exploration: Transcreation

Investigate the use of the term 'transcreation' by commercial companies on their websites. What definitions do they give? Which genres or text-types does it cover? How do the companies differentiate themselves from more traditional translation companies?

11.2 Localization, globalization and collaborative translation

In the digital age, translation has become big business and in industry (especially the software industry) the term is often subsumed into the acronym **GILT**

– Globalization, Internationalization, Localization, Translation
(Jiménez-Crespo 2013: 24–39):

- **Globalization** (g11n) in this context normally means the organization of business processes (management, marketing, consumer care) to support internationalization and localization.
- **Internationalization** (i18n) refers to the development stages of a digital product to ensure that it will function internationally.
- **Localization** (L10n) refers to the adaptation of the product to the target locale, 'the combination of a sociocultural region and a language in industrial setting' (Jiménez-Crespo 2013: 12). Localization may involve the substitution of inappropriate cultural symbols and the translation of text, including the need to fit specific space constraints on the screen/page, etc. Dunne (2006: 2) makes the important point that localization is a 'focal point in the corporate matrix', an intersection of development and authoring (as above), sales, marketing (promotional materials may need to be redesigned), legal advice (to comply with local legislation) and management (concerned to restrict costs).
- The difference between **localization** and **translation** is blurred (Mazur 2007, Jiménez-Crespo 2013: 11), but generally localization is seen by industry as a superordinate term that encompasses translation.[3] Thus, in the words of LISA, the Localisation Industry Standards Association, operational from 1990 to 2011, '**localization** involves taking a product and making it linguistically and culturally appropriate to the target **locale** (country/region and language) where it will be used and sold'.[4]

In this instance, it is industry that has been active in supplying theory with new conceptual terms such as 'localization' and 'locale', although in practice it has sometimes relegated 'translation' to the linguistic replacement of small, decontextualized chunks of language (Jiménez-Crespo ibid.: 52–3).

11.6 Exploration: Localization and translation

Investigate definitions of 'localization' in the commercial sector. Read the discussion of conceptualizations of localization in Jiménez-Crespo (2011, 2013: 8–23).

There is a growing number of publications explaining the mechanistic, day-to-day operation of new technologies in this new environment (starting with Esselink 2000, Austermühl 2001, and O'Hagan and Ashworth 2002; more recently Dunne and Dunne 2011 as well as Jiménez-Crespo 2013). Hartley (2009: 117–24) provides a useful summary of core concepts of both **computer-assisted translation** (CAT) and **machine translation** (MT) tools.

■ **Computer-assisted translation (CAT) tools** used by professional translators encompass tools for the alignment of ST–TT pairs, concordancing of search terms and term extraction. In particular, translation memory tools allow the creation of databases of previous translations. These are used to indicate matches with items in the text on which the translator is working. This increases work speeds and facilitates consistency in the translation of a given term in different texts by different translators.

■ **Machine translation (MT) tools** generate automatic translations. These are largely used for assimilation (Hartley 2009: 121), that is for comprehension. Among the most widely known are the free online translators such as Bing translator (https://www.bing.com/translator/), Google Translate (https://translate.google.com/) and Systran (http://www.systransoft.com/). However, Hartley (ibid.) points out that MT is increasingly used for **dissemination**, for example by the European Commission in order to provide a draft first translation of documents which are then post-edited by a human translator or editor.

The same technologies have also spawned innovative theoretical work that discusses what these changes mean for the translator and for our conceptualization of translation. Anthony Pym's *The Moving Text: Localization, Translation, and Distribution* (2004) is a major contribution to the theoretical discussion. It revisits common issues of translation within this new context. For example, a translation theory perspective is applied to **internationalization**, which leads to the adaptation of accepted communication models. Thus, the production of multiple TL versions (e.g. software localized for distribution worldwide in the local languages) modifies the 'simple' model of ST–TT transfer. An internationalized, **interlingua** version (a term taken from machine translation) is used as a basis for producing the versions for the TL locale. It is this interlingua version which is constantly updated, so that the status and role of the initial ST disappears (Pym 2004: 34–5, drawing on Lambert 1989). In internationalization, instead of representing a measure of TT against its ST, equivalence is above all concerned with the **functionality** of the target text. Pym identifies the differentiating features of this new industrial phenomenon as being complexity and size of environment:

> Perhaps the most obvious of these differences is that of size. Internationalization, indeed the whole discourse of localization, is traditionally concerned with narrow professional locales. Translational equivalence, on the other hand, is traditionally concerned with large-scale complex social entities [and] cannot help but engage in the complexity and overlaps of culture.
>
> (Pym 2004: 65)

The picture Pym paints of localization is one of a dehumanizing process focused on marketing locale rather than human cultures. Projects are conducted in teams of individuals who rarely see the larger picture and who are governed by deadlines, regulations and the market (ibid.: 198). In addition, a more recent phenomenon which needs to be taken into account is that of **collaborative translation** (in some cases also known as **crowdsourcing**) often among large groups of non-professional translators. Outstanding examples include the translation (or localization) of Facebook[5] or Wikipedia.[6] But such practices raise ethical questions of quality, fair pay and status – can or should a competent translation be attempted without payment and without the employment of professionals?

In Europe, the centre of the localization industry for many years has been Ireland. It is thus not surprising, perhaps, that the major theoretical critique has come from that country, in the form of Michael Cronin's *Translation and Globalization* (Cronin 2003) and *Translation in the Digital Age* (Cronin 2013). In a world increasingly dominated and revolutionized by information technology, Cronin investigates the concept of proximity of 'networks of (translation) exchange': so, while the ease of email and other communications may encourage translation agencies to prefer to contract translators in distant, lower-wage economies rather than the west, differentiated access to resources also means that translators in whatever country, however near, without access to such technology, are forever excluded from translation activity (Cronin 2003: 47). The technology of **globalization** has here come to redefine the role, relationship and status of translators. Not to be connected to the information superhighway is thus almost equivalent to not existing as a translator in the global economy.

The last chapter of the book revisits the issue of minority languages. Cronin discusses the fragile 'linguistic ecosystem', threatened by the major international languages but where he sees translation as having a positive as well as negative value. Cronin feels that translation theory is 'a vital necessity' for minority languages, enabling them to understand translation policies and thereby counteract or manipulate them for their own benefit (ibid.: 149). He sets out a 'translation ecology: a translation practice that gives control to speakers and translators of minority languages of what, when and . . . how texts might be translated into and out of their languages' (ibid.: 167). This presupposes an 'activist dimension' from translators, related to 'the equally urgent task of getting societies and cultures to realize how important translation is to comparative self-understanding and future development' (ibid.: 134). The task is urgent because translation is currently undervalued. This means, in monetary terms, that translators are underpaid and, in cultural and political terms, that translators and transnational policy-makers are ignorant of the historical context and importance of translation. This perhaps idealistic task would presumably be reliant on the translator's broadened role as active transmitter. It would also answer a lingering and not completely rhetorical doubt that jumps out of the book: 'Are translators, as incorrigible nomads who resist the confining lure of the local, not by definition sympathetic to the globalizing project?' (ibid.: 54). However, more recent work on translator activist networks (e.g. Boéri and Maier 2010, Wolf 2012) has begun to challenge this, highlighting the role played by translators in fighting for equity and in raising awareness of the social responsibility of the translation profession.

11.3 Corpus-based translation studies

In 1998, the 'corpus-based approach', as it has become known, was being suggested as a 'new paradigm in translation studies' (Laviosa 1998a). The approach drew on the tools and techniques of monolingual (mainly English) corpus linguistics that had initially been developed in the early 1980s by John Sinclair (1933–2007) and his team working on the *COBUILD English Dictionary* project at Birmingham, UK (Sinclair 1987, 1991). The rapid evolution of computer systems meant that it was possible to create an electronic 'corpus' (plural 'corpora') of naturally occurring texts (texts which had been written for a real communicative context and not artificially invented by the language researcher) that could then be processed and analysed with software to investigate the use and patterns of the word-forms it contained. The major reason for using computer corpora was the quality of linguistic evidence, particularly on collocations and typical uses of lexical items, vastly superior to the analyst's intuition (Sinclair 1991: 42). In translation studies, the corpus-based approach was pioneered in Oslo by the late Stig Johannson (1939–2010).

In a paper urging the use of computer corpora in translation studies research, the concept of **typicality** was considered by Baker (1993, 1995) to be related to the concepts of norms, laws and **universals** which Gideon Toury was working on (see Chapter 7). Baker's focus was on identifying typicalities of the language of a corpus of translated texts which could then be compared to non-translated language. The differences could potentially reveal elements that were due to the process of translating and the norms at work. Possible characteristic features of translations suggested by Baker (1993: 244–5) were explicitation, grammatical standardization and an increased frequency of common words such as *say*. Similar hypotheses have been made in the pre-computational past. For example, Levý (1969: 108) noted that translations are often characterized by grammatically correct but artistically clichéd terms. Blum-Kulka and Levenston (1983) suggested that lexical simplification is typical of translations, and Vinay and Darbelnet (1958/1995; see Chapter 4 in this volume) made many generalizations about the translation process, including the assertion that the TT is normally longer than the ST. It is with the advent of large computerized databases and readily available tools that these hypotheses could actually be tested on large amounts of text.

11.3.1 Different types of corpus

The papers in the special issue of *Meta* edited by Laviosa (1998b) were divided into those which discussed theoretical-methodological issues and those that used the new corpus-based tools for empirical research. In the years since that publication, and even with (or because of) the rapid development of technology and the much greater availability of electronic texts, these two issues have developed but are still not resolved into a generally accepted research methodology. This is in part because the methodology inevitably depends on the object of the research and because translation studies research normally has quite different goals from the original lexicographical projects for which the first corpora were developed. Perhaps the key question, though, is that of corpus type and design. Bernardini et al. (2003), in a volume on the use of corpora in translator training, briefly summarize corpus typology and the uses of each type, though admitting that 'terminology in this area is not consistent' (ibid.: 5). They discuss the following:

(1) **Monolingual corpora:** collections of texts in the same language. These may be analysed to identify characteristics of genre or author style or for the

use of specific word-forms. Translators may use them to check naturalness, including frequent collocation. It is important to add that large monolingual corpora, such as the British National Corpus[7] and the COBUILD Bank of English[8], may serve as representative **reference corpora**, a yardstick of the language against which to measure deviation (see below).[9]

(2)   **Comparable bilingual corpora**, which are normally specialized collections of similar STs in the two languages and which can be 'mined' for terminology and other equivalences (cf. Bowker and Pearson 2002, Bowker 2011). Such corpora – for instance, of documents on solar panel technology written in German and English – might be constructed by a translator working on the translation of this domain in those languages.

(3)   **Parallel corpora**, of ST–TT pairs, which, when aligned (sentence by sentence or paragraph by paragraph), can allow the strategies employed by the translator(s) to be investigated (cf. Kenny 2001, 2011). Examples are Linguee (http://www.linguee.com/), MyMemory (https://mymemory.translated.net/), OPUS (http://opus.lingfil.uu.se/) and the Canadian Hansard.

Importantly, Bernardini et al. (2003: 6) point out that '[w]hen used in conjunction with monolingual source and target corpora, a parallel corpus can also allow learners [or researchers] to compare features of texts produced under the constraint of translation with "original" texts in both languages'. That is, it is possible to identify salient lexical or grammatical features in TTs and then to see if such features are similarly salient in non-translated texts in the same language. Thus, Olohan and Baker (2000) examine the use of *that* in the Translational English Corpus (TEC) at the University of Manchester compared to its frequency in a reference corpus of original English, the fiction sub-corpus of the British National Corpus (BNC). Their tentative findings are that in the BNC the conjunction tends to be omitted more often when used with contractions (e.g. *I don't think [that] she saw me*), possibly indicative of informal texts. On the other hand, in the TEC *that* occurs more frequently with contractions. The suggestion is that this may be a feature of translated language.

11.3.2 Other corpus-based and corpus–driven studies

Maeve Olohan's *Introducing Corpora in Translation Studies* (2004) provides an overview of this area of research and includes other case studies of syntactic and other features. Most of Olohan's survey concerns the TEC corpus. That is, it looks at patterns in English TTs with little or no access to the STs. However, Olohan discusses commercially available software such as *Wordsmith Tools* (Scott 2012) and *Paraconc* (Barlow), to which we might add later software such as *Antconc* (http://www.laurenceanthony.net/software/antconc/) and *Sketch Engine* (https://www.sketchengine.co.uk/), the latter founded by the late Adam Kilgarriff (1960–2015). These facilitate the analysis of **researcher-constructed parallel corpora**, for example, a ST–TT pair or series of pairs in electronic format, which have been downloaded or scanned, copyright permitting. The kinds of analysis this enables are both **quantitative** (comparing ST and TT statistics for word frequency, distribution, lexical density, sentence length, keywords, etc.) and **qualitative** (close analysis of concordance lines of individual instances). Figures 11.1 and 11.2 (Case study 1 below) show an example of the type of data that is generated by concordance lines in comparable monolingual corpora. By such methods, the corpus-based approach links with other methodologies and approaches. These are notably **descriptive** studies, which study the translation product or seek to identify typical features of translation.

The combination of rapid access to the 'big picture' of quantitative data, supported with close critical analysis of the texts in their sociocultural environment, comprises a complementary interdisciplinary methodology that reveals patterns that may otherwise pass unnoticed. Olohan attempts to link stylistic patterns in a text with the ideology of the translator or the environment by searching for informal contractions and keywords. However, the success of this approach is limited by the results the computer is able to generate and the justified interpretations it permits. Still, by contrasting the work of different translators and triangulating the findings against a reference corpus (the BNC), intuition as to the **style** of a text may be confirmed and hypotheses generated regarding translated language. This thus follows the path marked out by Baker (2000), who analyses the style of translators Peter Bush (from Spanish) and Peter Clark (from Arabic) using the frequency of the verb *say* as a marker of standardization and reduced lexical variation. Baker finds that Clark uses *say* twice as often as Bush, but this may be due to the high frequency of the Arabic ST *qaal*. This is the problem with Baker's study. It claims to be developing a methodology for stylistic analysis, but there is little consideration at all of the SLs and STs. If we are to give any credence to Toury's law of interference (Toury 1995/2012; see our Chapter 7), these must have some effect on the TT.

One of the most innovative projects in parallel corpora has been the English–Norwegian bidirectional parallel corpus initiated by Stig Johansson. However,

Johansson (2003) discusses the difficulties of collecting suitable texts for multi-lingual corpora, one problem being that far more is translated from English than in the other direction (cf. Venuti, Chapter 9). One suggestion which Johansson pursued is to commission multiple translations of the same literary text from professional translators in order to study variation. These are collected as the Oslo Multilingual Corpus.[10] Such texts can also serve as training texts for apprentice translators and comparison with the professionals' work may aid the improvement of decision-making strategies (ibid.: 140–1).

It is also noticeable that a good number of studies adopt a **contrastive analysis** approach, using the analysis of comparable corpora that may be genre specific. The collection edited by Granger and Petch-Tyson (2003) specifically promotes itself as a bringing together of corpus linguistics, translation studies and contrastive analysis, while work from Ian Williams (e.g. 2007) is based on a 500,000-word corpus of biomedical research articles comprising English SL texts, Spanish TTs and a comparable corpus of non-translated Spanish STs of the same genre. Such a corpus design enables identification of statistical deviations in the Spanish TTs (compared to the English STs) and also of deviations between Spanish STs and TTs. Williams examines the frequency and collocation of the Spanish lemma *OBSERVAR* ('observe').[11] He finds (2007: 101) that *OBSERVAR* appears much more frequently n the Spanish TTs than the STs, and suggests that this shows 'a more restricted lexical range and greater homogeneity of the translations in spite of TL norms' (i.e. that Spanish TTs tend to show less variation than Spanish STs).

Although perhaps the most dramatic developments in this area are those that are producing practical results in the form of new statistical tools for the translator and for machine translation[12] (see section 11.3.1 above), there is continued interest in the ways in which the corpora approach can assist translation theory. The volume *Corpus-Based Translation Studies: Research and Applications* (Kruger et al. 2011), for instance, examines a range of phenomena, including translation units, textual norms, terminographic practice and explicitation. Importantly, too, the inclusion of corpus-based interpreting studies (Setton 2011) shows the fluid methodological overlap between research into translation and interpreting. Zanettin (2012) explores the applications of corpora for descriptive studies systematically in his *Translation-Driven Corpora*, echoing the distinction made by Saldanha and O'Brien (2013: 61–2), following Tognini-Bonelli (2001), between the **'corpus-based' approach** (which takes a pre-existing theory as its starting point) and **'corpus-driven' research** (which builds up from corpus data towards patterns and generalizations).

11.7 Exploration: Corpora and translation studies

Read Federico Zanettin's (2013) online article on corpus methods for descriptive translation studies. Make a note of the translation features analysed, the methods used and the ideal composition of the related corpora.

Case studies

We shall use examples of corpus-based translation studies and audiovisual translation as scenarios for a brief discussion of what they can bring to the theory and applications of translation studies, illustrated by reference to source material.

Case study discussion 1

The construction of new corpora is time-consuming and fraught with difficulties (investment in software and hardware, selection of texts, their preparation in a suitable format, revision of the texts to ensure deletion of unneeded tags, the insertion of tags to mark parts of speech or other features according to the purpose of the study, the interpretation of statistics, etc.). This is the reason that until recently there have been relatively few large-scale projects or even in-depth computer-assisted studies of translated books or authors. In addition, the results are sometimes treated with scepticism if they fail to relate to the sociocultural context of production and transmission. To some, the corpus-based approach smacks too much of the word- and text-restricted translation or may fit more closely into a contrastive analysis paradigm.

   A project of mine (Munday 2011) on **semantic prosody** (see Stewart 2009) or **association** in Spanish and English looked at the dictionary equivalents (English) *loom large* and (Spanish) *cernerse* based on an analysis of examples from the Leeds Collection of Internet corpora and the Spanish Real Academia Corpus (see Figures 11.1 and 11.2).[13]

Found 30 examples (0.165 ipm) of 'MU (meet [word="loom*"] [word="large"] -0 1) cut 100' in INTERNET-EN

□ >>	. However, in a genre where women may be expected to **loom large** , I was disconcerted to find that the men on this disc
□ >>	and savings. In such cases, among which nursing home costs **loom large** , Medicaid funding covers the shortfall between monthly
□ >>	, the challenges related to preservation of subsurface data **loom large** , the situation is not so dire as might be expected. Some of
□ >>	Second, although America's problems at home still **loom large** , traditional formulas for government action are now widely
□ >>	. Corporate consumerism and the power of advertising also **loom large** - the specialist, seductive language that lures Jack into
□ >>	, and the ineffable intentions of Alan Greenspan all **loom large** . Back to this month's issue Home	Subscribe	Media Kit	
□ >>	, and the ineffable intentions of Alan Greenspan all **loom large** . Back to this month's issue	Home	Subscribe	Newsstand
□ >>	, and the constraints on career choice and job satisfaction **loom large** . Because of increasing competition within the profession
□ >>	as threats of regulations, price controls and litigation **loom large** . Employers are no longer a secure source of health coverage
□ >>	the plan, the global ecological repercussions are bound to **loom large** . In the 1980s, western scientists feared that reducing the
□ >>	. If we view it *as a formal language*, then its flaws **loom large** . It lacks many key features, including implication and
□ >>	. I suppose at the start we imagined that money would **loom large** . Not so. The main reasons given for dissatisfaction were
□ >>	the future, though at the present moment their differences **loom large** . Our vast, dark Page 43 native population consists largely
□ >>	teaching of world history, these socially-derived judgments **loom large** . They invite further work on distinctive social profiles as
□ >>	possibilities of decentralisation of power and planning **loom large** before us. To make basic changes in the existing
□ >>	deicers is less well developed. If environmental concerns **loom large** for you, then you need information on the BOD and COD (
□ >>	at Everything2.com elaborates: ...the club foot was to **loom large** in Talleyrand's life. His parents obviously felt that
□ >>	affected ordinary men and women, how small everyday events **loom large** in individual lives. To her crisp style, reminiscent of
□ >>	it until last can cause ' the dreaded role play ' to **loom large** in people's minds, causing a negative distraction
□ >>	a problem with social roots, and political obstacles still **loom large** in some countries. Our world will be less secure if we fail
□ >>	capability for enforcing policy. Military considerations **loom large** in the " development pole " policy applied in the FTN
□ >>	. Nor do the choosy trout of cool rushing northern waters **loom large** in the angling of those of us who live on the Texas
□ >>	and examine two emerging common challenges that will **loom large** in the coming years. One such challenge is to ensure that
□ >>	a play-book than its original warrants. These changes might **loom large** in the mind of an editor, but to the average reader, not
□ >>	acts as a deterrent as long as the fear and hassle factors **loom large** in the minds of prescribers - - and this is where your
□ >>	the government seeks to rebuild its finances, continues to **loom large** on peoples' spending power. Financial performance In light
□ >>	. Along these lines, three targets for collaborative action **loom large** on the horizon; advocating for better funding for research
□ >>	have visualized the VLSI phenomenon that was starting to **loom large** outside of PARC - - all he saw was the tiny little piece of

Figure 11.1 Concordance sample of *loom large*

One of the results showed that in Spanish the typical lexical and syntactic collocation of *cernerse* was *una amenaza que se cierne sobre* ... ['a threat which hovers/looms over ...']; in the English corpus this corresponded to *a gathering threat* or *a threat gathering over* ... a different collocation and syntactic structure. Such findings are useful in gradually building up a contrastive picture of the languages that will then have applications for lexicographers and translators. It is not, however, the type of study that is in the mainstream of translation studies at present.

Case study discussion 2

Audiovisual translation has become more or less a separate branch within the field of translation studies. Yet the general absence of its own theoretical models is surprising. Its orientation has been above all prescriptive, describing and

Figure 11.2 Concordance sample of *se cierne(n)*

deciding how and where the subtitles should appear and what are the best techniques for producing a successful product. Descriptive studies are now becoming
more frequent, perhaps because of the popularity of the film medium and the
ready availability of multiple ST–TT pairs on DVDs and downloads. Areas such as
the translation of dialect and humour are flourishing (see Chiaro 2010).

However, many studies continue to limit themselves to the written word on
the screen and its comparison to a researcher-produced transcription of the
spoken dialogue, even though that is necessarily partial. A satisfactory theoretical
treatment of the visual image, most plausibly incorporating techniques and metalanguage from film studies (cf. Chaume 2004), would seem to be paramount.
One of the complications is that the visual image is hardly ever altered in the TT,
so it is easier to focus on the written word. The other is that the translation
studies theorist rarely has sufficient grounding in film theory. The same goes for
postcolonial or cultural theory when dealing with what is often known as 'world
cinema'. Let us take as an example the acclaimed Bengali film *Aparajito* (Satyajit

Ray, 1956), the second in a trilogy shot in black-and-white, with music from Ravi Shankar. The film follows the life of a poor family by the Ganges, focusing particularly on the young son, Apu. It won the Golden Lion award in Venice in 1957, showing both the impact on and acceptance by an international audience.

The visual and aural impact of the film is particularly impressive but the most striking feature of the subtitling of the opening scenes is the number of borrowings in the dialogue. Thus, we have many food items that are italicized in the English: *mung dal, mung, marou, khichree, paan masala, pedha*. At times, several appear in the same subtitles, often with other culture-specific words:

Apu's been asking for *khichree* since
he had some at the *ghat* the other day

where *khichree* is a dish of mung beans and rice and *ghat* refers to the steps leading down to the river for bathing. Occasionally, there is a mixture of explicitation and borrowing, such as:

A sweet made from milk [for ST *dinche ladoc*]
And a *pedha* as well

The explicitation may go unrecognized by most of the international audience. Yet the really interesting point to investigate would be the impact of these borrowings on the TT reception, the interaction between image and visual (how much of the sense can be gleaned from the picture?) and the positioning of the subtitler, viewer and subject through such choices. In particular, there are many culture-specific images and customs, mostly concerning the Hindu festival of Diwali, which are not explicated and which are conveyed by image alone. The in-depth analysis of this type of problem requires the associated expertise of theorists from film, postcolonialism and translation studies. A clearer example of the need for interdisciplinary collaboration would be hard to find.

Summary

This last chapter has examined three new scenarios for translation studies, each making use of or being determined by new technologies: audiovisual translation (section 11.1), localization and globalization (11.2) and corpus-based and corpus-driven approaches (11.3). Each has brought about a fundamental re-evaluation of translation practice and theory. Thus, the corpus-based approach, perhaps still undervalued by some, enables the more thorough analysis and discovery of major features of translated language and is driving the development of automatic machine translation of various types; audiovisual translation is the site of many descriptive studies as well as of new creative practice; but it is localization and globalization that perhaps presents the major challenge to translators and is the most evident locus of contact between technology, translator identity and the postmodern world. These are also sites that require very specific expertise and training from the researcher, and ideally necessitate interdisciplinary co-operation to maximize the effectiveness of different specializations.

Further reading

For all aspects of audiovisual translation, see Pérez-González (2014); see also Anderman and Díaz Cintas (2008), Chiaro (2010). For dubbing, see Chaume (2012). For non-verbal communication, see Poyatos (1997). For audio description and accessibility, see papers in Díaz Cintas et al. (2010). For multimodal texts, see the special issue of *JosTrans* (Issue 20, 2013), http://www.jostrans.org/archive.php?display=20. For video games, see Bernal Merino (2015) and O'Hagan and Mangiron (2013). For a study of fansubbing, see Massidda (2015). For the translation of music, see Susam-Saraeva (2008) and Minors (2013).

For translation technologies in general, see Chan (2015); for sociocultural issues, see Cronin (2013). For localization, see Esselink (2000), Dunne (2006) and Dunne and Dunne (2011). For corpus-based translation studies, see McEnery et al. (2006), Anderman and Rogers (2007), Kruger et al. (2011) and Zanettin (2012, 2013).

Discussion and research points

1 Read the detailed analysis of audiovisual translation in Chiaro (2009). Investigate which forms of audiovisual translation (e.g. subtitling, dubbing, surtitling, voice-over, audio description, etc.) are used in your country. Which are most prominent, and for which text genres or modes of communication? Why?

2 Read Michal Borodo's (2015) article on 'Multimodality, translation and comics', available on the companion website. Note the techniques employed for translating the visual image. Find an example of a translated graphic novel in your own languages. How far are similar techniques used?

3 How 'vulnerable' do you consider the subtitler really is? What other vulnerable translation contexts can you think of? To what extent does this fit with Anthony Pym's (2008) view of translation as characterized by risk avoidance?

4 Look at the study by Karamitroglou and discuss how you would go about studying norms of audiovisual translation in these ways. Do you think that the results will be very different from those of more conventional written translation?

5 What answer would you give to Cronin's question: 'Are translators . . . not by definition sympathetic to the globalizing project?' (Cronin 2003: 54). Read the papers in Boéri and Maier (2010) or Pérez-González and Susam-Saraeva (2012) to see an activist view on the translator's role.

6 Investigate what online corpus resources are available for your languages. What are the explicit objectives behind the creation of these corpora (e.g. language standardization, synchronic or diachronic analysis of language, contrastive analysis of languages, analysis of translation universals, etc.)?

The ITS website at www.routledge.com/cw/munday contains:

■ a video summary of the chapter;
■ a recap multiple-choice test;
■ customizable PowerPoint slides;
■ further reading links and extra journal articles;
■ more research project questions.

CHAPTER 12

Research and commentary projects

Key concepts

■ **The possibilities of 'consilience' (coming together) of trends in translation studies research.**

■ **The link between translation theory and practice.**

■ **Theory relevant to the writing of a reflective translation commentary.**

■ **Research project methodologies.**

Key texts

Chesterman, Andrew (2005) 'Towards consilience?', in Karin Aijmer and Cecilia Alvstad (eds) *New Tendencies in Translation Studies*, Göteborg: Göteborg University, pp. 19–28.

García Álvarez, Ana María (2007) 'Evaluating students' translation process in specialized translation: Translation commentary', *Journal of Specialised Translation* 7, http://www.jostrans.org/issue07/art_alvarez.pdf

Saldanha, Gabriela and Sharon O'Brien (2013) *Research Methodologies in Translation Studies*, Manchester: St Jerome.

Sewell, Penelope (2002) *Translation Commentary: The Art Revisited*, Dublin: Philomel.

Shei, Chris (2005) 'Translation commentary: A happy medium between translation curriculum and EAP', *System* 33.2: 309–25.

Williams, Jenny and **Andrew Chesterman** (2002) *The Map: A Beginner's Guide to Doing Research in Translation Studies*, Manchester: St Jerome.

12.0 Introduction

Watch the introductory video on the companion website.

The main aim of this book has been to present the major theories of translation in an objective way, underlining the strengths of each one and how each has contributed to the evolution of the discipline as a whole.

This final chapter seeks to respond to questions about the nature of the **link between translation theory and translation practice**. This is central to a discipline that straddles the academic subject of translation studies and the working practices of professional translators and is often located in universities that are heavily involved in training translators.[1] The focus of this chapter is as follows:

- 12.1 draws together the various strands of theory under the concept of 'consilience' (Chesterman 2005) and assesses their possible importance for the future.
- The last two sections then examine the application of theory to the two most common extended theoretical projects undertaken in universities: (section 12.2) commentary projects, where students have to write an extended commentary to accompany and explain a translation they have produced, and (12.3) more substantial research projects, most commonly at Masters or PhD level. The aim is to highlight those areas of theory that may have a particular bearing on such research.

12.1 Consilience in translation studies

The preceding chapters have, I hope, shown the **huge breadth of research** in translation studies, that is increasing at an ever faster pace. Chapter 1 set out to delimit what translation studies is, Chapter 2 gave a very brief introduction to the history of the ideas of the discipline, and then Chapters 3 to 6 presented the evolution of concepts from the more linguistically oriented theories. However, it is very important to note that translation studies has centred on applied rather than on theoretical linguistics. Indeed, it could scarcely be otherwise since translation is above all about communication. Hence the particular interest in forms of textual equivalence, text and discourse analysis and, in Chapter 5, the beginnings of incorporation of more cultural perspectives from translatorial action and skopos theory. Subsequent chapters investigate these. The descriptive studies paradigm developed by Toury (Chapter 7) is crucial in providing a framework into which individual case studies can be inserted, compared and replicated, and conclusions drawn. Without such a framework, such studies would have little if any generalizing power.

Chapters 8 and 9 gave some insight into the sociocultural and ideological factors that influence the process of translation and showed the ways that other disciplines, such as gender studies and postcolonial studies have interacted with translation studies. The important point is that translation is not limited to the words on the page. It is an intercultural and interlinguistic product of a complex process that involves human and institutional agents (author, commissioner, translator, editor, reviser, patron, political institutions, and so on) operating in specific sociocultural, geographical and historical conditions. Agents bring their own agendas, goals and subjectivity, while the conditions fluctuate over time according to changing political and historical circumstance. This provides a very rich source of material for research with the capacity for insight into language, communication, history, politics, sociology, culture and so on. The last two chapters extended the premises on which some of the traditional tenets of translation are built. Chapter 10 looked at hermeneutic and philosophical theories which have challenged the concept of equivalence and have extended the creativity of the translator. Chapter 11 then discussed the influence of new technologies on both practice and research.

12.1 Exploration: Revisiting the Holmes/Toury 'map'

Look again at the map presented in Chapter 1, p. 17 and locate the different theories and concepts introduced in the course of the book. Look at the websites of IATIS, EST and other associations for details of their most recent conferences. What seem to be the major trends in the latest research? In which ways do these suggest a broadening of the scope of translation studies? See the ITS companion website for a suggested revision of the map.

Even though the structure of the book might suggest an evolution from linguistic to cultural theories, this is far from the intention. With Andrew Chesterman,

I question the **simplistic linguistics–cultural studies divide** that has for some time marred the discipline by creating frictions and oppositions. Chesterman (2005) instead proposes a classification of four 'complementary [though overlapping] approaches' to research into translation: (1) the textual; (2) the cognitive; (3) the sociological; and (4) the cultural. Chesterman (ibid.: 24) perhaps optimistically feels that there is 'fairly widespread agreement' on some of the main research problems (e.g. the definition of 'translation' and 'equivalence', the description of translation universals, the explanation of causes and the justification of quality judgements) but not on the philosophical questions. Each of the four approaches has its own objectives and generates its own questions and methodologies. Thus:

(1)   The **textual** investigates the translation product, that is, individual ST–TT pairs or corpora of many texts or text fragments. It can be compared to undertaking field work in linguistics or anthropology, gathering primary data of translation phenomena (texts). The goal may be to find trends in one or more translations, to identify forms of equivalence, translation universals, difficult translation problems, to discuss and classify solutions adopted, to evaluate a translation, etc. (see Chapters 3 to 6).

(2)   The **cognitive** seeks to investigate the process of translation through empirical methods such as think-aloud protocols and eye-tracking (Chapter 4) to find out, among other things, what translation competence is comprised of and what marks out the experienced, successful translator's decisions.

(3)   The **sociological** looks at the role of the human agent, most notably but not exclusively the translator (see Chapter 8 and 9). Here, ethnographic methods of interviews and questionnaires may be useful, which brings in an ethical element to the study since special permissions may be required. Alternatively, historical data may be gathered through examination of translator correspondence, archives, writing.

(4)   The **cultural** places translation within a wider context, for example as part of a literary movement (see the polysystem theory, Chapter 7) or ideological power play (Lefevere, Chapter 8). It also pertains to the very nature of what we mean by translation, adaptation and related terms (Chapter 1). More forcefully, it brings translation into debate with critical and cultural theory (Chapters 8 to 10), extending and challenging the basis of traditional conceptualizations of translation.

Each of these approaches contributes to finding out more about the central object of study, translation. However, they are not discrete, hermetically sealed approaches. Quite the opposite. Thus, textual analysis of a ST–TT pair may take place within a descriptive studies framework (Chapter 7) that would locate the analysis within its wider cultural context. Just as linguistic analysis which does not consider the wider contextual factors is in some ways deficient, so too are culturally oriented studies which reject textual analysis. In my view, the two are complementary and a combination of the two essential for a fuller understanding of the role of translation. Similarly, the sociological and the cultural may overlap in studies of the history of specific translators or groups of translators, and there is no reason why such historical surveys should not also look at the texts and translation strategies adopted. What is important is that the boundaries of the discipline should be stretched by both empirical study and theoretical reflection. Reflective commentaries and research projects are the most common means by which students and translators (trainee and professional) can participate in this endeavour.

12.2 Translation commentaries

Students of translation, particularly at Masters level, are often required to translate a lengthy text of their choice for the summer project part of the programme. This text may vary between 3,000 and 10,000 words. In addition, a common requirement is to accompany it with a detailed commentary describing the translation strategies and procedures that have been adopted, and/or translation problems that have arisen. This provides the opportunity for reflective learning from the student and also gives insights into their process of translation that in some ways are as illuminating as methods such as think-aloud protocols (García Álvarez 2007, see also Chapter 4).

Each **commentary** is necessarily different, but there are several common factors that should be taken into account. Shei (2005) details what he terms the 'translation problem exploration space (TPES)', which includes the analysis of translation **purpose, method** and **readership** in order to establish the **norms** that are followed in the TT. These relate to theory covered in the following chapters of this book:

- purpose or skopos theory (Chapter 5);
- method (Chapters 3 to 6);
- readership (Chapters 3 and 5);
- norms (Chapter 7).

In addition, these factors will ideally be described in the **translation specification** of the text, mirroring and even formalizing real-life practice where the translator will generally be given more general instructions. Table 12.1 shows one example of a translation specification sheet:

Table 12.1 Example translation specification sheet[2]

*1 These are the **basic external features** of the **source text**.*

External features of source text	Example
Author (name and/or function)	Jonathan Amos, BBC science correspondent
Language variety	UK English, formal journalism
Genre or text type	Popular science report of specialized biology article. Informative text type
Publication outlet (e.g. newspaper title)	BBC News, Science and Environment
Date of publication	20 April 2011
Title of whole text	'Fossilized spider "biggest on record" '
Length (in characters or words)	489 words, including title and captions
Layout, font, visuals and other features	Font: Ariel point 11
	Visuals: 2 photographs
	Hyperlinks
Readership (e.g. lay, specialist)	Generally lay, educated, non-expert
Place of publication	Online http://www.bbc.co.uk/news/ science-environment-13134505

*2 These are any **particular constraints** that the person commissioning the translation has specified on features of the **target text**.*

Constraints of target text	Example
Language variety	Standard Chinese, simplified characters
Genre or text type	Popular science report. Informative text type; 'full' translation of ST
Length (in characters or words)	+/− 10%
Translator's notes (footnotes or endnotes)	Not acceptable
Layout, font, visuals and other features	Font: MingLIU, point 10.5
	Visuals: 1 photograph
Publication outlet (e.g. newspaper title)	Xinhuanet (of Xinhua news agency)
Readers' knowledge of subject	Generally lay, educated, non-expert
Date of publication	21 April 2011
Place of publication	Beijing and online, http://www.xinhuanet.com/

12.2.1 Extralinguistic information

The translation specification includes **extralinguistic information** which is needed by the translator in order to contextualize the ST and to decide on an overall translation strategy in the TL. Without such information (for instance, if the only instruction given to students were 'Translate this text into Chinese') translation would take place in a contextual vacuum where any procedure or strategy could potentially be justified. Some of the information in the sheet is similar to that listed by Christiane Nord in her model of ST analysis (see section 5.4).

The right-hand columns in Table 12.1 are completed as a sample with a description of an online text entitled 'Fossilised spider "biggest on record" ', a report on a 165-million-year-old fossil discovered in Inner Mongolia. As well as purely **informative details** such as the title and the author name, there are also more **subjective details** associated with the description of language variety and readership. For the ST, the values for the **language variety** can be inferred from an analysis of the text itself. So, the location of the publication and the spelling conventions suggest UK English rather than US English; the text is a piece of formal (rather than sensationalist) journalism which nevertheless includes direct quotation and some contracted forms (e.g. *There's a very distinct group of them*). But there are of course other values associated with language variety which have to do with such matters as participant relationship, author provenance and stance, social role and attitude, which we discussed in Chapter 6.2 when presenting Register analysis and Juliane House's model. Language variety is also bound up with questions of **genre** and **text type** which were discussed in Chapter 5.1. If we follow Reiss's schema set out in Table 5.1 and Figure 5.1, then we would locate this ST mainly as an informative text type. The precise labelling of the genre would depend on the sophistication and delicacy of the classificatory system. It is a popular science report and, in large part, a summary and popular 'rewriting' (to use Lefevere's term from Chapter 8) of scientific findings initially reported by a joint US–China scientific team in the specialist journal *Biology Letters*.[3] It is therefore in fact a form of intralingual translation (Jakobson, Chapter 1) from a technical to a popular report.

Although the ST **readership** has been described as 'generally lay, educated, non-expert', meaning that the readers will not usually have subject-specific knowledge, this is necessarily a generalization. It is of course quite possible that some experts will read the article. Equally, there will be different grades of expertise even among the general audience and there may be various reading purposes and positions.

The **length** in words (489) is important in order to delimit the boundaries of the text, especially if it is part of a larger macro-text, which in this case it is since it appears on a webpage that contains adverts and links to other stories and sites. It also serves as a way of roughly estimating the text size, important if the TT were expected to fit the same **layout** as the ST. For the professional, length is also a means to calculate payment, based on a fee per character, word, page or thousand words.

The **constraints of the TT** are the general extralinguistic factors that guide or determine some of the translator's decisions. In professional contexts, the constraints are normally formulated by the TT commissioner (see Holz-Mänttäri, section 5.2) and set out in the translation brief (see Nord, section 5.4). The sample values in Figure 12.1 are based on a hypothetical context of translation of the text for the Xinhua news agency in China. While the resultant TT could be sold to other publications, the brief limits itself to the publication by Xinhua for its own online outlet.

The constraints will go a long way to determining the macro-level characteristics of the TT and the overall translation strategy, but they will still leave the translator some freedom to determine micro-level procedures.[4] The decisions that are already made include the **language variety in the TL**. In this case it is Standard Chinese, simplified characters. Although it is beyond the limits of the current specification, it is entirely plausible that another translator would be asked to produce another TT in traditional characters – it is also very possible that one of these TTs would be an intralingual translation of the other.

The **genre** and **text type** are important, particularly in comparison with the ST. In the vast majority of cases, they will be very similar between ST and TT (here, 'popular science report', 'informative text type'). In some cases, though, there may be a genre shift – imagine ST advertorial copy being translated for use as a more explicit TT advertisement in a kind of 'adaptation' (see Chapter 1). More frequently, the translator's problem will be the different composition and expectations for the genre in SL and TL which might necessitate a particular translation strategy (see below). The term 'full translation' has been used to indicate that the translator is expected to translate the whole text and to distinguish it from summary, gist or other forms of translation. Nevertheless, text **length** will vary across languages, English or German, for example, generally being more concise than, say, Romance languages such as Spanish and French. Explicitation in translation may also add to text length (see Vinay and Darbelnet's claims in

Chapter 4). The accepted value +/− 10 per cent for the text length[5] is an acknowledgement of these factors while still determining that the TT must conform quite closely to the format of the ST layout. This is vital in areas such as webpage localization where text boxes and hyperlinks may have very restrictive sizes that cannot be overridden.

Linked to this are the values for translator's notes and layout. The **layout** of the TT determines the amount of space available to the translator and the form (including font) in which it will be displayed. The layout will often be checked and modified by an editor or copy-editor who has overall control for all pages. In genres such as the online news story, it would be highly unusual to allow **translator notes**. Other genres, such as the academic edition of a classical text, may demand them. Sometimes it may depend on the **purpose** ('skopos', see section 5.3) of the TT – a witness statement for use by the defence in preparation for a trial may require ambiguities, inconsistencies, culturally important information, etc. to be pointed out by the translator in a note so that they can be examined and pursued by the lawyers.

Those controlling the **publication outlet** of the TT may well have a say over the content of the translation. This will include the professionals and possibly political or cultural patrons discussed by Lefevere (see section 8.1). So, an editor may decide on the inclusion of visual material and the title, which may be crucial for the reading of the text, while a patron may decide on the selection of material and may promote or censor certain writers, ideas, texts or expressions.

Together with text purpose, it is the translator's view of the needs of the **TT readers** which will go a long way to deciding the overall translation strategy. Here, the translator will have the same reservations as we indicated above for the ST readership – it is impossible to fully generalize the readership since subject-specific knowledge, reading purpose and position will all vary. This casts huge doubt on the possibility of achieving **equivalent effect**, championed by Nida (Chapter 3). Nonetheless, it is almost impossible to translate without having some idea of who the target reader is. This may range from a wide audience ('generally lay, educated, non-expert') to a specific group (students of a textbook in a specific locale; biologists who are experts on the evolution of spiders) or to an individual (the translation of a personal letter). The audience may be described by the commissioner (say, advertising copy targeting a specific socio-economic group in a specific country). A translator will debate the needs and knowledge of the audience with the commissioner. Where it is difficult to determine (as might be the case with a literary translation of a popular author or with a tourist text aimed at a wide group), the translator might imagine a core audience. The assessment of the subject-specific knowledge and cultural distance of the TT reader will underpin decisions on how much **explicitation** to use (see Chapter 4). For example, a reader of a culture-specific text may need to be told that South Mumbai is a generally wealthier part of the city, that alcohol was legally prohibited in the USA in the 1920s or that the Japanese suffixes *san* and *sama* are honorifics. Such assessments of the readers' needs will not absolutely determine translation decisions, though, since the **purpose** of the translation and **intention** of the commissioner and translator play important roles. So, an overall decision may be taken to adopt a specific strategy, perhaps oriented using some of the well-known terms discussed throughout the book (see Table 12.2):

Table 12.2 Comparison of terminology for orientation of strategies

Theorist	Orientation of strategy	
	Target-oriented	Source-oriented
Schleiermacher (Chapter 2)	Naturalizing translation	Alienating translation
Nida (Chapter 3)	Dynamic equivalence (later called 'functional equivalence')	Formal equivalence (later called 'formal correspondence')
Newmark (Chapter 3)	Communicative translation	Semantic translation
Vinay and Darbelnet (Chapter 4)	Oblique translation	Direct translation
Nord (Chapter 5)	Instrumental translation	Documentary translation
House (Chapter 6)	Covert translation	Overt translation
Toury (Chapter 7)	Acceptability	Adequacy
Hermans (Chapter 7)	Target-oriented	Source-oriented
Venuti (Chapter 9)	Domestication	Foreignization

12.2 Exploration: Strategies

Look back at the earlier definitions and discussions of the different strategies that are listed in Table 12.2. What is the focus of each? How far do they differ from each other?

The selection of overall strategy may be influenced by the ideology or ethical stance of the translator (see Chapters 8 and 9), who may seek to produce a translation that challenges dominant ideology. Examples would be a feminist translation of a poet such as Emily Dickinson in a patriarchal society or the dissemination through translation of the ideas of a marginalized political group.

Table 12.1 describes the 'default' values but these may be overridden in specific circumstances. For instance, translator's notes may not usually be allowed but may be acceptable when there is information that would otherwise be confusing; or US English spelling may be required except for a specific term, such as *localisation*,[6] in a company's in house style guide.

12.2.2 Micro-level intratextual analysis

When it comes to the **micro-level** analysis of the TT, some discussion on the understanding of **equivalence** (see Chapter 3 and above) is crucial, but the form of analysis may draw on one or more of the models and theoretical contributions in Chapters 3 to 6 particularly (see Sewell 2002 for analysis of the strengths of different commentaries). The **metalanguage** of translation (e.g. *procedure, borrowing, calque, literal translation*, from Vinay and Darbelnet, Chapter 4) is essential to ensure precision of argumentation. The particular phenomena discussed may be covered by Nord's **intratextual factors** (see section 5.4) such as composition, non-verbal elements, lexis, sentence structure and suprasegmental features. Or they may be focused on the complex but more subtle **Register** and **discourse analysis** (House, Baker, Hatim and Mason, Munday, Chapter 6), where functional meaning is linked to the variables of (1) Field, (2) Tenor and (3) Mode and their corresponding lexicogrammatical realizations. Thus, the commentary may focus on a few particularly problematic aspects, such as the following:

> ### 12.3 Exploration: Register analysis
>
> Before looking at the discussion below, carry out your own analysis of the Register variables (Field, Tenor, Mode) of the BBC ST, identifying marked and/or potentially problematic features.

(1) **Technical or culture-specific terminology**, part of **Field**. In this text, this terminology is above all expressed by the semantic field of biology and the particular spider in question: *golden orb weaver, arachnid, invertebrate paleontology*, etc. But it is also realized in proper names. Some of these, such as the geographical region of *Inner Mongolia*, will probably have established equivalents. Organizations (*University of Kansas*) are more problematic, and the names of the journal *Biology Letters* and the position of the academic as *Gulf-Hedberg distinguished professor of invertebrate paleontology* will require careful thought and a more complex translation procedure linked to the overall translation strategy.

(2) **Writer–reader relationship**, part of **Tenor**, is complex, partly because the text is an amalgam of journalistic distance and the direct quotation of comments from the experts. So, on the one hand there are relatively impersonal statements of verifiable fact such as *Today's Nephila species are found around the globe in tropical and sub-tropical regions*. On the other hand, there is more informal opinion transmitted through the spoken words of the scientist which are nevertheless mixed with the specialized terminology of field: *You see not just the hairs on the legs but little things like the trichobothria which are very, very fine.*

Also crucial in Tenor are **modality** and **reporting verbs** which indicate the degree of commitment to truth, as in the following:

> The spider was encased in volcanic ash at the bottom of what would have been a lake. Perhaps the ash fall from an eruption pulled her from her web.

This describes the circumstances in which the spider was buried and preserved. *Was encased* is a categorical statement of fact but there are two modal forms that show more hedging: *what would have been a lake* shows deduction, presumably based on reliable evidence; *perhaps* is a more tentative hypothesis since it is impossible to know for sure how the spider ended up where it did.

(3) **Cohesive elements and word order**, part of **Mode. Cohesion** holds the text together, creating **'texture'** and contributing to the overall **coherence** of the argument. An example would be the **lexical chain** of synonyms that run through the text. Take the first three sentences of the piece:

> Scientists say a **fossilised spider** from the Inner Mongolian region of China is **the biggest** yet found.
>
> **The female**, which lived about 165 million years ago, belongs to a collection of spiders well known today – the **golden orb weavers**.

These creatures make webs from a very tough and distinctively golden silk.

All the items in bold refer to the golden orb weaver spider. They create a lexical chain that binds the text together but they rely on the reader's identification of that link. In one case (*the biggest*) this requires the recognition of the ellipsis and the filling in of the missing element – *the biggest **fossilised spider***. This crucial cohesive chain continues throughout the text, where the spider is referred to as *Nephila jurassica, their specimen, she* . . . and so on.

Word order and thematic structure are also noteworthy in these sentences. All three are relatively simple and begin with the grammatical subject in first position (*Scientists* . . . *The female* . . . *These creatures* . . .). In other words, the subject is the **'theme'** of the sentence, a common 'unmarked' order for this genre in English. In all three cases, the new information is located at the end of the sentence, in **rheme** position, and is taken up in the theme of the following sentence. Thus, sentence two ends with *the golden orb weavers* which, as *These creatures*, launches the third sentence.

These phenomena would need to be evaluated for **markedness** and importance. Such a **Register profile** (see House, Chapter 6) would then help in the decision-making of the TT, taking into account the typical conventions of that genre in the TL. The commentary might discuss the different options available to the translator and the constraints placed on translation by the difference in languages. Chinese might be able to retain the subject–verb order but might resort to different means of creating a lexical chain. The thematic profile of Arabic, which prefers a VS order, would be immediately different, but the aim would be to create something that was as unmarked as the English ST.

An important point to make is that the reflexive commentaries should be able to make generalizations from a consideration of specific problems (Shei 2005: 319). The Register profile classification is one way of assisting this.

12.3 Research projects in translation studies

In their book *The Map: A Beginner's Guide to Doing Research in Translation Studies*, Williams and Chesterman (2002: 69) liken the research process to 'a dialogue with . . . "reality" ' in which 'one of the secrets . . . is learning how to ask good **questions'**, types of which are summarized in Table 12.3.

These questions then lead on to potential **answers** from the analysis of the research findings and then to **claims** which may derive from the interpretation of

Table 12.3 Types of research questions (adapted from Williams and Chesterman 2002: 69–73)

Type of question	Example	Specifics
Definition	What does X mean? How can X best be defined?	How is 'translation' understood in the modern world and how is it differentiated from 'adaptation'?
Data	What can I find out about X ?	What are the skills that distinguish a professional subtitler from a fansubber in Japan?
Descriptive	What is this TT like compared with the ST?	What are the procedures and strategies employed in the translation of tourist brochures in Taiwan?
Causes and effects	Why was this text translated and not another one?	What were the norms in operation in the selection of translated texts in Soviet Russia?

the answers – for example, we may claim that in a given experiment professional translators adopted more efficient work practices because they completed the task more rapidly than non-professional translators.

Empirical research is so important for modern translation studies. It is the equivalent of field work for the linguist or an excavation for the archaeologist. Many TS excavations commence with a **hypothesis**, of which Williams and Chesterman give four types (see Table 12.4). These hypotheses may then be **tested empirically**, for example by examining translations or translation

Table 12.4 Types of hypotheses (following Williams and Chesterman 2002: 73–7)

Type	Definition	Example
Interpretive	Concept A is useful for understanding phenomenon B	A model of five types of equivalence can help to understand translation (see Koller, Chapter 3)
Descriptive	Phenomenon C occurs with feature D	TTs show greater explicitation than STs
Explanatory	Phenomenon E is caused by factor F	Crowdsourcing is sometimes used to reduce the costs of large-scale translation projects
Predictive	Factor G will cause phenomenon H	Increased use of technology will increase translation speed and quality

processes themselves and/or by researching the extralinguistic context of the society in which translation takes place. So, a study of borrowings from Arabic into modern-day Malay in an individual text (see Mansor 2011) would need to look at the relative strengths of the two languages, their openness to different forms of lexical transfer and, ideally, would research the translation conditions under which the TT had been produced.

Research projects of course may be undertaken at all levels, from an under-graduate assignment to a piece of cutting-edge postdoctoral research. But the development of a new research project, at whatever level, will typically need to consider the following:[7]

- What is your topic? Be as specific as you can. An indication of the area needs to be in the title, but you also have to be specific about the theoretical approaches and concepts you will be using in your dissertation. Importantly, there should be some indication of the motivation of the study and the antici-pated value and impact of the research.
- What is the scope of your study? For an MA dissertation you are not under obligation to develop a new theory, but you need to work on your own data in your language pair(s). You may, for example, investigate new translation phenomena in the light of an existing theoretical framework. You can also try to demonstrate that the phenomena you would like to investigate cannot be accommodated under any of the existing theoretical frameworks. A PhD dissertation needs to demonstrate an original contribution to knowledge, and may well adapt existing models or propose a new model as a theoretical advance.
- What research questions are relevant for your topic? Which specific question(s) are you going to investigate in your project? Usually, you would be working with some hypothesis or goal in mind, which may or may not be confirmed by the findings of your research.
- What work has already been done in your area of research? This would first of all locate the study within translation studies in general, using the Holmes/Toury map or van Doorslaer conceptualization discussed in Chapter 1. A more detailed literature review will cover work that has been done in the specific area of your research project. At the project planning stage, the basic texts should be discussed. This should provide the basis for the literature review in your dissertation which can be facilitated by the use of the electronic databases of material discussed in Chapter 1 and listed at www.routledge.com/cw/munday. The important role of the literature

review is to show critical evaluation of other work in the field, subtly identifying key work and pointing at gaps in the field which may be filled by your
study.

■ How will you conduct your study? What methodology will you use? This can
include the collection of corpora (e.g. ST–TT texts), the analysis of illustrative
examples (using a specific linguistic model), analysis of questionnaire
responses, etc. Are there any ethical issues involved in the data collection,
interviews, etc.?

■ Is your project manageable? A realistic timeline will help to determine this
and to guide the development of the research. It will also show if the topic
needs to be more narrowly focused.

12.4 Exploration: Research methodologies

Research methodologies in translation studies are becoming ever more
rigorous. Saldanha and O'Brien (2013) set out to build on *The Map* by
systematically presenting methodologies for mainly empirically-based
research projects. They cover: (1) principles and ethics in research; (2)
product-oriented research (including discourse and corpus studies); (3)
process-oriented research (including keystroke logging, eye-tracking and
think-aloud); (4) participant-oriented research (questions, interviews); and
(5) context-oriented research (case study design).

The above are typical questions, but are not meant to be restrictive. For
instance, I have made no attempt to promote the value of one specific model of
linguistic analysis over another. My own preference has often been for an adaptation of Hallidayan systemic-functional discourse analysis, but I am aware of potential limitations when analysing languages with more flexible word orders. And also
of the difficulties of accounting for meaning that is implied or associated rather
than explicit. For this reason, I recommend that readers examine a **range of the
models** presented in this book and evaluate them using their own data. Similarly,
the advance of **new technologies** (audiovisual translation, localization, electronic corpora . . .) is opening up enormous possibilities for the innovative study
of new modes and text types, including social media and automatic online
translation. Whole **new forms of interaction** have emerged (e.g. social media,
crowdsourcing) where translation is playing an important role. The 'traditional'

study of the translation of a 'stable' printed text is no longer the norm. Those entering the field at this time have the benefit of the firm foundations set by the pioneers of the discipline but also the opportunity to take translation studies into new areas. My hope is that this fourth edition of *Introducing Translation Studies*, together with its companion website, will serve as a useful aid and stimulus to many new research projects.

The ITS website at www.routledge.com/cw/munday contains:

- a video summary of the chapter;
- a recap multiple-choice test;
- customizable PowerPoint slides;
- further reading links and extra journal articles;
- more research project questions.

Notes

CHAPTER 1

Main issues of translation studies

1 See Pöchhacker (2004, 2009) and Pöchhacker and Shlesinger (2002) for detailed introductions to interpreting studies.
2 Used by the religious hermit and scholar Richard Rolle (c.1310–1349) in the preface to his *Psalter* (*Oxford English Dictionary*, online).
3 'New Zealand Government announces record surplus', *Wikinews* 11 October 2006, http://en.wikinews.org/wiki/New_Zealand_Government_announces_record_surplus
4 For a more detailed discussion on terms for 'translation', see Chesterman (2006). For India, see Ramakrishna (2000) and Trivedi (2006).
5 Commonsense Advisory (2015) *The Language Services Market 2015*. See http://ec.europa.eu/dgs/translation/faq/index_en.htm and http://ec.europa.eu/dgs/scic/about-dg-interpretation/index_en.htm.
6 See http://www.re-cit.eu/
7 BITRA, Bibliography of Interpreting and Translation, http://aplicacionesua.cpd.ua.es/tra_int/usu/buscar.asp?idioma=en
8 For further discussion of this background, see Gentzler (2001: Chapter 2).
9 In each case, 'translation' is used to cover both translation and interpreting.
10 See also subsequent work by McCarty (2003, 2005).

CHAPTER 2

Translation theory before the twentieth century

1 'Nec converti ut interpres, sed ut orator, sententiis isdem et earum formis tamquam figuris, verbis ad nostram consuetudinem aptis. In quibus non verbum pro verbo necesse habui reddere, sed genus omne verborum vimque servavi' (Cicero 46 @AC/1960 AC: 364). The full essay is given, in the English translation by H. M. Hubbell, in Robinson (1997b: 7–10).

2 Quoted in Robinson (1997b: 15).

3 In Robinson (1997b: 22–30).

4 'Ego enim non solum fateor, sed libera voce profiteor, me in interpretatione Graecorum, absque scripturis sanctis, ubi et verborum ordo et misterium est, non verbum e verbo, sed sensum exprimere de sensu' (St Jerome *Epistolae* Vol. II (395 AC/1565: 287)). The English translation is by Paul Carroll and is quoted in Robinson (1997b: 25).

5 Vermeer (1994: 7) sees 'word-for-word' translation as referring to the process of translating morpheme by morpheme and gives the example of the Greek συν-ειδηοις (*syn-éidêsis*), which was translated by the Latin *con-sci-entia* (with a literal meaning of 'knowledge with' but which has come to acquire an ethical dimension as 'conscience'). By contrast, Vermeer considers that 'sense-for-sense' refers to the translation of individual words or phrases 'according to their grammatical form and meaning in a given text', not according to the wider contextual meaning.

6 See the discussion by Lackner (2001: 361–5).

7 See Hermans (2003, online) for a discussion of the different English equivalents proposed for these terms.

8 Reprinted in Störig (1963: 14–32). A modern colloquial American English translation is to be found in Robinson (1997b: 83–9). English translations of the German given here are my own.

9 Quoted in Störig (1963: 15).

10 'Rein und klar Deutsch' (quoted in Störig 1963: 20).

11 'Man muß die Mutter im Hause, die Kinder auf der Gassen, den gemeinen Mann auf dem Markt drum fragen, und denselbigen auf das Maul sehen, wie sie reden und darnach dolmetschen; da verstehen sie es denn und merken, daß man Deutsch mit ihnen redet' (in Störig 1963: 21).

12 See Pountain (2008) for a discussion of the origins and demise of 'genius' of language.

13 Cited in Bassnett (1980/2002: 61), and given in full in Robinson (1997b: 95–7).

14 Translated in Chan (2004: 69–71).

15 Reprinted in Störig (1963: 38–70). A full translation is given in Robinson (1997b: 225–38) and Venuti (2004: 43–63).

16 'Entweder der Uebersetzer läßt den Schriftsteller möglichst in Ruhe, und bewegt den Leser ihm entgegen; oder er läßt den Leser möglichst in Ruhe, und bewegt den Schriftsteller ihm entgegen' (in Störig 1963: 47).

17 'Dem Leser durch die Uebersetzung den Eindruck zu geben, den er als Deutscher aus der Lesung des Werkes in der Ursprache empfangen würde' (in Störig 1963: 49).

18 *Diploma in Translation: Notes for Candidates* (1990) London: Institute of Linguists. These notes were later modified from the 1996 examination, but the type of language used to describe translation varied little.

19 Joan Kidd (1981, revised by Janet Doolaege 1990) *Guidelines for Translators*, document for UNESCO translators, Paris: UNESCO.

20 Marcel Proust (1996) *In Search of Lost Time*, Vol. 1: *Swann's Way*, London: Vintage.

21 Marcel Proust (2003) *The Way by Swann's*, London: Penguin Classics, originally published by Penguin in 2002.

CHAPTER 3

Equivalence and equivalent effect

1 Compare the examples given by Pinker (2007: 132) which show that language does have an effect through the selection of lexis and syntax even if it does not determine thought.

2 This work is now continued by the Nida Institute, http://www.nidainstitute. org/nida_school/

3 Now available at http://ebible.org/asv/

4 *J. B. Phillips New Testament*, London: HarperCollins Bibles, 1st edition 1958, updated 1972, new edition 2000. Now available online at http://www. ccel.org/bible/phillips/JBPNT.htm

5 Available online at http://www.erudit.org/revue/meta/1993/v38/n3/003147ar. pdf

6 See Table 12.2 in Chapter 12 for further discussion of related terms.

7 See the further reading section for references to the work of these scholars, and Chapter 5 for links to other work being conducted at the time by Reiss, Vermeer and Holz-Mänttäri in West Germany.

8 *Newsweek*, 21 May 2011.

9 See the online discussion of this and other examples by Chilukuri Bhuvaneswar at http://www.afriprov.org/index.php/african-proverb-of-the-month/30–2004 proverbs/208-dec2004.html

10 See http://www.scripture4all.org/OnlineInterlinear/Hebrew_Index.htm for the Hebrew text.

CHAPTER 4

Studying translation product and process

1 In the first edition of this book, we described van Leuven-Zwart's (1989, 1990) very detailed model of translation shift analysis. This is rarely used nowadays and therefore has been omitted from subsequent editions. However, that analysis is available on the *Introducing Translation Studies* website, www.routledge.com/cw/munday

2 References are made to the English edition unless otherwise stated. Where appropriate, the original French terminology is also given.

3 Note the similarity with recommendations by Nida and Newmark, which were discussed in Chapter 3.

4 The acute accent mark on the first letter of Équivalence distinguishes it from the general concept of equivalence of meaning (see Chapter 3).

5 This forms the basis of the discourse analysis models discussed in Chapter 6.

6 The British National Corpus (BNC) is a representative selection of British texts, amounting to some 100 million words, compiled in the 1990s. See Chapter 11 for more details of how searches may be carried out.

7 See Chapter 11 for more discussion of corpus-based translation studies.

8 In *The Royal River Thames: Westminster to Greenwich Cruise and Sail and Rail Guide* (1997), London: Paton Walker, pp. 7 and 14.

CHAPTER 5

Functional theories of translation

1 The German original *Möglichkeiten und Grenzen der Übersetzungskritik*, Munich: Max Hueber, 1971, is no longer in print.

2 Holz-Mänttäri's key work, *Translatorisches Handeln: Theorie und Methode* (1984), was published only in German. *Translatorisches Handeln* is sometimes translated as *translational action*, but here *translatorial action* is preferred in order to stress the emphasis on the translator's role; see also Christiane Nord's justification for such a translation in her preface to Reiss and Vermeer (2013: vi).

3 The phatic function figures in Roman Jakobson's influential typology of six types: referential, emotive, conative, phatic, metalingual and poetic (Jakobson 1960).

4 Neither this book nor Reiss and Vermeer's *Grundlegung einer allgemeinen Translationstheorie* in the next section is available in English. In this chapter, quotations from both works are my own translations.

5 Vermeer (1989/2012) states that the skopos can be considered in three ways: (1) the translation process; (2) the *translatum* itself; and (3) the translation mode and intention. A single text may have sections that exhibit various different aims or 'sub-skopoi'.

6 As Nord herself recognizes (2005: 80), this distinction is in some ways similar to House's (1977, 1997, 2015) 'covert' and 'overt' translation distinction, which is discussed in Chapter 6.

7 The model is based on the so-called 'New Rhetoric formula', a series of *wh*-questions ('Who says what in which channel to whom with what effect?'), quoted in Nord (2005: 42). Her text analysis model owes much to Beaugrande and Dressler's work (1981).

8 Roz Denny and Fiona Watt (1998) *Cooking for Beginners*, London: Usborne. The translation titles, also published by Usborne, are as follows: (Dutch) *Koken voor beginners* (1999); (French) *La cuisine pour débutants* (1999); (Italian) *Imparo a cucinare* (1999); (Spanish) *Cocina para principiantes* (2000).

CHAPTER 6

Discourse and Register analysis approaches

1 The crucial role of systemic functional grammar is to provide a precise grammatical terminology for what is known as discourse analysis. That is, it builds a specific linguistic description into the more general framework of language as communication and as an expression of the sociocultural process. 'Discourse analysis' itself is a wider term, employed differently by different scholars. In this chapter, it is used to mean a combination of: (1) analysis of the function of a text using the toolkit provided by SFL; and (2) the related analysis of social communication and power relationships as expressed in the text as a communicative act.

2 The most detailed description of the model is to be found in Halliday (1994) and Halliday and Matthiessen (2012). For a clear synthesis of these, see Eggins (2004) and Thompson (2004).

3 Called the *context of culture* in Halliday's model.

4 European Commission: Multilingualism 'EU languages and language policy' states: 'The European Union recognises that language and identity are closely intertwined, and that language is the most direct expression of culture', http://ec.europa.eu/education/languages/languages-of-europe/index_en.htm

5 Another criticism is the fact that the Hallidayan model of thematic analysis is mainly English-oriented. Baker (ibid.: 160–7) accepts this, and also outlines the alternative functional sentence perspective model of thematic structure, which, because it takes into account 'communicative dynamism' as well as word order, may be more suitable for languages with a frequent VS order.

6 See Discussion point 2 at the end of this chapter for more on this example.

7 In this example, and in the next sentence, all emphasis is added for ease of discussion.

8 For instance, *it is possible to hypothesize; this would suggest that; the likely conclusion is that . . .*

9 The German original is entitled *Jeder für sich und Gott gegen alle* ['Each for him/herself and God against everyone' (ZDF, 1974).

CHAPTER 7

Systems theories

1 See Chapter 3 for a discussion of this term.

2 See Chapter 9 for further discussion of this point.

3 Hermans prefers 'TT-oriented' and 'ST-oriented'.

4 See, for example, the promotion of translation into Arabic by organizations in the United Arab Emirates such as Kalima and the Mohammed Bin Rashid Al Maktoum Foundation.

5 Published in 1997 by Bloomsbury (London).

6 Translated by Marina Astrologo, published in 1998 by Adriano Salani editore (Florence).

7 Translated by Alicia Dellepiane, published in 1999 by Emecé (Barcelona).

8 This was supposedly to reflect the 'exciting' storyline, according to editor Arthur Levine of Scholastic Books, the US publishers of the Harry Potter series.

CHAPTER 8

Cultural and ideological turns

1 Lefevere here adopts the definition of Fredric Jameson (1974) *The Prison-House of Language*, Princeton, NJ: Princeton University Press, p. 109.

2 A more recent example is the decision of the Loeb Classical Library (since 1989 part of Harvard University Press) to commission 'more accurate and less cautious' translations of Greek and Roman texts, including Aristophanes (Steven Morris, 'Classic translations let obscenity speak for itself', *The Guardian*, 23 August 2000, p. 7).

3 The accuracy of Lowe-Porter's translations became the centre of a heated debate in *The Times Literary Supplement* in the autumn of 1995. See Venuti (1998: 32–3) and Hermans (1999: 1–7).

4 See M. L. Pratt (1987), 'Linguistic utopias', in N. Fabb, D. Attridge, A. Durant and C. McCabe (eds) *The Linguistics of Writing: Arguments between Language and Literature*, Manchester: Manchester University Press.

5 Published in 1992 by the Royal National Theatre and Nick Hearn Books, London.

6 Published by Panther Books, London. The translation, by Philippe Mikriammos, is *Un garçon près de la rivière*, Paris: Persona, 1981.

7 Tony Duvert (1973) *Paysage de Fantaisie*, Paris: Les Éditions de Minuit, translated by Sam Flores (1975) as *Strange Landscape*, New York: Grove.

8 Elsewhere called 'translationese'.

9 Spivak has, among others, translated Derrida and texts by Bengali writers including Mahasweta Devi.

10 Gurdial Singh (1991), *The Last Flicker*, translated by Ajmer S. Rode, New Delhi: Sahitya Akademi.

11 See http://jnanpith.net/awards/jnanpith-award

12 From the webpage of the Sahitya Akademi, http://sahitya-akademi.gov.in/sahitya-akademi/aboutus/about.jsp.

13 *Chachi* or *Tayyi* are used depending on whether a younger or elder aunt is being addressed.

CHAPTER 9

The role of the translator: visibility, ethics and sociology

1 Called 'strategies' in the first edition of *The Translator's Invisibility*.

2 Iginio Ugo Tarchetti (1977) *Racconti fantastici*, ed. N. Bonifazi, Milan: Guanda, translated by Lawrence Venuti (1992) as *Fantastic Tales*, San Francisco, CA: Mercury House.

3 A colloquial pronunciation of the hospital of St Mary of Bethlehem. From the seventeenth-century, *bedlam* became a common byword for 'mad confusion'.

4 Originally published in French as *Seuils* ['Thresholds'] in 1987.

5 See Simeoni (1998) below and also Gouanvic (2005: 157, fn. 15).
6 John Mort, Untitled, *Booklist*, 1 September 1993, p. 4.
7 Paul Gray, 'Twelve stories of solitude', *Time*, 29 November 1993, p. 80.
8 John Bayley, 'Singing in the rain', *New York Review of Books*, 17 February 1994, pp. 19–21.
9 Untitled, November 1993, p. 158.
10 John Sturrock, 'A wilder race', *Times Literary Supplement*, 17 September 1993, p. 20.
11 Janette Turner Hospital, 'García Márquez: Chronicle of a text foretold', *Independent*, 18 September 1993, p. 29.

CHAPTER 10

Philosophical approaches to translation

1 See Palmer (1969) for a standard introduction to hermeneutics from Schleiermacher to Gadamer, and Berman (1992) for a survey of German Romanticism from the perspective of translation theory.
2 Compare the discussion in Chapter 2 of the literal vs. free debate.
3 *Tableaux Parisiens*, translated by Walter Benjamin, originally published Heidelberg: Richard Weissbach, 1923, reissued Frankfurt-am-Main: Suhrkamp, 1963.
4 *Beowulf*, translated by Seamus Heaney (1999), London: Faber & Faber.
5 Published in *¡Cavernícolas!* (1985) Buenos Aires: Père Abbat editora, pp. 105–46.

CHAPTER 11

New directions from the new media

1 However, as we shall discuss in section 11.1.8, the development of technology now increasingly enables widespread manipulation of all kinds of digital material.
2 Krysia Driver, 'Germans in a hurry for Harry', *The Guardian*, 1 August 2005, http://www.guardian.co.uk/world/2005/aug/01/books.harrypotter; and Kim Willsher, 'Harry Potter and the boy wizard translator', *The Guardian*, 8 August 2007, http://www.guardian.co.uk/world/2007/aug/08/france.harrypotter.
3 The acronym is sometimes reduced to GIL, with translation counted as part of localization.

4 This was the definition that appeared on the LISA website until the association was dissolved in March 2011.

5 See http://www.insidefacebook.com/2008/04/02/now-you-can-help-translate-facebook-into-any-language/

6 http://en.wikipedia.org/wiki/Wikipedia:Translation

7 Available online at http://www.natcorp.ox.ac.uk/

8 Available online at http://www.collinslanguage.com/wordbanks/

9 Monolingual corpora in various languages are available from the Leeds collection of internet corpora: http://corpus.leeds.ac.uk/internet.html

10 Available online at http://www.hf.uio.no/ilos/english/services/omc/

11 A lemma comprises all the forms of the root word, which is usually written in QK?JJ A? NR?JQ. Thus, the lemma M@QCPT?P includes all morphological variants of the verb, such as *observo, observas, observa, etc*, as well as the infinitive form *observar*.

12 For example, Sharoff et al. (2009) and Babych and Hartley (2009).

13 Available online at http://www.rae.es

CHAPTER 12

Research and commentary projects

1 See Nida and Taber (1969), Bell (1991), Weissbort and Eysteinsson (2006) and Hyde Parker et al. (2010) for just a few of the volumes which bring together theory and practice in their titles.

2 Adapted from that in use at the University of Leeds, UK, in 2011.

3 Paul A. Selden, ChungKun Shi and Dong Ren, 'A golden orb-weaver spider (Araneae: Nephilidae) from the middle Jurassic of China', *Biology Letters*, 20 April 2011, http://rsbl.royalsocietypublishing.org/content/early/2011/04/16/rsbl.2011.0228.full

4 For the difference between translation strategy and procedure, see Chapter 1.

5 That is, that the TT may be 10 per cent under or over the length of the ST.

6 International use of *-isation* rather than US *-ization*.

7 Adapted from guidelines provided to prospective PhD students at the University of Leeds.

Bibliography

Abend-David, D. (ed) (2014) *Media and Translation: An Interdisciplinary Approach*, London and New York: Bloomsbury.

Adams, J. (2003) *Bilingualism and the Latin Language*, Cambridge: Cambridge University Press.

Aijmer, K. and C. Alvstad (eds) (2005) *New Tendencies in Translation Studies: Selected Papers from a Workshop, Göteborg 12 December 2003*. Göteborg: Göteborg University, Department of English.

Aixelà, J. F. (1996) 'Culture-specific items in translation', in R. Álvarez and M. C-Á. Vidal (1996), pp. 56–66.

Aksoy, N. (2010) 'The relation between translation and ideology as an instrument for the establishment of a national literature', *Meta* 55: 438–55.

Álvarez, R. and M. C-Á. Vidal (eds) (1996) *Translation, Power, Subversion*, Clevedon: Multilingual Matters.

Alves, F. (2003) *Triangulating Translation: Perspectives in Process-oriented Research*, Amsterdam and Philadelphia: John Benjamins.

Alvstad, C. and A. Assis Rosa (eds) (2015) *Voice in Retranslation*, special issue of *Target* 27.1.

Amos, F. R. (1920/1973) *Early Theories of Translation*, New York: Octagon.

Anderman, G. (2005) *Europe on Stage: Translation and Theatre*, London: Oberon.

Anderman, G. and J. Díaz Cintas (eds) (2008) *Audiovisual Translation: Language Transfer on the Screen*, London: Palgrave.

Anderman, G. and M. Rogers (eds) (2007) *Incorporating Corpora: The Linguist and the Translator*, Clevedon: Multilingual Matters.

Angelelli, C. (ed.) (2014) *The Sociological Turn in Translation and Interpreting Studies*, Amsterdam and Philadelphia: John Benjamins.

Archer, D., K. Aijmer and A. Wichmann (2012) *Pragmatics: An Advanced Resource Book,* London and New York: Routledge.

Arnold, M. (1861/1978) *On Translating Homer*, London: AMS Press.

Arrojo, R. (1998) 'The revision of the traditional gap between theory and practice and the empowerment of translation in postmodern times', *The Translator* 4.1: 25–48.

Arrojo, R. (1999) 'Interpretation as possessive love: Hélène Cixous, Clarice Lispector and the ambivalence of fidelity', in S. Bassnett and H. Trivedi (eds) (1999), pp. 141–61.

Austermühl, F. (2001) *Electronic Tools for Translators*, Manchester: St Jerome.

Austin, J. L. (1962) *How to Do Things with Words*, Oxford: Oxford University Press.

Babych, B. and A. Hartley (2009) 'Automated error analysis for multiword expressions', *Linguistica Antverpiensia New Series* 8: 81–104.

Babych, B., A. Hartley, K. Kageura, M. Thomas and M. Utiyama (2012) 'MNH-TT: A collaborative platform for translator training', http://www.mt-archive.info/Aslib-2012-Babych.pdf

Baker, M. (1992/2011) *In Other Words: A Coursebook on Translation*, 2nd edition, London and New York: Routledge.

— (1993) 'Corpus linguistics and translation studies: Implications and applications', in M. Baker, G. Francis and E. Tognini-Bonelli (eds) *Text and Technology: In Honour of John Sinclair*, Amsterdam and Philadelphia: John Benjamins, pp. 233–50.

— (1995) 'Corpora in translation studies: An overview and suggestions for future research', *Target* 7.2: 223–43.

— (2000) 'Towards a methodology for investigating the style of a literary translator', *Target* 12: 241–66.

— (2006) *Translation and Conflict: A Narrative Account*, Abingdon and New York: Routledge.

— (2009) *Critical Concepts: Translation Studies*, 4 volumes, London and New York: Routledge.

— (ed.) (2010) *Critical Readings in Translation Studies*, London and New York: Routledge.

Baker, M. and S. Hanna (2009) 'Arabic tradition', in M. Baker and G. Saldanha (eds), pp. 328–37.

Baker, M. and K. Malmkjær (eds) (1998), *The Routledge Encyclopedia of Translation Studies*, 1st edition, London and New York: Routledge.

Baker, M., M. Olohan and M. Calzada Pérez (eds) (2010) *Text and Context: Essays on Translation and Interpreting in Honour of Ian Mason*, Manchester: St Jerome.

Baker, M. and G. Saldanha (eds) (2009) *The Routledge Encyclopedia of Translation Studies*, 2nd edition, London and New York: Routledge.

Balderston, D. and M. Schwartz (eds) (2002) *Voice-overs: Translation and Latin American Literature*, Albany: State University of New York Press.

Bandia, P. (2008) *Translation as Reparation: Writing and Translation in Postcolonial Africa*, Manchester: St Jerome.

— (2010) 'Post-colonial literatures and translation', in Y. Gambier and L. van Doorslaer (eds), pp. 264–9.

Barlow, M. (no date) *Paraconc*, Athelstan, http://www.athel.com/mono.html

Barnstone, W. (1993) *The Poetics of Translation: History, Theory, Practice*, Yale: Yale UP.

Bassnett, S. (1980, 1991, 2002/2013) *Translation Studies*, London and New York: Routledge.

Bassnett, S. and P. Bush (eds) (2006) *The Translator as Writer*, London: Continuum.

Bassnett, S. and A. Lefevere (eds) (1990) *Translation, History and Culture*, London and New York: Pinter.

Bassnett, S. and H. Trivedi (eds) (1999) *Post-colonial Translation: Theory and Practice*, London and New York: Routledge.

Bastin, G. and P. Bandia (eds) (2006) *Charting the Future of Translation History: Current Discourses and Methodology*, Ottawa: Ottawa University Press.

Batchelor, K. (2008) 'Third Spaces, mimicry and attention to ambivalence: Applying Bhabhian discourse to translation theory', *The Translator* 14.1: 51–70.

— (2009) *Decolonizing Translation: Francophone African Novels in English Translation*, Manchester: St. Jerome.

Beaugrande, R. de (1978) *Factors in a Theory of Poetic Translating*, Assen: Van Gorcum.

Beaugrande, R. de and W. Dressler (1981) *Introduction to Text Linguistics*, London and New York: Longman, available online: http://www.beaugrande.com/introduction_to_text_linguistics.htm

Bell, R. (1991) *Translation and Translating: Theory and Practice*, London and New York: Longman.

Benjamin, A. (1989) *Translation and the Nature of Philosophy: A New Theory of Words*, London and New York: Routledge.

Benjamin, W. (1923/1963) 'Die Aufgabe des Übersetzers', in H. Störig (ed.) (1963), pp. 182–95.

— (1969/2004) 'The task of the translator', translated by H. Zohn (1969), in L. Venuti (ed.) (2004), pp. 75–82.

— (1923/2012) 'The translator's task', translated by S. Rendall, in L. Venuti (ed.) (2012), pp. 75–83.

Bennett, K. (2006) 'Critical language study and translation: The case of academic discourse', in J. Ferreira Duarte, A. Assis Rosa and T. Seruya (eds), pp. 111–28.

— (2007) 'Epistemicide: The tale of a predatory discourse', *The Translator* 13.2: 151–69.

— (2011) 'The Scientific Revolution and its repercussions on the translation of technical discourse', *The Translator* 17.2: 189–210.

— (2012) 'At the selvedges of discourse: negotiating the "in-between" in Translation studies', *The Place of Translation*, special issue of *Word and Text* 2.2: 43–61.

Berman, A. (1984/1992) *L'épreuve de l'étranger: Culture et traduction dans l'Allemagne romantique*, Paris: Éditions Gallimard; translated (1992) by S. Heyvaert as *The Experience of the Foreign: Culture and Translation in Romantic Germany*, Albany: State University of New York.

— (1985a/1999) *Traduction et la lettre ou l'auberge du lointain*, Paris: Seuil.

— (1985b/2012) 'La traduction comme épreuve de l'étranger', *Texte* 4 (1985): 67–81, translated by L. Venuti as 'Translation and the trials of the foreign', in L. Venuti (ed.) (2012), pp. 240–53.

— (2009) *Toward a Translation Criticism: John Donne*, translated and edited by F. Massardier-Kenney, Kent, OH: Kent State UP, originally published in French (1995) as *Pour une critique des traductions*, Paris: Gallimard.

Bermann, S. and C. Porter (eds) (2014) *A Companion to Translation Studies*, Malden, MA, Oxford and Chichester: Wiley Blackwell.

Bermann, S. and M. Wood (eds) (2005) *Nation, Language and the Ethics of Translation*, Princeton: Princeton University Press.

Bernardini, S., D. Stewart and F. Zanettin (eds) (2003) 'Corpora in translation education: An introduction', in F. Zanettin, S. Bernardini and D. Stewart (eds), pp. 1–14.

Bernal Merino, M. (2006) 'On the translation of video games', *Journal of Specialised Translation* 6: 22–36, http://www.jostrans.org/issue06/art_bernal.pdf

— (2009) 'Video-games and children's books in translation', *JosTrans* 11, http://www.jostrans.org/issue11/art_bernal.php

— (2015) *Translation and Localization in Video Games: Making Entertainment Software Global*, London and New York: Routledge.

Bhabha, H. (1994) *The Location of Culture*, London and New York: Routledge.

Bielsa, E. (2013) 'Translation and the international circulation of literature: A comparative analysis of the reception of Roberto Bolaño's work in Spanish and English', *The Translator* 19.2: 157–81.

Bielsa, E. and S. Bassnett (eds) (2009) *Translation in Global News*, London and New York: Routledge.

Billiani, F. (ed.) (2007) *Modes of Censorship and Translation: National Contexts and Diverse Media*, Manchester: St Jerome.

Blum-Kulka, S. (1986/2004) 'Shifts of cohesion and coherence in translation', in L. Venuti (ed.) (2004), pp. 290–305.

Blum-Kulka, S. and E. Levenston (1983) 'Universals of lexical simplification', in C. Faerch and G. Kasper (eds) *Strategies in Interlanguage Communication*, London and New York: Longman, pp. 119–39.

Boase-Beier, J. (2006) *Stylistic Approaches to Translation*, Manchester: St Jerome.

Bobrick, B. (2003) *The Making of the English Bible*, London: Phoenix.

Boéri, J. and C. Maier (eds) (2010) *Compromiso social y traducción/interpretación – Translation/Interpreting and Social Activism*, Granada: ECOS.

Booth, M. (2008) 'Translator v. Author (2007): *Girls of Riyadh* go to New York', *Translation Studies* 1.2: 197–211.

Borodo, M. (2015) 'Multimodality, translation and comics', *Perspectives in Translatology* 23.1: 22–41.

Bosseaux, C. (2007) *How Does It Feel?: Point of View in Translation; The Case of Virginia Woolf into French*, Amsterdam: Rodopi.

Bourdieu, P. (1977) *Outline of a Theory of Practice*, translated R. Nice, Cambridge: Cambridge University Press.

— (1991) *Language and Symbolic Power*, translated G. Raymond and M. Adamson, Cambridge: Polity Press.

Bowker, L. (2011) 'Off the record and on the fly: Examining the impact of corpora on terminographic practice in the context of translation', in A. Kruger, K. Wallmach and J. Munday (eds) *Corpus-based Translation Studies: Research and Applications*, London and New York: Continuum, pp. 211–36.

— (2015) 'Terminology and translation', in H. Kockaert and F. Steuers (eds) (2015) *Handbook of Terminology*, volume 1, Amsterdam and Philadelphia: John Benjamins.

Bowker, L. and J. Pearson (2002) *Working with Specialized Language: A Practical Guide to Using Corpora*, London and New York: Routledge.

Braden, G., R. Cummings and S. Gillespie (eds) (2010) *The Oxford History of Literary Translation in English*, volume 2: 1550–1660, Oxford: Oxford University Press.

Brems, E. and S. Ramos Pinto (2013) 'Reception and translation', in Y. Gambier and L. van Doorslaer (eds) *Handbook of Translation Studies Volume IV*.

Britt, B. (2003) *Walter Benjamin and the Bible*, Lewiston: Edwin Mellen Press.

Broeck, R. van den (1978) 'The concept of equivalence in translation theory: Some critical reflections', in J. S. Holmes, J. Lambert and R. van den Broeck (eds) *Literature and Translation*, Leuven: Academic, pp. 29–47.

Brown, M. H. (1994) *The Reception of Spanish American Fiction in West Germany 1981–91*, Tübingen: Niemeyer.

Brown, P. and S. Levinson (1987) *Politeness: Some Universals in Language Usage*, Cambridge: Cambridge University Press.

Brownlie, S. (2009) 'Descriptive vs committed approaches', in M. Baker and G. Saldanha (eds), pp. 77–81.

Bühler, K. (1934/1965) *Sprachtheorie: Die Darstellungsfunktion der Sprache*, Stuttgart: Gustav Fischer.

Buikema, R. and A. Smelik (1995) *Women's Studies and Culture: A Feminist Introduction*, London: Zed Books.

Burger, M. and N. Pozza (eds) (2010) *India in Translation Through Hindi Literature: A Plurality of Voices*, Bern: Peter Lang.

Butler, J. (1990) *Gender Trouble: Feminism and the Subversion of Identity*, London: Routledge.

Buzelin, H. (2005) 'Unexpected allies: How Latour's network theory could complement Bourdieusian analyses in translation studies', *The Translator* 11.2: 193–218.

Cabré, M-T. (2010) 'Terminology and translation', in Y. Gambier and L. van Doorslaer (eds) *Handbook of Translation*, Amsterdam and Philadelphia: John Benjamins.

Calzada Pérez, M. (ed.) (2003) *Apropos of Ideology: Translation Studies on Ideology – Ideologies in Translation Studies*, Manchester: St Jerome.

— (2007) *Transitivity in Translating: The Interdependence of Texture and Context*, Bern, Berlin, Brussels, Frankfurt: Peter Lang.

Carl, M. (2012) 'Translog-II: A program for recording user activity data for empirical reading and writing research' http://www.lrec-conf.org/proceedings/lrec2012/pdf/614_Paper.pdf

Carter, R. (1998) *Vocabulary: Applied Linguistic Perspectives*, 2nd edition, London and New York: Routledge.

Casanova, P. (1999/2004) *The World Republic of Letters*, translated by M. B. Debevoise, Cambridge, MA and London: Harvard UP.

— (2002/2010) 'Consecration and accumulation literary capital: Translation as unequal exchange', in M. Baker (ed.) (2010) *Critical Readings in Translation Studies*, London and New York: Routledge, pp. 285–303.

Cassin, B. (ed.) (2014) *Dictionary of Untranslatables: A Philosophical Lexicon*, Princeton: Princeton University Press.

Catford, J. C. (1965/2000) *A Linguistic Theory of Translation*, London: Oxford University Press (1965). See also extract ('Translation shifts') in L. Venuti (ed.) (2000), pp. 141–7.

Chamberlain, L. (1988/2012) 'Gender and the metaphorics of translation', in L. Venuti (ed.) (2012), pp. 254–68.

Chan, Leo Tak-hung (2001) 'What's modern in Chinese translation theory? Lu Xun and the debates on literalism and foreignization in the May Fourth period', *TTR* 14.2: 195–223.

— (ed.) (2004) *Twentieth-Century Chinese Translation Theory*, Amsterdam and Philadelphia: John Benjamins.

Chan, Sin-wai (ed.) (2015) *Routledge Encyclopedia of Translation Technology*, London and New York: Routledge.

Chan, Sin-wai and D. Pollard (eds) (1995) *An Encyclopedia of Translation*, Hong Kong: The Chinese University Press.

Chandler, D. (2007) *Semiotics: The Basics*, 2nd edition, London and New York: Routledge.

Chaume, F. (2004) 'Film studies and translation studies: Two disciplines at stake in audiovisual translation', *Meta* 49.1: 12–24.

Chaume, F. (2012) *Audiovisual Translation: Dubbing*, Manchester: St Jerome.

Chesterman, A. (ed.) (1989) *Readings in Translation Theory*, Helsinki: Finn Lectura.

— (1997) *Memes of Translation*, Amsterdam and Philadelphia, PA: John Benjamins.

— (2004) 'Beyond the particular', in A. Mauranen and P. Kujamäki (eds), pp. 33–50.

— (2005) 'Towards consilience?', in K. Aijmer and C. Alvstad (eds), pp. 19–28.

— (2006) 'Questions in the sociology of translation', in J. Ferreira Duarte, A. Assis Rosa and T. Seruya (eds), pp. 9–28.

— (2010) 'Why study translation universals?', HELDA – The Digital Repository of University of Helsinki, http://hdl.handle.net/10138/24319

Chesterman, A. and R. Arrojo (2000) 'Shared ground in translation studies', *Target* 12.1: 151–60.

Cheung, Martha (ed.) (2006) *An Anthology of Chinese Discourse on Translation: From Earliest Times to the Buddhist Project* (volume 1), Manchester: St Jerome.

— (ed.) (2009) *Chinese Discourses on Translation*, special issue of *The Translator* 15.2.

Cheyfitz, E. (1991) *The Poetics of Imperialism: Translation and Colonization from* The Tempest *to* Tarzan, New York and Oxford: Oxford University Press.

Chiaro, D. (2009) 'Issues in audiovisual translation', in Jeremy Munday (ed.) (2009), pp. 141–65.

— (2010) *Translation, Humour and Literature*, 2 volumes, London and New York: Continuum.

Chomsky, N. (1957) *Syntactic Structures*, Gravenhage: Mouton.

— (1965) *Aspects of the Theory of Syntax*, Cambridge, MA: MIT Press.

Christ, R. (1982) 'On not reviewing translations: A critical exchange', *Translation Review* 9: 16–23.

Chuquet, H. and M. Paillard (1987) *Approche linguistique des problèmes de traduction*, Paris: Ophrys.

Cicero, M. T. (46 bce/1960 ce) 'De optimo genere oratorum', in Cicero *De inventione, De optimo genere oratorum, topica*, translated by H. M. Hubbell, Cambridge, MA: Harvard University Press; London: Heinemann, pp. 347–73.

Classe, O. (2000) *Encyclopedia of Literary Translation into English*, 2 volumes, Chicago: Fitzroy Dearbon.

Cobley, P. (ed.) (2001) *The Routledge Companion to Semiotics and Linguistics*, London and New York: Routledge.

Connor, U. (1996) *Contrastive Rhetoric: Cross-cultural Aspects of Second-Language Learning*, Cambridge: Cambridge University Press.

Cook, G. (2010) *Translation in Language Teaching*, Oxford: Oxford University Press.

Cronin, M. (1996) *Translating Ireland: Translation, Languages, Cultures*, Cork: Cork University Press.

— (2003) *Translation and Globalization*, London and New York: Routledge.

— (2013) *Translation in the Digital Age*, London and New York: Routledge.

Cunico, S. and J. Munday (eds) (2007) *Translation and Ideology: Encounters and Clashes*, special issue of *The Translator* 13.2.

Davis, D. (2000) 'Omar Khayyām', in O. Classe (ed.) *Encyclopedia of Literary Translation into English*, volume II, Chicago: Fitzroy Dearbon, 1019–1020.

Davis, K. (2001) *Deconstruction and Translation*, Manchester: St Jerome.

de Campos, H. (1992) *Metalinguagem e outras metas: Ensaios de teoria e crítica literária*, São Paolo: Perspectiva.

Delabastita, D. (1989) 'Translation and mass-communication: Film and TV translation as evidence of cultural dynamics', *Babel* 35.4: 193–218.

Delisle, J. (1982, 2nd edition) *L'analyse du discours comme méthode de traduction*, Ottawa: University of Ottawa Press, Part I, translated by P. Logan and M. Creery (1988) as *Translation: An Interpretive Approach*, Ottawa: University of Ottawa Press.

Delisle, J. and J. Woodsworth (eds) (1995) *Translators through History*. Amsterdam and Philadelphia, PA: John Benjamins.

De Marco, M. (2012) *Audiovisual Translation Through a Gender Lens*, Amsterdam: Rodopi.

Derrida, J. (1974) 'White mythology', *New Literary History* 6.1: 5–74; original is 'La mythologie blanche', in *Marges de la Philosophie*, Paris: Minuit, 1972, pp. 247–324.

— (1985) 'Des tours de Babel', in J. F. Graham (ed.), French original pp. 209–48, translation in the same volume by J. F. Graham, pp. 165–207.

Devy, G. (1999) 'Translation and literary history: An Indian view', in S. Bassnett and H. Trivedi (eds), pp. 182–8.

Dharwadker, V. (1999) 'A. K. Ramanujan's theory and practice of translation', in S. Bassnett and H. Trivedi (eds), pp. 114–40.

Díaz Cintas, J. (2003) *Teoría y práctica de la subtitulación: Inglés–español*, Barcelona: Ariel.

— (2005) 'Back to the future in subtitling', *MuTra 2005 – Challenges of Multi-dimensional Translation: Conference Proceedings*, http://www.euroconferences.info/proceedings/2005_Proceedings/2005_DiazCintas_Jorge.pdf

Díaz Cintas, J. and P. Muñoz Sánchez (2006) 'Fansubs: Audiovisual translation in an amateur environment', *Journal of Specialised Translation* 6: 37–52.

Díaz Cintas, J. and A. Remael (2007) *Audiovisual Translation: Subtitling*, Manchester and Kinderhook, NY: St Jerome.

Díaz Cintas, J., A. Matamala and J. Neves (eds) (2010) *New Insights into Audiovisual Translation and Media Accessibility – Media for All?* Amsterdam and Atlanta: Rodopi.

Di Giovanni, N. T. (2003) *The Lesson of the Master*, London and New York: Continuum.

Di Pietro, R. J. (1971) *Language Structures in Contrast*, Rowley, MA: Newbury House.

Dickins, J. (2005) 'Two models for metaphor analysis', *Target* 17.2: 227–73.

— (2013) 'Procedures for Translating Culturally Specific Items', in A. Littlejohn and S.R. Mehta (eds), *Language Studies: Stretching Boundaries,* Newcastle: Cambridge Scholars Press, pp. 43–60.

Dimitriu, R. (2009) 'Translators' prefaces as documentary sources for translation studies', *Perspectives* 17.3: 193–206.

Dimitriu, R. and M. Shlesinger (eds) (2009) *Translators and their Readers: In homage to Eugene Nida*, Brussels: Éditions du Hasard.

Dolet, E. (1540/1997) *La manière de bien traduire d'une langue en aultre*, Paris: J. de Marnef, translated by D. G. Ross as 'How to translate well from one language into another', in D. Robinson (ed.) (1997b), pp. 95–7.

Dooley, R. (1989) 'Style and acceptability: The Guraní New Testament', *Notes on Translation* 3.1: 49–57.

Dryden, J. (1680/1992) 'Metaphrase, paraphrase and imitation'. Extracts of 'Preface to Ovid's Epistles' (1680) in R. Schulte and J. Biguenet (eds) (1992), pp. 17–31. An extract also appears in D. Robinson (ed.) (1997b), pp. 172–4, and L. Venuti (ed.) (2012), pp. 38–42.

— (1697/1997) 'Steering betwixt two extremes', from 'Dedication of the Aeneis' (1697), in D. Robinson (ed.) (1997b), pp. 174–5.

Dukmak, W. (2012) *The Treatment of Cultural Items in the Translation of Children's Literature: The Case of Harry Potter in Arabic,* PhD thesis, University of Leeds, UK.

Dunne, K. (ed.) (2006) *Perspectives on Localization*, Amsterdam and Philadelphia: John Benjamins.

Dunne, K. and E. Dunne (2011) *Translation and Localization Project Management: The Art of the Possible*, Amsterdam and Philadelphia: John Benjamins.

During, S. (2005) *Cultural Studies Reader*, 2nd edition, London and New York: Routledge.

Eco, U. (2003) *Mouse or Rat? Translation as Negotiation*, London: Weidenfeld and Nicolson.

Eggins, S. (2004) *An Introduction to Systemic Functional Linguistics*, 2nd edition, London: Pinter.

Ellis, R. (ed.) (2008) *The Oxford History of Literary Translation in English. Volume I: to 1550*, Oxford: Oxford University Press.

Englund-Dimitrova, B. (2005) *Expertise and Explicitation in the Translation Process*, Amsterdam and Philadelphia: John Benjamins.

Enkvist, N. E. (1978) 'Contrastive text linguistics and translation', in L. Grähs, G. Korlén and B. Malmberg (eds) *Theory and Practice of Translation*, Bern: Peter Lang, pp. 169–88.

Ericsson, K. and H. Simon (1984) *Protocol Analysis: Verbal Reports as Data*, Cambridge, MA: MIT Press.

Esselink, B. (2000) *A Practical Guide to Localization*, 2nd edition, Amsterdam and Philadelphia: John Benjamins.

Even-Zohar, I. (1978/2012) 'The position of translated literature within the literary polysystem', in L. Venuti (ed.) (2012). pp. 162–67. Also in I. Even-Zohar (1978) *Papers in Historical Poetics*, Tel Aviv: The Porter Institute, pp. 21–7.

— (1990) *Polysystem Studies*, Tel Aviv: Porter Institute of Poetics and Semiotics, Durham, NC: Duke University Press, special issue of *Poetics Today*, 11:1.

— (2005) 'Polysystem theory revised', in I. Even-Zohar (ed.) *Papers in Culture Research*, pp. 38–49, http://citeseerx.ist.psu.edu/viewdoc/download?doi=10.1.1.112.4768&rep=rep1&type=pdf

Faiq, S. (ed.) (2004) *Cultural Encounters in Translation from Arabic*, Clevedon: Multilingual Matters.

Fairclough, N. (1989, 2nd edition 2001) *Language and Power*, London: Longman.

— (2003) *Analysing Discourse*, London and New York: Routledge.

Fawcett, P. (1995) 'Translation and power play', *The Translator* 1.2: 177–92.

— (1997) *Translation and Language: Linguistic Approaches Explained*, Manchester: St Jerome.

Fedorov, A. V. (1953/1968) *Osnovy obshchey teorii perevoda* [Foundations of a General Theory of Translation], Moscow: Vysshaya shkola.

Felstiner, J. (1980) *Translating Neruda: The Way to Macchu Picchu*, Stanford, CA: Stanford University Press.

Ferreira Duarte, J., A. Assis Rosa and T. Seruya (eds) (2006) *Translation Studies at the Interface of Disciplines*, Amsterdam and Philadelphia: John Benjamins.

Firbas, J. (1986) 'On the dynamics of written communication in the light of the theory of functional sentence perspective', in C. R. Cooper and S. Greenbaum (eds) *Studying Writing: Linguistic Approaches*, Beverly Hills, CA: Sage.

— (1992) *Functional Sentence Perspective in Written and Spoken Communication*, Cambridge: Cambridge University Press.

Fish, S. (1981) 'What is stylistics and why are they saying such terrible things about it?', in D. Freeman (ed.) *Essays in Modern Stylistics*, London: Methuen, pp. 53–78.

Flotow, L. von (ed.) (2000) *Translation and Ideology*, special issue of *TTR* (*Traduction, Terminologie, Rédaction*) 13.1.

— (2011) *Translating Woman*, University of Ottawa Press.

Foran, L. (ed.) (2012) *Translation and Philosophy*, Bern: Peter Lang.

Forster, M. (2010) *After Herder: Philosophy of Language in the German Tradition*, Oxford: Oxford University Press.

— (n.d.) 'Hermeneutics', http://philosophy.uchicago.edu/faculty/files/forster/HERM.pdf.

Fowler, R. (1986, 2nd edition 1996) *Linguistic Criticism*, Oxford: Oxford University Press.

France, P. (2000) *Literature in English Translation*, Oxford: Oxford University Press.

France, P. and K. Haynes (eds) (2006) *The Oxford History of Literary Translation in English. Volume I: to 1550*, Oxford: Oxford University Press.

Frawley, W. (ed.) (1984) *Translation: Literary, Linguistic and Philosophical Perspectives*, Newark, London and Toronto: Associated University Presses.

Fung Chang, N. (2008) 'A missing link in Itamar Even-Zohar's theoretical thinking', *Target* 20.1: 135–48.

— (2010) 'Polysystem theory and translation', in Y. Gambier and L. van Doorslaer (eds) *Handbook of Translation*, Amsterdam and Philadelphia: John Benjamins.

Gaddis Rose, M. (1997) *Translation and Literary Criticism*, Manchester: St Jerome.

Gambier, Y. (ed.) (2003) *Screen Translation*, special issue of *The Translator* 9.2.

— (ed.) (2004) *Traduction audiovisuelle/Audiovisual translation*, special issue of *Meta* 49.1.

Gambier, Y. and L. van Doorslaer (eds) (2010) *Handbook of Translation Studies*, Amsterdam and Philadelphia: John Benjamins, and online.

Garcia, O. and Li Wei (2014) *Translanguaging: Language, Bilingualism and Education*, Houndmills: Palgrave Macmillan.

García Álvarez, A. M. (2007) 'Evaluating students' translation process in specialized translation: Translation commentary', *Journal of Specialised Translation* 7, http://www.jostrans.org/issue07/art_alvarez.pdf

García Yebra, V. (1982) *Teoría y práctica de la traducción*, Madrid: Gredos.

Gauvin, L. (1989) *Letters from an Other*, translated by S. de Lotbinière-Harwood, Toronto: Women's Press.

Genette, G. (1997) *Paratexts: Thresholds of Interpretation*, translated by Jane E. Lewin and foreword by Richard Macksey, Cambridge: Cambridge University Press.

Gentzler, E. (1993) *Contemporary Translation Theories*, London and New York: Routledge.

— (2001) *Contemporary Translation Theories*, 2nd edition, Clevedon: Multilingual Matters.

Gentzler, E. and M. Tymoczko (eds) (2002) *Translation and Power*, Amherst: University of Massachusetts Press.

Gerzymisch-Arbogast, H. (1986) 'Zur Relevanz der Thema-Rhema-Gliederung für den Übersetzungsprozeß', in Mary Snell-Hornby (ed.) *Übersetzungswissenschaft: Eine Neuorientierung. Zur Integrierung von Theorie und Praxis*, Tübingen: Francke, pp. 160–83.

Gerzymisch-Arbogast, H. and S. Nauert (eds) (2005) *Challenges of Multidimensional Translation: Proceedings*, Saarbrücken: Saarland University, http://www.translationconcepts.org/pdf/MuTra_2005_Proceedings.pdf

Gil Bardají, A. (2009) 'Procedures, techniques, strategies: Translation process operators', *Perspectives* 17.3: 161–73.

Gile, D. (2004) 'Translation research vs. interpreting research: Kinship, differences and prospects for partnership', in C. Schäffner (ed.) *Translation Research and Interpreting Research: Traditions, Gaps and Synergies*, Clevedon: Multilingual Matters, pp. 10–34.

Gillespie, S. and D. Hopkins (eds) (2005) *The Oxford History of Literary Translation in English. Volume III: 1660–1790*, Oxford: Oxford University Press.

Godard, B. (1990) 'Theorizing feminist discourse/translation', in S. Bassnett and A. Lefevere (eds), pp. 87–96.

Gottlieb, H. (1994) 'Subtitling: Diagonal translation', *Perspectives* 2.1: 101–121.

— (1997) 'Quality revisited: The rendering of English idioms in Danish television subtitles vs. printed translations', in A. Trosberg (ed.), pp. 309–38.

Gouanvic, J.-M. (1999) *Sociologie de la traduction: La science-fiction américaine dans l'espace culturel français des années 1950*, Arras: Artois Presses Université.

— (2005) 'A Bourdieusian theory of translation, or the coincidence of practical instances: Field, "habitus", capital and illusio', *The Translator* 11.2: 147–66.

Graham, J. F. (ed.) (1985) *Difference in Translation*, Ithaca, NY: Cornell University Press.

Granger, S. and S. Petch-Tyson (eds) (2003) *Extending the Scope of Corpus-Based Research: New Applications, New Challenges*, Amsterdam and New York: Rodopi.

Grice, H. P. (1975) 'Logic and conversation', in P. Cole and J. L. Morgan (eds) *Syntax and Semantics*, vol. 3: *Speech Acts*, New York: Academic Press, pp. 41–58.

Grossman, E. (2003/2005) 'Translator's note to the reader', in M. de Cervantes *Don Quixote*, New York: Ecco, pp. xvii–xx.

— (2010) *Why Translation Matters*, Yale: Yale UP.

Guenthner, F. and M. Guenthner-Reutter (eds) (1978) *Meaning and Translation: Philosophical and Linguistic Approaches*, London: Duckworth.

Gutas, D. (1998) *Greek Thought, Arabic Culture: The Graeco-Arabic Translation Movement in Baghdad and Early 'Abb sid Society (2nd–4th/8th–10th Centuries)*, London and New York: Routledge.

Gutt, E. (1991, 2nd edition 2000) *Translation and Relevance: Cognition and Context*, Oxford: Blackwell; Manchester: St Jerome.

— (2005) 'On the significance of the cognitive core of translation', *The Translator* 11.1: 25–49.

Haddadian-Moghaddam, E. (2014) *Literary Translation in Modern Iran: A Sociological Study*, Amsterdam and Philadelphia: John Benjamins.

Halliday, M. A. K. (1978) *Language as Social Semiotic*, London and New York: Arnold.

— (1994) *An Introduction to Functional Grammar*, 2nd edition, London, Melbourne and Auckland: Arnold.

Halliday, M. A. K. and R. Hasan (1976) *Cohesion in English*, London: Longman.

Halliday, M. A. K. and C. Matthiessen (2012) *An Introduction to Functional Grammar*, 4th edition, London: Arnold.

Halverson, S. (1999) 'Conceptual work and the "translation" concept', *Target* 11.1: 1–31.

Hansen, G. (2006) 'Retrospection methods in translator training and translator research', *Journal of Specialised Translation* 5: 1–40, http://jostrans.org/issue05/art_hansen.pdf

Hanssen, B. (2004) 'Language and mimesis in Walter Benjamin's work', *Cambridge Companion to Walter Benjamin*, Cambridge: Cambridge University Press, 54–72.

Hartley, A. (2009) 'Technology and translation', in Jeremy Munday (ed.) (2009), pp. 106–27.

Harvey, K. (1998/2012) 'Translating camp talk: Gay identities and cultural transfer', in L. Venuti (ed.) (2012), pp. 344–64.

— (2003) ' "Events" and "horizons": Reading ideology in the "bindings" of translations', in M. Calzada Pérez (ed.) *Apropos of Ideology: Translation*

Studies on Ideology – Ideologies in Translation Studies, Manchester: St Jerome, pp. 43–69.

Hatim, B. (2009) 'Translating text in context', in J. Munday (ed.) *The Routledge Companion to Translation Studies*, London and New York: Routledge, pp. 36–53.

Hatim, B. and I. Mason (1990) *Discourse and the Translator*, London and New York: Longman.

— (1997) *The Translator as Communicator*, London and New York: Routledge.

Hatim, B. and J. Munday (2004) *Translation: An Advanced Resource Book*, London and New York: Routledge.

Heaney, S. (1999) *Beowulf: A New Translation*, London: Faber and Faber.

Heidegger, M. (1962) *Being and Time*, translated by J. Macquarrie and E. Robinson, New York: Harper and Row.

— (1971) *On the Way to Language*, translated by P. D. Hertz, New York: Harper and Row.

Heilbron, J. (1999/2010) 'Towards a sociology of translation: Book translations as a cultural world system', in M. Baker (ed.) (2010) *Critical Readings in Translation Studies*, London and New York: Routledge, pp. 304–16.

Heilbron, J. and G. Sapiro (2007) 'Outline for a sociology of translation', in M. Wolf and A. Fukari (eds) (2007) *Constructing a Sociology of Translation*, Amsterdam and Philadelphia: John Benjamins, pp. 93–107.

Henry, R. (1984) 'Points for inquiry into total translation: A review of J. C. Catford's *A Linguistic Theory of Translation*', *Meta* 29.2: 152–8.

Hermans, T. (ed.) (1985a) *The Manipulation of Literature: Studies in Literary Translation*, Beckenham: Croom Helm.

— (1985b) 'Translation studies and a new paradigm', in T. Hermans (ed.) (1985a), pp. 7–15.

— (1995) 'Revisiting the classics: Toury's empiricism version one', *The Translator* 1.2: 215–23.

— (1996) 'Norms and the determination of translation: A theoretical framework', in R. Álvarez and M. Carmen-África Vidal (eds), pp. 25–51.

— (1997) 'The task of the translator in the European Renaissance: Explorations in a discursive field', http://discovery.ucl.ac.uk/955/1/97_Task_Translator_Renaissance.pdf

— (1999) *Translation in Systems: Descriptive and System-Oriented Approaches Explained*, Manchester: St Jerome.

— (2003) 'Cross-cultural translation studies as "thick" translation', *Bulletin of the School of Oriental and African Studies* 66.3: 380–89, http://www.soas.ac.uk/literatures/satranslations/Hermans.pdf

— (ed.) (2006a) *Translating Others: Volume I*, Manchester: St Jerome.

— (ed.) (2006b) *Translating Others: Volume II*, Manchester: St Jerome.

— (2007) *The Conference of the Tongues*, Manchester: St Jerome.

— (2009) 'Translation, ethics, politics', in J. Munday (ed.) *The Routledge Companion to Translation Studies*, London and New York: Routledge, pp. 93–105.

Holmes, J. S. (ed.) (1970) *The Nature of Translation: Essays on the Theory and Practice of Literary Translation*, The Hague and Paris: Mouton.

— (1972) 'The name and nature of translation studies', in J. Qvistgaard et al. (eds) *Third International Congress of Applied Linguistics (Copenhagen, 21–26 August 1972): Congress Abstracts*, Copenhagen: Ehrverskøkonomisk Forlag, http://www.eric.ed.gov/PDFS/ED074796.pdf

— (1988a) *Translated! Papers on Literary Translation and Translation Studies*, Amsterdam: Rodopi.

— (1988b/2004) 'The name and nature of translation studies', in L. Venuti (ed.) (2004), pp. 180–92.

Holmstrom, L. (2006) 'Let poetry win: The translator as writer – an Indian perspective', in S. Bassnett and P. Bush (eds), pp. 33–45.

Holub, R. C. (1984) *Reception Theory: A Critical Introduction*, London and New York: Methuen.

Holz-Mänttäri, J. (1984) *Translatorisches Handeln: Theorie und Methode*, Helsinki: Suomalainen Tiedeakatemia.

— (1986) 'Translatorisches Handeln – theoretische fundierte Berufsprofile', in M. Snell-Hornby (ed.) *Übersetzungswissenschaft: Eine Neuorientierung*, Tübingen: Franke, pp. 348–74.

House, J. (1977) *A Model for Translation Quality Assessment*, Tübingen: Gunter Narr.

— (1997) *Translation Quality Assessment: A Model Revisited*, Tübingen: Gunter Narr.

— (1998) 'Politeness in translation', in L. Hickey (ed.) (1998) *The Pragmatics of Translation*, Clevedon: Multilingual Matters, pp. 54–71.

— (2002) 'Universality versus culture specificity in translation', in A. Riccaardi (ed.), pp. 92–110.

— (2006) 'Text and context in translation', *Journal of Pragmatics* 38.3: 338–58.

— (ed.) (2014a) *Translation: A Multidisciplinary Approach*, Houndmills and New York: Palgrave Macmillan.

— (2014b) 'English as a Global Lingua Franca: A Threat to Multilingualism, Intercultural Communication and Translation?', talk at the Free Linguistics Conference 2014, https://www.youtube.com/watch?v=dLHuwsQgQcU

— (2015) *Translation Quality Assessment: Past and Present*, London and New York: Routledge.

Huang, Ko-wu (2003) 'The reception of Yan Fu in twentieth-century China', in C. Yik-yi Chu and R. Mak, *China Reconstructs*, Lanham: University Press of America, pp. 25–44.

Hung, E. (2005) 'Cultural borderlands in China's translation history', in E. Hung (ed.) *Translation and Cultural Change: Studies in History, Norms, and Image Projection*, Amsterdam and Philadelphia: John Benjamins, pp. 43–64.

Hung, E. and D. Pollard (1998) 'The Chinese tradition', in M. Baker and K. Malmkjær (eds) (1998), pp. 365–74.

— (2009) 'Chinese tradition', in M. Baker and G. Saldanha (eds), pp. 369–78.

Hung, E. and J. Wakabayashi (eds) (2005) *Asian Translation Traditions*, Manchester: St Jerome.

Hurtado Albir, A. (2001) *Traducción y traductología: Introducción a la traductología*, Madrid: Cátedra.

Hurtado Albir, A. and F. Alves (2009) 'Translation as a cognitive activity', in J. Munday (ed.), pp. 54–73.

Hyde Parker, R., K. Guadarrama and A. Fawcett (eds) (2010) *Translation: Theory and Practice in Dialogue*, London and New York: Continuum.

Inggs, J. and L. Meintjes (eds) (2009) *Translation Studies in Africa*, London and New York: Continuum.

Inghilleri, M. (ed.) (2005a) *Bourdieu and the Sociology of Translation and Interpreting*, special issue of *The Translator* 11.2.

— (2005b) 'The sociology of Bourdieu and the construction of the "object" in translation and interpreting studies', *The Translator* 11.2: 125–46.

— (2009) 'Sociological approaches', in M. Baker and G. Saldanha (eds) *The Routledge Encylopedia of Translation Studies*, pp. 279–82.

Ivir, V. (1981) 'Formal correspondence vs. translation equivalence revisited', *Poetics Today* 2.4: 51–9.

Jääskeläinen, R. (2009) 'Think-aloud protocols', in M. Baker and G. Saldanha (eds), pp. 290–3.

Jakobsen, A. L. (2003) 'Effects of think aloud on translation speed, revision and segmentation', in F. Alves (ed.), pp. 69–95.

Jakobsen, A. L. and L. Schou (1999) 'Translog documentation', *Copenhagen Studies in Language* 24: 149–84.

Jakobson, R. (1959/2012) 'On linguistic aspects of translation', in L. Venuti (ed.) (2012), pp. 126–31.

— (1960) 'Closing statement: Linguistics and poetics', in T. Seboek (ed.) (1960) *Style in Language*, Cambridge, MA: MIT Press, pp. 350–77.

James, C. (1980) *Contrastive Analysis*, London: Longman.

Jauss, H. R. (1982) *Toward an Aesthetic of Reception*, translated from the German by T. Bahti, Brighton: Harvester Press.

Jerome, E. H. (St Jerome) (395 ce/1997) 'De optime genere interpretandi' (Letter 101, to Pammachius), in *Epistolae D. Hieronymi Stridoniensis*, Rome: Aldi F., (1565), pp. 285–91, translated by P. Carroll as 'On the best kind of translator', in D. Robinson (ed.) (1997b), pp. 22–30.

Jiang, C. (2010) 'Quality assessment for the translation of museum texts: Application of a systemic functional model', *Perspectives* 18.2: 109–26.

Jiménez-Crespo, M. (2011) 'To adapt or not to adapt in web localization', *JosTrans* 15, http://www.jostrans.org/issue15/art_jimenez.php.

— (2013) *Translation and Web Localization*, London and New York: Routledge.

Johansson, S. (2003) 'Reflections on corpora and their uses in cross-linguistic research', in F. Zanettin, S. Bernardini and D. Stewart (eds), pp. 135–44.

Jones, F. (2011) *Poetry Translating as Expert Action: Processes, Priorities and Networks*, Amsterdam and Philadelphia: John Benjamins.

Kade, O. (1968) *Zufall und Gesetzmäßigkeit in der Übersetzung*, Leipzig: VEB Verlag Enzyklopädie.

Kaindl, K. and K-H. Spitzl (eds) (2014) *Transfiction: Research Into the Realities of Translation Fiction*, Amsterdam and Philadelphia: John Benjamins.

Kang, J-H. (2015) 'Conflicting discourses of translation assessment and the discursive construction of the "assessor" role in cyberspace', *Target* 27.3: 454–71.

Karamitroglou, F. (2000) *Towards a Methodology for the Investigation of Norms in Audiovisual Translation*, Amsterdam and Atlanta: Rodopi.

Kearney, R. (2007) 'Paul Ricœur and the hermeneutics of translation', *Research in Phenomenology* 37: 147–59.

Kelly, L. (1979) *The True Interpreter*, Oxford: Blackwell.

Kenny, D. (2009) 'Equivalence', in M. Baker and G. Saldanha (eds), pp. 96–9.

— (2001) *Lexis and Creativity in Translation: A Corpus-Based Study*, Manchester: St Jerome.

— (2011) 'Translation units and corpora', in A. Kruger, K. Wallmach and J. Munday (eds), pp. 76–102.

Kharmandar, M. A. (2015) 'Ricœur's extended hermeneutic translation theory', *Études Ricœuriennes/Ricœur Studies* 6.1: 73–93, (DOI 10.5195/errs.2015.281).

Kittel, H. and A. Polterman (2009) 'The German tradition', in M. Baker and G. Saldanha (eds) (2009), pp. 411–18.

Koller, W. (1979a) *Einführung in die Übersetzungswissenschaft*, Heidelberg-Wiesbaden: Quelle und Meyer.

— (1979b/1989) 'Equivalence in translation theory', translated from the German by A. Chesterman, in A. Chesterman (ed.) (1989), pp. 99–104.

— (1995) 'The concept of equivalence and the object of translation studies', *Target* 7.2: 191–222.

Komissarov, V. (1993) 'Norms in translation', in P. Zlateva (ed.) *Translation as Social Action: Russian and Bulgarian Perspectives*, London and New York: Routledge, pp. 63–75.

Koskinen, K. (2000) 'Institutional Illusions: Translating in the EU Commission', *The Translator*, 6.1: 49–65.

Koster, C. (2000) *From Word to Word: An Armamentarium*, Amsterdam and Atlanta: Rodopi.

Kothari, R. (2003) *Translating India: The Cultural Politics of English*, Manchester: St Jerome.

Kress, G. and T. van Leeuwen (1996/2006) *Reading Images: The Grammar of Visual Design*, 2nd edition, London and New York: Routledge.

Krings, H. (1986) 'Translation problems and translation strategies of advanced German learners of French (L2)', in J. House and S. Blum-Kulka (eds), *Interlingual and Intercultural Communication*, Tübingen: Gunter Narr, pp. 263–75.

Krishnamurthy, R. (2009) 'The Indian tradition', in M. Baker and G. Saldanha (eds) (2009), pp. 449–58.

Kruger, A., K. Wallmach and J. Munday (eds) (2011) *Corpus-Based Translation Studies: Research and Applications*, London and New York: Continuum.

Kuhiwczak, P. (1990) 'Translation as appropriation: The case of Milan Kundera's *The Joke*', in S. Bassnett and A. Lefevere (eds), pp. 118–30.

Lackner, M. (2001) 'Circumnavigating the unfamiliar: Dào' n (314–385) and Yan Fu (1852–1921) on western grammar', in M. Lackner et al. (eds), pp. 357–70, http://www.wsc.uni-erlangen.de/pdf/lackner.pdf

Lackner, M., I. Amelung and J. Kurtz (eds) (2001) *New Terms for New Ideas: Western Knowledge and Lexical Change in Late Imperial China*, Leiden: Brill.

Lakoff, G. and M. Johnson (1980) *Metaphors We Live By*, Chicago: University of Chicago Press.

Lal, P. (1964) *Great Sanskrit Plays in New English Transcreations*, New York: New Directions.

Lambert, J.-R. (1989) 'La traduction, les langues et la communication de masse: Les ambiguïtés du discours international', *Target* 1.2: 215–37.

Lambert, J.-R. and H. van Gorp (1985/2006) 'On describing translations', in J. Lambert, D. Delabastita, L. d'Hulst and R. Meylaerts (2006) *Functional Approaches to Translation and Culture: Selected Papers by José Lambert*, Amsterdam and Philadelphia: John Benjamins, pp. 37–47.

Larkosh, C. (ed.) (2011) *Re-engendering Translation: Transcultural Practice, Gender/Sexuality and the Politics of Alterity*, Manchester: St Jerome.

Larose, R. (1989) *Théories contemporaines de la traduction*, 2nd edition, Quebec: Presses de l'Université du Québec.

Larson, M. L. (1998) *Meaning-Based Translation: A Guide to Cross-Language Equivalence*, 2nd edition, Lanham, New York and London: University Press of America.

Laviosa, S. (1998a) 'The corpus-based approach: A new paradigm in translation studies', *Meta* 13.4: 474–9.

— (ed.) (1998b) *The Corpus-Based Approach/L'approche basé sur le corpus*, special issue of *Meta* 13.4.

Lederer, M. (1994) *La traduction aujourd'hui: le modèle interprétatif*, Paris: Hachette, translated (2003) by Ninon Larché as *Translation: The Interpretive Model*, Manchester: St Jerome.

Lee, T-K. (2013) *Translating the Multilingual City: Cross-lingual Practices and Language Ideology*, Bern: Peter Lang.

Leech, G. (1983) *Principles of Pragmatics*, London: Longman.

Leech, G. and M. Short (1981) *Style in Fiction: A Linguistic Introduction to English Fictional Prose*, London and New York: Longman.

Lefevere, A. (1977) *Translating Literature: The German Tradition from Luther to Rosenzweig*, Assen: Van Gorcum.

— (1985) 'Why waste our time on rewrites?: The trouble with interpretation and the role of rewriting in an alternative paradigm', in T. Hermans (ed.) (1985a), pp. 215–43.

— (1992a) *Translation, Rewriting and the Manipulation of Literary Fame*, London and New York: Routledge.

— (ed.) (1992b) *Translation/History/Culture: A Sourcebook*, London and New York: Routledge.

— (1993) *Translating Literature: Practice and Theory in a Comparative Literature Context*, New York: The Modern Language Association of America.

Leuven-Zwart, K. M. van (1989) 'Translation and original: Similarities and dissimilarities, I', *Target* 1.2: 151–81.

— (1990) 'Translation and original: Similarities and dissimilarities, II', *Target* 2.1: 69–95.

Leuven-Zwart, K. van and T. Naaijkens (eds) (1991) *Translation Studies: State of the Art*, Amsterdam: Rodopi.

Lévi-Strauss, C. (1958) *Anthropologie structurale*, Paris: Plon, translated (1963) by C. Jacobson and B. Grundfest Schoepf as *Structural Anthropology*, New York: Basic Books.

Levine, S. J. (1991) *The Subversive Scribe: Translating Latin American Fiction*, St Paul, MN: Graywolf Press.

Levinson, S. C. (1983) *Pragmatics*, Cambridge: Cambridge University Press.

Levý, J. (1963/1969) *Umění překladu,* Prague: Československý spisovatel, translated by W. Schamschula (1969) as *Die Literarische Übersetzung: Theorie einer Kunstgattung*, Frankfurt: Athenäum.

— (1967/2000) 'Translation as a decision process', in L. Venuti (ed.) (2000), pp. 148–59.

— (2011) *The Art of Translation*, translated by P. Corness, edited by Z. Jettmarová, Amsterdam and Philadelphia: John Benjamins.

Lewis, P. (1985/2012) 'The measure of translation effects', in L. Venuti (ed.) (2012), pp. 220–39.

Linde, Z. de and N. Kay (1999) *The Semiotics of Subtitling*, Manchester: St Jerome.

Loffredo, E. and M. Perteghella (eds) (2006) *Translation and Creativity: Perspectives on Creative Writing and Translation Studies*, London: Continuum.

Loh, D. (1958) *Translation: Its Principles and Techniques*, Beijing: Times Publishing.

Longhurst, B., G. Smith, G. Bagnall, G. Crawford, M. Ogborn, E. Baldwin and S. McCracken (eds) (2013) *Introducing Cultural Studies*, 2nd ed., London and New York: Routledge.

Lörscher, W. (1991) *Translation Performance, Translation Process, and Translation Strategies: A Psycholinguistic Investigation*, Tübingen: Gunter Narr.

Louw, T. van der (2007) *Transformations in the Septuagint: Towards an Interaction of Septuagint Studies and Translation Studies*, Leuven: Peeters.

Luo, X. and Hong Lei (2004) 'Translation theory and practice in China', *Perspectives* 12.1: 20–30.

Luther, M. (1530/1963) 'Sendbrief vom Dolmetschen', in H. Störig (ed.) (1963), pp. 14–32.

Luyken, G. M., T. Herbst, J. Langham-Brown, H. Reid, and H. Spinhof (1991) *Overcoming Language Barriers in Television: Dubbing and Subtitling for the European Audience*, Manchester: European Institute for the Media.

Lyons, J. (1977) *Semantics*, Cambridge: Cambridge University Press.

McCarty, W. (1999) 'Humanities computing as interdiscipline', available online: http://www.iath.virginia.edu/hcs/mccarty.html

— (2003) 'Humanities computing', http://www.mccarty.org.uk/essays/McCarty, %20Humanities%20computing.pdf

— (2005) *Humanities Computing*, Basingstoke: Palgrave Macmillan.

McDonough Dolmaya, J. (2012) 'Analyzing the crowdsourcing model and its impact on public perceptions of translation', *The Translator* 18.2: 167–91.

McElduff, S. (2009) 'Living at the level of the word: Cicero's rejection of the interpreter as translator', *Translation Studies* 2.2: 133–46.

McElduff, S. (2013) *Roman Theories of Translation: Surpassing the Source*, London and New York: Routledge.

McEnery, T., R. Xiao and Y. Tono (2006) *Corpus-Based Language Studies: An Advanced Resource Book*, London and New York: Routledge.

Maier, C. (1990) 'Reviewing Latin American literature', *Translation Review* 34.5: 18–24.

— (2007) 'The translator as an intervenient being', in J. Munday (ed.) (2007b), pp. 1–17.

Malblanc, A. (1944/1963), *Stylistique comparée du français et de l'allemand*, 2nd edition, Paris: Didier.

Malmkjær, Kirsten (2003) 'What happened to God and the angels: HW Dulken's translations of Hans Christian Andersen's stories in Victorian Britain OR An exercise in translational stylistics', *Target* 15.1: 37–58.

— (2005) *Linguistics and the Language of Translation*, Edinburgh: Edinburgh University Press.

— (ed.) (2011) *The Linguistics Encyclopedia*, 3rd edition, London and New York: Routledge.

Malmkjær, K. and K. Windle (eds) (2011) *The Oxford Handbook of Translation Studies*, Oxford: Oxford University Press.

Mangiron, C. and M. O'Hagan (2006) 'Game localisation: Unleashing imagination with "restricted" translation', *Journal of Specialised Translation* 6: 10–21, http://www.jostrans.org/issue06/art_ohagan.pdf

Mansor, I. (2011) *Procedures and Strategies in the Translation into Malay of Cultural Elements of* Rihlat Ibn Battuta, PhD thesis, University of Leeds, UK.

Marais, K. (2014) *Translation Theory and Development Studies*, London and New York: Routledge.

Martin, J. and P. White (2005) *The Language of Evaluation: Appraisal in English*, Basingstoke: Palgrave.

Mason, I. (2000) 'Audience design in translating', *The Translator* 6.1: 1–22.

— (2003/2012) 'Text parameters in translation: Transitivity and institutional cultures', in L. Venuti (ed.) (2012), pp. 399–410.

Mason, K. (1969/1974) *Advanced Spanish Course*, Oxford: Pergamon.

Massidda, S. (2015) *Audiovisual Translation in the Digital Age: The Italian Fansubbing Phenomenon*, Houndsmills: Palgrave Macmillan.

Matejka, L. and K. Pomorska (eds) (1971) *Readings in Russian Poetics: Formalist and Structuralist Views*, Cambridge, MA: MIT Press.

Mauranen, A. and P. Kujamäki (eds) (2004) *Translation Universals: Do They Exist?*, Amsterdam and Philadelphia: John Benjamins.

Mayoral, R., D. Kelly and N. Gallardo (1988) 'The concept of constrained translation: Non-linguistic perspectives of translation', *Meta* 33.3: 356–67.

Mazur, J. (2007) 'The metalanguage of localization: Theory and practice', *Target* 19.2: 337–57.

Mehrez, S. (1992) 'Translation and the postcolonial experience: The francophone North African text', in L. Venuti (ed.), pp. 120–38.

Miao, Ju (2000) 'The limitations of equivalent effect', *Perspectives* 8.3: 197–205.

Miko, F. (1970) 'La théorie de l'expression et la traduction', in J. S. Holmes (ed.), pp. 61–77.

Millán, C. and F. Bartrina (eds) (2013) *The Routledge Handbook of Translation Studies*, London and New York: Routledge.

Milton, J. and P. Bandia (eds) (2009) *Agents of Translation*, Amsterdam and Philadelphia: John Benjamins.

Minors, H. (ed.) (2013) *Music, Text and Translation*, London and New York: Bloomsbury.

Mitchell, S. (2005) *Gilgamesh: A New English Version*, London: Profile.

Morini, M. (2013) *The Pragmatic Translator: An Integral Theory of Translation*, London and New York: Bloomsbury.

Mossop, B. (2007) 'The translator's intervention through voice selection', in J. Munday (ed.), pp. 18–37.

— (2013) 'Andrei Fedorov and the origins of linguistic translation theory', http://www.yorku.ca/brmossop/Fedorov.htm

Mounin, G. (1955) *Les belles infidèles*, Paris: Cahiers du Sud.

— (1963) *Les problèmes théoriques de la traduction*, Paris: Gallimard.

Munday, J. (1998) 'The Caribbean conquers the world? An analysis of the reception of García Márquez in translation', *Bulletin of Hispanic Studies* 75.1: 137–44.

— (2001/2008/2012) *Introducing Translation Studies*, 1st/2nd/3rd edition, London and New York: Routledge.

— (2002) 'Systems in translation: A systemic model for descriptive translation studies', in T. Hermans (ed.) *Crosscultural Transgressions. Research Models in Translation Studies* II: *Historical and Ideological Issues*, Manchester: St Jerome, pp. 76–92.

— (2007a) 'Translation and ideology: A textual approach', *The Translator* 13.2: 195–217.

— (ed.) (2007b) *Translation as Intervention*, London: Continuum and IATIS.

— (2008) *Style and Ideology in Translation: Latin American Writing in English*, New York: Routledge.

— (ed.) (2009) *The Routledge Companion to Translation Studies*, London and New York: Routledge.

— (2010) 'Evaluation and intervention in translation', in M. Baker, M. Olohan and M. Calzada Pérez (eds) *Text and Context*, Manchester: St Jerome, pp. 77–94.

— (2011) 'Looming large: A cross-linguistic analysis of semantic prosodies in comparable reference corpora', in A. Kruger, K. Wallmach and J. Munday (eds), pp. 169–86.

— (2012) *Evaluation in Translation: Critical Points of Translator Decision-Making*, London and New York: Routledge.

— (2013) 'The role of archival and manuscript research in the investigation of translator decision-making', *Target* 25.1: 127–40.

— (2014) 'Using primary sources to produce a micro-history of translation and translators', *The Translator* 20.1: 64–80.

Munday, J. and M. Zhang (eds) (2015) *Discourse Analysis in Translation Studies*, special issue of *Target* 27.3.

Nabokov, V. (1955/2004) 'Problems of translation: *Onegin* in English', in L. Venuti (ed.) (2004), pp. 115–27.

Newmark, P. (1981) *Approaches to Translation*, Oxford and New York: Pergamon, republished 2001 by Shanghai Foreign Language Education Press.

— (1988) *A Textbook of Translation*, New York and London: Prentice Hall.

— (2009) 'The linguistic and communicative stages in translation theory', in J. Munday (ed.), pp. 20–35.

Nida, E. A. (1964a) *Toward a Science of Translating*, Leiden: E. J. Brill.

— (1964b/2012) 'Principles of correspondence', in L. Venuti (ed.) (2012), pp. 141–55.

— (2002) *Contexts in Translating*, Amsterdam and Philadelphia: John Benjamins.

Nida, E. A. and C. R. Taber (1969) *The Theory and Practice of Translation*, Leiden: E. J. Brill.

Niranjana, T. (1992) *Siting Translation: History, Post-structuralism, and the Colonial Context*, Berkeley, CA: University of California Press.

Nord, C. (1988) *Textanalyze und Übersetzen: Theoretische Grundlagen, Methode und didaktische Anwendung einer übersetzungsrelevanten Textanalyze*, Heidelberg: J. Groos, translated.

— (1997) *Translating as a Purposeful Activity: Functionalist Approaches Explained*, Manchester: St Jerome.

— (2003) 'Function and loyalty in Bible translation', in M. Calzada Pérez (ed.), pp. 89–112.

— (2005) *Text Analysis in Translation: Theory, Methodology and Didactic Application of a Model for Translation-Oriented Text Analysis*, translated by C. Nord and P. Sparrow, 2nd edition, Amsterdam: Rodopi.

Nornes, A. (1999/2004) 'For an abusive subtitling', in L. Venuti (ed.) (2004), pp. 444–69.

— (2007) *Cinema Babel: Translating Global Cinema*, University of Massachusetts Press.

Norris, C. (2002) *Deconstruction: Theory and Practice*, 2nd edition, London and New York: Routledge.

O'Brien, S. (2006) 'Eye tracking and translation memory matches', *Perspectives* 14.3: 185–205.

— (ed.) (2011) *Cognitive Explorations of Translation*, London: Continuum.

O'Hagan, M. (2009) 'Evolution of user-generated translation: Fansubs, translation hacking and crowdsourcing', *Journal of Internationalization and Localization* 1: 94–121.

O'Hagan, M. and D. Ashworth (2002) *Translation-Mediated Communication in a Digital World: Facing the Challenges of Globalization and Localization*, Clevedon: Multilingual Matters.

O'Hagan, M. and C. Mangiron (2013) *Game Localization: Translating for the Global Digital Entertainment Industry*, Amsterdam and Philadelphia: John Benjamins.

Olohan, M. (2004) *Introducing Corpora in Translation Studies*, London and New York: Routledge.

Olohan, M. and M. Baker (2000) 'Reporting *that* in translated English: Evidence for subconscious processes of explicitation', *Across* 1.2: 142–72.

Orero, P. and J. Sager (eds) (1997) *The Translator's Dialogue: Giovanni Pontiero*, Amsterdam and Philadelphia, PA: John Benjamins.

Osgood, C., G. Suci and R. Tannenbaum (1957) *The Measurement of Meaning*, Urbana, IL: University of Illinois Press.

O'Sullivan, C. (2013) 'Multimodality as challenge and resource in translation', *JosTrans* 20, http://www.jostrans.org/issue20/art_osullivan.pdf

Palmer, R. (1969) *Hermeneutics: Interpretation Theory in Schleiermacher, Dilthey, Heidegger and Gadamer*, Evanston, IL: Northwestern University Press.

Parks, T. (2007) *Translating Style: The English Modernists and their Italian Translations*, 2nd edition, Manchester: St Jerome.

Peden, M. S. (1987) 'Telling others' tales', *Translation Review* 24.5: 9–12.

Pedersen, J. (2005) 'How is culture rendered in subtitles?', MUTRA 2005, http://www.euroconferences.info/proceedings/2005_Proceedings/2005_Pedersen_Jan.pdf

— (2011) *Subtitling Norms for Television*, Amsterdam and Philadelphia: John Benjamins.

Pedrola, M. (1999) 'An interview with Peter Newmark', in G. Anderman and M. Rogers (eds) *Word, Text, Translation: Liber Amicorum for Peter Newmark*, Clevedon: Multilingual Matters, pp. 17–22.

Pérez-González, L. (2014) *Audiovisual Translation: Theories, Methods and Issues*, London and New York: Routledge.

Pérez-González, L. and S. Susam-Saraeva (eds) (2012) *Non-Professionals Translating and Interpreting*, special issue of *The Translator* 18.2.

Pinker, S. (1994) *The Language Instinct: The New Science of Language and Mind*, London and New York: Penguin.

— (2007) *The Stuff of Thought: Language as a Window into Human Nature*, London and New York: Penguin.

Pöchhacker, F. (2004) *Introducing Interpreting Studies*, London and New York: Routledge.

— (2009) 'Issues in interpreting studies', in J. Munday (ed.) (2009), pp. 128–40.

Pöchhacker, F. and M. Shlesinger (eds) (2002) *The Interpreting Studies Reader*, London and New York: Routledge.

Popovič, A. (1970) 'The concept "shift of expression" in translation analysis', in J. S. Holmes (ed.), pp. 78–87.

Pound, E. (1915) *Cathay*, London: Elkin Mathews.

— (1918/2012) 'Guido's relations', in L. Venuti (ed.) (2012), pp. 84–91.

— (1951) *ABC of Reading*, London: Faber and Faber.

— (1953) *The Translations of Ezra Pound*, London: Faber and Faber.

— (1954) *Literary Essays*, ed. T. S. Eliot, London: Faber and Faber.

— (1963) *Translations*, New York: New Directions.

— (2010) *New Selected Poems and Translations*, New York: New Directions.

Pountain, C. (2008) 'The genius of language', lecture given at Newcastle University, 27 October 2008, http://www.ncl.ac.uk/sml/research/seminars/Pountain.pdf

Poyatos, F. (ed.) (1997) *Nonverbal Communication and Translation*, Amsterdam and Philadelphia: John Benjamins.

Proust, M. (1996) *In Search of Lost Time*, Vol. 1: *Swann's Way*, London: Vintage.

— (2003) *The Way by Swann's*, London: Penguin Classics.

Pym, A. (1992) *Translation and Text Transfer: An essay on the principles of intercultural communication*, Frankfurt am Main, Berlin and Bern: Peter Lang.

— (1998) *Method in Translation History*, Manchester: St Jerome.

— (ed.) (2001) *The Return to Ethics*, special issue of *The Translator* 7.2.

— (2004) *The Moving Text: Localization, Translation, and Distribution*, Amsterdam and Philadelphia: John Benjamins.

— (2006) 'On the social and cultural in translation studies', introduction to A. Pym, M. Shlesinger and Z. Jettmarová (eds), pp. 1–25.

— (2007) 'Natural and directional equivalence in theories of translation', *Target* 19.2: 271–94.

— (2008) 'On Toury's laws of how translators translate', in A. Pym, M. Shlesinger and D. Simeoni (eds), pp. 311–28.

— (2010/2014) *Exploring Translation Theories*, London and New York: Routledge.

— (2016) *Translation Solutions for Many Languages: History of a Flawed Dream*, London and New York: Bloomsbury.

Pym, A., M. Shlesinger and Z. Jettmarová (eds) (2006) *Sociocultural Aspects of Translating and Interpreting*, Amsterdam and Philadelphia: John Benjamins.

Pym, A., M. Shlesinger and D. Simeoni (eds) (2008) *Beyond Descriptive Translation Studies*, Amsterdam and Philadelphia: John Benjamins.

Qian, H. (1992a) 'On the implausibility of equivalent response (Part I)', *Meta* 37.2: 289–301, available at http://erudit.org/revue/meta/1992/v37/n2/003148ar.pdf.

— (1992b) 'On the implausibility of equivalent response (Part II)', *Meta* 37.3: 491–506.

— (1993a) 'On the implausibility of equivalent response (Part III)', *Meta* 38.2: 226–37.

— (1993b) 'On the implausibility of equivalent response (Part IV)', *Meta* 38.3: 449–67, http://www.erudit.org/revue/meta/1993/v38/n3/003147ar.pdf

— (1994) 'On the implausibility of equivalent response (Part V)', *Meta* 39.3: 418–32.

Qvale, P. (2003) *From St Jerome to Hypertext: Translation in Theory and Practice*, translated by L. Sivesind and K. Malmkjær, Manchester: St Jerome.

Rabassa, G. (1984) 'The silk purse business: A translator's conflicting responsibilities', in W. Frawley (ed.) (1984), pp. 35–40.

— (2005) *If This Be Treason: Translation and its Dyscontents*, New York: New Directions.

Rafael, V. (1993) *Contracting Colonialism: Translation and Christian Conversion in Tagalog Society under Early Spanish Rule*, Durham, NC: Duke University Press.

Rajak, T. (2009) *Translation and Survival: The Greek Bible of the Ancient Jewish Diaspora*, Oxford: Oxford University Press.

Ramakrishna, S. (2000) 'Cultural transmission through translation: An Indian perspective', in S. Simon and P. St-Pierre (eds), pp. 87–100.

Rao, S. (2006) 'From a postcolonial to a non-colonial theory of translation', in N. Sakai and J. Solomon (eds), pp. 73–94.

Raw, L. (ed) (2012) *Translation, Adaptation and Transformation,* London and New York: Continuum.

Rebenich, S. (2002) *Jerome*, London and New York: Routledge.

Reiss, K. (1971/2000) *Möglichkeiten und Grenzen der Übersetzungskritik*, Munich: M. Hueber, translated (2000) by E. F. Rhodes as *Translation Criticism: Potential and Limitations*, Manchester: St Jerome and American Bible Society.

— (1976) *Texttyp und Übersetzungsmethode: Der operative Text*, Kronberg: Scriptor Verlag.

— (1977/1989) 'Text types, translation types and translation assessment', translated by A. Chesterman, in A. Chesterman (ed.) (1989), pp. 105–15.

— (1981/2004) 'Type, kind and individuality of text: Decision making in translation', translated by S. Kitron, in L. Venuti (ed.) (2004), pp. 168–79.

Reiss, K. and H. J. Vermeer (1984/2013) *Towards a General Theory of Translational Action: Skopos Theory Explained*, translated by C. Nord, English reviewed by M. Dudenhöfer. Manchester: St Jerome.

Reiss, K. and H. J. Vermeer (1984) *Grundlegung einer allgemeinen Translationstheorie*, Tübingen: Niemeyer.

Rener, F. (1989) *Interpretation: Language and Translation from Cicero to Tytler*, Amsterdam and Atlanta: Rodopi.

Reynolds, M. (2006) 'Principles and norms of translation', in P. France and K. Haynes (eds) (2006), pp. 59–84.

Riccardi, A. (ed.) (2002) *Translation Studies: Perspectives on an Emerging Discipline*, Cambridge: Cambridge University Press.

Richardson, D. and V. Robinson (eds) (2007) *Introducing Gender and Women's Studies*, 3rd ed. Houndmills and New York: Palgrave Macmillan.

Ricœur, P. (2004/2006) *On Translation*, translated by E. Brennan, London and New York: Routledge.

Robinson, D. (1997a) *Translation and Empire: Postcolonial Theories Explained*, Manchester: St Jerome.

— (ed.) (1997b) *Western Translation Theory from Herodotus to Nietzsche*, Manchester: St Jerome.

Rogers, M. (2006) 'Structuring information in English: A specialist translation perspective on sentence beginnings', *The Translator* 12.1: 29–64.

Rosenthal, F. (1965/1994) *Das Fortleben der Antike im Islam*, translated (1994) by E. and J. Marmorstein as *The Classical Heritage in Islam (Arabic Thought and Culture)*, London and New York: Routledge.

Rundle, C. (ed.) (2014) *Theories and Methodologies of Translation History*, special issue of *The Translator* 20.1.

Rundle, C. and K. Sturge (eds) (2010) *Translation under Fascism*, Basingstoke: Palgrave Macmillan.

Said, E. (1978) *Orientalism*, London: Penguin.

Sakai, N. and J. Solomon (eds) (2006) *Translation, Biopolitics, 'Colonial Difference'*, Hong Kong: Hong Kong University Press.

Salama-Carr, M. (1995) 'Translators and the dissemination of knowledge', in J. Delisle and J. Woodsworth (eds) *Translators Through History*, Amsterdam and Philadelphia: John Benjamins, pp. 101–30.

Saldanha, G. (2011) 'Style of translation: The use of foreign words in translations by Margaret Jull Costa and Peter Bush', in A. Kruger, K. Wallmach and J. Munday (eds), pp. 237–58.

Saldanha, G. and S. O'Brien (2013) *Research Methodologies in Translation Studies*, Manchester: St Jerome.

Santaemilia, José (ed.) (2005) *Gender, Sex and Translation: The Manipulation of Identities*, Manchester: St Jerome.

Sato-Rossberg, N. and J. Wakabayashi (eds) (2012) *Translation and Translation Studies in the Japanese Context*, London and New York: Bloomsbury.

Saussure, F. de (1916/1983) *Cours de linguistique générale*, Paris: Éditions Payot, translated (1983) by R. Harris as *Course in General Linguistics*, London: Duckworth.

Schäffner, C. (ed.) (1994), *Translation Research and Interpreting Research: Traditions, Gaps and Synergies*, Clevedon: Multilingual Matters.

— (1998a) 'Action (Theory of "translatorial action")', in M. Baker and K. Malmkjær (eds), pp. 3–5.

— (1998b) 'Skopos theory', in Baker and K. Malmkjær (eds) (1998), pp. 235–8.

— (ed.) (1999) *Translation and Norms*, Clevedon: Multilingual Matters.

— (2010) 'Norms of translation', in Y. Gambier and L. van Doorslaer (eds), pp. 235–44 and online.

Schiavi, G. (1996) 'There is always a teller in the tale', *Target* 8.1: 1–21.

Schleiermacher, F. (1813/2012) 'On the different methods of translating', in L. Venuti (ed.) (2012), pp. 43–63.

Schulte, R. and J. Biguenet (eds) (1992) *Theories of Translation*, Chicago and London: University of Chicago Press.

Scott, M. (2012) *Wordsmith Tools*, Stroud: Lexical Analysis Software, http://www.lexically.net/wordsmith/

Selim, S. (ed.) (2009) *Nation and Translation in the Middle East*, special issue of *The Translator* 15.1.

Seruya, T. and M. Lin Moniz (2008) *Translation and Censorship in Different Times and Landscapes*, Newcastle: Cambridge Scholars Press.

Setton, R. (2011) 'Corpus-based interpreting studies (CIS): Overview and prospects', in A. Kruger et al. (eds), pp. 33–75.

Sewell, P. (2002) *Translation Commentary: The Art Revisited*, Dublin: Philomel.

Sharoff, S., B. Babych and A. Hartley (2009) ' "Irrefragable answers": Using comparable corpora to retrieve translation equivalents', *Language Resources and Evaluation* 43: 15–25.

Shei, C. (2005) 'Translation commentary: A happy medium between translation curriculum and EAP', *System* 33.2: 309–25.

Shuttleworth, M. and M. Cowie (eds) (1997) *Dictionary of Translation Studies*, Manchester: St Jerome.

Simeoni, D. (1998) 'The pivotal status of the translator's habitus', *Target* 10.1: 1–39.

Simon, S. (1996) *Gender in Translation: Cultural Identity and the Politics of Transmission*, London and New York: Routledge.

Simon, S. (2012) *Cities in Translation: Intersections of Language and Memory*, London and New York: Routledge.

Simon, S. and P. St-Pierre (eds) (2000) *Changing the Terms: Translating in the Postcolonial Era*, Ottawa: University of Ottawa Press.

Simpson, P. (1993) *Language, Ideology and Point of View*, London and New York: Routledge.

Sinclair, J. (ed.) (1987) *Looking Up – An Account of the COBUILD Project in Lexical Computing*, London: Collins.

— (1991) *Corpus, Concordance, Collocation*, Oxford: Oxford University Press.

Sinn, E. (1995) 'Yan Fu', in Chan Sin-Wai and D. Pollard (eds) *An Encyclopaedia of Translation*, Hong Kong: Chinese University Press, pp. 432–6.

Snell-Hornby, M. (1988, revised 1995) *Translation Studies: An Integrated Approach*, Amsterdam and Philadelphia, PA: John Benjamins.

— (1990) 'Linguistic transcoding or cultural transfer: A critique of translation theory in Germany', in S. Bassnett and A. Lefevere (eds), pp. 79–86.

— (1991) 'Translation studies: Art, science or utopia?', in K. van Leuven-Zwart and T. Naaijkens (eds), pp. 13–23.

— (2006) *The Turns of Translation Studies*, Amsterdam and Philadelphia: John Benjamins.

— (2010) 'The turns of translation studies', in Y. Gambier and L. van Doorslaer (eds), pp. 366–70.

Snell-Hornby, M., F. Pöchhacker and K. Kaindl (eds) (1994) *Translation Studies: An Interdiscipline*, Amsterdam: John Benjamins.

Sperber, D. and D. Wilson (1986/1995) *Relevance: Communication and Cognition*, Oxford: Blackwell.

Spira, I. (2015) *A Conceptual History of Chinese -Isms: The Modernization of Ideological Discourse 1895–1925*, Leiden: Brill.

Spivak, G. (1993/2012) 'The politics of translation', in L. Venuti (ed.) (2004), pp. 312–30.

St André, J. and H-Y. Peng (eds) (2012) *China and Its Others: Knowledge Transfer Through Translation, 1829–2010*, Amsterdam: Rodopi.

Steiner, G. (1975/ 1998) *After Babel: Aspects of Language and Translation*, 3rd edition, London, Oxford and New York: Oxford University Press.

Stephenson, C. (2007) 'Seeing red: Soviet films in fascist Italy', in F. Billiani (ed.), pp. 235–56.

Stewart, D. (2009) *Semantic Prosody: A Critical Evaluation*, London and New York: Routledge.

Störig, H.-J. (ed.) (1963) *Das Problem des Übersetzens*, Darmstadt: Wissenschaftliche Buchgesellschaft.

Sturge, K. (2004) *'The Alien Within': Translation into German during the Nazi Regime*, Munich: Iudicium.

Susam-Saraeva, S. (ed.) (2008) *The Translation of Music*, special issue of *The Translator* 14.2.

Švecjer, A. D. (1987) *Übersetzung und Linguistik*, translated from the Russian by C. Cartellieri and M. Heine, Berlin: Akademie.

Taylor, C. (2003) 'Multimodal transcription in the analysis, translation and subtitling of Italian films', *The Translator* 9.2: 191–205.

Thibault, P. (2000) 'The multimodal transcription of a television advertisement: Theory and practice', in A. Baldry (ed.) *Multimodality and Multimediality in the Distance Learning Age*, Campobasso: Palladino Editore, pp. 311–85.

Thompson, G. (2004) *Introducing Functional Grammar*, 2nd edition, London: Arnold.

Tirkkonen-Condit, S. (2004) 'Unique items: Over- or under-represented in translated language?' in A. Mauranen and P. Kujamäki (eds), pp. 177–84.

Tirkkonen-Condit, S. and R. Jääskeläinen (eds) (2000) *Tapping and Mapping the Process of Translation: Outlooks on Empirical Research*, Amsterdam and Philadelphia: John Benjamins.

Titford, C. (1982) 'Subtitling: Constrained translation', *Lebende Sprachen* 27.3: 113–16.

Tognini-Bonelli, E. (2001) *Corpus Linguistics at Work*, Amsterdam and Philadelphia: John Benjamins.

Toury, G. (1978/2012) 'The nature and role of norms in literary translation', in L. Venuti (ed.) (2012), pp. 168–81.

— (1980) *In Search of a Theory of Translation*, Tel Aviv: The Porter Institute.

— (1985) 'A rationale for descriptive translation studies', in T. Hermans (ed.) (1985a), pp. 16–41.

— (1991) 'What are descriptive studies in translation likely to yield apart from isolated descriptions?', in K. van Leuven-Zwart and T. Naaijkens (eds), pp. 179–92.

— (1995/2012) *Descriptive Translation Studies – And Beyond*, 2nd ed, Amsterdam and Philadelphia: John Benjamins.

— (2004) 'Probabilistic explanations in translation studies: Welcome as they are, would they qualify as universals?', in A. Mauranen and P. Kujamäki (eds), pp. 15–32.

Trivedi, H. (2005) 'Translating culture vs. cultural translation', *91st Meridian* 4.1, http://iwp.uiowa.edu/91st/vol4-num1/translating-culture-vs-cultural-translation

— (2006) 'In our own time, on our own terms', in T. Hermans (ed.) (2006a), pp. 102–19.

Trosberg, A. (1997) *Text Type and Typology*, Amsterdam and Philadelphia: John Benjamins.

— (2000) 'Discourse analysis as part of translator training', *Current Issues in Language and Society* 7.3: 185–228.

Tymoczko, M. (2003) 'Ideology and the position of the translator: In what sense is a translator "in between"?', in María Calzada Pérez (ed.), pp. 181–201.

— (2005) 'Trajectories of research in translation studies', *Meta* 50.4: 1082–97, http://www.erudit.org/revue/meta/2005/v50/n4/012062ar.html

— (2006) 'Reconceptualizing western translation theory', in Theo Hermans (ed.) (2006a), pp. 13–22.

— (2007) *Enlarging Translation, Empowering Translators*, Manchester: St Jerome.

— (ed.) (2010) *Translation, Resistance, Activism: Essays on the Role of Translators as Agents of Change*, University of Massachusetts Press.

Tynjanov, J. N. (1927) *Arkhaisty i novatory*, Moscow: Akademia, translated (1971) by C. A. Luplow as 'On literary evolution', in L. Matejka and K. Pomorska (eds), pp. 66–78.

Tyulenev, S. (2012) *Applying Luhmann to Translation Studies*, London and New York: Routledge.

— (2014) *Translation and Society: An Introduction*, London and New York: Routledge.

Tytler, A. F. (Lord Woodhouselee) (1797) *Essay on the Principles of Translation*, Edinburgh: Cadell and Davies, extracted in D. Robinson (ed.) (1997b), pp. 208–12.

van Doorslaer, Luc (2007) 'Risking conceptual maps', in Y. Gambier and L. van Doorslaer (eds) *The Metalanguage of Translation*, special issue of *Target* 19.2: 217–33.

Vázquez-Ayora, G. (1977) *Introducción a la Traductología*, Washington, DC: Georgetown University Press.

Venuti, L. (ed.) (1992) *Rethinking Translation: Discourse, Subjectivity, Ideology*, London and New York: Routledge.

— (1995/2008) *The Translator's Invisibility: A History of Translation*, London and New York: Routledge.

— (1998) *The Scandals of Translation: Towards an Ethics of Difference*, London and New York: Routledge.

— (1999) *L'invisibilitá del traduttore: una storia della traduzione*, translated by M. Guglielmi, Roma: Armando Editore.

— (ed.) (2000/2004/2012) *The Translation Studies Reader*, 1st/2nd/3rd edition, London and New York: Routledge.

— (2003) 'Translating Derrida on translation: Relevance and disciplinary resistance', *The Yale Journal of Criticism* 16.2: 237–62.

— (2013) *Translation Changes Everything: Theory and Practice*, London and New York.

— (ed.) (forthcoming) *The Oxford History of Literary Translation in English. Volume 5: 1900–2000*, Oxford: Oxford University Press.

Vermeer, H. J. (1989/2012) 'Skopos and commission in translational action', in L. Venuti (ed.) (2012), pp. 191–202.

— (1994) 'Translation today: Old and new problems', in M. Snell-Hornby, F. Pöchhacker and K. Kaindl (eds) *Translation Studies: An Interdiscipline*, Amsterdam and Philadelphia: John Benjamins, pp. 3–16.

Vieira, E. (1997) 'New registers in translation for Latin America', in K. Malmkjær and P. Bush (eds) *Rimbaud's Rainbow: Literary Translation and Higher Education*, Amsterdam and Philadelphia: John Benjamins, pp. 171–95.

— (1999) 'Liberating Calibans: Readings of Antropofagia and Haroldo de Campos' poetics of transcreation', in S. Bassnett and H. Trivedi (eds), pp. 95–113.

Vinay, J.-P. and J. Darbelnet (1958/1995) *Comparative Stylistics of French and English: A Methodology for Translation*, translated and edited by Juan Sager and Marie-Jo Hamel, Amsterdam and Philadelphia: John Benjamins. Original French published 1958 as *Stylistique comparée du français et de l'anglais: Méthode de traduction*, Paris: Didier.

— (1995/2004) 'A methodology for translation', in L. Venuti (ed.) (2004), pp. 128–37.

Viswanatha, V. and S. Simon (1999) 'Shifting grounds of exchange: B. M. Srikantaiah and Kannada translation', in S. Bassnett and H. Trivedi (eds), pp. 162–81.

Vorderobermeier, G. (ed.) (2014) *Remapping Habitus in Translation Studies*, Amsterdam: Rodopi.

Wakabayashi, J. and R. Kothari (eds) (2009) *De-centering Translation Studies: India and Beyond*, Amsterdam and Philadelphia: John Benjamins.

Wallmach, K. (2006) 'Feminist translation strategies: Different or derived?' *Journal of Literary Studies* 22.1–2: 1–26.

Warren, R. (ed.) (1989) *The Art of Translation: Voices from the Field*, Boston: North-eastern University Press.

Weaver, W. (1989) 'The process of translation', http://www.arts.ed.ac.uk/italian/gadda/Pages/resources/babelgadda/babeng/weavertranslation.html

Weissbort, D. and A. Eysteinsson (eds) (2006) *Translation – Theory and Practice: A Historical Reader*, Oxford: Oxford University Press.

Weissbrod, R. (2009) 'Philosophy of translation meets translation studies', *Target* 21.1: 58–73.

Whorf, B. (1950/1956) 'An American Indian model of the universe', in J. B. Carroll (ed.) (1956) *Language, Thought and Reality: Selected Writings of Benjamin Lee Whorf*, Cambridge, MA: MIT, pp. 57–64.

Williams, I. (2007) 'A corpus-based study of the verb *observar* in English-Spanish translations of biomedical research articles', *Target* 19.1: 85–103.

Williams, J. (2013) *Theories of Translation*, Houndmills and New York: Palgrave Macmillan.

Williams, J. and A. Chesterman (2002) *The Map: A Beginner's Guide to Doing Research in Translation Studies*, Manchester: St Jerome.

Wilss, W. (1977) *Übersetzungswissenschaft. Probleme und Methoden*, Stuttgart: E. Klett, translated (1982) as *The Science of Translation. Problems and Methods*, Tübingen: Gunter Narr.

— (1996) *Knowledge and Skills in Translator Behavior*, Amsterdam and Philadelphia: John Benjamins.

Wolf, M. (2000) 'The third space in postcolonial representation', in S. Simon and P. St-Pierre (eds), pp. 127–45.

— (2012) 'The sociology of translation and its "activist turn"', *Translation and Interpreting Studies* 7.2: 129–43.

Wolf, M. and A. Fukari (eds) (2007) *Constructing a Sociology of Translation*, Amsterdam and Philadelphia: John Benjamins.

Woods, M. (2012) *Censoring Translation: Censorship, Theatre and the Politics of Translation*, London and New York: Continuum.

Wright, David (2001) 'Yan Fu and the tasks of the translator', in M. Lackner et al. (eds), pp. 235–56.

Young, R. (2003) *Postcolonialism: A Very Short Introduction*, Oxford: Oxford University Press.

Zanettin, F. (2012) *Translation-Driven Corpora: Corpus Resources for Applied and Descriptive Translation Studies*, Manchester: St Jerome.

— (2013) 'Corpus methods for descriptive translation studies', *Procedia* 95: 20–32, http://www.sciencedirect.com/science/article/pii/S1877042813041384

Zanettin, F., S. Bernadini and D. Stewart (2003) *Corpora in Translator Education*, Manchester: St Jerome.

Zanettin, F., G. Saldanha and S-A. Harding (2015) 'Sketching landscapes in translation studies: A bibliographic study', *Perspectives* 23.2: 161–82.

Zhang, M. and Pan Li (2009) 'Introducing a Chinese perspective on translation shifts: A comparative study of shift models by Loh and Vinay and Darbelnet', *The Translator* 15.2: 351–74.

Zürcher, E. (2007) *The Buddhist Conquest of China: The Spread and Adaptation of Buddhism in Early Medieval China*, Leiden: Brill.

Index

Figures in **bold** indicate a major entry; <u>underlinings</u> indicate a reference in a case study.

Abbāsids 36–7
Abend-David, D. 220
abusive fidelity *see* fidelity
acceptability 41, 175, 179, 188, 280, 311
accuracy 41, <u>50</u>, 51, 54, 68, 72, 177, 234, 325
action theory **124**, 128
Adams, J. 56
adaptation 9, 10, 27, 43, 70, 81, 123, 130, 198, 215, 219–20, 230, 277, 284, 289, 305, 309, 315; Vinay and Darbelnet's adaptation procedure 91, 108
adequacy 61, 117–18, 127, 129, 138, 139, 173–4, 179, 188, 311; functional adequacy 127–9, 139
adequate translation 173, 176–9, 183; *see also* Toury, G.
advertising 10, 121, 123, 260, 275, 282, 310
aggression (stage in Steiner's hermeneutic motion) 253, 267
Aijmer, K. 26
Aixelà, J. F. 111
Akkadian 240
Aksoy, N. 204
Allende, I. 234
Alves, F. 87, 100, 104, 110
Alvstad, C. 26, 110, 248, 302
American Translation and Interpreting Studies Association (ATISA) 13
Amos, F.R. **40–3**, 56
amplification 92
Anderman, G. 280, 300
Angelelli, C. 237, 247

Anglo-Saxon 192, 218, 235, 258, <u>266–9</u>
anuvad 10
applied linguistics 12, 16, 141, 142
appropriation 198, 214, 244–5; stage in Steiner's hermeneutic motion 254
Äquivalenz 59, **74–7**
Arab world 10, 22, 33, 56, 220; in Baghdad 36; translation methods in 36–7
Arabic 36, 61, 70, 77, 89, 99, 110, 119, 150, 153, 154, 155, 157, 172, 181, 193, 203, 220, 294, 314, 316, 324
area-restricted theories 18
Aristophanes 203, 325
Arnold, M. 49
Arrojo, R. 26, 214, 272
art of translation 44, 235
Ashworth, D. 289
Asian traditions 36, 56; *see also* China; India; Japanese
assessment of translations <u>50–1</u>, 54, 114, 141, 142, **145–9**, <u>161–3</u>
audio description 11, 278, 285, 300
audiovisual translation 1, 5, 11, 20, 22, 121, 168, 184, 214, 220, **274–87**, <u>296–9</u>, 300–1, 317; *see also* dubbing; subtitling
Austermühl, F. 289
Austin, J. L. 166
Australia 21, 232

Babel (journal) 12
Babych, B. 126, 327
back transformation 63–4

Baker, M. 11, 12, 22, 56, 134, 177–8; Arab tradition 36–7; corpus linguistics 99, 292–4; discourse analysis 5, 21, **149–55**, 157, 160, 165, 167, 312, 324; equivalence 77; key texts 29, 141; narrative theory 214

Balderston, D. 247

Bandia, P. 220, 237, 240, 247; key text 222

Barnstone, W. 38, 56, 110

Bartrina, F. 12

Basque 216

Bassnett, S. 12, 21, 247, 320; cultural turn 22, 197; equivalence 77; key texts 29, 58, 198; literal vs. free debate 31, 49; postcolonialism 210, 211–12, 213; rejection of linguistic approaches 198, 247, 320

Bastin, G. 247

Baudelaire, C. 260

Bayley, J. <u>244</u>

Beaugrande, R. de 112, 151, 323

Belgium 11, 21, 189, 199, 277, 278, 326

Bell, R. 21, 100, 109, 166, 327

belles infidèles 177, 205

Bengali 3, 10, 22, 209, <u>298</u>, <u>325</u>

Benjamin, A. 272

Benjamin, W. 5, 49, 250, 258, **260–2**, 271, 272, 273; Derrida's reading of <u>263–4</u>; key text 249

Bennett, K. 179, 212, 215

Berman, A. 5, 223, **229–33**, 246, 247, 257, 326; key text 222; negative analytic 223, 229–33; positive analytic 232–3

Bermann, S. 13, 220, 247

Bernal Merino, M. 287, 300

Bhabha, H. 212, 220, 235

Bible translation 4, 13, **31–2**, 33, **38–41**, 42, 55, 56, 57, **62**, <u>79–81</u>, 83, 121, 176, 206, 252, 253, 261

Bielsa, E. 243

Biguenet, J. 56

Billiani, F. 220

Blum-Kulka, S. **151**, 167, 292; key text 141

Boase-Beier, J. 110

Bobrick, B. 38–9, 56

Boéri, J. 22, 236, 291, 301

Böll, H. 182

Booth, N. 233

Borges, J-L. 234

Borodo, M. 301

borrowing 24, 36, 88, **89**, 99, <u>107–8</u>, 181, 266, 296, 312, 316

Bosseaux, C. 110, 159, 166

Bourdieu, P. 5, **237–9**, 240, 246

Bowker, L. 84, 293

Boyle, D. 279

Braden, G. 55

Brazil 22, 27, 102, 150, 214, 259, 260, 272, 287

Brems, E. 247

Britt, B. 261

Brittan, L. 154–5, 166

Broch, H. 255

Brown, M. 241, 247

Brown, P. 155

Brownlie, S. 213

Bruni, L. 30, 40

Buddhist tradition 13, **33–4**, 55, 133

Bühler, K. 114–15, 143

Burger, M. 220

Bush, P. 99, 247, 294

Butler, J. 220

Buzelin, H. 238, 247

Cabré, M.-T. 84

Cabrera Infante, G. 207, 235

Caillé, F. 13

calque 24, **89**, 101, 181, 227, 258, 312

Calzada Pérez, M. 21, 214, 220

Campos, H. de **259–60**, 272, 287

Camus, A. 156–7

Canada 5, 12, 22, 102, 205, 213, 217, 219, 293

Canadian Association for Translation Studies/Association canadienne de traductologie 13

cannibalist theories 22, 259, 272

capital (Bourdieu) 237, 296

Carl, M. 104

Carroll, P. 320

Carter, R. 84

Cassin, B. 272

Catford, J. C. 4, 15, 84, 87, **95–7**, 109, 112; criticisms of 97; key text 86

causation 238

Cavalcanti, G. 259

censorship 186, 215, 220

Chamberlain, L. 257

Chan, L. T. 22, 34, 36, 44, 56, 320

Chan, S. W. 300

Chaume, F. 281, **283–5**, 298, 300

Chesterman, A. 6, 26, 27, 116, 170, 238, 319; consilience 303, 304–5; key texts 169, 302; norms **186–8**, 194, 195; research questions 314–15; universals 185

Cheung, M. 22, 56, 220; key text 29

Cheyfitz, E. 220

Chiaro, D. 280, 298, 300; key text 274

China 10, 13, 33, 38, 55, 220, 308, 309, 313

Chinese 4, 15, 33–6, 46–7, 55, 61, 66, 69, 87, 95, 110, 133, 193, 216, 256, 258, 279, 287, 307–14

Chomsky, N. 4, 16, 257; influence on Nida **62–5**

Christ, R. 242, 245

Churchill, W. 147

Cicero, M. T. 4, 13, 30, **31**, 32, 34, 41, 46, 55, 319

Cixous, H. 214

Clark, P. 99, 294

Classe, O. 55

COBUILD 291, 293; Bank of English 293

codes (audiovisual) 281, **283–5**

cognitive: processing 73, 87, **100–4**, 228, 237; sciences 3, 4, 18, 25; theories of translation 109, 110, 166, **305**

coherence 50–1, 151, 153, 154, 167, 168, 284, 313; coherence rule 127, **128**

cohesion 50–1, 69, 81–82, 92, 93, 125, 132, 142, 144–5, 149, **151–3**, 160, 162, 163–4, 165, 166, 167, 168, 264, 312

Coindreau, M.-E. 238

co location 99, 145, **152**, 166, 181, 185, 208, 291, 293, 295, 297

colonization 197, 198, **209–11**, 212–13

commentary **302–14**

commission 124, **129**, 132, 134–5, 138, 164, 187, 188, 215, 224, 237, 240, 281, 295, 304, **307**

communication theory 124

communicative translation 4, 58, 59, **71–4**, 138, 311

comparative literature 5, 7, 12, **15**, 21, 25, 27, 189, 199

compensation 92, 108, 160, 163; stage in Steiner's hermeneutic motion 254, 268, 269

componential analysis **66–7**

computer-aided translation; computer-assisted translation (CAT) 18, 20, 26, 78, **289**; see also corpus; machine translation

concordancing 289, 294, 296–7, 297–8

connectors, conjunctions 64, 93, 106–7, **152**, 293

Conrad, J. 232

consilience 6, 302, 303, **303–4**

context 93, 94, 95, 100, 101, 123, 127, 132, 138, 143–4, 145, 147, 154, 156–60, 166, 174, 190, 193–4, 198, 282, 291, 305–6, 308–9, 317; see also sociocultural context

contrastive analysis 7, 295–6, 296–7, 301

conventions **177**

Coover, R. 242

Copenhagen Business School 104

corpus: -based translation studies 274, 291–6, 296–9, 300, 322; British National (BNC) 293, 322; -driven studies 280, 284, 289; linguistics 3, 185, 291, 295; Spanish Real Academia (RAE) 296; stylistics 159; Translational English (TEC) 293; types of 292–3

correspondence **74–6**, 84; formal **68–9**, 95–7, 262, 311

Cortázar, J. 152

covert translation 22, 74, 147, **148**, 165, 166, 311, 323

Cowie, M. 12

Cowley, A. 42, 152
creative writing 15, 25
creativity 31, 41, 42, **47–9**, 61, 77, 98, 99, 115, 121, 230, 230, 254, 256, **258–62**, 270, 287, 300, 304
Critical Discourse Analysis 215
Croatian 216
Cronin, M. 22, 214, 219, 268, 290–1, 300, 301; key text 274
crowdsourcing 290, 315, 317
cultural: context 127, 217, 305–6, see also sociocultural context; difference 67, 126, 154, 160, **212**, 226, 240; filter **148**; turn **197–9**, 208, 214
cultural studies: -oriented approaches 22, 25, 246, 293; split with linguistic approaches 304–5; varieties in translation studies **197–221**
culture 5, 47–8; in audiovisual translation studies 280; and ideology 160; and language conventions 155, 157; link with translation strategies and procedures 65–8, 72, 89, 91, 97; link to text analysis 118, 120, 127, 131–4, 147–8; translations as facts of target culture 175; see also cultural studies; domestication; hermeneutics; norms; polysystem theory
culture-specific items 111, 134–8, 181, 185–6, 280, 284, 291, 311, 313
Czechoslovakia 98, 109

Damasus, Pope 32
Dào'ān **34–6**, 57
Darbelnet, J. 4, 15, 86, 87, **88–95**, 95, 99, 104–8, 109, 110, 111, 179, 181, 231, 292, 309, 311, 312; key text 87
Davis, D. 199
Davis, K. 272
Davis, L. 53–4
decision-making 21, **98**, 103, **176–7**, 180, 184, 237, 295, 314
deconstruction 5, 25, 70, 211, 249, **262–6**, 272
deforming tendencies **230–2**
Delabastita, D. **276–7**, 277, 284; key text 274

Delisle, J. 36, 56, 97, 101
De Marco, M. 220
Denham, J. 42
Derrida, J. 5, 211, 249, 250, 262, **263–4**, 269, 271, 272, 325; key texts 249; translations of **264–5**
descriptive translation studies (DTS) 5, 17, 79, 169, 170, 174–91, 191–3, 194, 195, 237, 281, 296
de-verbalization 101
Devy, G. 213
Dharwadker, V. 213
Di Giovanni, N. T. 234, 247
Di Pietro, R. J. 15
dialect 39, 99, 133, 157, 185, 217–18, 226; in audiovisual translation studies 266, 276, 280, 287, 298
dialectic of embodiment 254
Díaz Cintas, J. 20, 278, **279–80**, 281, 283, 285, 286, 300; key text 275
Dickins, J. 111, 119
Dickinson, E. 312
différance 262, **263–4**
Dimitriu, R. 84
direct translation 22, 36, **88–9**, 108, 191, 281, 311
directness of translation **179**, 188
discourse analysis 21, 55, 100, **141–68**, 215, 264, 265, 303, 312, 317, 322, 323
documentary translation **131**, 134, 275, 311
Dolet, E. 29, 30, **38–9**, 39, 42; five principles of translation **44–5**, 46, 57
Dolmetscher (Schleiermacher) 47
domestication 49, 88, **225–9**, 230, 243, 245, 247, 248, 253, 257, 287, 311
Dooley, R. 102
Dostoevsky, F. 206, 231
double linkage 75
Dressler, W. 151, 323
Dryden, J. 29, 30, **42–4**, 45, 48, 49, 52, 55, 225, 245
Duarte, J. Ferreira 26, 238
dubbing 121, 220, 277, 278, 281, 283, **284–5**, 300
Duhamel, M. 238

Dukmak, W. 70, 155
Dunne, E. 300
Dunne, K. 300
During, S. 219
Dutch 3, _135–7_, 203–4, 215, 277, 323
Duvert, T. 208

'ear' **234**. 248
Eco, U. 272
editors 215, 224, 229, 237, 239, 240,
    281, 289, 304, 310
Eggins, S. 144, 166, 323
elective affinity 256–7, 257, _267–8_, 273
ellipsis 152
Englund-Dimitrova, B. 103
enhancement 35, 255
Enkvist, N. E. 151, 166
Enright, D. J. _52–3_
epitexts 223, **242**, 243
equivalence 2, 4, 6, 19, 21, **58–85**,
    232, 303–4, 312; in Catford **95–7**;
    in Chesterman's relation norm 188;
    criticisms of **69–70**, 77–9; directional
    (in Pym) 78; dynamic **67–9**, 71, 73,
    _79–83_, 84–5, 174, 311; ethnocentrism
    of 232; formal **67–9**, 71, _79–83_;
    functional 118, **129**, 138, 147–8,
    289–90; in House's model **147–8**; in
    localization 289–90, 293; in meaning
    58, **60**, 322; Koller's five types of
    74–6, 315; natural (in Pym) 78; non-
    prescriptive definition (in Toury) 177,
    180, 183; semantic 117; at text level
    113; textual 113, 114, 174, 303; at
    various levels in Baker **149–50**, 153;
    Vinay and Darbelnet's use of **91**, 108,
    322
equivalent effect 4, 58, 59, **67–9,** 72–3,
    _81–2_, 83, 115–18, 119; criticisms of
    69–70, 71, 310
Erasmus, D. 39
Ericsson, K. 103
Esquivel, L. 234
Esselink, B. 289, 300
ethics of translation 5, 25, 46, 100,
    222–41, 247, 248
Euclid 37

European Association for Studies in
    Screen Translation 13
European Society for Translation Studies
    13
evaluation (attitude) 158
Even-Zohar, I. 5, 21, 169, **170–4**, 175,
    189, 194, 195, 254; key text 169
exoticizing translation 131, 232
explicitation **92**, 108, 115–17, 136, 151,
    154, 160, 167, 184, 185, 231, 292,
    295, _299_, 309, 311, 315
eye-tracking 18, 104, 109, 305, 317
Eysteinsson, A. 56, 327

Faiq, S. 220
Fairclough, N. 215
faithfulness _see_ fidelity
false friends 51, 74, 89
fan yi 10
fansubbing 265, 300
Fawcett, P. 77, 84, 109, 119, 154, 166,
    239, 320; key texts 86, 141
Fédération Internationale des Traducteurs
    (FIT) 13
Fedorov, A. V. 15, 88, 109
Felstiner, J. 234–5
feminist theories 197, 198, **205–7, 208–10**,
    213–14, 219, 235, 253, 257, 312
fidelity 10, **40–1**, 46, 205; abusive 249,
    264–6, _270_; rule 127, **128**
fidus interpres 41
Firbas, J. 166
Firth, J. R. 95
Fish, S. E. 159
Fitzgerald, E. 199, 200
fluency 46, 51, 187, 228, 241, 247
foreign, the 5, 29, **47–9**; Schleiermacher
    _53–4_; _see also_ Berman
foreignization 49, 88, **225–33**, 247, 248,
    249, 262, 311
form vs. content 32, 41, 46, 53, 68–9, 72,
    115, 241
Formalism 21, 170–1, 174, 195
Forster, M. 47, 48, 272
Fowler, R. 159
France 91, 109, 172, 177, 208, 263
France, P. 56, 57

Frank, A. 203–4
Frank, O. 203–4
Frawley, W. 246
free translation 4, **30–44**, 48, 59, 284
Freihoff, R. xiii, 116
French 3, 8, 15, 16, 19, 42, 44, 45, <u>52–4</u>,
  61, 82, 83, **87–95**, 96–7, <u>104–8</u>, <u>110</u>,
  <u>134–8</u>, 156–7, <u>163–4</u>, 172, 181, 205–8,
  229–30, 238, 253, 263–5, 276, 277,
  278, 280, 286, 309, 322, 323, 325
Fukari, A. 22, 237, 247
function of translation 119, *see also*
  equivalence: functional
functional grammar 21, 141, 149, **323**
functional sentence perspective 166, 324
functional theories **113–40**
functions of language **113–18**;
  communicative 119, 121, 134, 144,
  162; ideational **144–5**, 147, 144, **150,
  282–3**; interpersonal **132, 144–5**,
  147–8, 150, **156**, <u>157–8</u>, 163–4,
  282–3; semiotic 158, <u>163–4</u>; textual
  144–6, 151; *see also* functional
  grammar
Fung Chang, N. 195

Gadamer, H.-G. 251, 326
Gaddis Rose, M. 247
gain 46, 72, **92**, 108
Galen 37
Galicia 172
Gambier, Y. 12, 277–8, 285
Garcia, O. 220
García Álvarez, A.-M.: key text 302
García Márquez, G. xiii, 3, 144, <u>243–5</u>
García Yebra, V. 88
Garnett, C. 206
gate-keepers 240
Gauvin, L. 206
gay issues **207–8**, 219
gender: and translation 5, 22, 25, 190, 197,
  205–7, 208–9, 213–14, 219, 220, 304
generalization: as procedure **93**, 231,
  281, 308; in descriptive studies **182**
generative grammar 4, 15, 16, **62–3**,
  238, 257
Genette, G. 242

genre **118–20**, 125, 132, 134, 138, 139,
  144–5, 157, 175, 187–8, 194, 241,
  307–9; in audiovisual translation 276,
  279, 287; in corpora 292, 294; digital
  123–4
Gentzler, E. 12, 16, 70, 173–4, 176,
  183–4, 195, 214, 220, 259, 319
German 3, 15, 16, 29, 39–40, 47–8, 56,
  60, 61, 74, 75, 84, 88, 89, 93–4, 98,
  99, 109, 110, 126, 131, 136, 139,
  148–9, 151, <u>161–3</u>, 164, 172, 173,
  176, 182, 204, 206, 232, 253, 255–6,
  260, 262, 272, 286, 293, 309, 320,
  322, 324, 326
German Democratic Republic 74
Germany 21, 47, 71, 84, 113, 114, 138,
  172, 200, 204, 215, 229, 241; *see
  also* West Germany
Gerzymisch-Arbogast, H. 151
Gil Bardaji, A. 88
Gile, D. 8, 26
Gilgamesh 240
Godard, B. 205, 220
Goethe, J. 47, 182, 251
Google Translate 289
Gorp, H. van 169, **189–90**, <u>191</u>
Gottlieb, H. 277, **285–6**
Gouanvic, J.-M. **237–8**, 326; key text
  222
Graham, J. F. 249, 272
grammar-translation method 14
Granger, S. 295
Greece: ancient Greece 31, 71, 250,
  253; audiovisual translation in modern
  Greece 281
Greek 10, 13, 14, 31–2, 36, 38–9, 41,
  42, 60, 64, 80, 81, 202–3, 216, 255,
  256, 258, 320, 325
Grice, H.P. **165–6**
Grossman, E. 234, <u>243–5</u>
Guadarrama, K. 327
Guaraní 102
Guenthner, F. 272
Guenthner-Reutter, M. 272
Gutas, D. **37**; key text 29
Gutt, E. 5, **101–2**, 109, 110, 112, 160,
  166; key text 86

habitus 26, **237–8**, 248
Haddadian-Moghaddam, E. 240
Halliday, M.A.K. 5, 21, 95, 141, **142–7**, 149, 151, 152, 156, <u>163</u>, 165–7, 283, 317, 323–4; criticisms of 159–60
Halverson, S. 10
Hamel, M.-J. 87
Hanna, S. 36–7
Hansen, G. 104
Hanssen, B. 260
Harvey, K. **207–8**, 219, 247; key text 197
Hasan R. 111, 151, 152, 165
Hatim, B. 5, 20, 21, 75, 76, 102, 110, 112, 141, 142, 150, **156–61**, 164, **165**, 215, 312; key text 141
Hausa 78
Haynes, K. 56
Heaney, S. 258, <u>266–9</u>
Hebrew 31–2, 38, 39, 41, 67, <u>79–81</u>, 151, **172–3**, 174, 176, 181, 182, 321
hegemonic languages **209–11**, <u>216–18</u>
Heidegger, M. 251, 253, 272
Henry, R. 97, 112
Henry VIII, King of England 38
Herder, J. 47, 250
Hermans, T. 21, 42, 46, 56, 57, 61, 98, 109, 188, 220, 238, 247, 272, 311, 320, 324, 325; key texts 169; and Manipulation School 189–91; and systems theories 176, **183–4**, 195
hermeneutic motion 5, 49, 249, **250–5**, 257–8, <u>266–9</u>, 272; see also G. Steiner
hermeneutics 25, 47, 49, 249, **250–5**, 272, 326
Herzog, W. <u>161</u>
Hindi 10, <u>217</u>, 279
Hippocrates 37
historiography 5, 18, 22, 170, 200, 210, 236
history of translation 13–16, 18, 30–42, 49, 55–6, 210, 306
Hölderlin, F. 251, 255, 262, 306
Holmes, J. S. 4, 7, 11, **16–21**, 27, 28, 174, 182, 183, 194, 241, 276, 304, 316; key text 7

Holmstrom, L. 287
Holub, R. C. 247
Holz-Mänttäri, J. 113, 114, **124–6**, 127, 131, 134, 138, 187, 309, 321, 322
Homer 71, 131
Hopi 60
Horace 13, 31, 41
horizon of expectation 241, <u>245</u>
House, J. 5, 26, 74, 142, **145–9**, 155, 157, 160, <u>161–3</u>, 164, 165, 166, 215, 285, 308, 311, 312, 314, 323; key text 142
Huang, K. 46
Humanists **38–40, 42**
humanities computing 25
Humboldt, W. von 47, 251
Hung, E. **33–6**, 56, 220
Hungarian 154
Hurtado Albir, A. 16, 100, 104, 110; key text 87
Huxley, A. 46
hybridity 212
Hyde-Parker, R. 327
hypotheses of translation **315**

ideational see functions of language
ideology 20, 46, 109, 183, 186, 190, 312; in cultural and ideological turn 197–221; in new media 285, 294; and positionality 233–40; textual approach 157–60; of theorists **213–14**
Ilusio (Bourdieu) 237
imitation 29, 30, **43–4**, 46, 55
implicature **153–4**
In Other Words (journal of Translators' Association) 12
in-betweenness 212
incorporation (stage in Steiner's hermeneutic motion) 253, 254
India 5, 10, 172, 211–13, <u>216–18</u>, 219, 220, 319; Anglo-Indian writing 232
inferencing **101–2**, 154
Inggs, J. 220
Inghilleri, M. 22, 237, 238, 239, 247
Institute of Linguists, The Chartered (CIoL) 12; Diploma in Translation of <u>50–1</u>, 57, 321

Institute of Translating and Interpreting (ITI) 12
instrumental translation **131**, 134, 311
integrated approach 11, 113, 114, **120–3**, 276, 283
intercultural: communication 127, 138; transfer **124–6**
interdisciplinarity **24–7**, 190, 265, 294, 299, 300
interference 68, 75, 169, **181, 184–6**, 294
interlinear translation 249, 261–2
interlingua 289
interlingual translation 4, **9–10**, 22, 59, 61, 124, 251, 263; in audiovisual translation 277, 278, 279; *see also* Jakobson
International Association for Translation and Intercultural Studies (IATIS) 13
internationalization 8, **288,** 289, 290
interpersonal *see* functions of language
interpretation: of sense/text 9, 47, 80–1, 101, 128, 228, 250, 269, 282; *see also* hermeneutics (NB for 'spoken translation' *see* interpreting)
interpreter: used by Cicero 31; by Horace 41
interpreting 7, 8, 11–2, 13, 18, 20, 168, 277, 319; studies 20, 26, 100, 295, 319
interpretive model 5, **100–1**
interpretive translation (Gutt) 101
intersemiotic translation 4, **9**, 59, 251, 263; *see also* Jakobson, R.
intertextuality 127–8, 190
intervenient being 236
intervention, interventionist approach 98, 197, 211, 218, 222, 226
intralingual translation 4, **9–10**, 22, 59, 193, 263, 308, 309; in audiovisual translation 278; *see also* Jakobson, R.
invariant concept **77–8**, 176; *see also* tertium comparationis
(in)visibility of translator 5, 222, 223, **224–5**, 227, 228, 229, 234, 241, 243–5, 246, 248, 285, 286, 325; *see also* Venuti, L.

Ireland 268, 290
Irish 213, 214, 216, 266–9
Israel 189
Italian 3, 42, 61, 96, 102, 110, 134–8, 191–4, 224, 226, 258, 259, 323
Italy 186, 191
ITI Bulletin, The (journal of The Institute of Translating and Interpreting) 12

Jääskeläinen, R. **103**; key text 87
Jakobsen, A. L. **103–4**
Jakobson, R. 4, 119, 322; categories of translation **9–10**, 251, 263, 277, 308; equivalence and meaning 58, **59–62**, 83; key texts 7, 58
James, C. 15
Jameson, F. 324
Japanese 93, 151, 155, 202, 256, 265, 279, 284, 286, 287, 311
Jauss, H. R. **241–2**, 247
Jerome, E. H. (St Jerome): *Latin Vulgate* translation 31, 38–42; sense for sense translation 13, **31–2**, 33, 34
Jiang, C. 149
Jiménez-Crespo, M. 123–4, 139, 288–9; key text 275
Johannson, S. 291
Johnson, M. 119
Jones, F. 238
Jonson, B. 43
Joyce, J. 117, 232

Kade, O. 8, 16, 74
Kaindl, K. 236
Kang, J.-H. 247
Karamitroglou, F. 184, **281–2**, 301
Kassovitz, M. 163
Kay, N. 279
Kearney, R. 235
Kelly, L. 41, 56
Kenny, D. 77, 84, 99, 293
kernel **63–4**, 70
Kharmandar, M. A. 255
Khayyam, O. 199
Kilmartin, T. 52–3
Kittel, H. 48

Koller, W. 4, 16, 59, 71, **74–7**, 77, 84, 95, 315; key text 58
Komissarov, V. 195
Korrespondenz *see* correspondence
Koskinen. K. 85
Koster, C. 110
Kress, G. 283
Krings, H. 103
Krishnamurthy, R. 39, 319
Kuhiwczak, P. 239
Kujamäki, P. 195
Kumārajīva 33
Kundera, M. 239–40, 244
Kushner, T. 207

Labé, L. 253
Lackner, M. 35–6, 320
Lakoff, G. 119
Lal, P. 287
Lambert, J.-R. 21, **189–91**, 194, 289
language: determinism **60–1**; relativity **60–1**; teaching and learning 14, 19, 26–7 universalism **60**
langue 59–60, 74
Larose, R. 69, 109
Larson, M. L. 84
Latin 8, 10, 13–14, 31, 38–9, 45, 55, 89, 216, 267
Latour, B. (actor-network theory) 5, 238, 246
Laviosa, S. 291–2
Lawrence, D. H. 280
laws of translation 17, 169, 170, **180–6**, 193, 194, 224; criticism of 174; of growing standardization 93, **180–1**; of interference **181**, 184; of reduced control over linguistic realization 184; Tytler's 45–6
Lederer, M. **100–1**
Leech, G. 84, 166
Lefevere, A. 5, 56, 69, 190, 195, 224, 233, 305, 308, 310, 324; and cultural turn 22, 209; key texts 197, 198; and polysystemists 21; rewriting 199–205, 214, 219, 220
Leipzig School 16, 74
letter, the 49, 270; in Berman 232–3

Leuven-Zwart, K. M. van 322
Levenston, E. 292
Levine, A. 324
Levine, S. J. 207, 234–5
Levinson, S. C. 155, 166
Lévi-Strauss, C. 257
Levý, J. 73, **98**, 292; key text 98
Lewis, P. 249, **264–5**, 269, 270, 272; key text 249
lexicogrammar **144**, 164, 165
Li, P. 15, 95; key text 87
Libertella, H. 269–71
Linde, Z. de 279
lingua franca 215, 221
Linguist, The (journal of The Chartered Institute of Linguists) 12
linguistic: hospitality 262; sign 9–10, 59, 60, 61, 258, 262–6, 271; toolkit approach 159, 323
linguistically oriented approaches 16–18, 21, 24–6, 62, 65–7, **86–112**, 123, **142–58**, 303–5; criticisms of 112, 159–60, 170, 262–3
Lin Moniz, M. 220
Lispector, C. 214
literal translation 24, 38, **43–5**, 52–4, 71–3; in Benjamin 260–3; in Berman 230–2; contextually motivated 86; as documentary translation 131; in Hatim and Mason 156; in Vinay and Darbelnet 89, 107–8, 313
literary agents 224, 240
literary theory 3
literary translation 7, 11, 14, 21, 51, 55, 98, 99, 121, 131, 152, 166, 169, 170, 177, 184, 189, 196, 206, 210, 219, 233–48, 250–1, 255, 258, 260, 271, 276, 310
literary translators 5, **233–6**
locale 10, 123, 288–90
Localisation Industry Standards Association (LISA) 288
localization 4, 5, 10, 22, 274, 275, **287–91**, 299, 300, 310, 317
Loffredo, E. 247
Loh, D. 4, 15, 87, 95, 109
Longhurst, B. 219

Lörscher, W. 103
loss **34–5**, 46, 57, 72, **92**, 108, 181, 231, 232, 254, 265; *see also* compensation; gain
Lotbinière-Harwood, S. 206
Lowe-Porter, H. 206, 325
loyalty 53–4, 128–9; *see also* fidelity
Luhmann, N. 5, 238, 239, 246
Luo, X. 47
Luther, M. 29, 30, **39–40**, 49, 54, 253
Luyken, G. 277
Lyons, J. 84

McCarty, W. 25, 319
McDonough Dolmaya, J. 139
McElduf, S. 31, 56
McEnery, A. 300
machine translation 18, 21, 97, 289, 295, 300
Maier, C. 222, 236, 242, 245, 247, 291; key text 222
Malblanc, A. 15, 88, 109
Malmkjær, K. 9, 12, 84, 98, 109
Mangiron, R. 260, 286–7, 300
Manipulation School, the 5, 21–2, 170, **189–91**, 194, 195, 199
Mann, T. 123
Marais, K. 22
markedness **98–9**, 150, 314
Martin, J. 158
Mason, I. 5, 21, 130, 142, 156–7, 160, 163–5, 215, 312; key text 142
Mason, K. 14
Massardier-Kenney, F. 233
Massida, S. 300
Matejka, L. 195
Mauranen, A. 195
Mayoral, R. 276
meaning 4, 25, 32, 34, 37, 39, 41, 45–7, 49, 50, 53, 54, 58, 78, 92, 101, 132, 147, 152, 153, 211, 212, 225, 249, 259, 260, 261, 282, 283, 317, 320; analysis of **62–7**, 80–4; communicative or pragmatic 71, 133, 138, 141–5, 153–4, 159, 164–5, 312–13, 317; in hermeneutic motion 250–5; instability in deconstruction **262–6**, 266–70;

interpretive model 5, 100–1; nature of **59–67**; preservation of 89; stylistic 69
Meintjes, L. 220
message-transmitter compounds 124, 126
Meta (journal) 12, 21
metalanguage 22–4, 88–93, 21–3, 86–90, 298, 312
metaphor: *belles infidèles* 177, 205; cannibalism 259–60; captive 253; colonization 208–11; Steiner's 205, 250–4, 257; tight-rope walker 52; translation of 10, 46, 52, 67, 72, <u>76</u>, 80, 91, **118–20**, 154, 198, 210, 245, 253, 257, 261, 267
metaphrase 29, 43, 55
Miao, J. 70
Miko, F. 100
Millán, C. 12
Minors, H. 300
mismatches 146, 147, 160, 162, 163, 164, 166
Mitchell, S. 240
modality **145**, 156–7, 163, 166, 190, 313
modulation **90–1**, 93, <u>107–8</u>
Mounin, G. 15, 109, 205
Muir, E. 206
Muir, W. 206
multidisciplinarity 11, 26
multilingualism 197, **216**, 220
multimedia translation 277
multimodal transcription 282–3
multimodality 274, 301
Munday, J. 20, 76, 102, 142, 165, 236, 239; corpus-based translation studies 296–7, discourse analysis 21, 144–5, 157–8, 166, 215, 312; ideology 158–9, 214; translator style 99, 110, 144
Muñoz Sánchez, P. 286
mutation 171

Nabokov, V. 53, 253
Nā'ima al-Himsi, I. 36
narrative 190, 202; theory 215
narrative point of view 166, 190
naturalizing translation 5, 48, 49, 53, 54, 311

naturalness 51, **68**, 81, 293
negative analytic 222, 223, **229–33**, 247
neologisms 37, 99, 192, 206, 287
Neruda, P. 234–5
Netherlands, the 12, 38, 189
Neubert, A. 16, 74
new media **274–301**
Newman, F. 49
Newmark, P. 4, 30, 59, **71–4**, 77, 311,
    322; key texts 58
Nida, E. A. 4, 16, 51, 59, **62–71**, 73, 74,
    75, 79–84, 101, 154, 310, 311, 322,
    327; key text 59
Nida Institute 321
Niranjana, T. 22, **210–11**, 213, 218, 219,
    272; key text 198
nominalization 145, 150
non-verbal elements 9, 101, 133, 136; in
    audiovisual translation 276, 283, 300
Nord, C. 5, 113, 114, 119, 128–30,
    131–4, 136, 138, 139, 142, 177, 180,
    195, 308, 309, 311, 312, 322, 323;
    key text 113
norms of translation 23, 169, 170–2, 175,
    176–80, 184, 190, 191, 193, 194,
    195, 224, 237, 306, 315; in audiovisual
    translation 266, 272, 281, 283;
    Chesterman's **186–8**, 194; in corpus-
    based studies 292, 295; criticisms
    of 188, 223–4; definitions of 188; of
    language 72
Nornes, A. 265–6
Norris, C. **263**, 272
Northern Ireland 268
Novalis 251

O'Brien, S. 26, 104, 295, 317; key text
    302
O'Hagan, M. 126, 260, 286, 287, 289,
    300
oblique translation 88–91, 95, 108, 311
Olohan, M. **293–4**; key text 275
option (Vinay and Darbelnet) **89, 93,
    98–9**, 99, 179
orator: used by Cicero 30
Orero, P. 246
Osgood, C. 84

overt translation 22, 74, **147**, 148, 163,
    165, 166, 285, 311, 323
Ovid 43

Palmer, R. 272, 326
Pammachius 31
paraphrase (Dryden) 30, **43–4**, 55
paratext 35, 99, 242
Parks, T. 110
parole **60–1**, 75
patronage 190, **200–3**, 185, **194–7**,
    218–19
Pearson, J. 293
Peden, M. S. 234
Pedersen, J. 184, 281–2
Pedrola, M. 74
Peng, H.-Y. 220
Pérez-González, L. 278, 300–1; key text
    275
peritexts 242–4
Persian 199, 203
Perspectives (journal) 12
Perteghella, M. 247
Petch-Tyson, S. 295
Phillips, J. B. 65, 321
philosophical theories 5, 233, 246,
    249–72, 304
philosophical works: translation of 36–8,
    42, 46, 52
Pinker, S. 60, 321
Pinter, H. 151
Pirandello, L. 280
Plato 38
Pöchhacker, F. 20, 319
poetics 172, **199–204**, 219, 242, 249;
    see also style
Polish 173
politeness: maxim of 155, 207
politics of translation 198, 209
Pollard, D. 33–4
Polterman, A. 48
polysystem theory 21, 23, 169, **170–4**,
    175, 182, 184, 189, 190, 194, 195,
    199, 202, 237, 246, 254, 305; in
    audiovisual translation **281–2**
Pomorska, K. 195
Popovič, A. 100

Porter, C. 13, 220, 247
Portuguese 3, 81–3, 99, 102, 150, 153, 179, 215, 232, 80–1, 96, 99, 144, 145, 147, 173, 209, 224
positionality 223, **233–6**
postcolonialism 5, 22, 25, 190, 197, 199, **208–13**, 214, 218–20, 225, 268, 269, 287, 298–9, 304
postmodernism 208, 262
poststructuralism 190, **208–11**, 263, 272
Pound, E. 5, 49, 256, **258–60**, 271–3; key text 250
power 40, 142, 157, 165, 197, 200, 217, 218, 219, 220, 225, 228, 237, 271, 285, 323; in literary translation, 198–9, **201–3, 239–41**, 246, 270, 305; in postcolonial contexts 209–13, 214–16
Pountain, C. 320
Poyatos, F. 300
pragmatics 15, 25, 62, 65–7, 77, 92, **153–5**, 165–6
Prague School 98
prefaces: of translator 19, 34, 40–3, 46, 52–5, 99, 189, 220, **242**, 266–9, 278, 311
Prendergast, C. 53–4
presupposition 132, 135–7, 153–4
problems of translation: functional hierarchy of 132–4
procedures *see* translation procedures
process *see* translation process
project management 126
Proust, M. 3, 19, 50, 52–4
pseudo-translation 22
psychology 18, 103
publishers 5, 12, 149, 178, 187, 191, 193, 200–1, 208, 217, 224–5, 228–9, 233, 237, 239, 240, 242, 245–6, 271
Punjabi 3, 216–19, 232
pure language (Walter Benjamin) 5, 249–50, **261–2**, 264, 271
Pym, A. 12, 15, 20, 56, 58, 78, 84, 247; on ethics 237–8; key texts 59, 87, 275; on localization 289–90, 301; on translation solutions 88, 109–10; on Toury 169, 186

Qian, H. 69–70, 84
Quebec 205
queer theory **207**
Qvale, P. 247

Rabassa, G. 234, 247
Rafael, V. 220
Rajak, T. 31–2, 56
Ramakrishna, S. 319
Ramanujan, A. K. 211, 213
Ramos Pinto, S. 247
rank: of language 95; -restricted theories 18; shifts 97
Rao, S. 212–13
Rebenich, S. 31
reception theory 223, **241–3**, 245–7
reception of translation 189, 222, 223, 241–3, 245, 246, 247
receptor-oriented translation **68–70**, 71
recreation of text in translation 259–61
Reformation, Protestant 13, **38–40**
register: of lexis 50, 133, **136**, 207, 217, 218; in audiovisual translation 280, 284, 285
register analysis 102, **141–6**, 157, 164–5, 308, **311–14**, 323; criticisms of 159–60, 166
Reiss, K. 5, 19, 21, 49, 52, 75, **113–20**, 138, 275, 308, 321–3; key texts 113–14; and skopos theory 126–30, 131, 134
relevance 5, 97, 233; Derrida 264; Grice's maxim 155, 160; theory 86, 101–2, 109, 112, 160
Remael, A. 20, 278, 279–81, 286; key text 275
Rener, F. 41, 56
research: projects **314–17**; questions **316–17**
resistance 22, 209, 246, 257, 268
retranslation 22, 110, 185
reviews 19, 56, 178, 191, 200, 202, 215, 233, **241–5**, 246, 247; analysis by Venuti 222, 223, 224, 225, 227, 229
rewriting 197, 198, **199–204**, 214, 219, 231, 261, 308
Richards, I. A. 15

Richardson, D. 220
Ricœur, P. 250, 255, 262, 272
Rilke, R. M. 253
risk: avoidance 186, 301; -taking 186, 264, 270, 273
Robinson, D. 32, 41, 42, 43, 220, 319, 320; key text 30
Robinson, V. 220
Rode, A. S. 217
Rogers, M. 166, 300
Rolle, R. 319
Roman tradition 30; see also Cicero, M. T.
Romanticism 253, 326; see also hermeneutics; Schleiermacher
Rosenthal, F. 36
Rowling, J. K. 191
Rundle, C. 22, 56, 220
rupantar 10
Rushdie, S. 212
Russian 3, 60, 61, 89, 96, 173, 185, 206, 217, 232, 253

Sábato, E. 234
Sager, J. 85, 246
Said, E. 220
Salama-Carr, M. 36
Saldanha, G. 11–12, 26, 37, 56, 99, 104, 110, 159, 295, 317; key text 29, 302
Sanskrit 33, 35, 36, 216, 287
Santaemilia, J. 220
Sapir-Whorf hypothesis 60
Sato-Rossberg, N. 22, 56
Saussure, F. de 59, 60, 74
Schäffner, C. 130, 195
Schlegel, A. W. 47, 251
Schleiermacher, F. 29, 47, 48, 49, 52, 54, 121, 225, 226, 256, 250, 272, 311, 326; key text 30; see also hermeneutics; Romanticism
Schou, L. 104
Schulte, R. 56
Schütz, A. 204
Schwartz, M. 247
science of translating 58, 62; see also Übersetzungswissenschaft
Scott Moncrieff, C. K. 52
Seleskovitch, D. 100

Se im, S. 22, 220
semantic prosody 296
semantic structure analysis **67**, 80
semantic translation 4, 58, **71–3**
semantics 25, 62, 65, 90, 92, 101, 164
semiotics 9, 168, 279
sense for sense translation 32, 36, 43
Septuagint, Greek 13, 31, 32, 56
Serbian 216
Serbo-Croat 216
Seruya, T. 220
servitude: of translator's habitus 237; in Vinay and Darbelnet 93, 99, 179
Sewell, P.: key text 312
Shakespeare, W. 18
Shei, C. ii, 306, 314
shifts in translation 37, 98
Short, M. 166
Shuttleworth, M. 12
sign language 20
signified 60, **262**, 264; see also linguistic sign
signifier 60, **262**, 263, 264; see also linguistic sign
Simeoni, D. 170, 223, 237, 247, 326
Simon, H. 103, 206
Simon, S. 22, 96, **205–9**, 213, 216, 219; key text 220
Simpson, P. 159, 166
Sinclair, J. 291
Singh, G. 216, 218, 325
Sinn, E. 46
skopos theory 5, 21, 113, 114, **126–7**, 129–30, 138, 170, 304, 306; see also Reiss, K.; Vermeer, H. J.
Snell-Hornby, M. 7, 11, 16, 20, 47, 74, 84, 114, 120–2, 124, 139, 198, 276; integrated approach **113–14**; key texts 56, 139
sociocultural context: 21, 27, 125, 138, 233, 235, 296; constraints 177
sociolect 136, 164, 168, 218, 280; see also dialect
sociolinguistics 165
sociology 2, 3, 5, 18, 22, 25, 222–3, **236–9**, 246–7, 304, 325

source language (SL) 8, 33, 36, 68, 185, 279
source text (ST) 8–9, 53, 124, 129, 133, 148, 250, 253, 307
Spain 172, 243
Spanish 3, 14, 16, 38, 60–1, 88, 93–4, 96, 99, 109–10, 120, 135–7, 150, 157, 172, 181, 191–4, 231–2, 234–5, 243, 269–71, 294–7, 309, 323
Sperber, D. 101
Spira, I. 46
Spitzl, K.-H. 230
spirit 40–1, 43–4, **46, 49**, 67–8, 80, 244, 256
Spivak, G. 22, **209**, <u>218–19, 325</u>
Srikantaiah, B. M. 213
St André, J. 220
St Augustine 41
St-Pierre, P. 220
Steinbeck, J. 280
Steiner, G. 30, 49, 56; criticisms of 250–8; hermeneutic motion 5, 49, 249, **250–2**, <u>254–5</u>, 257, 258, 267, 269, 272; key text 249
Stephenson, C. 186
Stewart, D. 296
Störig, H.-J. 56, 272, 320–1
strategies *see* translation strategies
structural linguistics 98
Sturge, K. 215, 220
stylistics 87; *see also* translational stylistics
substitution 152, 276, 281, 288
subtitling 18, 186, 220, **265–6**, <u>272</u>, <u>274</u>, <u>276–9</u>, 281, 284–6, 299, 300; abusive 266
superdiversity 221
surtitling 278, 300
Susam-Saraeva, ?. 300, 301
Švecjer, A. D. 109
Sweden 26
Swedish 281
syntax 3, 35–6, <u>53–4</u>, 65, 73, 82, 144, 227, 234, 255, 261, 321
Syriac 36
systems theories 5, 219
Systran 289

Taber, C. R. **62–4**, 68, 327
Tarchetti, I. 226, 241, 235
Target (journal) 12, 21, 26, 58–9
target language (TL): definition 8
target text (TT): definition of 8
tarjama 10
taxonomies 50, 87, 109, 134, 146, 194
Taylor, C. **281–3**
terminology 84, 133, 145, 313
tertium comparationis 78, 84
text analysis 5, 76, 113–14, **130–1**, 134, 138–9, 142, 323
text linguistics 18, 151, 330
text-type 5, 17, 19–20, 52, 127, 188
thematic structure 93, 133, 144, 149–51, 153, 166, 314, 324
theory of contact 207
think-aloud protocols 18, 103, 109, 305–6; retrospective 103
third space 212, 235, 324
Thomas, M. 126, 329
Thompson, G. 166, 323
Tirkkonen-Condit, S. 103
Titford, C. 276
Tognini-Bonelli, E. 295
Toury, G. 73, 311; criticisms of 174–82, 233; descriptive translation studies 4–5, 79, **174–80**, <u>181–4</u>, <u>191–4</u>, 292; key texts 169; laws **180–4**, 233, 292, 294; and literary translators 233; map of translation studies 4, 16–17, 28, 311; norms **174–82**, 184; polysystem theory 23, 169–73, 182
Tracy, D. de 214
traductología 16, 88
traductologie 13, 16
transadaptation 278
transcreation 27, 121, 269, 272, 274, 286–7
transcription 89, 168, **281–3**, 298
transformational grammar *see* generative grammar
transitivity **144–5, 156**, 160, 166
translanguaging 220
translatability 47, 58, **61–2**; limits of 97, 250

translated literature: as system **169–73**, 182, 189–90, 194

translatese 209, 218; *see also* language of translation; universals of translation

translating *see* translation

translation: aids 19–20; as art 44, 235; assessment 50–5, 114, **146–8**; as craft 74, 256; criticism 19, 200; definitions 8; as derivative 5, 170, 205, 225; ecology 291; as higher order act of communication 110; minoritizing 226; policy 19–20, 171, 179, 188, 214; political act 185, 206; as product 8, 17, **86–100**, 178; project **55, 205–8**, 213; purpose of *see* skopos theory; specification 307; technical 11, 19, 11, 72, 89, 123, 160, 184, 236, 284; translations as facts of target culture 175; workshop 14–15; *see also* literary translation

translation flows 241

translation procedures **24, 86, 92–3**, 105, 108–10, 276; in audiovisual translation 274, 281

translation process 8, 17, 22, 43, 63–4, 71, **100–12**, 124, 131, 138, 166, 175, 176, **178–80**, 187, 195, 218, 233, 264, 287, 316

translation shifts **86–7**, 95–6, 98–100, 104, 111, 114, 175–6

translation strategy **23–4**, 32, 36, 39, 49, 51, **86–95**, 131–2, 191–4, **309–15**; alienating **48–9**, 54, 311; archaicizing 258–9; definition of **23**; experimental 249, 258–9, 265, 270–2; link to text type **113–15**; *see also* abusive fidelity; domestication; foreignization; translation procedures

translation studies: applied 19–21; as emerging discipline 16; fragmentation 26; integrated approach to 120–3; main issues of **7–28**; name and nature of discipline 16–17; 'pure' 16–19; *see also* consilience; descriptive translation studies; history of translation; interdiscipline; integrated approach

translation theory: criticism of Western theories 10, 209; early theory **29–57**; general 17, 127

translational stylistics 86, **98**

translatology 16; *see also* translation studies

translator: activism 236, 247; contracts of 239, 280; as expert 48, 125; ideology of 233–6; payment of 201, 290, 309; statements by 178; status of 237; training of 11, 14, 19, 22, 62, 71, 79, 83, 103, 123, 126, 132, 138–9, 295, 300; types of (Schleiermacher) 47–8; working practices of 21, 27, 126, 138, 237, 303; *see also* (in)visibility; literary translators

Translator, The (journal) 12

translatorial action 113, 114, **124–6**, 127, 128, 138, 139, 149, 187, 312

Translators Association, the 12

Translatum 127, 130, 323

transliteration 33–4, 37

Translog 104

transmutation 9, 25, 276

transposition 61, 90, 93, 107, 108

Trivedi, H. 197, 211–13, 220

Trosberg, A. 139, 166

trust (Steiner's hermeneutic motion) 252, 255

truth 40–1, 47, 50, 74, 157, 163, 210, 233

Turkish 203

Turner Hospital, J. 244

Twain, M. 182

Tymoczko, M. 10, 212, 214, 220, 235, 236, 247

Tyndale, W. 38–9

Tynjanov, J. N. 170

Tytler, A. F. (Lord Woodhouselee) 29, 30, 42; laws or rules of translation **45–6**, 69

Tyulenev, S. 237–8, 247

Übersetzer (Schleiermacher) 47, 260, 272

Übersetzungswissenschaft 16, 74, 84

UNESCO 3, 51–2, 148, 321

unit of translation 94

universals of translation 2, 19, 92, 184; S-universals 185; T-universals 185; *see also* translated language

University of: Antwerp 189; Austin 21, 199; Göteborg 26; Heidelberg 16, 74, 132, 326; Iowa 14; Leeds 296, 324; Leuven 189, 199; Manchester 293; Princeton 14; Saarland 16, 74; Tel Aviv 189

Untermeyer, J. S. 206, 255

untranslatability 47

Urdu 203

van Doorslaer, L. 7, 12, 20, **22–4**, 28, 316; key text 7

van Leeuwen, T. 283

Vázquez-Ayora, G. 16, 88, 109, 150

Venuti, L. 5, 22, 44, 49, 56, 160, 214, **222–5**, 234, 243, 245–6, 247, 272, 295, 325; foreignization and domestication **225–9**, 257, 311; influence of Berman **229–30**; key texts 223; on Pound 258–9; on publishing industry **239–41**; translation of Derrida 264; *see also* (in)visibility

Vermeer, H. J. 5, 19, 21, 32, 113, **126–30**, 134, 138, 329, 321, 322, 323; criticisms of **130–1**; key text 114

version 9, 10, 27, **148**, 163, 287, 289

Vian, B. 238

Vidal, G. 207

video games 10, 260, 277, **286**, 287, 300

Vieira, E. 22, 259, 260, 272, 287

Vinay, J.-P. 4, 15, 86, **88–95**, 95, 99, 104–8, 109, 110, 111, 179, 181, 231, 292, 309, 311, 312; key text 87

Virgil 44, 255

visual 116, 117, 162, 165, 265, **274–7, 281–5**

Viswanatha, V. 213

voice (narrative and creative) 53, 110, 209, 231, **234**, 238, 248, 266–9

voice-over 123, 278, 300

Vorderobermeier, G. 22, 237, 247

Wakabayashi, J. 22, 56, 220

Wallmach, K. 206

Warren, R. 246

Weaver, W. 246

Weissbort, D. 56, 327

Weissbrod, R. 272

West Germany 11, 74, 241, 321; *see also* Germany

White, P. 158

Williams, I. 295

Williams, J. 12, **314–15**; key text 302

Wilson, D. 101

Wilss, W. 16, 49, 74, 84

Windle, K. 12

Wolf, M. 22, 212, 222, 236, 237, 247, 291

Wood, M. 220, 247

Woods, M. 220

Woodsworth, J. 36, 56

Word-for-word translation **29–33**, 37, 39, 41, 42, 43, 45, 46, 48, 55, 69, 73, 89, 256, 261, 320

Wordsmith Tools 294

Xuan, Zang 33

Yán Fù **46–7**, 57

Young, R. 220

Zanettin, F. 27, 295–6, 300

Zhang, M. 15, 95, 165; key text 87

Zohn, H. 260, 273

Zürcher, E. 34–6